Sir Ranulph Fiennes was the first man to reach both poles by surface travel and the first to cross the Antarctic Continent unsupported. In the 1960s he was removed from the SAS Regiment for misuse of explosives but, after joining the army of the Sultan of Oman, received that country's Bravery Medal on active service in 1971. He is the only person yet to have been awarded two clasps to the Polar medal for both Antarctic and the Arctic regions. Fiennes has led over thirty expeditions, including the first polar circumnavigation of the Earth, and in 2003 he ran seven marathons in seven days on seven continents in aid of the British Heart Foundation. In 1993 Her Majesty the Queen awarded Fiennes the Order of the British Empire (OBE) because, on the way to breaking records, he has raised over £14 million for charity. He was named Best Sportsman in the 2007 ITV Great Briton Awards and in 2009 he became the oldest Briton to reach the summit of Everest.

Also by Ranulph Fiennes

A Talent For Trouble
Ice Fall In Norway
The Headless Valley
Where Soldiers Fear To Tread
Hell On Ice
Bothie The Polar Dog (With Virginia Fiennes)
Living Dangerously
The Feather Men
Atlantis Of The Sands
Mind Over Matter
The Sett
Fit For Life
Beyond The Limits
The Secret Hunters
Captain Scott: The Biography
Mad, Bad And Dangerous To Know
Mad Dogs And Englishmen
Killer Elite
My Heroes
Cold

TO THE ENDS OF THE EARTH

Circling the World from Pole to Pole

RANULPH FIENNES

SIMON & SCHUSTER

London · New York · Sydney · Toronto · New Delhi

A CBS COMPANY

First published in Great Britain by Hodder and Stoughton Ltd, 1983
This paperback edition published by Simon & Schuster UK Ltd, 2014
A CBS COMPANY

A CIP catalogue record for this book
is available from the British Library

ISBN: 978-1-47113-570-5
ebook ISBN: 978-1-47113-571-2

Typeset in the UK by M Rules
Printed and bound by CPI Group (UK) Ltd, Croydon, CRO 4YY

For Poul Andersson
Whom we will not forget

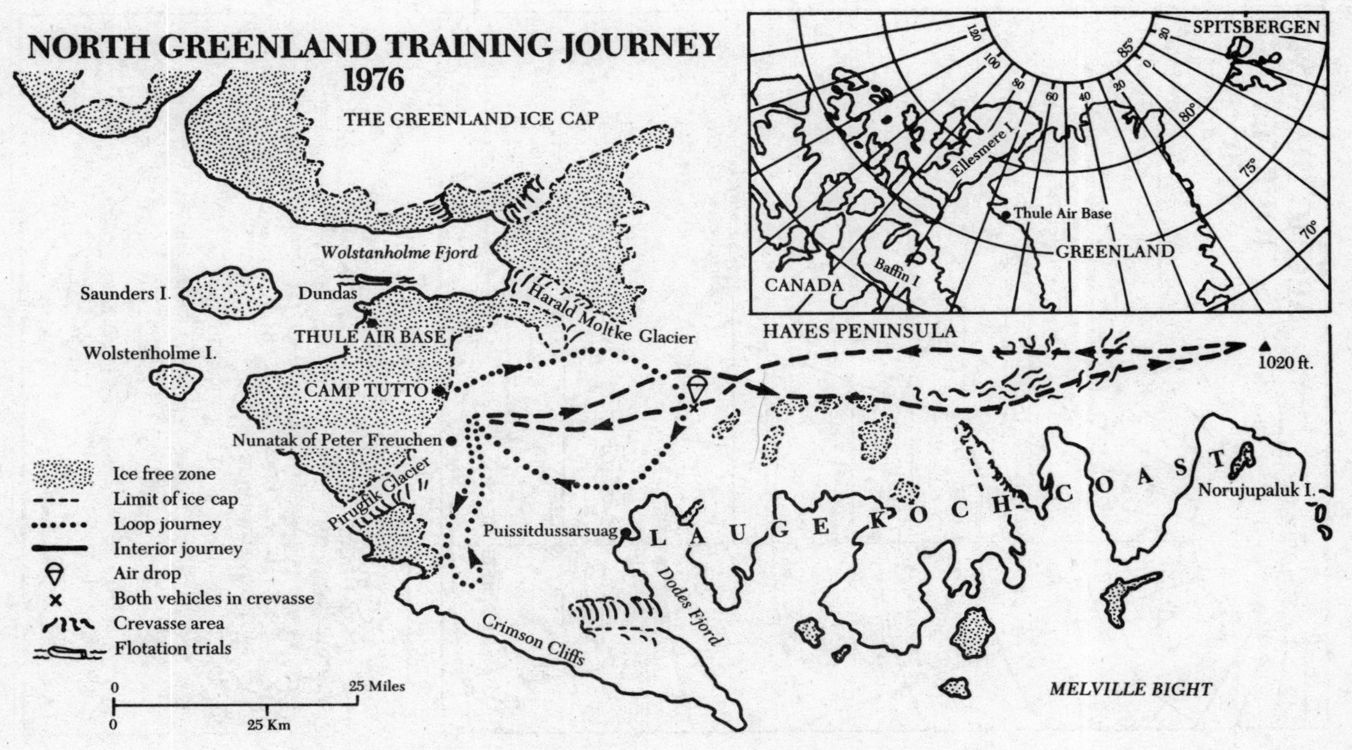
NORTH GREENLAND TRAINING JOURNEY
1976
THE GREENLAND ICE CAP
Wolstanholme Fjord
Saunders I.
Dundas
THULE AIR BASE
Wolstenholme I.
CAMP TUTTO
Harald Moltke Glacier
Nunatak of Peter Freuchen
Pirughik Glacier
Puissitdussarsuag
LAUGE KOCH COAST
Dodes Fjord
Crimson Cliffs
HAYES PENINSULA
1020 ft.
Norujupaluk I.
MELVILLE BIGHT
Ice free zone
Limit of ice cap
Loop journey
Interior journey
Air drop
Both vehicles in crevasse
Crevasse area
Flotation trials
0
25 Miles
0
25 Km
SPITSBERGEN
Ellesmere I
Thule Air Base
GREENLAND
CANADA
Baffin I
120
100
80
60
40
20
0
20
85°
80°
75°
70°

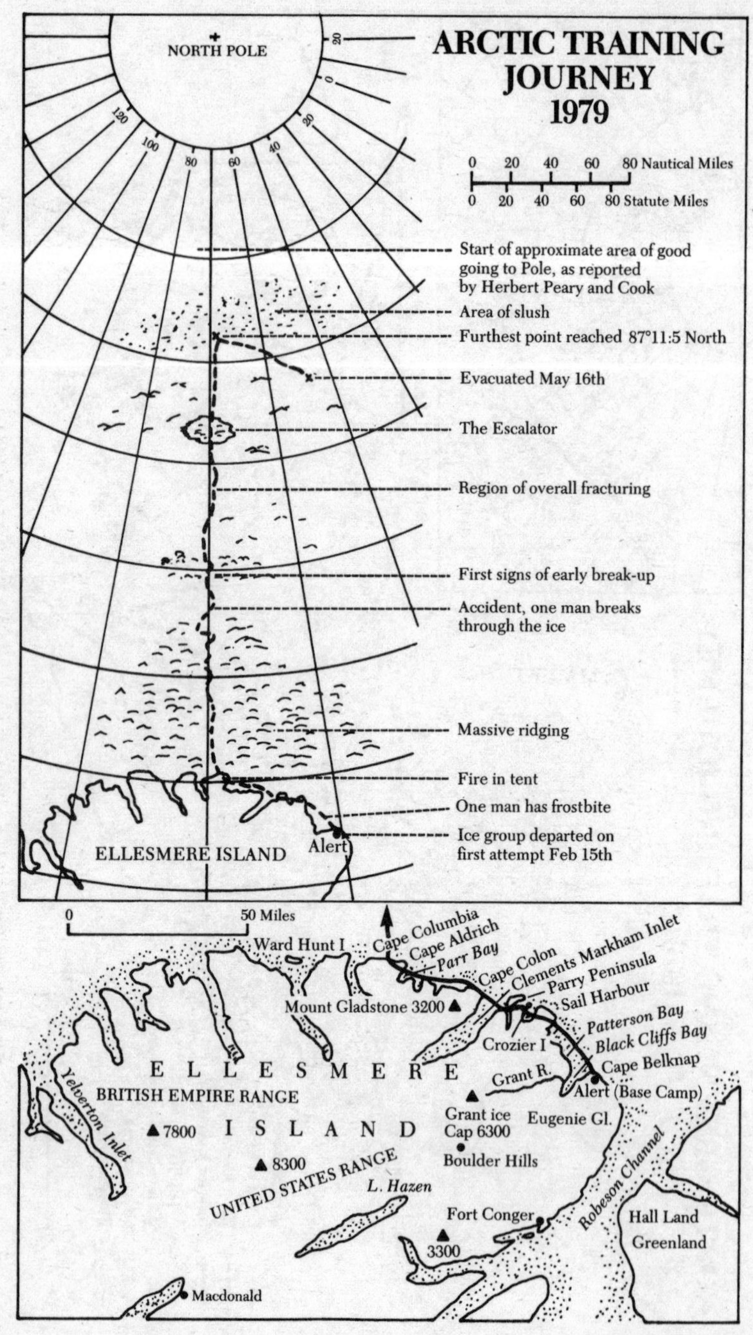
ARCTIC TRAINING JOURNEY 1979
NORTH POLE
0 20 40 60 80 Nautical Miles
0 20 40 60 80 Statute Miles
Start of approximate area of good going to Pole, as reported by Herbert Peary and Cook
Area of slush
Furthest point reached 87°11:5 North
Evacuated May 16th
The Escalator
Region of overall fracturing
First signs of early break-up
Accident, one man breaks through the ice
Massive ridging
Fire in tent
One man has frostbite
Ice group departed on first attempt Feb 15th
ELLESMERE ISLAND
Alert
0 50 Miles
Ward Hunt I
Cape Columbia
Cape Aldrich
Parr Bay
Cape Colon
Clements Markham Inlet
Parry Peninsula
Sail Harbour
Mount Gladstone 3200
Crozier I
Patterson Bay
Black Cliffs Bay
Cape Belknap
Grant R.
Alert (Base Camp)
E L L E S M E R E
I S L A N D
BRITISH EMPIRE RANGE
Yelverton Inlet
7800
8300
UNITED STATES RANGE
Grant ice Cap 6300
Eugenie Gl.
Boulder Hills
L. Hazen
Fort Conger
Robeson Channel
Hall Land
Greenland
3300
Macdonald

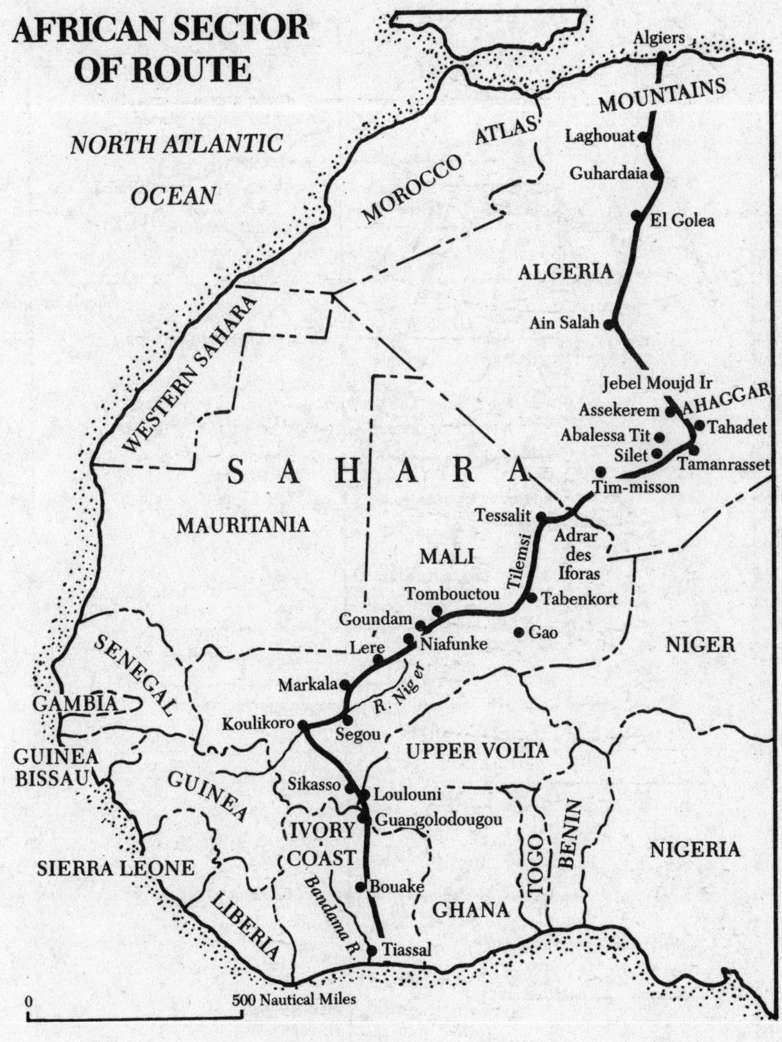
AFRICAN SECTOR
OF ROUTE
NORTH ATLANTIC
OCEAN
MOROCCO
ATLAS
MOUNTAINS
Algiers
Laghouat
Guhardaia
El Golea
ALGERIA
Ain Salah
WESTERN SAHARA
Jebel Moujd Ir
AHAGGAR
Assekerem
Abalessa Tit
Tahadet
Silet
Tamanrasset
S A H A R A
Tim-misson
Tessalit
MAURITANIA
MALI
Tilemsi
Adrar
des
Iforas
Tombouctou
Tabenkort
Goundam
Gao
Niafunke
NIGER
Lere
SENEGAL
Markala
R. Niger
GAMBIA
Koulikoro
Segou
GUINEA
BISSAU
UPPER VOLTA
GUINEA
Sikasso
Loulouni
Guangolodougou
IVORY
COAST
TOGO
BENIN
NIGERIA
SIERRA LEONE
Bouake
Bandama R.
LIBERIA
GHANA
Tiassal
0
500 Nautical Miles

REGION OF SANAE/BORGA

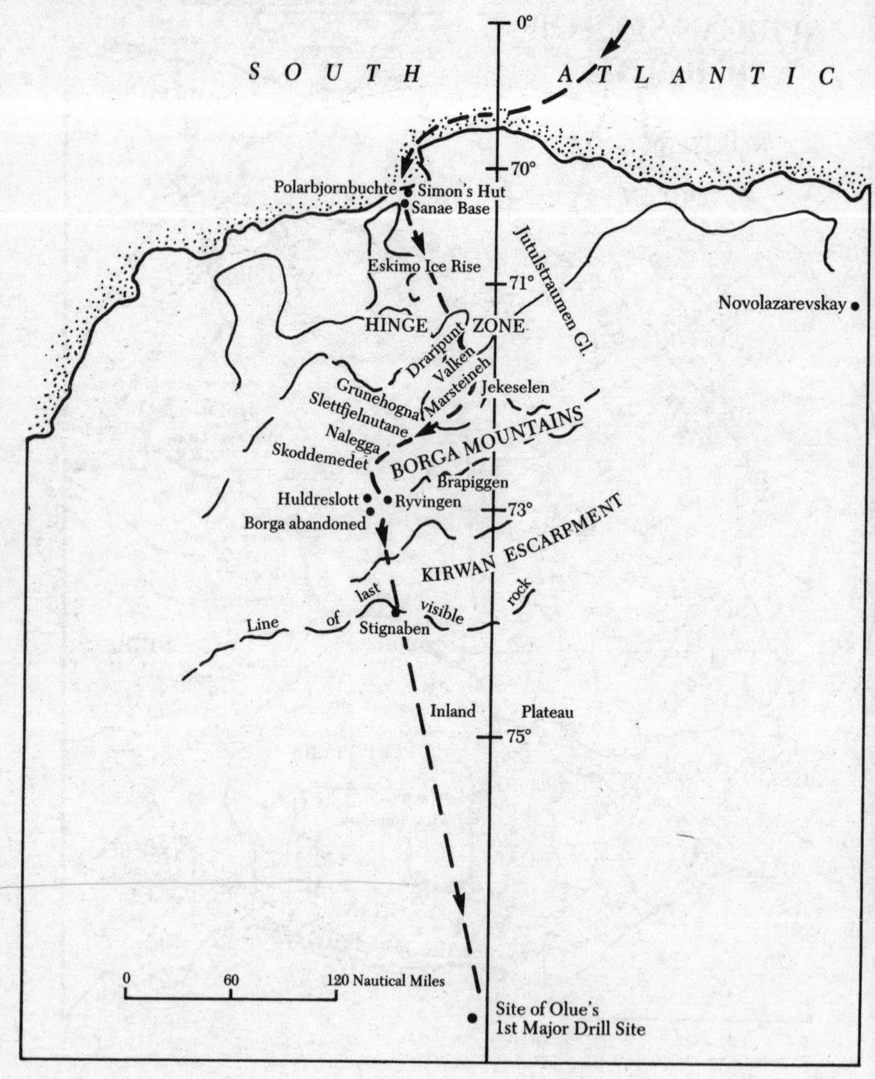

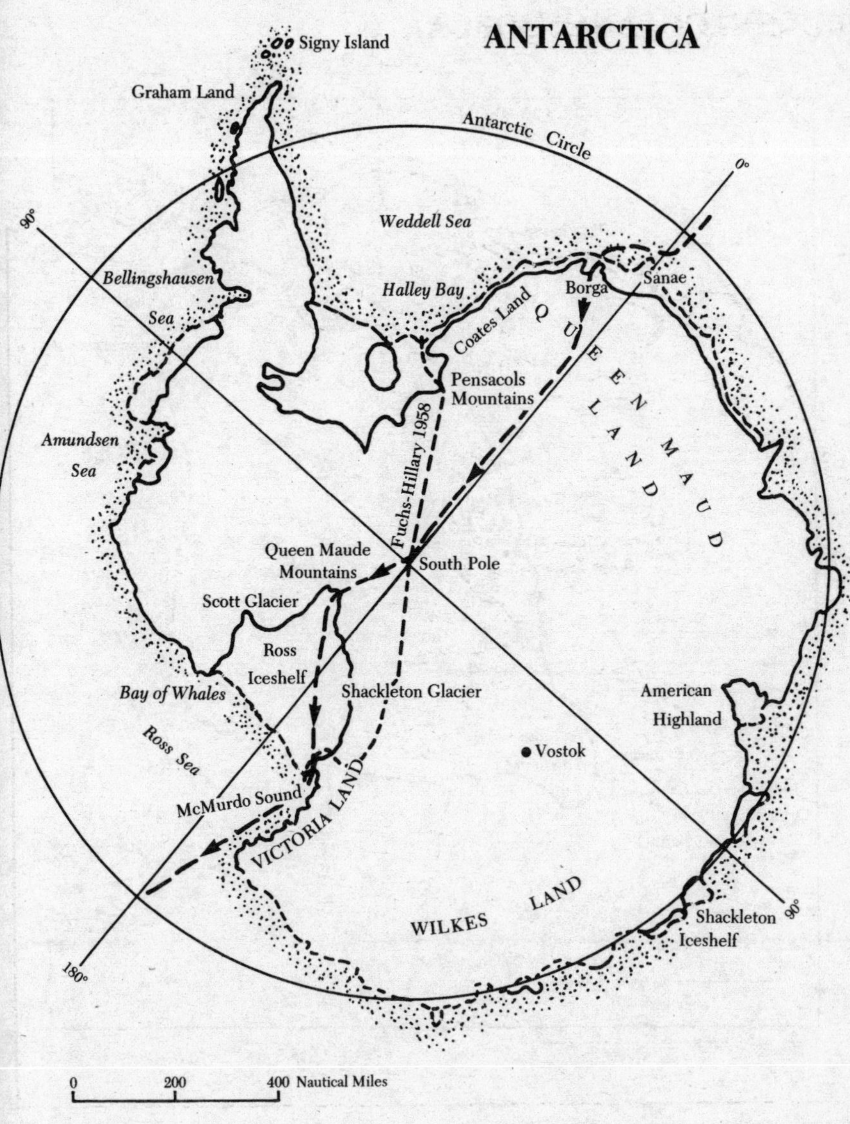
ANTARCTICA
Signy Island
Graham Land
Antarctic Circle
0°
90°
Weddell Sea
Bellingshausen
Sea
Halley Bay
Coates Land
Borga
Sanae
QUEEN MAUD LAND
Pensacols
Mountains
Amundsen
Sea
Fuchs-Hillary 1958
Queen Maude
Mountains
South Pole
Scott Glacier
Ross
Iceshelf
Bay of Whales
Shackleton Glacier
American
Highland
Ross Sea
Vostok
McMurdo Sound
VICTORIA LAND
WILKES
LAND
Shackleton
Iceshelf
90°
180°
0
200
400 Nautical Miles

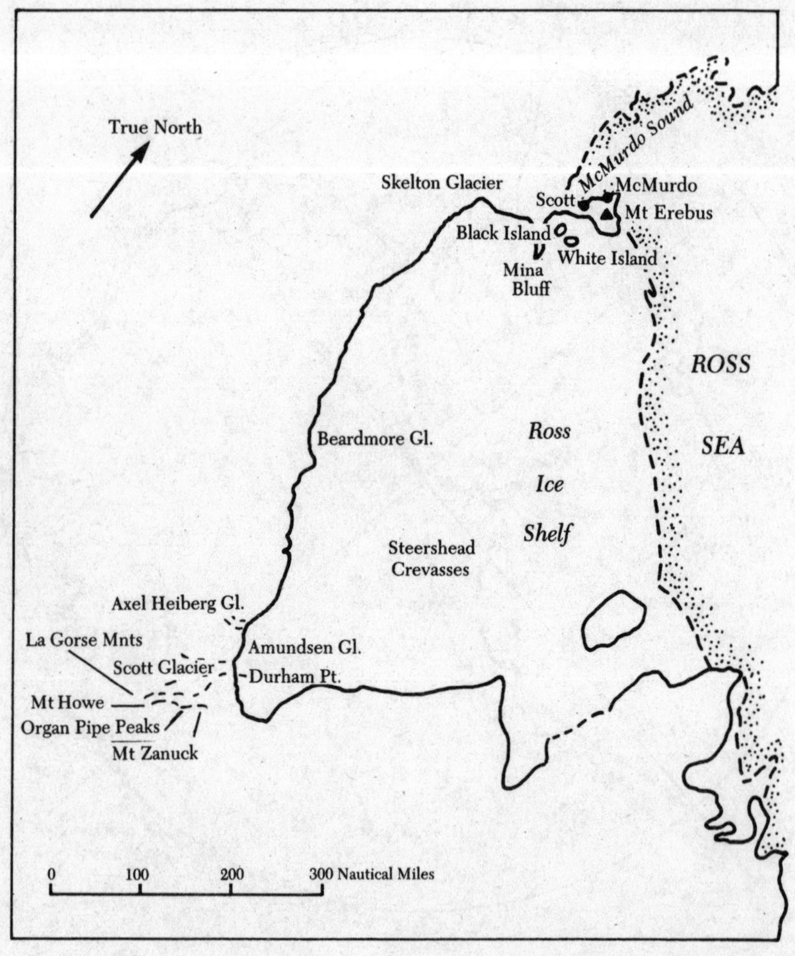
True North
McMurdo Sound
Skelton Glacier
McMurdo
Scott
Mt Erebus
Black Island
White Island
Mina
Bluff
ROSS
SEA
Ross
Ice
Shelf
Beardmore Gl.
Steershead
Crevasses
Axel Heiberg Gl.
La Gorse Mnts
Amundsen Gl.
Scott Glacier
Durham Pt.
Mt Howe
Organ Pipe Peaks
Mt Zanuck
0
100
200
300 Nautical Miles

TO TUKTOYAKTUK

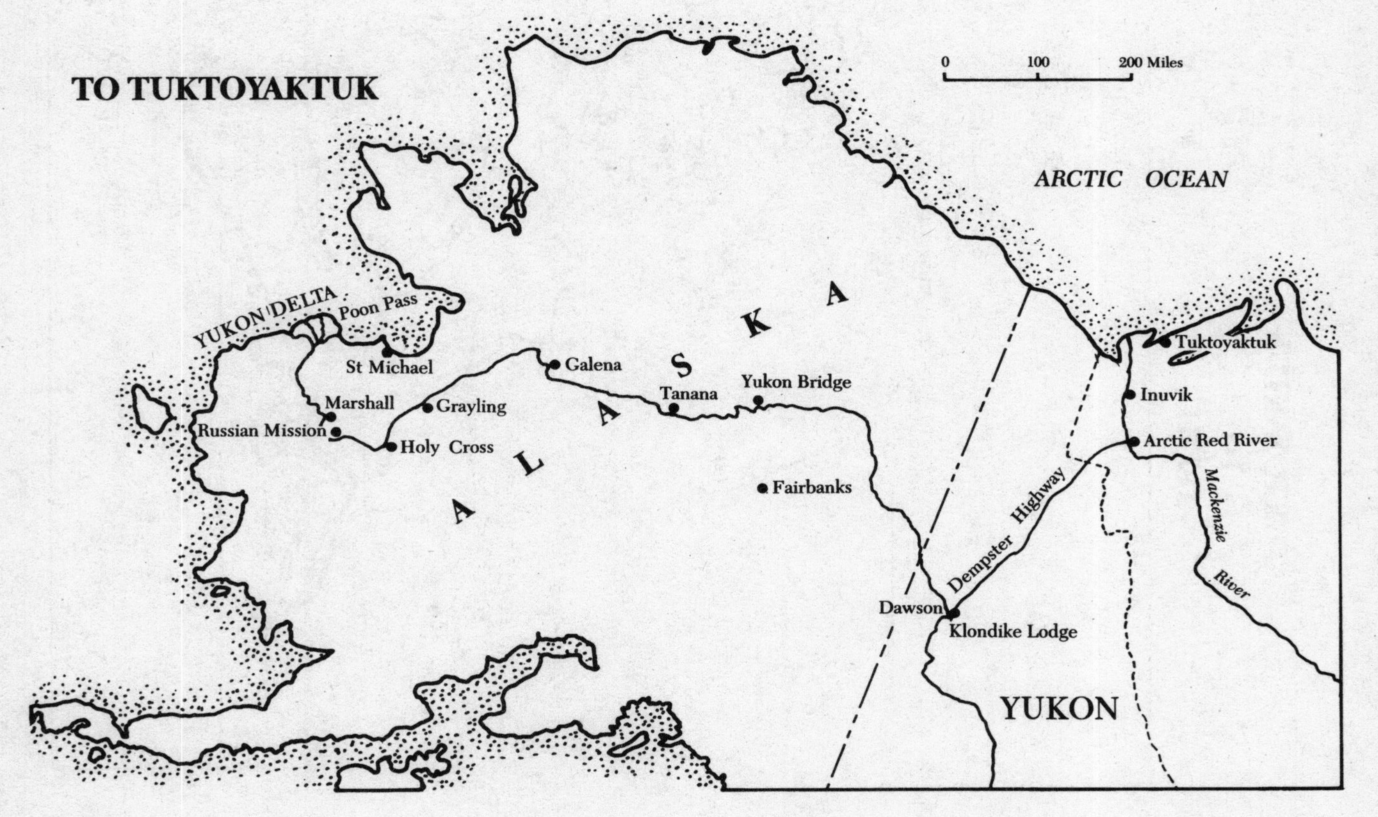

TUKTOYAKTUK
TO
ALERT

H I S L A N D S
Alert
Lake Hazen
ISLAND
Tanqary Fjord
AXLE
HEIBERG
ISLAND
Eureka
ELLESMERE
GREENLAND
Great Bear
Cape
Noregian
Bay
Thule
Hell Gate
Craig Harbour
ST
D
Jones Sound
Cornwallis
Island
DEVON ISLAND
te Bay
B A F F I N
Barrow Strait
Lancaster Sound
Peel Sound
SOMERSET
ISLAND
BOOTHIA
PENINSULAR
B A Y
BAFFIN ISLAND
Palsey
Bay
Spence Bay
Gjoa Haven
R I T O R I E S

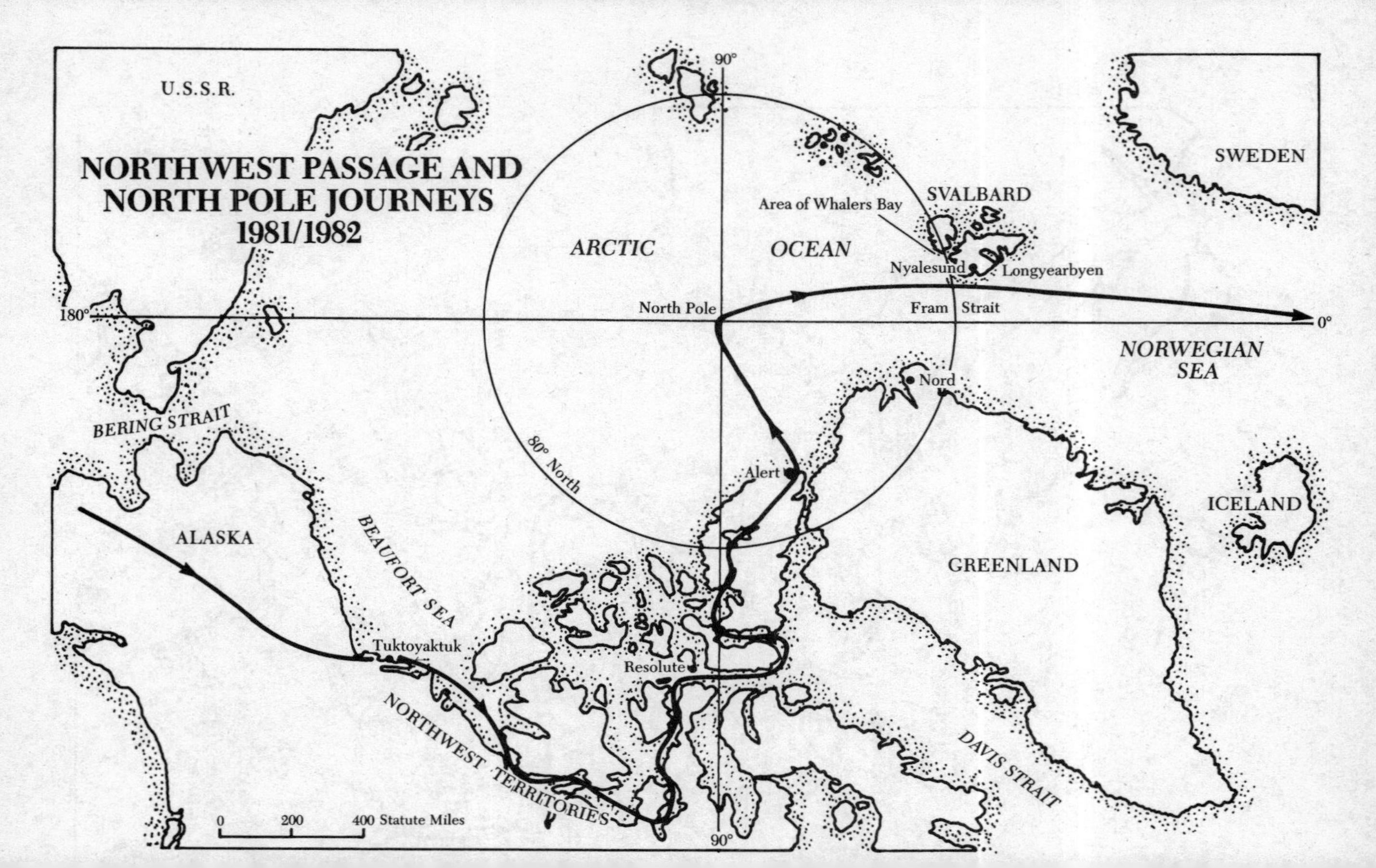
NORTHWEST PASSAGE AND
NORTH POLE JOURNEYS
1981/1982
U.S.S.R.
SWEDEN
SVALBARD
Area of Whalers Bay
Nyalesund
Longyearbyen
ARCTIC
OCEAN
North Pole
Fram Strait
90°
180°
0°
NORWEGIAN
SEA
Nord
Alert
80° North
BERING STRAIT
ALASKA
BEAUFORT SEA
Tuktoyaktuk
Resolute
ICELAND
GREENLAND
NORTHWEST TERRITORIES
DAVIS STRAIT
0
200
400 Statute Miles
90°

Contents

Foreword by H. R. H. Prince Charles

BUCKINGHAM PALACE

I was lucky enough not only to be present at the start and at the finish of the Transglobe Expedition in London but also to be able to meet Ran Fiennes and his team when the *Benjamin Bowring* was moored in Sydney Harbour. For someone who participated in what I suspect were the only comfortable parts of the entire voyage to write a foreword may seem presumptuous. I am, however, delighted to be able to record my admiration for the extraordinary ingenuity, courage, imagination and sheer hard work of the entire expedition. I know that Ran himself would acknowledge that the party would never have left London, let alone returned there, without the work and support of the Committee at home and the incredibly generous help and sponsorship of so many different individuals and companies. This is, of course, true, but it is also true that notwithstanding the immensely important contributions made by everyone else, the ultimate success of Transglobe was due to the efforts of those who carried out this unprecedented adventure. How they endured the hardships that confronted them or survived the astonishing risks they took is beyond my comprehension. Their exploits have added another stirring chapter to the long history of polar explorers, whose heroic example has contributed greatly to man's knowledge as well as stimulating the imagination of countless people all over the world.

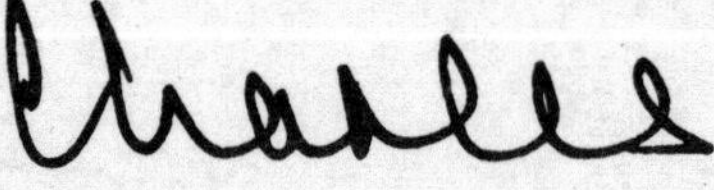

Chapter One

Great floods have flown from simple sources.

SHAKESPEARE

In February 1972 my wife suggested we travel around the world. I looked up from the boots I was polishing with a mixture of spit and black kiwi in readiness for a weekend with the Territorial SAS regiment.

'Ginnie, we can't pay the mortgage. How the hell can we go round the world?'

'Get a contract from a newspaper, a book publisher and a TV company.' She was peering into the simmering Irish stew. I knew it was Irish stew because that was, with very few exceptions, the only dish she had produced since our marriage eighteen months earlier.

'They won't be interested,' I replied. 'Everybody goes round the world.'

'They all do it horizontally.'

I glanced at her, not sure I was understanding. She continued to poke at the stewpot without elaborating. 'Of course they do. There is no other way.' I tried to keep my tone unsarcastic. Our life together was at the time a series of minor volcanic eruptions touched off by the tiniest sparks. 'You can't get over the top because of the Arctic Ocean and the Antarctic ice cap happens to cover the bottom.'

She stopped prodding our supper and looked up. 'So?' Her glacier-blue eyes were on me, unblinking.

'So no sane person even tries to do it. If it were possible it would have been done. All oceans have been crossed west to east, north to south, solo, on rafts, backwards and sideways. All major mountains have been climbed and all rivers travelled up to their source and back down again. People have gone round the world by horse, bicycle and probably by broomstick. They have parachuted from over thirty thousand feet and gone paddling to the deepest spots in the deepest seas. Quite apart from messing around on the moon and planets.'

I spat for emphasis at one toecap but it went inside the boot. She was unimpressed. 'You are saying it can't be done because it hasn't been done. Is that it? That's pathetic.'

'It may be pathetic but it's practical. Even to look into the possibilities would take months. We know nothing about polar travel. Nothing. How do we pay the gas bill if I spend months in libraries and polar institutes doing the necessary research? Answer me that.'

'You knew nothing about parachuting before your Norwegian glacier trip. Nothing about hovercraft before the Nile journey and nothing about inflatable boats and rapids until last summer in British Columbia. So why should ignorance get in the way of a polar journey?'

'The poles are different—'

But she was not finished. 'And as for research, I did most of that for the other trips even before we were married. You can finish the Dhofar book and carry on with your lecturing . . .' The matter continued to be thrashed out over the Irish stew and by bedtime had become a tender topic.

That weekend my territorial unit parachuted by night into

Denmark and 'blew up' a number of radar installations in the Frederikshaven area. The activity erased from my mind Ginnie's absurd circumpolar suggestion.

It was not the first time she had bruited the idea. On a recent Highland holiday it had surfaced and I'd ignored it as a romantic rambling inspired by the wild and glorious scenery.

It may seem odd in the twentieth century to plan and carry out expeditions as a means of making a living, yet I'd been doing just that since leaving the army in 1970.

Why did I choose such a way of life? I didn't really; it just sort of came about. Things worked out that way despite youthful intentions to be a hundred and one other things from fireman to spy. In 1943, four months before I was born, my father died of wounds received not far north of Monte Casino while commanding a tank regiment, the Royal Scots Greys.

By the time I was sixteen a career in the army preceded by university and two years at the Officer Training College at Sandhurst seemed like a good idea. Perhaps I had secret visions of one day becoming commanding officer of the Greys like my father.

Unfortunately, I had inherited his title but not, frankly, his brains. Considerable grey matter is needed in today's technically oriented fighting forces to the point where would-be regular officers are not accepted for Sandhurst without two A-level certificates of education in English and mathematics.

After four and a half years at Slough Grammar, local vernacular for Eton College, I had defeated all attempts to push my mathematical abilities up to 'ordinary' level standard. The same applied to physics and chemistry. If Eton had handed out certificates for boxing and climbing the college spires by night I would have been fine. As it was I left with only four 'ordinary' levels and that had been a classic case of squeezing blood from a stone. So Sandhurst was out of the question but there was another way. You applied for a short service commission, three years only, and at the end of it, you could stay on if they liked you. Instead of two years at Sandhurst there would be five months concentrated training at Mons Officer Cadet School.

At Mons, half of us were white; the rest black, brown and yellow. Everyone got on fine so long as they pulled their weight. There were three major exams: Military Knowledge, Papers I and II, and Signals. Another prospective Scots Grey, Brassey, was also unusually thick. The exam results were announced on boards around the camp for all to see. They were always the same. A mass of whites followed by a mass of blacks followed by Fiennes and Brassey followed by Wanga Dong, a remarkable Thai cadet whose mind was at all times in the lotus position. I was warned that my career was in danger. So was Brassey's. It did not help when the police apprehended me one night seventy feet up the wall of the west wing of nearby Heathfield School for Girls. With me was Lord Richard Wrottesley, the only man at Mons with a monocle. In our attempted withdrawal he damaged the school's bursar and so was thrown out of Mons. I received another warning and fifty-six days of 'restrictions of privileges' – a standing record.

At the final test, Battle Camp, basic fitness and above-average skill with a spade saw me through. Brassey was made to complete the whole weary five months a second time while I went straight to the Greys. Life is most unfair for some. Brassey said it was not because I was the better cadet, but that Mons could not risk my presence for another term.

In 1941 the Greys had been in Palestine. My father, as training major, witnessed their six hundred grey horses being given away to the local police when tanks came on the scene. But in 1963 in Germany I found most Greys officers spent their spare time with horses: polo, steeplechasing or the local drag-hunt. Such sports as boxing, orienteering and climbing were not popular.

I had a troop of Conqueror tanks. We exercised all over northern Germany, tearing up cornfields and crashing through pine forests. Our training seemed to involve mostly withdrawal from east to west. This was doubtless realistic but not exactly inspiring.

For three years I became involved with what the military call 'adventure training', mainly canoeing along European rivers in the summer with dozens of brawny jocks. This was an open struggle: me trying to improve their canoeing talents, the jocks to increase their experience of Lowenbrau, frauleins, gasthaus brawls and Danish nudist camps. The winter I spent instructing langlauf skiing in Bavaria. All this gave me a taste for travel and a desire to escape tank exercises in the Prussian mud.

A chance came in 1965 with an SAS recruitment notice. The Special Air Service did not normally accept short service officers with only two years military service but there was no harm in trying.

Their selection course in North Wales was an interesting experience. At first there were fourteen officer applicants and one hundred and thirty other ranks. After a week there were six officers and forty-two other ranks. Most of the survivors were hardened soldiers from the parachute regiments, marines and infantry units. 'Tank people' were the scum of the earth, on a level with the veterinary corps.

One test was to draw up realistic plans of a bank robbery in the local town, Hereford. My plans, based on a fraudulent talk to a bank manager, were left in error in a restaurant on my Sunday off. This resulted in a police alert in Herefordshire followed by a full and publicised ministerial inquiry.

The commanding officer, one Colonel Mike Wingate-Gray, did not approve of the realism of my bank raid but refrained from sacking me. Within a month the selection staff had ruthlessly cut us down to three officers and twelve men. We passed into the regiment and began our specialist training, including a demolition course.

Over the weeks I collected a certain amount of plastic explosive, detonators and other such bric-a-brac. Also, a civilian friend in the wine business was at the time incensed by the outcry in England's prettiest village, Castle Combe in Wiltshire. The village was, he said, being ruined by concrete and sandbags because 20th Century-Fox was turning it into a film set for *Doctor Dolittle* with Rex Harrison and Samantha Eggar. Since the villagers' protests were going unheard, my friend devised a plan to destroy the mock lake the movie people had built and thereby publicize the whole outrage. My part would be to provide the explosive side of the affair. No one would be hurt but the point would be made.

As it was, the police were tipped off in advance and pounced. I evaded capture but my car did not. So, needing to report at camp the very next morning for a jungle training course in Borneo, I approached the police. Far from releasing my car they put me up for the night in Chippenham jail. At the subsequent local assizes I was fined and Colonel Wingate-Gray sacked me from the SAS.

Returned to my old three tanks, I spent a year festering in the same old mud, repenting my sins. An official circular called for officers volunteering for a two-year posting to the Sultan of Oman's forces. I applied at once to the colonel. He appeared delighted and signed my form without delay (or with indecent haste).

Visions of sun and sand.

Reality was otherwise. The day I arrived in Oman the only other Greys officer with the sultan's forces was flown out with his shoulder smashed by a bullet.

For two long years with thirty Muslim soldiers, phosphorous grenades and ten light machine guns, I learned that real soldiering was not the romantic existence I had looked forward to.

By the 1970 monsoon the three-hundred-strong army of the sultan in Dhofar with its eleven British officers had been forced back to a small coastal plain. Nine-tenths of the terrain fell under

Marxist control. Muslim tribesmen with no government protection got short shrift unless they altered their beliefs. We moved only by night to mount mobile ambushes.

I learned that to kill a man face to face, even though to delay by a second would mean one's own death, was a foul experience. I had seen, too, what man could do to man: what befell those Muslims, young and old alike, who failed to switch allegiance. Backs burned with hot charcoal, eyes gouged out with sticks. All in the name of Marxism, just as the Inquisition lay at Christianity's door.

Nonetheless I think I would have stayed in the army had it been possible. The end of my term in Oman coincided with my eighth and last year in the British army; I had stretched my short service commission as far as it would go.

What to do in 'Civvi Street' – that sand sea beyond the secure khaki oasis which had been my home and the confines of my thinking since schooldays? With no business connections, no qualifications and no unearned income, I could hardly linger. My only skills lay outside the city. I had enjoyed the planning and the organising of adventure training, but in the army taxpayers had provided the funds, the transport and the paid participants.

Starting small with a journey to a Norwegian glacier, a hovercraft trip up the Nile and the transnavigation of British Columbia by river, I made contacts with some fifty companies willing to help either through altruism or in return for publicity. In 1970 I married Ginnie. We worked well together but craved a bigger challenge than the rivers and mountains of the early expeditions. In the summer of 1972, after three months' study in geographical libraries, I took Ginnie's circumpolar idea to my literary agent, George Greenfield. George acted for John Le Carré, David Niven and other notables, but his particular interest was and is the field of exploration. Through his ability to interest publishers and newspaper editors in the rights of proposed expeditions he had helped to make financially feasible such journeys as Vivian Fuchs' crossing of Antarctica, Wally Herbert's crossing of the Arctic Ocean and Francis Chichester's solo circumnavigation.

I had learned that the seal of George's approval on a scheme was very much a step in the right direction. But he was far from ecstatic. His observations as devil's advocate were sobering. To follow the polar axis would mean crossing Antarctica. Even in the 1950s that had cost Sir Vivian Fuchs, director of the British Antarctic Survey, and Sir Edmund Hillary over £1 million even though they had the practical and financial support of their governments and Sir Anthony Eden's personal backing. Four years of full-time planning, two aircraft and two ice-breakers had been involved. The venture itself had lasted nearly two years in remote Antarctica. It involved men, many of them scientists, who were among the world's leading polar authorities.

No private nongovernment expeditions had operated in Antarctica since the last world war. Why not, in a period when private expeditions blossomed like pop groups and ventured to the most remote deserts, glaciers and peaks? The answer was simple: there is nowhere as remote as Antarctica. No commercial shipping or air lines can be appealed to for sponsored transport to its frozen wastes. And should you get there, the *only* bases that exist are scientific outposts operated by governments, not private concerns. And none looking kindly on helping 'unauthorised' visitors. Together the governments present a hostile wall to private inquiries for assistance. Try to cross the coldest continent on earth with no outside support, no hospital, no fuel, no spares and no available rescue facilities. To do this would mean total self-sufficiency. At the least it would mean owning or charting an ice-breaker and an aircraft.

George Greenfield was not finished. Suppose we somehow crossed Antarctica and reached the top of the world. Whatever route we followed, the Arctic Ocean would bar the way. In history, the Arctic Ocean has only once been crossed. Wally Herbert with three companions and forty huskies carried out his remarkable sixteen-month journey in 1968. Herbert was a man of great polar experience, as were two of his team, yet the preparations for the venture took him four years, involved re-supply from Hercules C-130 transport aircraft and final evacuation by helicopters from a British navy ship. Ignoring any problems there might be with *other* parts of our route, it could be seen that the polar zones alone could take us twelve years to cope with, given the success rate in planning and travel of Fuchs and Herbert. Cold winters in Sussex were the limit of our polar experience.

We left George's office and sat in silence with two cups of coffee at the nearest sandwich bar. 'Oh well,' Ginnie sighed.

'Yes,' I agreed.

Still ...

W. H. Smith used to produce six-inch tin globes. We bought one and pencilled out various possible routes. It did not seem worth the risk of mounting the whole scheme in the knowledge that, at any minute, political permission might be withdrawn, so we rubbed off all the pencilled routes passing through any part of the USSR. Only one line remained – just off the Greenwich Meridian.

On the aged theory that the shortest route is a straight line between two points, we decided to plan a route adhering to the Greenwich Meridian unless a good reason cropped up to add mileage with detours. The Arctic Ocean, though less remote than Antarctica, appeared to provide more difficult travel conditions. Better to leave it until last. Our route from Greenwich, then, would go south through Europe and the bulge of West Africa, by sea to Cape Town, then on to Antarctica.

By chance, close to where the meridian touches Antarctica's coastline, there is a South African scientific base called Sanae (standing simply for South African National Antarctic Expedition). From the region of Sanae our pencil line skimmed over some fourteen hundred miles of white nothingness to the South Pole, and on the other side of the world jinked north to a New Zealand coastal base named after Captain Scott; from there up the Pacific along the International Date Line all the way to the Bering Straits between Russia and Alaska.

At this point we made a critical route-planning decision. Wally Herbert's Arctic Ocean crossing was made from Point Barrow in Alaska up to the North Pole, then down to Spitsbergen. I had not wanted to emulate his route. There was one other possible starting point on the North American coastline: Ellesmere Island in the Canadian archipelago. To reach it from the Bering Straits I traced a line up the Yukon River to Dawson City, then north to the Mackenzie River and down to its mouth at Tuktoyaktuk. From there to Ellesmere Island my pencil ran east, then north along the coast between various islands for two or three thousand miles. This was the largely ice-bound corridor known as the Northwest Passage, made infamous in the nineteenth century by the deaths of over two hundred explorers and pioneers along its barren shores. From Ellesmere Island the route ran on to the North Pole, where it rejoined the Greenwich Meridian for the last stretch back to England.

Man had reached the moon and beyond, but no one had travelled to both poles in one expedition, let alone travelled the course of the earth's polar axis. By the route we marked on our six-inch globe we would try to correct this omission.

A friend in Los Angeles told us of four Americans who had travelled to the North Pole in 1968 on snowmobiles. One of them, Walt Pederson, intended to reach the South Pole overland and become the first man to reach both ends of the earth. In terms of planning he had a few years start on us, but perhaps he would fail. The Norwegians had by four short weeks beaten the British to the South Pole in 1911. The Americans had beaten several British attempts to the top of the world when Peary claimed ninety degrees north in

1910. Some say neither Peary nor his rival American claimant, Cook, reached the Pole. Nonetheless, if they didn't, Plaisted – Walt Pederson's leader – certainly clinched American priority in 1968.

What we were considering amounted to the last major polar challenge. The joining-up of the feats of the Antarctic, Arctic Ocean and Northwest Passage pioneers into a logical conclusion. None of the stages of Sir Francis Chichester's great ocean circumnavigation were individually virgin; other sailors had been there before him. But his was the ultimate challenge in his chosen field of endeavour: give or take doing the same thing backward, in a smaller boat, or at age ninety.

I learned later that the longest single stage of our planned route, some one thousand miles to the South Pole along the zero meridian, was one of the last remaining truly unexplored regions on earth.

Patriotism in the mid-1970s was no longer openly considered a totally worthwhile motive. To admit to it was to invite denigration and even scorn. Perhaps I was born too late in the scheme of things because to me a man's own country can be worth living for, dying for and doing for. Later on more tangible benefits to be gained as a result of our venture, mainly through scientific research work in the polar regions, became apparent, but initially our sole reasoning was the acceptance of challenge for its own sake.

George Greenfield had made clear that without the blessing of the British government we could not hope to receive help from any base in Antarctica, and without such help the journey would stand little chance. So my next visit was to the Foreign Office. The so-called Polar Desk, a sub-office of the Latin Americas Department, was housed near Waterloo Bridge. I wore my grey pin-striped suit and got an old regimental tie out of mothballs. The gentleman I was to meet looked after Britain's responsibilities north of the Arctic Circle and south of the Antarctic Circle virtually by himself. He was an ex-biologist and, quite apart from his diplomatic position, was a leading figure in Antarctic circles, owing to his past activities with the Falkland Islands Dependencies Survey (now called the British Antarctic Survey). He knew about our plans and naturally treated them as yet another private expedition which must be put in its place, quickly and unequivocally. He did just that, making it plain that we would get to Antarctica, much less cross it, over his dead body.

That meeting, I think in retrospect, finally removed my last doubts about the desirability of pursuing the whole endeavour. This pillar of the establishment had flung down the gauntlet. As far as he and, I later discovered, a number of other Antarctic pundits in the country were concerned, I was to be blocked at every turn. He knew where I would have to go, whom I must approach and lost no time in putting the word out in those quarters.

For the next four years we were to batter our heads against an unyielding wall of officialdom. But, practice making perfect, we got quite good at it. And the eminent Foreign Office gentleman died some five years later.

We found it best, when chatting up important people, to have a firm date to aim for. They are then less inclined to think you are building castles in the air. Obviously we could not get going in a year. But two might be possible. So early in 1973 we drew up plans to depart in September 1975 (the month being obligatory and based on the short summer season in Antarctica). The Royal Greenwich Observatory celebrated their Tercentenary in 1975. Thinking of a nice tie-up, we visited the observatory. Owing to pollution Greenwich skies are no longer good for observing stars, so the observatory has moved, lock, stock and Isaac Newton's telescope, down to the clear skies of Sussex, to the spacious grounds of Herstmonceux Castle.

Normally I find my full family name, Twisleton-Wykeham-Fiennes, something of a burden, ripe for the barbed wit of *Private Eye*, who once rearranged it as Twizeewick Piston Steam, but as far as our standing with the observatory's director was concerned it could do no harm, inasmuch as he was a local history buff. Back in 1066 my ancestor, Count Eustache de Boulogne, was appointed number two to William the Conqueror when they attacked the Brits. King Harold, defending Hastings, was inhibited by a Norman arrow in his eye. Cousin Eustache grabbed his chance and, as recorded in the Bayeux Tapestry, removed the royal head with a clean sweep of his axe. William gave him five castles or the ground on which to build them for this brave act, and the Fynes or Fiennes clan flourished.

One Ranulph Fiennes, killed at the Battle of Bosworth five centuries back, had owned Herstmonceux, and the castle's current inmate agreed to a tie-up between his observatory and our voyage.

Starting, then, in 1975, when would it end? For this the six-inch globe was inadequate. Back to the map room and libraries of the Royal Geographical Society. I kept my original notes:

Year One	1)	England to Cape Town via France, Spain, Algeria, Mali and Ivory Coast (Land Rovers) 3½ months. Start 1st September. Arrive mid-December (no floods nor great heat at this season).
	2)	Cape Town to Sanae. (Boat averages ten knots for all ocean phases.) Fourteen days if no bad pack ice. Arrive early January mid-Antarctic summer.
Year Two	3)	Set up base camp for winter period and set out for Pole in November at beginning of Antarctic summer.
Year Three	4)	Crossing trip of one hundred days (dogs or machines) via South Pole to Scott Base. Get there in February for collection by boat before sea ice closes up in area.

	5)	Up Pacific to Yukon mouth. Boat drops off rubber boats in mid-June (Yukon ice breaks up by then even in a bad year). By Land Rover to Northwest Passage at Tuktoyaktuk (sea ice in Passage passable some years but only in mid-July to late-August).
	6)	Arrive North Ellesmere Island before sun disappears in mid-October. Spend winter there.
Year Four		Set out for North Pole at sunup (early March). Reach North Pole by mid-May. Reach Spitsbergen before ice breakup in early June. Back to Greenwich in boat by 1st September.

Three whole years to go around the world? This must be wrong. We both doublechecked and tried to cut corners. But no, the seasons when polar travel are possible are short. Worse yet was the obvious likelihood that we might not complete the Antarctic crossing in one season. From the start we had to plan against such bad luck and allow an extra year down there for another winter and another attempt from where we left off. This contingency planning applied equally to the Northwest Passage and the Arctic Ocean. Take an umbrella with you and it won't rain. Plan for the worst, six years, and you might do it in three.

By the time the enormity of our self-imposed undertaking had fully sunk in with the slow unearthing of more information, we had spent over a year doing nothing else. We were like rolling stones. Having gone a little way down a hill, the realisation that the hill was more like a mountain with no yet-visible bottom was not going to stop us.

For the first year we lived in a basement flat at Earl's Court just behind the underground station, a grotty, noisy spot. 'We need an office,' Ginnie said. 'With a free telephone. There's no way we can set up everything here. The cost of phone calls and postage alone will be crippling.'

'I'll ask the colonel,' I replied. 'There must be spare space in the barracks.'

The 21st SAS Territorial Regiment is based in the Duke of York's barracks in Sloane Square. Mistakenly, the IRA believed that regular Special Air Service men used the place and had recently bombed it twice, both times damaging the Victorian brickwork but not much else.

The colonel was sympathetic; he even liked the idea. As a territorial or weekend soldier, I was in charge of a troop. My earlier explosive sins with the regular SAS had been forgotten – or so I thought. But the 21st SAS and its Scottish territorial counterpart, the 23rd SAS, are administered by a brigadier who also commands the regular regiment and when my colonel asked for his blessing, memories were revived. Was it the same Fiennes who had caused trouble six years previously? It was. How do we know he's changed his ways? We don't, but his scheme sounds worthwhile. We'll back it officially only if a responsible SAS man oversees Fiennes.

They obviously had a wry sense of humor because the man they chose was Mike Wingate-Gray, the man who had slung me out of the regiment and was now a retired brigadier. Surprisingly, he agreed to become nominal boss of the venture to keep me on the path of righteousness.

They gave us an office – an attic room in an unused indoor rifle range. There was no window and no light bulb, but on the plus side it was so quiet you could hear the mice pass wind, and there was a telephone. Ten days, two light bulbs and some purloined furniture later, the quartermaster visited us without an appointment and found Ginnie using the telephone (to a potential stationery sponsor).

He looked at me.

'That is a telephone.'

'Yes,' I agreed. 'Would you like some tea? We've installed a kettle –'

'That telephone is not on our establishment; it was removed last year.'

My blood ran cold. The telephone must be guarded at all costs. I decided not to annoy him.

'That's correct. It was removed. Do you take milk? Sugar?'

The quartermaster drank his tea but next morning our phone was gone. I knew the admin captain downstairs had many friends. The advantage of a territorial unit is the number of civilian professions represented. My friend Alf knew a post office technician and part-time supply corporal. Late one night, after minimal fiddling with the wiring, a new phone was installed and kept in a desk drawer when not in use. We were back in business.

By the end of 1973 a mountain of equipment from some two hundred sponsor companies was stored around the barracks in half-empty garages and armories.

When depressed by a bad morning of sponsors saying no we could always listen to the Irish Rifles recruits downstairs learning to play the bagpipes or watch the cast of *Upstairs Downstairs* rehearsing in the old gymnasium next door.

When our finances grew serious one of us would disappear for a while to recoup. I spent three weeks doing an expedition in the London sewers in the company of a statuesque blond actress as part of the BBC 'World About Us' series. Ginnie went to Oman for a month to live as a nominal third wife of a local sheikh in order to write a feature for *Woman's Own*. For two months I went to Brunei with a detachment of the regular SAS on a jungle-tracking course – the same course I had missed by a day seven years before owing to *Doctor Dolittle*. And in the evenings or at weekends I lectured at schools, universities, ladies' luncheon clubs and borstals about previous expeditions.

At that time our policy was to prepare all the equipment needed for the polar crossings. First things first. The oceans could wait. A smallish boat with a crew of volunteers would suffice. And as for aircraft support, I was assured by those polar men who would meet me that only a Hercules C-130 transport plane with skis could cope with the vast distances involved with our proposed Antarctic route.

The RAF had Hercules aircraft and I worked slowly but surely on gaining the support of the Ministry of Defence.

Whatever type of boat we used we would need fuel. I visited Sir David Barran, a top executive of Shell, in their skyscraper beside the Thames. He was friendly and tried hard to press my case with the rest of his board. No luck. British Petroleum was also negative so I approached the only other British-owned gasoline company – ICI Petrochemicals. After a year of correspondence they agreed to help.

The Army Mountain and Arctic Warfare Committee saw an opportunity at no cost for prolonged cold-weather tests for recently developed clothing and rations. Through them we obtained Arctic rations, excellent polar clothing and three hundred equipment parachutes.

To travel over the ice we needed dogs or machines to pull our sledges. Wally Herbert, Britain's most experienced polar traveller, writes: 'The partnership of man and dogs is the safest form of surface travel in the Arctic Ocean when beyond the range of light aircraft ... If a dog dies, he and his food supply are eaten by his teammates and the team carries on.' Geoffrey Hattersley-Smith, one of the few men to have worked with machines and dogs along the edge of the Arctic Ocean, stresses that his dog team could move a great deal faster over patches of rough ice than any type of snow machine. The superiority of dogs over machines for day-to-day travel in areas of broken polar ice was never in doubt, whoever we asked. Dogs do not refuse to start in low temperatures, nor do they break down and thereby waste weeks, and not just days, of good travel weather. But when I wrote to Wally Herbert in 1974 for his advice, his answer had been adamant. We should *not* use dogs unless we were prepared to spend a year or two learning how to handle them.

But a decision involving further prolonged delay was not easily acceptable and there were other factors to be considered, even if we had two years to spend learning to master the difficult art of dog driving and dog care. Our expedition would of necessity be under some public scrutiny, and the media can be quick to spotlight any real or imagined cruelty to animals. Although our intentions might be humane, the results could misfire. A Japanese polar expedition flew 180 huskies from Thule to Alert in specially built cages but the dogs panicked in the air and 105 died. Wally Herbert bought forty dogs in Qanaq but on the way back to his base a quarter either died or chewed through their traces and deserted. So, having weighed the pros and cons, we decided to use snow machines. Even if they made travel more difficult over the Arctic Ocean, they were financially and administratively within our scope. Dogs were not.

When a man who has never sailed but wants to goes to a boat show, he is confronted by a thousand different shapes, sizes and types. Bewildering, especially if he's uncertain of the conditions in the seas he will eventually visit. To help myself I categorised all of them in two groups. Snowcats, bigger machines with closed driving cabins; and snowmobiles, little ones with no protection from the elements. Previous homework indicated our sledge loads would be around one thousand pounds, so the machines selected had to be able to pull that weight in soft powder snow or on ice and have protection to save us from exposure. They also had to be light enough for two or three people to manhandle. Unable to make up my mind, I opted for one of each type, and after much letter writing obtained a Swedish snowmobile and an Austrian Snowcat big enough for two passengers in a little raised cabin. Since this looked like a groundhog on a Sugar Puffs package, that's what we called it.

I knew even less about the pros and cons of sledges except that if they broke up everything would come to an abrupt halt and wood repairs in low temperatures can take up huge amounts of precious time.

Wally advised me: 'I personally would *never* take a metal sledge. A sledge must be flexible and easy to repair as well as strong.' The Antarctic travelers I spoke to said the same thing. Nonetheless, anxious to take advantage of anything the twentieth century might offer, I approached the British Steel Corporation. They were interested. How would the Austenitic 316 special steel stand up to extreme temperatures? Using thin tubes welded by hand to the design of medical professor Noel Dilley, four eight-foot six-inch sledges for the Arctic and four twelve-foot nine-inch sledges for the Antarctic were fashioned by young BSC apprentices as part of their training under the watchful eye of expert steel welder Percy Wood, recently retired. 'We'll show these wood merchants a thing or two,' Percy muttered as the sledges were handed over to the expedition.

Meanwhile, my attempts to get approval for the Antarctic plans were going nowhere fast. The crossing plan depended on Hercules transport aircraft dropping parachutes with fuel and food. Only the RAF could provide this aid, but without the Royal Geographical Society's approval of the plans, they would not. The RGS committee would not even convene unless the Foreign Office gave the green light. *They* would not. An impasse.

After two years of turned-down proposals, my military patrons, the SAS, were becoming impatient. When any aspect of the plan was criticised, I altered it and reapplied. But the Foreign Office simply found new criticisms. Concentrating for a change on my Arctic plans for the Canadian Arctic sector, they found a new tack. Referring to my previous expedition in Canada, they said: 'A trail of litter had been left behind and the public had been critical.' I wrote to the Government of British Columbia and finally received a letter from their agent-general in London: '... The reports of littering and other charges were exaggerated and in some cases unfounded and the expedition was well-received by the public.' This left the false impression that there had been *some* litter and *some* genuine charges of complaint. Nonetheless, it put a stop to Foreign Office obstruction on that front. But that allegation alone took fourteen months to deflect and the Foreign Office simply reverted to new Antarctic objections. For example: 'No assessment by any experienced polar authority of the expedition's feasibility has been made ... There appear to be considerable risks in using metal sledges ... the technical details are not satisfactorily presented ... An expedition of this sort is a highly hazardous undertaking in which the chances of failure must be rated as high, however well-planned the logistics.' There were other points too, and the appraisal ended by suggesting that the proposal 'should be reconsidered in the light of these comments'.

Robin Knox-Johnson, single-handed yachtsman of common sense and experience, agreed to help advise on the maritime side. Until 1975 I had been content with the offer of a friend of Mike Wingate-Gray to skipper a steel-hulled fishing trawler fifty-four feet long, with an eighteen-foot beam, one hundred and thirty-horse-power motor and a crew of four. Robin shot this idea down in flames. The smallest crew we would need, he wrote, would be ten men. The cheapest boat, secondhand, that he advised for a voyage such as we projected would cost £350,000. As Ginnie said when we read this: 'Al Humdu lillah' [an Arabic expression of wonder meaning 'To God be the praise'].

Our route across Antarctica passed through terrain nominally held by South Africa, New Zealand and the United States. Since 1973 I had tried to woo the relevant officials. In December 1974 the

South Africans replied: 'Our Scientific Council for Antarctica Research has come to the conclusion it is unable to support the principle of your expedition to the South Pole via the Greenwich Meridian nor is it able to propose any worthwhile scientific mission which in its opinion your expedition could fruitfully undertake. I trust you will appreciate the implications of this decision.' The New Zealand reply came next: 'My principals have considered your proposals. I am instructed to advise that all New Zealand's resources in the spheres of logistics and scientific manpower are already over-committed to supporting . . . scientific programmes of national and international importance. New Zealand is not in a position to make commitments to support private expeditions . . . I regret that we cannot consider becoming involved in a supporting or a scientific role.'

After the first two years of learning how not to approach the Foreign Office, foreign governments and the individual members of Britain's polar circles, years in which we had on the plus side amassed a great deal of specialist equipment, we began to concentrate more on finding people for our team. We could forget aircraft crewmen, since if the RAF did help their Hercules would be fully manned. The ship's crew would have to wait. I went into a state of shock even thinking about a £350,000 boat. So the land team, those who would travel across the Poles and all the jungles, deserts, swamps and rivers in between, were my first target.

Previous journeys had made me a firm believer that the fewer people involved the better, since human beings seem to be badly designed for getting on with each other. Shove them together in a confined space and the sparks will usually fly: witness the one-in-three divorce rate.

Three or four seemed about as small an ice-travel team as we could get away with. There also had to be a mobile radio base to maintain communications. From previous trips I knew the job of base leader was a key position. If an expedition leader has a totally loyal and committed person watching his back in base, half the battle is won. Ginnie found herself volunteering for the job. But she would need someone to help run things. Not wanting her alone with some husky he-man, I thought it seemed a good idea to find a second girl. So we needed three men and a woman. The word was put about through friends and adventure organisations.

Andrew Croft, well known in polar circles, was in the early days almost the only member of those circles prepared to be seen to help and advise us. He was always forthright in his advice. On the ideal number for a travel group, he said: 'With three men, two can gang up against the leader. My experience suggests that you as leader should only decide whether to have two or three companions *after* you have seen your potential colleagues in action during Arctic training. The success or failure of the enterprise will largely depend on you, your leadership qualities and, above all, your judgement and choice of colleagues. Do not decide on them until you have lived and operated with them under extreme difficulties.'

This seemed sound advice, and since I was not at first planning any Arctic training, Snowdonia would have to do for the selection and training.

Between 1972 and 1978 a hundred and twenty volunteers for the land team tried their luck. Some lasted no longer than the interview stage. I had a stock approach which I called the black talk. 'If you want to join you must apply to the Territorial SAS Regiment in the corridor just below this attic. They have a weekend selection course in Wales.'

'What, just the weekend?'

'No, twelve weekends and a final two-week test in the hills. You will need to get rid of your beard and some of that hair, of course.' If this last point did not get rid of them at once, the black talk continued. 'If the SAS accepts you as a trooper, come back again and we'll have another talk. If you're still interested, you must leave your job and help us here full-time to get the expedition going.'

'What's the pay?'

'Pay? This is an expedition. There is no pay.'

'But you say the journey may last three years. How do I live?'

'The expedition will last at least three years. But it could be that we aren't ready to leave as planned in 1975. If so, we just keep working till we're ready. We only work during the day normally, so you can get a job in the evenings and weekends to keep alive.'

'What if you can't get the support? You've got no ship, no aircraft, they say.'

'We *will* get going one day.'

'Yeah, but if I give up my job, I won't get it back again. I've got to be sure there's at least going to be an expedition.'

'You can be.'

'You're a captain and a sir. You don't need to work.'

This one made me swallow. 'Look, friend, I may have a title but I don't have any income except what I earn. I lecture at sixty-five pounds a crack plus travel. Evenings and weekends. Ginnie and I don't entertain, we don't drink. We don't have a home life. *This* is our life. You either commit yourself or you don't.'

The bulk of them we never saw again. But some made it into the Territorial SAS and worked on and off to help us. Those who were most interested had already joined the unit and heard about us at first hand. But few could make the final decision to pack in their jobs. Dan Oxbury, a 21st SAS trooper, sent us a letter, one we had many others like. '... I'm writing, somewhat sadly, to tell you, after a lot of careful thought, I've decided to withdraw from the expedition while you still have time to find another candidate. Believe me, this has been one of the most difficult decisions I've ever made.' Then followed the explanations.

I knew a very special man, Geoff Holder, from the Royal Engineers from a previous expedition. Tough but warmhearted, he would be ideal, I thought. I traced him to a helicopter unit in Hong Kong. His reply in late 1974: 'I would like to take part but there are a couple of constraints. I am now married with three daughters. If I am to take part I must obtain an income no less than my current one so as to clothe, house and educate family. Also I would expect my wife to be able to fly to the various stopping points en route. If these two problems and a few other minor ones can be overcome, I would much like to join you.' No comment.

Whoever did make the grade I took on weekends in Snowdonia each winter and spring from 1973 until 1976. Usually there was freezing rain, thick mist and strong winds. Sometimes, for good measure, snow and ice covered the rocks. The route was always the same, the course of an annual army race called the Welsh 3000. Twenty-four miles if you did not add a bit getting lost. One man fell three hundred feet and cut his knee open. On his way down he knocked two civilians off. They fared worse, ending up with helicopter evacuation to a hospital. A good time for the course was between seven and nine hours. But it didn't matter if they took fourteen so long as they finished. I was trying to find out about their character under stress, not their physical ability – the SAS selection would have made sure that was above average.

Whoever I ended up with would need to be good astronavigators, deft mechanics, capable radio operators and medics to the extent of removing an appendix or tooth in a tent. But I looked only for good nature and patience, the first virtue being the cardinal point. Ginnie and I were not necessarily either, but there wasn't much we could do about that. At least I could try to ensure that the rest of the group were. How we succeeded in our choice only time would tell. The plan was, when we found our paragons, to have them trained in the necessary skills on army courses which, like the

Welsh 3000 weekends, were army activities and so cost us nothing. So long as we put in time with the regiment they were happy to help.

Our mountain team became fit. Most years we won the territorial army trophy. Once we beat all regular army entries apart from the Gurkhas and they were discounted as being hardly human when moving in the hills. In 1974, after seven hours we finished two minutes behind the little brown greyhounds. That year four men looked like good material for the expedition: a surveyor, an engineer, a shutterer (concrete mouldmaker) and a scaffolding erector. We took all four to the Cairngorms' Arctic Plateau for two weeks in the winter with snowmobiles and sledges. But twelve months later I decided two were not suitable, one started his own company filling roofs with insulating foam, and the best of them had his passport revoked by the income tax department after his scaffolding activities 'on the lump' were discovered.

About that time George Greenfield suggested a cautious approach to Sir Vivian Fuchs to obtain his personal support for the venture. Sir Vivian made two things clear. The Antarctic Treaty precluded *any* form of military exercise, training or activity (including the use of an RAF Hercules) unless purely in support of scientific activities. His advice was for ours to become a purely civilian venture. Secondly, he insisted that my proposals would never be taken seriously unless we gained experience. We must train in polar regions, *then* put forward the more ambitious plan.

I came to accept this as inescapable and with a heavy heart told Dr Hunter of the Greenwich Observatory that a 1975 start was out.

How to gain polar experience? We could not get to Antarctica, but the Greenland ice cap was similar in many ways and much more accessible. On its northwest coast at Thule is an American BMEWS site. The bachelor staff there say this stands for Balmy Men Existing Without Sex. It is in fact one of a chain of Ballistic

Missile Early Warning Sites set up during the cold war of the fifties along with the Nome site in Alaska and Fylingdales in Yorkshire.

The RAF, I discovered, operated three polar navigation training flights to Thule each summer using Hercules C-130s, often with no cargo. Ideal to get our kit and ourselves there.

I quickly formulated a new proposal for summer 1976 – three months ice-cap travel near Thule followed by five months training on the Arctic Ocean to the north. Canadian Air Force C-130s fly weekly from Thule to their Arctic base Alert on Ellesmere Island, the most northern inhabitation in the world. The vicinity of Alert would be ideal for our Arctic training camp.

We set to work to get a new set of permits: from the Danes who owned Greenland; the Americans for Thule; and the Canadians for Alert. Unlike Antarctica, the Arctic had no hangup about 'military training'.

But in June 1975 our Foreign Office friends turned down the new scheme. Perhaps they perceived the thin end of the wedge. This time all their comments were focused on the Alert training. So I played our last hand by asking simply to go to Thule for three months of ice-cap travel and mentioned that if such an exercise was successfully completed, I would *then* press to go to Alert for further ice experience.

At last less opposition. We'd been at it for four years before our first 'approval in principle' was given for this diluted plan. The RAF agreed to take our cargo to Thule but not team members even though all were territorials. After five visits to the United States Embassy in London I met an air attaché who was prepared to listen. Colonel Paul Clark was obviously no textbook officer. He liked the circumpolar scheme and nodded with sympathy at my tale of official delays.

'So all you guys want from us is a trip to Thule care of the United States Air Force?'

I nodded, holding my breath.

'Well, we're here to help. I'll call you.'

So although the RAF would not fly British soldiers to Greenland, for $2,000 the USAF agreed to take us there via New Jersey. Paul Clark was later to give up a promising career with the United States armed forces to join us as an unpaid deckhand.

The long weary years in the attic were nearing an end. They were an investment we had made of our own free will. We had learned patience, and in the process had grown much closer together.

As for the stonewalling ... the army did what they could to help but they, like us, were hidebound by the Foreign Office. And as for the Foreign Office, it had long since learned that to keep private individuals out of Antarctica, which it considered its unwritten duty, it had only to turn aside all approaches until the applicant just gave up.

We were stubborn.

Chapter Two

Failure has no friends.

JOHN F. KENNEDY

In 1975 we were promoted downward to a ground-floor office with two telephones.

One day a well-dressed man with an air of mild debauchery walked in. Oliver Shepard was tall and dark and wanted to join us. Mentally I denounced him as unsuitable on sight. For starters I remembered him from Eton days as a pompous-sounding character with pompous-sounding friends. We had joined the 21st SAS at the same time by chance but seldom met. For three years I had seen nothing of him but heard through the grapevine that he had expensive tastes, was separated from his wife and lived a life as far removed from expeditions as chalk from cheese.

A quick interrogation revealed that he was working for a wine and beer distributor, managing their Chelsea pubs and enjoying a good salary complete with Volvo estate car and healthy expense account which was reflected in his paunch. Altogether not a propitious background for our purposes, but there was no harm in letting him try his luck. So he rejoined the Territorials and began to suffer weekends in Snowdonia.

Mary Gibbs came to us through friends of friends. She was dark and pretty. Ginnie got on well with her, and she gave up her job with a book publisher. Not able to join the SAS, she signed up with a Territorial hospital unit based in the barracks. Ginnie was likewise attached to a signals regiment.

Geoff Newman, tall and fair and powerfully built, gave up a printing job to join us, and in July that year Oliver took me to a local party where I met one Charlie Burton who had just left a job in South Africa. The next morning he turned up at the barracks in an old tweed overcoat and smoking an evil-smelling briar. Geoff and he began their SAS selection course early in 1976. In March the six of us, with one or two others, went training in the Cairngorms.

Again I ran through the basics of cross-country skiing, how to erect a polar tent and how to cook dehydrated rations. And again I wondered how long *this* group would last.

I needn't have worried. All four seemed ideal – in fact, they improved with time. Geoff and Mary became quietly attached. Oliver and Charlie, both extroverts and accomplished beer-drinkers, developed a close and lasting friendship. They took my initial black talk in their stride.

With the kit more or less ready, we intended to leave in June 1976 for Greenland and to come back in September to push through the Arctic proposal and, presuming the authorities gave it a fair wind, head north again to Alert in January 1977.

Out of his job, Ollie Shepard took up residence within the barracks, sleeping on our office floor and eating dehydrated expedition rations. His paunch disappeared.

One night our friend Andrew Croft asked us to supper. The key Foreign Office man was also there, not our initial bête noire but a younger, friendly man who had taken over the Polar Desk. He was prepared to help from now on but warned us it would be a long uphill struggle and the main expedition's chances would depend on our success or otherwise in Greenland and the Arctic.

Spring fled by. The team trained hard. Charlie and Geoff were accepted into the SAS; Charlie and Geoff as troopers, Ollie and I as captains. Ginnie and Mary in their separate outfits were privates.

Ollie took numerous courses. On April 25 his diary recorded: 'I am now a doctor.' On May 18: 'Now I am a dentist.' (This was after a one-day course with the Royal Army Dental Corps.)

'What's the secret of good dentistry?' I asked him.

'You've got to be cruel to be kind,' he said.

I made a mental note to keep my teeth well away from him.

Two weeks after his general hospital attendance Ollie was itching to get at our appendixes but two years later, out on the ice, it was all he could do to remember which side they were on.

In the past, expeditions for me were hermetically sealed units. You left England, carried out your set task and returned. All the team went too. None stayed behind as United Kingdom representatives. But things were different now. Work toward the main venture had to go on while we were away training. Mike Wingate-Gray and Andrew Croft together with Peter Booth, a friend from previous travels, agreed to carry on in London.

Ginnie, our communications planner, would be unable to telephone them from polar bases so she visited the Cove Radio and Navigation Department of the Royal Aircraft Establishment at Farnborough. With the permission of their departmental boss, the three officers there agreed to act as Ginnie's United Kingdom radio base. They would then phone Andrew Croft or the others in London. This way we could have speedy communications even from the Poles whenever ionospheric conditions were favourable.

Throughout June and July the RAF and the USAF got the jitters about carrying us and our cargo to Thule. In Greenland the short summer season sped by. Finally in late July, all in uniform, we flew to New Jersey with one hundred and fifty United States nuclear submariners. From there, in a windowless transport plane, to Sondrestrom in Greenland, and soon after to Thule Missile Warning Site. We settled into an empty wooden house the Americans kindly let us use and awaited the RAF with our cargo.

The sun did not go away at all, just spun a yellow hula-hoop above the dead and gravel hills. To the east by ten miles crouched the rim of the giant ice cap.

In August the RAF brought our kit including sledges and two groundhog machines. On our Cairngorms trials the groundhogs proved much more punchy than the smaller snowmobile, so I'd ordered a second – a duplicator company and some breakfast cereal manufacturers kindly paid for them.

The ice cap above Thule was well mapped. The crevasse fields were localised and could be crossed or avoided as one wished. I planned to squeeze two trips into what remained of the short summer season. First, an eighty-mile loop journey swinging around the Haynes Peninsula and passing through two known crevasse zones. If all went well with the untested machines, the steel sledges and the inexperienced participants, the second, more ambitious, journey would follow immediately, heading east toward the interior of the ice cap for one hundred and fifty miles along the fissured slopes which parallel the jagged coastline of Melville Bight.

If the weather held, we thought we should complete both journeys by the end of September, with a sound knowledge of problems similar to those encountered in Antarctica and, as important, in time to catch the early October flight back to England. This last would enable me to face the Royal Geographical Expedition Society's committee meeting on November 1 to decide the fate of my 1977 Arctic training proposal.

*

On a brisk August morning three of us set out from the edge of the ice cap. None of us knew what lay ahead; none of us 'knew' ice or how to deal with its obstacles, its moods and its terrors. There were three of us for a number of reasons: mainly because I subconsciously suspected three would prove ideal for the Arctic, and partly because our tents were designed for three, not four. There was, too, an apparent advantage in leaving one male with our otherwise all-woman radio base. After Greenland I hoped to know the good and bad points of the three men. Oliver, who had been with me longest, was a good radio operator, a sound medic and a solid, if sometimes snappy, person. It was generally agreed that he should be groomed as our future chief mechanic, and so he should stay with his groundhog throughout the Greenland journey. I was uncertain about Charlie and Geoff and so decided to take one on the loop journey, the other on the inland route.

When asked who would like which, Charlie had wrinkled his dark eyebrows, thought for a while and, looking at Geoff, muttered: 'Not fussy. What about you, Geoff?' Geoff had not hesitated. 'I'll do the loop journey.' I skied ahead with one eye never far from my compass and my ski sticks, prodding hard to reveal any false surface. A man with his weight spread on skis should be safe enough over all but the weakest crevasse ceilings. Geoff drove a yellow groundhog and Oliver, far behind, a red vehicle, and each towed two sledges loaded with tents, food, petrol, aluminium ladders, ropes and radio. Slowly we crept up the side of the rolling escarpment of ice.

When we finally halted, the stillness of the ice cap weighed down on our conversation so that we too were quiet, stopping what we were doing just to listen and get the feel of silence. A bowl of ice like a shallow amphitheatre hid the true horizons. Streamers of blue-black cloud swelled into mushrooms and thunderheads. The air was cool yet electric in its stillness. I erected the tent while Geoff prepared his air-sampling gear and Oliver checked the groundhogs, working from a manual. The sounds they made seemed unnaturally loud. Eerie. We spoke little. The orange cloth of the tent flapped idly. There was no wind and I wondered if air pressure caused the movement. None of us had ever experienced a blizzard. The finest grains of spindrift touched my cheeks, and looking up, I saw a soft film of vapour move across the sky above the horizon. By my feet, like dust devils in a desert, scurrying fingers of snow suddenly were blowing in all directions. And suddenly stopped. And then blew afresh with greater energy and more direction. A gentle motion animated the tent. My nose and ears felt cool, and through the light silk covering of my face mask I heard the faintest sound, like the saturation of wind in some unseen forest.

A pall of grey cloud covered our white saucer world. I remembered the words of a Greenland pundit back in London: 'Watch the winds of the west coast. Never mind the interior where the gradient's easy. It's the coastal slopes that cop the sudden hammer blows. The wind starts up on top at eight thousand feet and gathers speed as she roars down towards the sea. They've recorded one hundred and eighty knots at Thule, and that would tear down the toughest tent on the market.'

Now that we were on the ice sheet right above Thule, despite the gentle incline and general docility of the terrain, I began to wonder if the weather could suddenly turn that nasty. Half-afraid that the others would accuse me of overcaution, I began to shovel snow onto the wide skirt of the tent, tightening the material and pinning it down. We were in no position to predict the weather on the ice cap and, as it turned out, ignorance was bliss.

More snow fell on Greenland that year than had ever been recorded before. Early in 1977 Professor Hubert Lamb, the climate expert at the University of East Anglia, was quoted as saying there had been so heavy a snowfall in 1976 that the Greenland ice cap was made unduly heavy in terms of the world's balance. An enormous weight had been added to the earth's surface at a particular point. Since the earth wobbles on its orbit in the best of times, this unbalancing weight might well have altered the natural vibration. Which could have changed the atmospheric circulation and so too the fragile weather pattern.

Within thirty minutes of the first light breeze the air was thick with driven snow, great wet flakes that clogged in the wolverine rime of our parkas and the wool of gloves and socks. Body warmth quickly thawed the snow, so our clothes were soon damp. Inside the tent, snow from our clothes and boots fell to the groundsheet and, once the cooker heated the air, the snow turned to water and everything began to get damp.

For a while the wind hovered, playing cat-and-mouse, then pounced with the rush of a breaking wave. The three ten-foot aluminium tent poles creaked, twanged and settled to a jerking vibration. The cloth strained taut and palsied with the violence of the onslaught, shaking off its moisture onto our bags.

After a night of silent wonder, of introduction to a side of nature so easily ignored in an urban lifetime, we went outside to dig away snow that threatened to bury the tent.

Outside the particular feeling of helplessness was familiar. I remembered too clearly a sandstorm in Arabia when just such a maelstrom of confounding, omnipotent energy had blurred my senses and concentrated all my thought processes on the immediate search for shelter from the cutting blast of the elements. To face away from the wind was not enough: a thousand whipping ice spicules lashed the eyes, spun down the smallest gaps in clothing, clustered on eyebrows and came from everywhere, it seemed, at once.

In five minutes we were all back inside the tent feeling, for the first of many times, what a wonderful place it was after all. The most physically miserable moments of my life were to pass in that tent but never once, at the end of a day, would my pleasure at entering its little world be cloyed by the evil memories of the night before. The intense relief of removal from the frying pan before commencing the new sensations of the fire.

For three days the storm lashed the featureless world about us and we began to learn the art of doing nothing in a small space. There is no room for privacy, no room to stand, no food beyond the daily dehydrated ration. Water comes from snow scooped from just right of and outside the inner lining. The lavatory area is just to the left of and outside the inner lining. Unless the storm should last for longer than there is snow to be scooped up, there should be no reason to open the outer entrance sleeve.

Until the end of August we travelled to the limit of the peninsula, to such moonlit fairylands as the tumbled icefall of Puissitdlussarsuaq. Each day brought less sun and more moon. It was a wild land of immense beauty.

On August 28 we celebrated Oliver's birthday with a squashed fruitcake. As we munched, the evening radio call came through. Ginnie sounded weary.

'Hello, Two Four. This is Zero Alpha.' After wishing Oliver a happy thirtieth birthday she continued in a quiet voice. 'Some bad news. The weekly United States passenger plane left here this morning with a mixed load of Americans and Danes. It crashed on landing at Sondre Stromfjord. The fuselage caught fire and twenty-seven passengers were killed, others cruelly burned. A message has just come through from Mildenhall in Suffolk. Another USAF passenger plane crashed there early this morning. Seventeen dead. It could be a coincidence but naturally the United States authorities are suspicious, especially of foreigners like us.'

*

The eighty-mile loop journey was finished a month behind schedule but we had learned a good deal. Geoffrey was quite the opposite sort of character to Ollie, but both seemed tough and resilient.

The time had come for a changeover.

Charlie and the girls met us at the edge of the ice sheet. Ginnie seemed ill at ease. I told her all had gone well on the ice cap, in particular that Geoffrey and Oliver had lived up to our expectations. I asked about Mary and Charlie. Mary, she said, was hardworking and cheerful. She was worried about Charlie.

If he behaved on the ice, she said, as he had at the base hut, we could be in for trouble. It was not so much what he had done as what he had not done. Mary and he had not hit it off, to put it mildly. There was a great deal to do maintaining the base, fetching water, servicing generators and manning radio watch, but Charlie was morose and idle. He would spend long hours on his mattress in the hut reading cowboy books, of which he had discovered an inexhaustible supply. He had made friends with a local Danish fire chief and often disappeared on boozing sessions in one of Thule's many private bars. Mary was inclined to be bossy with him and Ginnie short tempered, so the combination was not ideal.

Since Geoff had volunteered to do the first journey, the loop, it was now Charlie's turn to come on the main inland route. Oliver as mechanic and I as navigator would do both. I was not alone in my doubts about Charlie. Oliver's diary at the time said: 'It's a pity Geoff is off tomorrow. I know he has a much better personality than Charlie and I can work with him better. He is more stable and quiet. The next three weeks could be very interesting.'

The girls departed, taking Geoff with them. Oliver found a rounded gully and taught Charlie the tricks of driving a groundhog with two heavy sledges. I was determined to watch Charlie's weaknesses during the inland journey with a critical eye and, if necessary, remove him from the team before we went any further; after all, any basic failing revealed in Greenland was likely to recur in magnified form in the harsher environment of the Arctic. We hoped to spend up to six years of enforced togetherness in tough circumstances if all our plans materialised.

In terms of the Arctic, Greenland was not cold, but at the time we were all struck by the sudden temperature drop as the evening advanced. It was also the first time the sun fell below the horizon and stayed there while we travelled. Oliver, the toughest of us, wrote in his diary: '... minus 14 degrees Centigrade. It is unbelievably cold.' My own recorded comments were somewhat more basic: 'The cold has made the surface firm. The skis slide well and fast now. Two balaclavas keep the ears warm but my nose cracked for the first time. It's a pity it's so large. On the other hand, while trying to relieve myself just before we set out, I decided some things *would* be better larger. With mittens on, it was difficult to locate owing to the overlap of three layers of underwear, top and bottom, two pairs of trousers and a very long front shirttail. Owing to the puffy nature of my duvet jacket I could not see below my chest and did everything by touch. When I thought all was ready, it turned out that my mitt was holding one end of my belt whereas the offended item, scared by the cold wind, had in fact retreated. This I discovered too late in the day.'

Ollie, acting as radio operator as well as mechanic, gave a shout of triumph from inside the tent.

'How's that for communications? Washington – clear as a bell.' Greatly impressed, Charlie and I placed an earpiece close to the headset. Two men with American accents were talking about geology and the terrible weather. The conversation ended with one of them saying, 'Till tomorrow, Washington Land. Over and out.'

'That can't be bad, eh?' chuckled Oliver. 'Over two thousand miles and perfect reception.'

I had studied our small-scale Greenland map with care and

remembered seeing a peninsula some two hundred miles north of Thule. It was totally devoid of any significant features other than the grand-sounding name of Washington Land.

I waited until Oliver had regaled Charlie with various bits of technical know-how about obtaining such long-distance clarity before showing Charlie Washington Land's actual location on the map.

There was much laughter that evening in the tent. We were elated at the thought of the journey ahead. Charlie was happy to be away from Thule. He showed no signs of evil humour and pulled his weight at whatever we did, being unusually quick at copying our actions – with our earlier journey behind us, we thought of ourselves as experts. This might have been annoying for Charlie but he never showed it. He took over the signalling duties although his Morse was painfully slow. Every morning and evening, when conditions allowed, he sent back our location with detailed observations of the prevailing cloud formations, the minimum temperature, the barometer reading, the wind speed and the visibility factor.

Geoff's job for the Meteorological Office had been the measuring of ice nuclei in the atmosphere above the ice cap. He did this by attaching a suction pipe to a pump driven by a mini-generator, the whole apparatus acting like a vacuum cleaner. To the working or sucking end he attached filters on which the nuclei were trapped, and by using a special processing technique he was able to count their number.

Although colder, the second and longer journey at first went well. Our destination was the lofty ridge line running north to the inland plateau from the island of Norujupaluk. To reach it involved a tortuous up-and-down journey some forty miles along shoulders of falling ice, almost certainly crevassed but sufficiently well covered with snow bridges, we hoped, to provide a safe enough passage providing we kept our eyes open.

We passed at length along a natural corridor through rising mountains, and once through it, the ice began to show its jaws: ploughed fields with bottomless furrows.

We tied nylon ropes between the two tracked snow vehicles. Each weighed half a ton and each towed two sledges. We called them groundhogs because of their comic appearance. Charlie drove the first, Oliver the second. My weight was well distributed on seven-foot-long skis, so at least in principle I was less likely than the machines to break through the thin snow crust that disguised many of the crevasses. Nonetheless I moved with caution, prodding the crust with a ski stick and checking my compass only when I stopped.

We climbed all day. At first our bearing and the lay of the land agreed with each other, but by evening, as the temperature dropped to minus 9 degrees Fahrenheit, the great white dune angled north away from our axis. Reluctantly I sidestepped, rechecked the compass and began to tack in long obtuse zigzags across the face of the gradient.

Almost at once the metallic bark of a horn sounded. Both machines were in first gear and straining, the diagonal angle of ascent creating an uneven pull. Charlie's gloved hand was signalling from his cab. His rear sledge had overturned, but he hadn't stopped, out of fear of losing momentum.

I skied back and heaved the slowly moving sledge onto its runners. The boxes were lashed in place, so none had spilled its contents. No sooner had I struggled back to the front to set the correct trail than a horn barked again. This time it was Oliver. Same thing all over again.

The next four hours were exhausting as the slope grew steeper yet and the overturns more frequent. Darkness found us lost and groping. The machines would no longer pull two sledges, so each driver took one sledge forward a mile or so, then cautiously turning on the steep face of the ice field, retraced the trail to bring up his other sledge. In this manner, tired and very thirsty, we came to the crest of the climb shortly before midnight. Charlie lit the Optimus to melt snow and make tea, but the wind cut into us on this high ridge, the sweat of exertion damp under our vests.

Oliver, who had gone to the far edge of the crest with binoculars, now called me over. We stood on a knife-edge above a Christmas land of fragile beauty. Under a million brilliant stars the silvered rock of distant ranges danced along wraiths of valley mist. A silence brooded here, a beautiful silence that lay alike over the virgin snow-fields and the menace of the fissure zones, black veins in the moon-pink valley. I forgot the wind. This was the hidden Valley of Dreams, glimpsed once and never again. The answer to life's search might lie in such a place.

Charlie's voice came over the rise. Our tea was getting cold. Horrors! The moment went. When next we saw the valley a bank of sea mist covered all but our own target peak and the upper ramparts of the scattered giants.

Tacking up the hill had not been possible with the groundhogs roped together . . . the tracks kept tangling and fraying the nylon. Now that we were no longer attached we began the descent. Back in England the learned pundits had said: 'The steeper the slope the greater the danger.' But we were committed.

I entered the mist. All ahead was grey. Behind, the groundhogs eased on to the knife-edge, their tracks cutting deep, sledges jostling and colliding. In the yellow murk they loomed monsterlike over the crest, nosing down the faint runnels of my ski tracks.

My thighs ached with the strain of stemming the skis. The slope was steep. I felt the edge of fear as the void fell away in the gloom. There was no sense of distance, no shadow or perspective, no noise other than the snow thrown against my goggles and the sharp hiss of the hickory skis biting ever faster. A long dark shadow lay directly ahead. How close I could not tell but I swerved and it was gone. This was a fool's game. Bending low, I began a curving telemark, leading with the left knee. It seemed an age. Then before I knew it, I had stopped. Turning to listen for the others I overbalanced. My ski stick, thrust out to stop me falling, broke straight through the surface snow and disappeared. My arm followed up to the shoulder. With slow movements, carefully keeping my body weight over both skis, I moved away from the small black hole in the snow, the only indication of hidden danger.

I cursed myself again for a fool. This was no place for travel by night. There could be no way of knowing how steep or how long the descent below was. But the groundhogs would certainly not make it back up this same slope. Nor could we safely wait where we were – it was cold and too steep to pitch a tent. Should a blizzard come without warning we couldn't risk being caught here unprotected.

The machines eased downward, close together. Both drivers gave a thumbs-up, travelling in first gear, using the steering brakes as sparingly as possible. I held on to Charlie's cab, using it as a brake to rest my legs but keeping both skis clear of the churning tracks; the groundhog was no bigger than a two-door family car.

'My arm went through a crevasse back there,' I shouted through his window. 'And you've just driven over it.'

Charlie looked strained in the faint light of his cab, but he managed to grin. 'Pull the other leg – it's got bells on.'

I shook my head, but two gloved fingers appeared against the plastic window.

The descent had begun to ease. I let go of the groundhog and immediately sped away, this time under control. The farther we descended the darker it became. It seemed an age before the slope levelled out and only then, when we were well and truly committed to the valley, did it reveal its unpleasant nature.

I slid to a halt and threw back the fur-rimmed hood of my parka to listen. Looking back and around I saw nothing but the hostile grin of the mist, heard only the imagined echo of my skis cutting the snow. Then a distant fox barked. Twice, short and sharp. I kick-turned the light Norwegian skis and langlaufed back up my trail. Suddenly a groundhog appeared with Charlie half out of its cab.

Oliver, he said, had gone down a crevasse.

At first I could see nothing. Charlie pointed to a vague line of darker gloom. I skied toward it. Oliver's groundhog had a flag on its cabin roof, and it was this Charlie had seen. The rest of the vehicle had completely disappeared from view.

Cresting the rise, I finally saw the trapped groundhog, and catching my breath, came to an abrupt halt. My ski tips hung over a narrow canyon in the snow that led in zigzag fashion to the hole that had swallowed Oliver's machine.

I inspected the fissure and could see no bottom to it. Oliver had been driving almost parallel to its course when his groundhog's right-hand track had punctured the rotten bridge concealing its presence. The vehicle must have lurched sideways and downward. Fortunately, for the moment at least, the left-hand track had caught on the lip of the crevasse and balanced there. But the least movement could dislodge the machine and send it plunging downward.

As I watched, Oliver began to wriggle out of his tiny cabin door, his parka catching on the controls as he did so. The groundhog rocked to and fro; snow fell away from the bank which held it, and Oliver, realising his danger, redoubled his efforts. Soon he was on the catwalk beside the cab and, keeping his weight central, edged toward the safer side, away from the void. Each time the machine lurched and slipped a bit, he froze. When it quieted he moved, eel-like, nearer terra firma. He did well, escaping without disturbing the machine. Now we had only to pull it out, an event we had long prepared for. Oliver, without the safety of skis, stayed where he was. I moved over to Charlie and motioned him forward.

On paper we had agreed on the best method of recovery: a straightforward pull by the still mobile groundhog using Kevla, a towrope endowed with a great deal of elastic strength. Once enough elasticity was induced by the towing machine, the other should by rights pop out of its predicament like a cork from a champagne bottle.

Charlie reversed, then slowly nosed through the moving wraith of mist into the best approach angle. He was perhaps eighty yards from Oliver and well away from the crevasse when it happened.

The only noise was a sharp thud as Charlie's head hit the windscreen. What I saw, as the snow unzipped in front of me, was a long black cavern.

The groundhog was moving slowly at the time. Charlie was quick. He slammed on both steering brakes as he felt himself fall, coming to an abrupt halt as his vehicle jammed its upper catwalks between the lips of the new crevasse. Then, unseen, the moon edged behind the southern hills, and the darkness was complete. By torchlight and wary as long-tailed cats in a room full of rocking chairs, we tested the snow yard by yard until we came to Charlie. He was out before we reached him and unlashing his tent from his leading sledge.

We made camp between the two crevasses, hoping that the spot we chose was solid. We were tired, miles from anywhere, and caught between an escarpment we could not climb and a deeply crevassed valley through which we must travel to escape.

For two days we shovelled, dug, chipped and cursed. At first the task had seemed beyond us. To extricate the groundhogs from the dizzy perches meant moving them backward or forward. Yet the slightest movement in either direction would only serve to widen the gap in the delicate snow bridges and send the machines plunging downward.

Oliver's diary records: 'We spent the day roped together as crevasses are all around us. One, close to the tent, is about five feet wide and has infinite depth.'

After many hours we completed tunnels for our aluminium crevasse ladders well beneath the sunken groundhogs. The recovery operation was dicey but it worked.

Our timetable was now in the red. Winter and darkness were upon us. The journey back to Thule was splattered with crevasse alarms, boggings and countless breakdowns. But Oliver always coped. With spindrift settling down his neck and some of his fingers split from the nails back to the first knuckle, he continued patiently and thoroughly, 'botching up' where he had no spare part to do the job. As he worked Charlie watched, helping where he could. Oliver was often short and sharp with him but he ignored this: it was Oliver's way when embroiled with details. Theirs was a close and easy friendship. Luckily, however, the two did not form an alliance against me. In the back of beyond where there are no links with normal life, friendship is vitally important.

Two things, I believe, saved us from a triangle situation. Both men were strong individualists and at all times stuck rigidly to their independent theories on how things should best be done. They did not experience the temptation of forming a united front for the sake of it or the better to disrupt my own way of doing things. When each disagreed with my theories he did so separately and openly, avoiding the behind-the-back consultations which are the most poisonous ingredient even a short expedition can suffer. Secondly, I had been through life without feeling the need for close friends, probably due to a youth spent amusing myself, as my three elder sisters had different tastes. Most days I could speak to Ginnie on the radio or at least listen to her Morse signals, so there was never a feeling of personal isolation. I had been lucky enough to be able to select with care individuals without malice. Such people are surprisingly rare. With Charlie the malice content was minimal, with Oliver, nonexistent.

Despite the holdups our pace was faster than before. Oliver's mechanical work was slicker; we could strike or break camp in under an hour and many little short cuts learned over the weeks saved us much previously wasted time.

We returned to Thule not a day too soon. The weather clamped down on the icecap and stayed there, a grim, grey blanket hiding the whole feature from the camp. But the wind spilled down the valley, battering at the manmade installations and tearing through Thule to lash the icebergs and the black islands beyond.

Once again six in number, we stored all the kit, cleaned and greased for the winter, and told the authorities, Danish and American, that we hoped to be back in about three months' time to pick it all up by transport plane on our way north to Alert and the Arctic Ocean.

I returned from Greenland fit and weighing 185 pounds. Over the next three months in London, the most harassing I can remember, I lost fourteen pounds without exercise or a diet. My first grey hairs also sprouted during this period.

There are those who think of expeditions as fun and games for the rich. Had we been attempting to gain recognition and support for an expedition to raid a bank in Moscow, the authorities could hardly have shown a more suspicious, antagonistic attitude. Every hurdle that could be produced was shoved in our way – or so it seemed. Our official route to the Arctic was as straight as a butcher's hook. If our funds had been limitless we could probably have bought our way around many of the obstacles, but the vital political permissions would still have proved elusive.

Just before we left Thule I had been offered a quick visit on the weekly supply plane to Alert. During the forty-minute stop-off at the Canadian base I saw the station commander and told him our intentions. Two miles north of his camp, on the very edge of the ocean, was a huddle of empty shacks owned by Polar Shelf – an Arctic research group based in Ottawa. Their boss had kindly said we could use his huts as our base. This did not mean we could *get* there. The airstrip was maintained and lit up by the military, the only people physically at Alert.

I explained to their boss that as yet we did not have the British army's blessing, but when we did I would like to ask for Canadian forces' support to take us and our cargo from Thule to Alert using existing flights, not extra ones.

Within a week of returning to London my unofficial visit to Alert rebounded with a vengeance. The Canadians had asked the British High Commission in Ottawa about my plans. The latter burst a blood vessel and scattered signals like confetti, or, more aptly, like ashes. Mike Wingate-Gray fielded one and showed it to me. Distinctly unflattering.

Somehow SAS support stayed with us, but the wider army backing withered away. One of its suggestions was:

> In view of the revised policy for territorial training and the security restrictions placed on expeditions operating in the Alert area, it is strongly recommended that no further action is taken to have this project submitted as an Army Adventurous Training Exercise.

Which meant that any chance of RAF Hercules transport aircraft supporting our planned travels in the Arctic or Antarctic was now out of the question. Yet such flights were crucial to the whole venture.

Since, as they say, crying over spilled milk is a waste of time, I inquired about the cost of chartering a Twin Otter ski-plane for our Arctic work. I found out it came to £50,000 if we could get away with only three resupply flights after the initial ones between Thule and Alert. Awesome.

An old friend of mine was an ex-soldier who lived and worked in Arabia. At the time he was visiting London and he offered to introduce me to his friend Dr Omar Zawawi, an Omani businessman who had built up a business in Zanzibar and subsequently in Europe. Dr Omar, a charming man with a wealth of good humour and razor-sharp perception, saw me at his Knightsbridge house. Nothing seemed to escape his dark brown eyes. For two hours I described our aims and our problems. He approved of free enterprise. He had read and enjoyed a book I had written about Oman. Most of all he was grateful to the individual Britons who had risked their lives for the freedom of his country. The upshot of the meeting was a dinner at which he introduced Ginnie and me to a Yorkshireman, Jack Codd, the managing director of Tarmac International. A month later we received £58,000 from Dr Omar and Jack Codd as well as promises of support for the main circumpolar journey. The money would deal with resupply during our northern travels but not with the England-to-Thule-to-Alert problem.

This was partly solved by Scandinavian Airline Systems. They would take us and our baggage from England to Thule and, after the training, back again. As a rule they sponsored only such as Bjorn Borg, the then-local tennis hero, but two coincidences attracted them to us. Their trade name was SAS, and the start date of our polar training journey coincided with their celebrations to mark the twentieth anniversary of their first transpolar flight.

Next question: what machines should we use on the broken ice rubble of the Arctic Ocean? Greenland had confirmed the groundhogs' superior pulling power but had revealed two defects which boded ill for the Arctic Ocean. On bare ice we had lost all control of the vehicles. They had skidded about in response to gravity and the metal tracks, unable to dig in, had slithered powerless sideways or backward. This wouldn't do on ocean pack ice. Perhaps the smaller Skidoos would be better.

Clearly we needed advice, but there were more individuals in Britain who had climbed Mount Everest than had travelled even briefly on Arctic sea ice. The most knowledgeable of those who had was said to be Dr Hattersley-Smith. I'd corresponded with him before but only about sledges. Now he assured me the groundhogs would be fatal on sea ice.

'What about snowmobiles?' he suggested.

'I tried them in Scotland. Not enough power.'

'Ah, but were they Bombardier from Canada?'

'No, we had some Swedish machines.'

'You get onto Bombardier. Their machines are tough with plenty of poke. They call them Skidoos.'

If my research had unearthed this information years before, I would not have rejected the snowmobiles so quickly. But regret was no good: time was short. We had either to risk using the groundhogs or conjure up some Skidoos. But could we obtain them immediately? Would we be able to get them to Alert on time? Would they prove as good as the doctor made out? Would Oliver be able to repair them? With only thirty days to go I tried to contact anybody who might have used them. The models appeared to be powered by a 640-cc air-cooled Rotax engine made in Austria and mounted on a robust chassis made near Montreal by the Bombardier Company. They had a history of reliability with woodsmen, farmers and hunters in the Canadian Arctic and had been used by the British Antarctic Survey.

I telexed Bombardier in Montreal and asked them if they would like to sponsor us. They were immediately, and probably sensibly, hostile in their reaction. Had we driven snowmobiles before? Had we travelled on the Arctic Ocean? Did we have a trained mechanic going with us? Did we intend to take a comprehensive supply of spare parts? All our answers being negative, Bombardier sensed bad, not good, publicity. In no way would they sponsor us. So we quickly reverted to existing sponsors to purchase the machines for us. From them we were soon able to send a large cheque to Bombardier in Montreal requesting that they quickly send four Alpine Skidoos, each with £500-worth of backup spares, to the nearest commercial airfield to Alert, which appeared to be Resolute, six hundred miles to the south.

Oliver immediately arranged to travel out to Giinskirchen, where the engines and gearboxes were manufactured. The friendly director of Bombardier's Austrian branch sponsored Oliver with his accommodation, transport and tuition. Despite no money and little knowledge of German, in which language all Oliver's instruction was given, he came back after a week slightly less perturbed than he had been on first hearing of my last-minute switch. Anyone but Oliver might well have thrown up his hands in disgust at this inefficiency and flatly refused the job. As it was he set about ordering supplies of spares, tools and lubricants for machines he had never seen, all with his usual cheerful optimism.

The major problems we still faced – government permission and air transport – were entwined and could only be broached if our Arctic training plan was approved by the Royal Geographical Society.

Although four months spent in Alert training locally on the sea ice might give us an idea of Arctic travel, only the test of a race to a set objective could indicate our adequacy sufficiently to attract the tremendous sponsorship our main circumpolar journey would require: for instance, by 1980 we would need a Twin Otter aircraft for resupply in both polar zones and an ice-strengthened vessel to take us to both ends and both sides of the world. Those items alone would cost £1 million, and who could we find to *give* this to a group of nobodies who had messed around on the edge of the Arctic for a few months?

So my proposal involved, as the clearly stated objective, the North Pole itself. On November 1, 1976, I went before the Royal Geographical Society's Expeditions Committee.

The committee's chairman, Sir Vivian Fuchs, questioned me closely on many technical details. He noted the precise results of our Greenland journey and asked the opinion of Colonel Andrew Croft, who had accompanied me to the interview. The other committee members, all exalted figures in the world of geography and expeditions, posed a variety of questions from astronavigation to personality difficulties.

No reaction was evident, favourable or otherwise, when we left, but Andrew Croft told me he felt it had gone well. We would be told the result soon enough. It could not be too soon from my point of view. Even with the RGS approval there was a chance the army might remain totally against any support.

That October, awaiting the Royal Geographical Society's decision, all problems seemed magnified because of the need for urgency. If we wanted to make our assault on the North Pole during the coming spring, then we would have to be ready to leave England again within three months with permits, equipment and stores complete. In the polar zones timing is critical to survival, let alone success. This is summed up neatly by Charles Kuralt writing of the unsuccessful 1967 American attempt on the North Pole: 'There is only a short span of time, mid-March to mid-May, when man can safely walk on the Arctic ice. Earlier in the year total darkness and severe cold make travel hazardous. Later, the rising sun turns the ocean snow cover to mush, high winds break the ice pack into thousands of individual floes and higher temperatures keep the resulting leads from freezing over quickly.'

No expedition, however experienced, leaving land after March 15 can hope to reach the North Pole. To get ourselves into a position with a chance of success from our intended base at Alert would mean setting out by February 28. This in turn meant reaching Alert at least a month earlier, the end of January, since it takes time to set up a self-contained base in permanent darkness and sub-zero temperatures – even for trained men. To move the thirty-one thousand pounds of fuel, food and equipment we had left in the warehouse in Thule five hundred miles farther north to Alert demanded departure from England in mid-January at the latest. Otherwise our journey would crumble in dismal failure, as had the majority of North Pole attempts; the most recent only three miles from its starting point.

So, at best, there were three months including Christmas – when I knew ten days could be written off in terms of productivity – in which to navigate a number of Chinese-like obstacle courses. A series of problems kept the six of us busy every day for six and often seven days a week. The winter was the only time we could make an income from lectures, so at least three evenings a week were used up talking to audiences all over the country. Nor did the Territorial Army allow us an office for nothing. Every Tuesday evening found all six of us in khaki in various London drill halls. I obtained leave, but the three other men had to spend two weeks with the Special Air Service in Bavaria as soon as we returned from Greenland.

Weekends when we could have been greasing, painting, packaging, weighing and listing the tons of sponsors' stores which were again piling up inside and outside the office were instead spent parachuting by night into Denmark to disrupt NATO installations with tear gas and mock explosives or wading along Scottish lochsides to attack nuclear submarine pens. Our polar experience was not widened by these things, but our base of goodwill at the Duke of York's headquarters was strengthened.

At last the Royal Geographical Society's approval came. I immediately wrote to the Ministry of Defence. Everything, I explained, was now ready except for two things: Canadian army permission for us to be based at the old shacks near their Alert camp; and the use of their weekly transport planes to fly our cargo up from Thule.

Five short weeks before we *had* to leave England, a reply was sent by the Director of Army Training to our own brigadier. It was a final and irrefutable no. The author was obviously of a kindly nature. He ended by saying: 'I wish Fiennes all possible success and regret in the present circumstances it is not possible to give him official or semiofficial support. I realise this will be a bitter blow to Fiennes, but even if the expedition had been put forward by an experienced team from the Regular army it would *not* have been approved due to the high financial risks to Her Majesty's government.'

There was one last hope of leaving in January. It meant flying to Ottawa to try to get Alert permission direct from the Canadian army. Except I knew no one in Ottawa, let alone the Canadian forces. Our United States air attaché friend booked me to New York and back, and Air Canada, through the good offices of the government of Alberta, sponsored my onward flight to Ottawa. Once there the Rowley family kindly let me stay in their house. Dr Rowley, an internationally respected Arctic scientist, took me to a government liaison officer whose specific area of interest was foreigners visiting the Northwest Territories – of which Ellesmere Island is the northeastern tip.

Stewart Shackell listened patiently to my dilemma and immediately plotted a course of action. Over the next five days he drove me about Ottawa via a maze of governmental departments, introducing me with a sympathetic account of my problems. He approached the minor problems first, ones which I had not even considered: radio licences, customs' permits, explorers' licences and so on.

Then, after a number of telephone calls, came a visit to the defence headquarters at Tunney's Pasture, which bristled with security. I had my British army I.D. card and used it. Somewhere along a maze of corridors and further check-in desks we came to the correct department. Army and air force personnel – all with the same smart olive green uniforms, polite manners and close-cropped hair – nodded as we passed.

The security colonel who greeted us had specific responsibility for Alert. He knew all about our earlier unorthodox approaches, the hornet's nest that had been stirred at the British High Commission in Ottawa and the urgency of our current position. The whole matter had obviously been discussed at a high level and on learning of my arrival in Ottawa, the authorities had made a decision.

I felt the strain of the past two months ease as the colonel stated the position concisely. We *could* base ourselves at the deserted huts two miles north of the Canadian camp since we already had the permission of their owners, the Polar Continental Shelf Project. We must be totally self-contained and must expect no help from the Canadian forces. We must produce proof of insurance coverage up to £100,000 for search-and-rescue costs. We must keep clear of all security areas at all times. All these things were fair and I agreed without question, overwhelmingly thankful for the permission. For so long Alert had seemed like a distant, unobtainable paradise.

There remained only one question: would the weekly resupply flights from Thule to Alert help us move equipment north if space was available on the existing flights? This was a request I had mentioned in all my papers to the Ministry of Defence over the past three years. Although it should cost the Canadians nothing, it would save us up to £30,000. On the other hand it was the thin end of the wedge, as indeed was the permission granted for our presence at Alert. Others would point to favours granted and clamour for similar treatment. Things could go dangerously wrong for us, and only the Canadians would be held responsible if no intensive search-and-rescue operations were mounted. Furthermore, the Arctic is a fragile area. Too many expeditions trampling the wild beauty and fragile fauna of Ellesmere Island, soon to be protected in parts as a national park, would leave pollution in their wake. And there was the delicate matter of Canadian sovereignty. Individual Canadians had often objected strongly to foreign expeditions exploring their Arctic territory.

The colonel registered my request, promised to pass it to the relevant authority and saw us out past the security desk.

Stewart Shackell had moved mountains for us. On the Air Canada Boeing back to New York I reflected how, despite the stubborn opposition and antagonism of many officials and civil servants, our endeavour was to go ahead through the goodwill of a few who believed there was still room for such activities despite the cramped outlook of officialdom in general.

With two weeks until our deadline I returned to London to find the others engaged in a flurry of last-minute business.

We would need a patron for the main journey. H.R.H. Prince Charles was my first choice. I saw no reason why he should agree, but there was no harm in asking. I wrote a letter requesting this honour and took it by hand to Buckingham Palace.

It was raining and few tourists were about. I asked one of the sentries at the gate where I should go regarding the matter of royal patronage. The soldier gave no reply so I moved round to the left flank, where there appeared to be a tradesmen's entrance. My identity card saw me past two policemen but a security officer stopped me well before I made it to the main palace. He relieved me of the letter. 'Don't worry, sir. I'll make good and sure this reaches His Royal Highness. A fine day to you, sir.' I had been politely seen off.

With only three weeks to go, I still had no permission from the Americans to land at Thule nor any means of transporting our cargo from Thule to Alert. But our free SAS flight left Heathrow on January 24, which was already three weeks behind my original schedule.

On January 11 a telegram came from the United States authorities in Thule. It was directed to the United States air attaché in London and stated simply that the request to visit Thule was granted.

Armed with the telegram I telephoned Ottawa to expedite clearance of our gear from Thule, the last remaining hitch. The kindly colonel said he had no clear answer and, in view of the time factor, advised me to cable directly to the Ministry of National Defence. This I did, and a week later his assistant replied, saying that all Thule-Alert flights were fully committed, and in any case there were commercial reasons against such help being given.

I immediately contacted the director of Bradley Air Services, whose Otter aircraft would be resupplying the expedition. He promised to try to move all our cargo from Thule, but now a new problem came up. There was no fuel in Thule available for Bradley Otter or DC-3-type aircraft. Without refuelling, no Canadian-based medium aircraft could then fly on to Alert – where again there was no suitable fuel.

On January 23 a giant flatbed truck was loaded at the barracks with our crates, prefabricated hut and other stores, and departed for Harwich en route for the SAS terminal at Copenhagen Airport. Even with the knowledge that Thule might prove a dead end, I felt we had to leave the next day and let the future look after itself.

SAS had reserved first-class seats for us – a luxury unexpected and very welcome. By now, feeling fatalistic, I expected our cargo truck to have sunk along with its North Sea ferry or crashed en route to Copenhagen.

At Thule the airstrip seemed unfamiliar. We descended the ramp to a twilit knot of parka-clad officials. The Danish naval commander was there as before, a new United States colonel and a furry blur of juniors in the background. No one smiled. The atmosphere went with the temperature, minus 23 degrees Fahrenheit, and neither struck me as pleasant.

A good friend, Palle Hansen, drove us to Dundas village adjacent to the United States base in a pickup truck. The Dundas radio boss, Eigil Jensen, had kindly made a house in the village available to us on our way to and from the Arctic, and while the girls set about making bedspaces and a meal, we drove to the warehouse, where we had left thirty thousand pounds of equipment and the groundhogs from our last journey.

The equipment was in fine condition because the Danish commander who used the store had kept it locked up at all times. However, both groundhogs were deep-frozen up to their sprockets in a solid block of ice. Someone had left an overflow pipe running free into the low shed. Its door was now frozen shut and nothing short of oxyacetylene would extricate the groundhogs.

Since we were to use Skidoos – if they ever materialised from Montreal – we temporarily abandoned the frozen groundhogs and concentrated on moving bit by bit all the applicable stores up to the airstrip. We had earlier packed everything for a groundhog journey. Now much of it had to be repacked and all groundhog gear left behind.

On our second day Ginnie came to the warehouse and took me to one side. She was in tears; rare for her. Unable to locate me, the new American colonel had summoned her and various other top functionaries on the base, including the Danish commander, to his inner office. We had come without United States permission, Ginnie was told. She had protested that this was not so but naturally did not have the vital telegram on her person at the time. I was to see the colonel as soon as possible.

I ran through the dark of the day to the headquarters building, homing in on its metal Christmas tree lights and painted light bulbs. I found that my lungs hurt breathing the cold air. I was not fit – nor were the others, I suspected.

The colonel's direct junior took the telegram from me. (I had copied it in an adjacent office and kept the copy.) He made no comment as I left, informed me that no Bradley Air Service aircraft had permission to land at Thule even if there had been fuel for them. Except, of course, for emergency landing.

After several attempts I managed to telephone the Bradley boss, Dick de Blicquy, in Ottawa. He promised he would somehow find an aircraft big enough to take all our cargo to Alert and still carry sufficient fuel for itself. Bradley's own Thule permit had indeed lapsed some months previously. He said he would try Pacific Airlines, which owned a Hercules C-130, provided we could get them a Thule permit.

I phoned a contact in the Pentagon who, three days later, managed to clear the Pacific Airlines application, but by then Dick de Blicquy had already contacted an old friend, the director of Northwest Territorial Airlines, who agreed for £15,000 to fly a DC-6 from faraway Yellowknife, stop at Resolute and collect our Skidoos which had just arrived there, then collect half our cargo and ourselves from Thule and drop us at Alert. Stopping only long enough to unload, he would then return to Thule via Resolute's fuel dump with only two of us to load the remaining cargo for a second flight to Alert. All this to happen in the polar darkness with temperatures down to minus 40 degrees Fahrenheit. Bad weather at any point en route would cause delay and add cost. But it was the only way out and I immediately thanked Dick. He said we could expect the DC-6 on February 2, weather and United States permits willing.

Later that evening it was all smiles again at Thule. Even the base commander came to wish us well. His junior explained that an

English couple bound for Qanaq, north of Thule, to film the Eskimo way of life, had applied for the same date and we had been sent their clearance. But as the original telegram had not explained which request had been granted but just 'the request', the United States air attaché in London had passed it on to us. Thule had checked back with London and now knew that we had arrived in good faith. (The other couple was also allowed in.) The fact that the United States air attaché was Paul Clark, by now a good friend of the expedition, was on the face of it irrelevant. Ignorance is and was bliss.

Our flight north was in the pitch darkness of an Arctic winter. Our huts were half-full of snow but provided a shelter from the elements. It took a week to make them habitable. I would not say we made them comfortable during the first month. Ginnie, in her wolfskin, began to set up her communications system. Working with a lantern on the exposed hill above the camp she trudged back and forth with buckets of water. Each was the result of hours warming ice hacked from the sea. She poured the water around empty drums she had dug into the snow in strategic positions on the hillside. The water froze the drums in place to serve as anchor points for the mast's guy ropes.

The first time we attempted to erect the snaking tube of the aerial, its brittle metal snapped and the whole contraption collapsed in a tangle of tubing and wire. The next attempt was successful although the mast could never have been described as straight. The silicone coating of the antennae wires, Ginnie discovered, tasted good to the local Arctic foxes. Their sharp teeth snapped the wires and called for counteraction. Eventually Ginnie hoisted all antennae onto a series of poles stuck in the snow, replaced all coaxial cables that broke due to the cold and finally made voice contact with our radio base over two thousand miles away, the radio station at Cove in England.

Perhaps her pleasure at the successful communications put her in a forgetful state, because later that day she visited the wooden shack, five feet by five feet, which was our lavatory, and was careless. There was a drill involved with this unavoidable but dreaded activity which called for the undoing of all buttons, zips and belts. Then clutching paper, flashlight and of course one's clothes, one rushed to the hut, bared a minimal portion of one's backside and tried to complete the operation in seconds. Our tinned and dehydrated diet, however, did not contribute toward quick results. Ginnie's error was the failure by flashlight to check that the polyethylene liner covered the metal rim of the rusty open-ended fuel drum that served as our throne. She found out soon enough, as did anyone in the neighbourhood, for her yelps were magnified by the echo-chamber characteristics of the hut.

Rushing into the warmth of our shack she mistakenly sought comfort by shoving the painful area close to the metal stove. In her agitation she brushed against the red-hot heater and so achieved the probably unique distinction of scarring one cheek with a cold burn and the other with a hot one, all within five minutes.

On February 26 we left the girls in the dark and set out for the Pole. Three days later we were static some six miles to the west. The machines refused to start no matter what Ollie and Charlie did to them with blowtorches, heater and even hot tea.

When we moved, our clothes cracked, taking on any shape the wearer reclined in for a certain length of time and objected when strained to another pose. A mitten, for instance, after holding a Skidoo handlebar for a while, would stay in that position until the fingers were banged or manipulated with the other hand.

Despite three layers of socks, two of felt boots and outer canvas mukluks, our feet were a problem. When possible we stood on a sledge box, Skidoo seat or a couple of shovels laid on the ice –

anything but the ground itself. We decided to test Geoff's ice-drilling kit and took it in turns to turn the handle so many times each. After drilling four feet the bore became jammed and defied all our efforts with Oliver's antifreeze and alcohol to get it out again.

Geoff persevered and after three hours' jiggling about he retrieved the bits. We decided to delay such research work until we were truly under way farther north.

On March 1 we were still staring at the nearby Black Cliffs. There was already a noticeably long period of twilight. We spoke little ... our thoughts were sombre. Ginnie informed us on the radio that Alert meteorological station had just recorded their lowest ever temperature, and that to our south the United States was experiencing their coldest winter ever recorded. After this news our communications broke down. The Morse key froze up and the coaxial cable cracked internally – Geoff had bent it slightly, which was understandable since it's customary to coil it up in a neat roll once communications have been made. The headset's mouthpiece became inoperative because when Geoff had spoken into it his breath had condensed and then frozen inside the fine wire mesh.

We were getting nowhere, but at least we were learning a great deal. Which, of course, was the idea.

Early on March 3 we rose after another bad night. There was no wind. The temperature was minus 51 degrees Centigrade. At quarter past three that afternoon Oliver shouted, 'She's coming up. Look at Alert.'

The three of them left what they were doing, forgot their feet and their hands, their ears and their noses and stood watching the low hills of the eastern horizon. Directly over the long black tongue of the airstrip a slowly spreading film of red light suffused the twilit sky. Then a speck of royal red appeared on the ridgeline, growing in size like a fresh wound until, for the first time in a month ... the sun.

Oliver, optimistic as ever, waxed lyrical in his diary: 'The sun at last. Oh, what a feeling to shed the grim cloak of darkness. My spirits rose immediately and things looked better. The effect on us all was dramatic.'

I decided to record the moment on camera. My Bolex ciné-camera, set at top speed and fully wound, gave a quick groan and then refused to budge. My Nikon's standard lens was jammed as was its zoom lens. Both had been fully winterised, but not with minus 50 degrees in mind. I carried an underwater Nikonos camera in my inner pocket and was pleased to discover that although the focus was jammed on infinity and the shutter was sluggish, it at least worked. Looking at the photograph now, I still find it difficult to recall the feel of life at minus 50 degrees. I remember no feeling of elation, only an increasing realisation of impending failure. From now on we had to average ten miles a day every day to reach the Pole before the ice breakup, *if* it was to be a normal year. But as people all over the world were to discover, 1977 was no normal year. Even in Britain people died trapped in snowdrifts that winter.

About this time Geoffrey became unusually quiet. I lived in one tent with him; the others were next door. In the evenings and, worse still, in the mornings we would hear their cooker roaring gently and soon the smell of their food would emanate through the thin tent walls. Our own cooker was a freakish contraption or, perhaps, our mechanically minded brethren were just better at cooker-starting. Either way, the fiddling and the frustrations in our dark refrigerator of a tent intensified in the knowledge that next door things were better.

The following day Oliver managed to start up one of the machines. I leapt onto it with no equipment, and cursing in apprehension every time the engine spluttered, headed back for Alert. My plan was to take it to a Canadian army mechanic there for diagnosis, then return with 'the facts' so that Oliver could put the others right.

While I was away Geoffrey's state deteriorated. In particular his feet lost all feeling. That night the others invited him to dinner in their tent and while they ate a delicious Kesp soya bean stew in its gravy of freshly boiled seawater, they tried to massage some life back into his yellow-white toes. Frostbite had to be avoided, especially so early on in the journey.

The next day I returned to the forlorn little ice camp, not by Skidoo but in a Bombardier Snowcat with the base commander and mechanic. Sympathetic with our delays and fascinated with the root cause of our Canadian machines' bad behaviour, they had decided to risk their big Bombardier out on the sea ice.

They had brought with them an aircraft heater to dry out the Skidoos, and in no time at all the machines were throbbing away. We abandoned the tents and the equipment on the ice and decided to spend as long as necessary back at camp manufacturing built-in heater systems for each Skidoo. Once these were ready we would come back to the tents and carry on.

Geoffrey, Oliver and Charles left on their Skidoos, and as mine was already back at base I travelled with the major in his heavy Snowcat, which almost immediately struck a hidden bar of ice with one of its skis. The steel ski broke cleanly, making steering practically impossible. The mechanic drove on, and with his ginger beard thrust forward and his barrel muscles heaving at the heavy controls, he resembled a pirate at the helm in heavy seas. Whatever, thanks to determination and despite painfully slow progress, he managed to reach the camp.

We arrived after the others to hear that Geoff had frostbite.

I hurried down to the huts. Mary had put dry bandages on the six fingers worst affected and sedated Geoff, who was in pain.

It had happened without warning on the journey back. The three drivers had been exposed to minus 49 degrees Fahrenheit with a wind speed of their own making of fifteen knots. Although each man wore silk gloves, woollen gloves, heavy quilt gauntlets and thick leather outer mitts the cold had penetrated these with ease and every so often it had been necessary to stop to swing both hands about until the blood was forced back right to the fingertips.

Geoff's dilemma had been the worry that any stop would either oil up the plugs or, through briefly letting go of the hand throttle, the engine would stop. And once one engine stopped, even immediate attempts to start up again were often fruitless. Probably wishing to avoid risking this and since the other two kept going, Geoff in his already run-down state had let six of his fingers go numb.

For six days Oliver and the Canadians worked on ways of starting the vehicles, mainly a preheating system using petrol cookers and ducting. On March 10 we set out again without Geoff. By now it was mostly daylight.

Twilight was fading into night as Oliver, Charlie and I Skidooed back to our abandoned tents. Although I had marked their position in my mind, the site of our recent frustrations looked very different in the dim light. We only found them because our last set of tracks were still visible in many places.

Inside and out the tents were heavy with hoarfrost. We next made the mistake of lighting our cookers – it was soon very wet. And the tent was more uncomfortable, it seemed to me, without Geoff.

That night Oliver mended his wolfskin parka with tough thread, dental floss. It took him a long while because of his fingers, and I could hear him muttering through the tent walls. On the way he had received a bad knock against a sharp ice block and ripped his parka. The rest of that day had been a misery for him with an average chill factor of minus 105 degrees. We had stopped many times to thump legs and arms against each other. The lesson Geoffrey had suffered was at the front of our minds.

I couldn't sleep that night and spent an hour in the morning lighting my cooker. When it finally caught I shouted to the others to wake up. From then on Oliver gave me Valium tablets to induce sleep, but I never took more than two every other day – it's easy to sleep too well and ignore creeping frostbite of the nose or cheeks. I dreaded the moment when at intervals through the night it was necessary to turn over and the layer of frost particles from my breath dropped off the bag lining and slid down my neck.

The new heaters were cumbersome and difficult to light but they did the trick along with a number of intricate preparations that Ol and Charlie performed like surgeons. Great was their pride that first morning when all three vehicles, one by one and at long intervals, coughed and spluttered their way to life after their night out.

When every last item, including the ten-foot-long tent rolls heavy with clinging ice, was lashed to the sledges of Skidoo rear platforms, I felt my eyebrows rise under their twin crusts of ice. No way will we move over pressure ridges like this, I thought. There must be everything but the kitchen sink aboard despite our cautious planning. A lot of it was due to Geoff's absence. Many items from his sledge had been added to ours, contrary to original planning.

Sure enough there was trouble even on the comparative calm of the bay ice. Because of the complete lack of shadow we could not see the bumps, ridges and ditches which made up the surface of the sea. Time and again Skidoos and their drivers rolled over. Even more often the sledges tipped and, at each overturn, the other two were forced to turn back or go forward to help, since no sledge would reright without all three of us heaving on ropes. Often even this was not enough, in which case lashings had to come off, fixed on with so much care a few minutes before, then tents, fragile antenna coils and heavy boxes. Clearly our lashing system was wrong, and it would be many days before we found the answer . . . The Arctic puts great strain on a laden sledge. All Eskimo sledges are made loosely, each piece of wood lashed on with hide that absorbs the ceaseless bumps and bangs coming from every angle. But even this is insufficient to prove a lasting answer, as every previous expedition to the Pole has shown. Time was always wasted repairing wooden runners and slats. Which was why, four years before, I had begun work on our stainless steel sledges. And now I anxiously watched for cracks, broken welds and contortions as the supercool steel thudded against the iron-hard ice.

The violent vibrations of the rigid sledges shook each box and tore at every lashing or knot so that no matter how we tried to prevent it, every mishap ended with equipment scattered all over the place.

Charlie's machine, leading us along a seemingly smooth corridor, struck a low wall and flung him forward. His back hit an angular ice block and he lay still.

I stopped and waded up to him. He groaned. His back was all right but a sharp knock on the knee caused him pain. Over the next fortnight a swelling developed about the knee which Oliver bandaged. Charlie suffered in silence now that he really had something to worry about.

For the first time since the Greenland journey, when the problem had anyway been mild, I began to suffer from piles – which for the next three months I found difficult to forget despite some excellent things that Oliver gave me that he called 'bombs'.

Along the coast we travelled long hours, ten or eleven a day. Britain's greatest Arctic traveller, Wally Herbert, had written: 'We were travelling about eight hours a day which meant ten hours a day outside in a temperature of minus 50 degrees Fahrenheit. The fatigue was crippling.'

Ollie's diary recorded: 'What a night! Firstly, had to thaw out my sleeping bag which was solid with ice and had a frozen zip. Then the cooker wouldn't start so the tent was perishing. Eventually I got up and fetched one of the Skidoo start-cookers, which although warm, emitted eye-stinging fumes. Supper was too salty. I shivered all night long and woke with a freezing nose. I hate this f—— place.'

In the morning we rose more or less together. Outside there was always a chilling breeze which brought on the desire to crawl back into the tent. Yet once there in its damp, cramped confines, scarcely warmer than outside if the cooker was off, a strong wish to be outside again began to grow. I recalled a favourite bit of doggerel of my mother: 'As a rule man's a fool. When it's hot he wants it cool. When it's cool he wants it hot, always wanting what is not.'

Eighty miles or so along the coast, close by Parr Bay, we came to a narrow ledge between the sea ice and the snout of a glacier. The southward push of the ocean currents had forced up a wall of broken ice against the cliffs which the ice poured over.

A strong wind blew down the glacier and caught between the fifty-foot-high wall of sea ice and the cliffs themselves, just as we were. This wind rushed east, knifing through our clothes. Oliver got the anemometer from under his seat. 'Gusting to fifty,' he shouted. After each minute or so of travel each man stopped to kick and jump and windmill his arms. Without these frequent delays our extremities would have frozen because we were experiencing for the first time a wind-chill factor of minus 120 degrees. The liquid on our eyeballs kept freezing up, and this made it difficult to negotiate the rough ice of the glacier tongue.

Oliver's fingers were agony that day.

The mountain feature behind us was Cape Aldrich, the most northerly feature of the Canadian continent. On its summit Admiral Peary had built a cairn, but our concentration was fully committed to spotting obstacles a yard away through ice-caked eyes without trying to admire the local points of historical interest.

The corridor into which we were forced was ten yards wide and dark. Despite this the colour of the ice cubes on our right was a spectacular pellucid green. I tried to photograph this with my Nikonos, but for the first time the camera's shutter had frozen inside my wolfskin parka.

The power of the elements could not fail to impress. The ice wall resembled a curling wave poised ready to strike against the cliff. An overwhelming sense of impending motion made us scuttle along between the rock and the precarious wall like mice under a portcullis.

The rampart of blue-green ice blocks, some twelve metres high, was a testimony to the great driving and cutting power of the pack ice. Peary, in an account of his journey along Greenland's northern coastline, talked of pressure ice stacked a hundred feet high against the cliffs.

Thankfully we passed out of this bottleneck as the cliffs gave way to high rolling hills. But the way west was blocked. The level ice couloir between the hillside and the high rim of the sea ice soon tapered away to a dead end. We could go no further by land.

Here we axed a ramp down to the sea ice and once on it left the coast to turn north and head out over the ice rubble of the semi-frozen sea. Now a new fear would always be with us – breaking through the ice.

Radios and aircraft can't prevent frostbite or save a man who falls into the freezing sea. Unless a pilot knows roughly where to look, his ability to rescue polar travellers is minimal. Still, the very presence of such modern accoutrements is a great morale booster. True, almost as many expeditions with radios have suffered casualties and disappeared as those without. Radios can't be depended on, but the presumption that they will work at least allows for more ambitious plans. The ability to receive aerial resupply, so long as communications, navigation and the weather work according to plan, makes a North Pole attempt conceivable.

Most modern geographers and polar historians believe that neither Dr Cook nor Admiral Peary reached the North Pole. Of the four expeditions that undisputedly did complete the journey, all relied heavily on air support and all were experienced Arctic travelers.

In 1968 the Simpson Expedition determined to reach the Pole with no air support and set out from Ward Hunt Island, which they reached by Twin Otter aircraft, manhauling their own sledges. Because of the rough ice and the breakdown of their communications equipment, they turned back some hundred miles out from the coast. My own personal belief is that the journey can only be done with air support. When science advances to the point where a man can live on one hundred pounds of food for fifty days despite strenuous activity all day at extreme temperatures, then perhaps it will be possible. Certainly the easiest method of getting to the North Pole is on foot towing a small narrow sledd, but since the sledd load must be kept to around one hundred and fifty pounds maximum, air support is still necessary.

During our first day on the sea ice we made about half a mile to the north. This seemed terrible. Later we were to realise it was very respectable.

Two things then happened: the Skidoos, all three of them, began to lose power, even to stop completely for a while, until much play with the throttle would temporarily clear their systems. And still more discouraging, a wall of ice rubble fifteen feet high blocked the way north and could not, like the earlier muck, be detoured around because it stretched away for as far as we could see to the west and east ... Standing on a broad slab at the top of the wall I could see much better and almost wished I had stayed at ground level. To the north a chaotic jumble of blocks, large and small, made up the entire view. Nothing else except the sky. No one could possibly get through that lot, was my immediate reaction. Carefully I looked around for another route. There was, of course, no other way, for Moses was not available with his rod to open up a path. The chaos was complete to the west and east, resembling Hiroshima after the bomb.

Oliver tried to fix the machines, but in the process tipped petrol onto his hand and blistered the skin. His hands struck me as unworkable, but he had an extremely stubborn streak and would listen to no suggestion of rest while there was light. However, he wrote that, 'The cold is intense and my hands are letting me down badly. The pain is indescribable and permanent. I cannot sleep because of it.'

The weather seemed settled so I went off with Charlie. After four hours we had cut a gap in the nearby high wall just big enough for everything to pass through.

We had been informed by the Polar Continental Shelf Project authorities in Ottawa that pressure ridges could occur at a rate of seventy per mile and that bad ridging would stretch back from the coast for about thirty miles. This was, and probably is, the case during most normal years. If it had held true in 1977 we would have travelled a great deal faster. But 1977 was not normal. The famous American Impact Team, sounding a warning in 1978 of impending climatic changes, wrote: 'The winter of 1976–77 was something else again. Unprecedented in its ferocity, it seemed to last forever ... Upper New York State lay under twenty-six feet of snow, and Chicago had many days of their lowest temperatures on record ... In Kansas the earth froze to a depth of four feet ...'

The polar weather cauldron from which this vicious weather stemmed proved equally abnormal. We had selected the wrong year to travel on the Arctic Ocean. At the time, though, the overall picture was not evident: all that mattered was our immediate progress and, anticipating normal obstacles, we now discovered something well beyond our blackest expectations.

It was not a question of seventy or even a hundred pressure ridges to the mile. Certainly the ridges were there – we had spent four whole hours dealing with just one of them – but the really unpleasant discovery was the incredible debris *between* the ridges, making us walk and hack every foot of the way north.

A team of huskies would make short work of such rubble; their paws could scrabble where no Skidoo would travel, even without a sledge. But for what seemed good reasons we had deliberately chosen Skidoos, and the heaviest models, and now had to accept that all progress north depended on our physical ability to hack a road through the ice, wide and smooth enough to take the machines.

With four of us at work, things would have been better. Geoff was tough and a hard worker but his frostbitten hands meant a long period back at base: there was no knowing when he would rejoin us. The Skidoos needed Oliver's constant attention, which effectively left only two pairs of hands, two axes. At low temperatures the human body, making no allowance for the encumbrance of bulky clothing and footwear, works at four-fifths of its normal efficiency. I became quickly exhausted.

'Come on, Ran,' Charlie said. 'You're like a constipated woodpecker with a bent beak. Hit the bloody ice, don't stroke it.'

But he too soon felt the effort. Each time an axe struck, bits of ice flew about. But so *little* ice for so *much* activity. Feather-soft snow lay over cracks in between ice blocks, and we kept falling into these. On one occasion Charlie disappeared up to his shoulders. On another, one of my boots became stuck in a cranny. We laughed weakly at each other. What else could we do? To strike a stance from which to use the axe gainfully it was often necessary first to dig out a flat platform. Otherwise the act of swinging the axe had us sliding all over the place. The exertion meant taking deep breaths of freezing air, and this created a burning sensation in the chest.

The reflected glare made me want to wear my tinted glasses, but they either misted up or my nose was exposed to the wind, depending on whether my face mask was up or down. Since my nose was already raw I gave up the glasses and never wore them again until, weeks later, the temperatures warmed up to the minus twenties.

After seven hours and two hundred yards of axe work we trudged and slid back to the tent. Oliver was sitting on a Skidoo, cleaning a spark plug. He didn't appear to notice our return, although we approached from the direction he was facing.

'How's it going, Ol?' Charles offered.

Oliver looked up sharply and I noticed the whites of his eyes were completely bloodshot.

'I don't seem able to see much,' he said, 'and it's not just my squint.'

'Could be a touch of sun-blindness,' I suggested.

He shook his head. 'There's no real pain, just a general blur.' Oliver didn't blame the glare, and thought it more likely that cooker fumes were the culprit.

Our tents each had a ventilation hole at the peak, but these became quickly clogged with ice despite daily attention, and because of the extreme temperatures the fumes seemed reluctant to rise. As all the carburettors were cleaned with petrol in the other tent, the fumes were worse there, which explained why the eye problems of the other two started first.

One night a whole range of little things went wrong. Even in the Arctic disasters can come in small packages. After a supper of dehydrated chicken chunks and carrot flakes I was chewing at my daily Mars bar when a sizeable piece of filling came out of one tooth and I swallowed it. The cavity left a rough edge which the raw piece on my tongue kept touching.

Next, as was our custom, I used a polythene bag after supper to avoid going outside. I propped this up, after securing the neck with a double hitch, at the end of my sleeping bag. Normally by morning the bag would be frozen solid and easy to bury. But that night the bag leaked over the end of my sleeping bag.

And next: soon after I had placed my metal one-pint mug, full of ice slush, on the cooker, my eyes began to sting. This grew quickly intolerable, as though a spike was being screwed in behind the upper lid of each eye. I lay on my back to see if that lessened the pain. In doing so, my feet kicked the cooker and the mug fell over onto my only two dry items – a khaki face mask and my blue Damart mitts, which I only wore at night. Not seeing much with my watering eyes, I grabbed the hot base of the metal mug. For long minutes in the dark I thought of nothing but my eyes. I squirmed about, pressed my eyeballs with my mitts, knelt and looked downward, even scraped frost off the tent liner and held it against each eye in turn. But the feeling of grit lumps moving about under the lids persisted, intensified. And the tent grew quickly colder.

I lit the candle which came with the day's rations and propped it on the cooker board, the only flat space in the tent. Not thinking, I picked up my spoon from the end of the bed and received another cold burn through a hole in the mitt. One eye got better for a while, and I decided I'd drink hot cocoa before trying to sleep. I kept the half-gallon petrol can well away from the inner tent lining, which, by nature of its breathability, is made from a material that is also highly flammable. As I filled the cooker tank a second unseen spurt escaped to the ground-sheet and flowed away in several directions. This had happened several times before, but I had always noticed it in time to mop up the spillage before lighting up.

Perhaps because of my eye problems, that night I lit the cooker without noticing the rivulets of petrol.

There was a sudden *woomf* as the fumes and the liquid ignited.

My thoughts went immediately to the advice of Bill Gundry, the airstrip chief sergeant. 'Moses and willikers, man. When you got yourself a tent fire there's no time to grab a knife and cut your way out. No, siree. That's Brit army pi-jaw. You just lie in that there bag of yours and tuck in your hands, face and all. Before you can say skunk there'll be red-hot nylon a-raining down on you like so much molten metal. And she eats into your skin like phosphorous. Jeez, man, that nylon grafts itself to you before she cools. No sir, you fergit your fancy escape ideas. When that liner goes you got half a lousy second to hide your pride or you'll be a-hopping all over that ice cap like a hot blueberry pie.'

I wasn't inside my bag and the groundsheet *was* on fire all over the place. None of the flames were as yet touching the flammable liner, so I tried to smother them with the bag. Each time I moved the bag to a new area, the place I'd just snuffed out caught fire again. I grabbed for the Chubb fire blanket always carried in our camp boxes. The fire was soon out, my second mug of cocoa water had tipped over and acrid black smoke curled about the tent.

The lacing that tied the inner sleeve of the tent in place had frozen solid. Eventually I cut it open to let the fumes out, and the rest of the night became a succession of very long minutes to be lived through . . .

That was the first of many nights that my eyes kept me awake. I can remember no dentist, limb breakage, nothing in my life that caused such a memorable sensation as the 'eye thing' during our first month on the Arctic Ocean.

Part of my tent troubles, I realised, was the absence of my tent partner, Geoff, including his body warmth. One evening Oliver suggested we all sleep together the way we had in Greenland. 'Geoff won't be with us for a while. It will save putting up two tents, cooking on two cookers and besides, the more bodies around the warmer it is.'

The idea struck me, particularly at the moment of imminent departure to my own tent, as highly acceptable. I said nothing. After a brief and pregnant silence Charlie muttered, 'That's it. That's the last straw. Work all day on the bloody Burma Highway cutting my boots open with axes, half-blind from fumes, lame like a stuck pig and now my last remaining comfort in life is ruined. I know how it'll end too – with you two taking up four-fifths of the tent and old Charlie squeezed up against the liner like a frozen sardine. *No.* Definitely not. You stay in your own damn tent.'

If Charlie really didn't like an idea, you soon knew it by his black looks and uneasy silence. Tirades like this one could usually, though not always, be safely ignored, so I thanked them both and brought in my sleeping bag, mug and spoon.

Ol's diary, which I only read many months after our return, showed his subsequent approval of the new regime. He always slept in the middle because everyone liked it that way. The disadvantage was the lack of privacy, but this didn't worry him at all. Charlie's diary, a very threadbare and noncommunicative affair, revealed his dislike of the reversion to a threesome. Certainly the tent was a close fit for three people over six feet. It was difficult to move without causing your neighbour discomfort, and any morsel of snow left on your clothes after brushing down in the entrance area was likely to fall on someone else's gear and cause a good deal of silent indignation. Since I was next to Oliver I found myself silently cursing him on many occasions for the most trivial offences. By nature impatient and selfish, I must have been an exceptionally objectionable tent companion. Fortunately for our continued survival as a workable team, the others were blessed with more easygoing natures . . .

For many days our average progress was half a mile to the north and, to achieve even that, many miles to the west, east and south had to be axed. Any attempt at cutting a route due north, whatever the obstacles, had soon proved unrealistic.

Long journeys on foot in all directions always preceded the making of our Burma Highway, since there was little point in hacking our way through solid ice when a perfectly good passageway just *might* run a few yards away to either side. Indeed, the feeling that if we hauled our way over just one more wall we might be rewarded by some treasure such as an open lane to the north prolonged many a useless recon journey, slithering, sliding, plunging into sharp-edged crevasses hidden by drifts and ever wary of the creeping attack of frost on the cheeks and nose.

The twin aches of hunger and thirst always travelled with us. The hunger was each day with coffee for breakfast and nothing but deep-frozen Mars bars or a packet of pelletlike Rollos and eight sweets aptly called Fox's Glacier Mints. The Mars bars were great once you managed to gnaw a piece off small enough to close your mouth over and suck. But they were also tooth killers. By the end of the following June when we returned to London, we had among the six of us lost a total of nineteen fillings. Oliver had been trained to take out teeth and fill up holes, but despite the professional-looking set of dental instruments, which he would show Charlie and me with loving pride from time to time and despite the unpleasantness of our gaping holes, neither of us ever approached him to undertake molar repairs of any sort.

The thirst was fourteen hours in the arid atmosphere of a polar desert with nothing to drink but little balls of snow. Little lollipops of ice looked nicer but I avoided them after once cutting a thin sliver off a big block. I put it in my mouth. There was a fizzling noise and stinging sensation. I felt around with my mitt and removed the ice. I tasted blood. For days afterward my tongue remained raw where the ice had burned it.

'What we need,' Charlie explained, 'is a female with big tits. D-size cups would allow us to heat up quite a decent supply of snowballs.' I remembered reading about Myrtle Simpson, the only female participant in a North Pole attempt, who had kept the expedition butter in her bra. Despite the hot butter, that team foundered some ninety miles from the coast. I didn't mention this to Charlie.

Travelling up front and needing to look constantly at the horizon for the line of apparent least resistance, I wore no goggles, my eyes shielded from the lethal glare by the ice beads that formed on my eyelashes. I learned never to rub these off until either eye could see nothing at all and then only to remove enough to unstick the lashes.

Our kit was now constantly damp or frozen up depending on whether it was inside or outside the tent.

We averaged only four hours of sleep a night despite taking Valium tablets from time to time.

Oliver had hell with his fingers, the ends of which had gone black, and layers of skin peeled off all but the little fingers.

Three of my fingers had gotten frostnip, and the throbbing was always worst at night. My nose and one ear also suffered, and I could only sleep on one side or on my back.

If you tried to snuggle down inside your bag, tying the draw-strings tight above your head, your breath formed a thick coating of frost all around your head, particles of which fell down your neck or settled on your face and ears. If you left a hole at the top of the bag just big enough for your nose and mouth and somehow managed to keep them in that position through the sleeping hours, then your nose grew extremely painful – the temperature was around minus 40 degrees once the cooker's heat had vanished.

A great boon in the tent was the little polythene bag hanging from a hook at the apex. This was full of luminous beads called Beta Lights and provided a green and restful, if rather satanic, light when it was dark.

For three years in our London office and for four months in the same tent on the Greenland ice cap, relations between the three of us had remained near-idyllic. This state of affairs did not remain total proof against the strains of the Arctic . . .

It began in many small ways, few of which could be pinpointed. But there were occasions which stuck out; moments when tempers flared, hours of silent annoyance. I record some of the incidents realising that few polar journeys, if any, have escaped such troubles, though most avoid mentioning them because they don't reflect so well on the participants, least of all on the leader – who is often the book writer and who selected his companions in the first place.

Because of our slow progress I decided we needed to make up more time in the morning. The easiest way to do that appeared to be to knock a quarter of an hour off the normal getup time and to have one mug of coffee, not two, since the extra water-boiling time was effectively half an hour.

For many days we had no normal schedule, so my decision did not apply for a while. Then one morning I woke Oliver at 5:45 A.M. instead of 6:00 A.M. (since he usually made the coffee). He was irritated, but his only comment this time was to mutter darkly, 'Too early.' Another morning I rose to put my boots on after my cup of coffee, it having been agreed that we would have no second cup that day. But Charles and Ol had thought the half hour thereby saved could be best employed by a post-coffee doze. There was a lot to be said for this since we were desperately short of sleep and with the cooker going and warm liquid inside us we could really relax. But I persisted and could feel the atmosphere crackle as I crawled out of the tent.

Day by day I felt myself increasingly irritated by Oliver for no good reason. Sometimes I found his unabashed optimism hard to take. On a day when things had gone well I always steeled myself for a coming downturn of events. And that was as well because that's how things went in the Arctic. Ol on the other hand was elated by each bit of progress, and noticing my determined depression, decided to cheer me up to his own high level of optimism.

On March 27 he recorded: 'Morale is high and we will make it.'

Cherry Garrard, writing of Bowers, Scott's companion to the Pole, said: 'There were times when his optimism seemed forced and formal although I believe it wasn't really so. There were times I have almost hated him for his infernal cheerfulness.' I was right with Garrard on Bowers.

Oliver, like myself, had a fiery temper that usually evaporated as quickly as it boiled up. The catalysts which sparked us off, though, were two different sets of chemicals. He wasn't too worried about his few possessions and didn't fuss when ice scattered by Charles or me went over his bag and clothing. Equally, he was careless on entering the tent, when ice from his clothes flew about.

At the time of the daily meal, however hard I tried to act with care, my tent behaviour was dogged by President Ford-type accidents. Pots full of stew went flying. Spoons or bits of radio sank into the beverage. Lighting the cooker, I allowed too much petrol to leak and ignite Ol's sleeping bag. Sugar ended up in the stew and salt in the cocoa. And so on. It's a wonder, in retrospect, that the others didn't execute me in desperation – certainly they must have found it difficult to contain their annoyance.

Our diaries served to a large extent as safety valves. Feelings which were red-hot at the time and recorded as such were more often than not totally forgotten by the following week. My own diary noted '. . . he [Oliver] lost the rifle this morning. It fell off his sledge. I saw him pack both the Skidoo heaters and the Flametamer fuel can in the rear of his sledge tarpaulin although it had a hole in it. Everything soon fell out, though fortunately not when he was travelling last. I told him what he'd done but there was no apology. He leapt immediately to the defence without logic, saying, "But there was nowhere else." He is very careless.' A day later, I wrote: 'After his irritated mood and cold this morning, Ol is this evening almost childish in his loud playfulness. Charles, though silent and morose when cold or in pain, is more solid, understandable and dependable. Ol's saving grace is his incredible patience with the vehicles despite his lack of knowledge . . .'

At about the same period Oliver's diary was equally filled with strong feeling. Naturally unable to understand either my carefully cultivated cocoon of pessimism or my irritation toward him, he wrote: 'A good day and we travelled a good distance. Ran is getting very odd. Sarcastic and short-tempered. I don't think he is physically well. He can't sleep properly, seems to be peeing a hell of a lot, and is getting frostbite, etc. No problems with the vehicles for once so we stopped late with a good outlook for tomorrow.'

Each unaware of the reasons behind the other's behaviour, and determined to control our petty reactions, we would have appeared to a casual observer a remarkably tight-knit group. We had come to the Arctic to test ourselves as well as each other and the equipment. It was proving a very genuine trial. If I did not like the others they need not be selected for the main expedition. If they did not like me they need not join the main expedition. If I was unsuited to my task in such conditions I could withdraw from my own expedition and find a suitable replacement.

During the early days there was very little outward sign of our frustration with each other. But things were bound to get worse ... polar extremes worry a man all day and every day, nagging at his temper and sapping his ability to stay calm; every weakness is aggravated, every characteristic exaggerated.

On one occasion in the tent I noticed an especially menacing silence. Charlie clambered out to get something and Ol muttered, 'Charlie has really got the hump because I didn't heave kit from the plane.' In his diary he wrote: 'Charlie got bad-tempered for some unknown reason,' and 'the barometer is very low, like me.' For the rest of the day life in the tent was sour, but with coffee the next morning all was well again. And Charlie was not a man to hold a grudge for a moment longer than he felt necessary.

As we moved about, axeing the route, often separated by two or three miles and away from each other for many hours, the possible presence of bears lurked in the back of the mind. Had we had dogs, especially when we slept, they might have warned us, though they don't really scare bears off. (A year after our own journey the Japanese explorer Naomi Uemura *was* awakened by his dogs but a visiting bear, ignoring the yapping huskies, slashed his tent open, ate all his dogmeat and began to sniff at the sleeping bag in which Uemura crouched. Soon afterward he shot the bear, but he'd come perilously close to being meat for the bear himself.)

Fly over the Arctic Ocean from anything more than a few hundred feet up and you are unlikely to see bears. Indeed you will probably think the ice is all a great flat skating rink. This is because the uneven nature of the ice loses any white object in the overall glare. And where the surface looks white it also appears firm and safe. But below a few hundred feet, and if your aircraft is going slowly enough, you will see an endless succession of small fields enclosed by hedges, broken by large areas of rubble, split by endless streams and a few great rivers. Little else, though.

To learn the true nature of the place you must experience more than a cursory glimpse from above, so grab your parachute and land on the sea ice. If you should strike lucky, you will land in a soft drift. It might be so soft that your body will sink up to your armpits. You will find fields covered with such drift where walking is a problem. You might on the other hand land on solid ice, angled and sharp, full of cracks and cavities or on apparently sound ice that is in fact slush – with all the characteristics of quicksand. All around you there will be walls of ice from five to thirty feet high. These are the hedges, but you will find no gateway into the next field unless you are lucky. So you decide to cut through the hedge. There is, after all, no option. But which way? Look around for the highest part of the highest hedge, climb it and look around again. If your eyesight is in good shape you should be able to see other paddocks, all with their own enclosing hedges. Some will stretch north twenty paces, others as much as a mile. Knowing that once you've decided to start hacking down the first hedge you are committed to entering that particular field, you will want to know that *its* hedges are not of the thirty-foot variety. This, of course, means walking on ahead to check before you even touch your axe. When you wearily climb the second hedge you may well find a chaos of broken blocks as far as you can see. If so, you will change your mind about where to make that first gateway. The variations, or 'courses open', are infinite. Perhaps the most frustrating fact is that only a mile or so to the west or east while you hack through hedges and rubble, there could well be a newly frozen river, smooth and without obstacles running north for a hundred miles. In 1968 explorer Ralph Plaisted struck lucky. His reconnaissance pilot Weldy Phipps noticed a seventy-mile northerly lead, so his Skidoo completed in two days what might otherwise have taken weeks. A rare chance, indeed, but the possibility that you might be missing such an opportunity will always nag at the back of your mind.

Often the good paddocks lead mostly west or east with only a little northerly gain. How much fuel should you waste following them? Or would it be better to waste energy hacking at a region of rubble that at least takes you north? Even in the open paddocks and fields all is not exactly rosy. There are deep splits partially filled with snow or bridges over like miniature crevasses. There are hummocks, endless ranks of them, often twenty feet high and joined to each other like sand dunes. Here your sledge will overturn at the least misjudgement, so although you are concentrating on navigation, on keeping various parts of you free from frostbite, and on your Skidoo not throwing you off, don't forget to keep the eight-hundred-pound sledge behind you on as even a keel as possible.

When the temperature rises, the composition of the ice pack weakens. Then, when the winds blow and the ocean beneath moves with the currents and the natural swell of all seas in response to the moon's pull or the wind acting on the sail surface of the ridges, then the ice cracks and your troubles really begin . . .

By the first week of April the temperature had risen to the minus twenties with frequent brief colder spells. Only at night could we tell the effect this was having on the floes. A ground-sheet and a thin Karrimat separated the ear from the ice. Each vibration, crack or thud jangled the nerves.

Generally, the rule is 'White ice is thick, grey ice thin.' On April 4 Oliver led the way into an avenue with huge, isolated slabs lining its route. Then his Skidoo broke down. This was nothing new. We were averaging nine or ten breakdowns daily. Charlie stayed to help, and leaving my sledge with them, I carried on down the avenue with Skidoo and axe to work on whatever obstacles lay ahead. I noticed the sky was darker than usual. The lane lay north-east, narrowed into a bottleneck alley and then to a wide paddock.

As though a vice had squeezed the whole paddock inward, the floes which formed its floors had broken and tipped at various angles. Seawater had flooded onto the low parts, and in the middle of the paddock several of the floes had floated apart. Here the water seemed to be freshly frozen over. It looked passable.

I stopped the Skidoo and walked forward to check.

The ice felt spongy at first, then more like rubber. Without warning it began to move. A few feet ahead black water gushed up and spread rapidly over a wide area. I stopped at once but the water rushed past me, covering my boots and, perhaps because of its weight or my involuntary movements, the whole mass of new ice began to rise and fall as though a motor boat had passed by. The undulating movement of a swell approached in slow motion, and as it passed under me the ice rind broke up beneath my boots and I began to sink.

Afraid of disturbing the ice further, I kept rigid, like a mesmerised rabbit.

As the water closed over my knees the remaining layer of crust broke, and I sank quietly and completely. My head could not have been submerged more than a second – the air trapped under my wolfskin acted as a life jacket. At first I had no thoughts but to get out fast. But the nearest solid floe was thirty yards away. Instinctively I shouted for the others, then remembered they were a good half-mile away on the other side of who knew how many slabs and ridges.

I leaned both arms on the new ice that hung suspended under two or three inches of water, then kicked with my boots to lever my chest up onto this fragile skin. I succeeded and felt a rush of hope. But the thin skin broke beneath me and I sank again.

I tried several more times. Each time I clawed and crawled until half out, and each time I sank I was weaker.

My mind began to work overtime but not constructively. Perhaps a passerby might see me and throw a rope. Realisation hit like a bombshell. There would be *no* passerby.

Was it deep? A vivid picture of the Arctic Ocean's floor mapped in the *National Geographic* magazine flashed to mind and gave me a sort of watery vertigo. Yes, it was deep. Deep. Directly under my threshing feet was a cold drop to the canyons of the Lomonosov Ridge between fourteen and seventeen thousand feet below. I vaguely remembered that sailors on the Murmansk convoys reckoned on survival in the waters of the North Sea for about one minute before the cold got them. And this thought brought back the words of an SAS lecturer on survival: 'Never struggle, don't even try to swim, just float and keep as still as you can. Give the water trapped in your clothes a chance to warm up a bit, then keep it there.'

So I tried doing nothing except paddle my arms to keep afloat. But, from a great distance it seemed, I sensed a numbness in my toes. My inner boots filled up, my trousers were sodden. Only in the wolfskin could I feel myself. Inside the gloves there was no sensation in my fingers. And all the while my chin inside the parka hood was sinking slowly lower as the clothes became heavier.

It might work in the Mediterranean or even in the North Sea but not here. I felt a rising panic. I *must* get out now or never. I smashed at the ice with one arm while the other thrashed wildly to keep my head above water.

The seconds seemed like minutes and the minutes like hours. The precarious platform of ice rind was too strong to smash with one arm. Only with the weight of my chest could I crack it, a few inches at a time, and my strength was draining quickly. My arm slapped down on a solid chunk, inches thick, suspended in the skein like a layer of clay in quicksand. I levered my chest onto it. It held. Then my thighs, and finally my knees.

For a second I lay gasping on this island of safety, but once out of the water the cold and the wind zeroed in. It was minus 38 degrees Fahrenheit that morning with a seven-knot breeze. At 20 degrees below zero with a nineteen-knot wind, dry exposed flesh freezes in one minute.

Moving my stomach and wriggling legs and arms like a turtle in soft sand I edged to the nearest floe with the nilas (newly formed ice) bending and pulsating under me as though it were alive. But it held. Standing up I watched the water dribble out of boots, trousers and sleeves. When I moved I heard the trousers crackle as they froze. The shivering began, and I could not control it. I tried press-ups but five had always been my limit in the best of times. I slumped over to my Skidoo. The air movement was bitter on my face and legs. It would be foolish to walk back to the others. My Skidoo had stalled. I couldn't start it again without taking off my thick outer mitts. This I couldn't do; the leather had gone rigid and shrunk.

For fifteen, twenty minutes I plodded round and round my

Skidoo with a sodden heavy jog, flapping my arms in wheeling windmills and shouting all the while.

Then Ol arrived.

'I've fixed her,' he said. 'What's the next bit like?'

'Unsafe,' I told him. 'I went in.'

'Is there a way round?' he asked, and then finally, 'Good Gawd, so you *did* . . .'

After that, all was action. I got on the back of his Skidoo and we went back slowly to where Charlie was stopped with an overturned sledge. They quickly erected the tent, started the cooker, cut my boots and wolfskin off with a knife and between them found bits and pieces of spare clothes to replace my soaked ones. Soon the wet items were strung dripping above while tea brewed, and Ol rubbed the blood back into my fingers and toes.

I had been damn lucky, and assured the others as well as myself that future ice-testing forays would be conducted with greater care. The rule of 'White ice is thick, grey ice thin' would no longer be gospel. After that we would use an axe or a prod in all dubious places.

Twelve hours later my clothes were damp but wearable. My mountain-equipment duvet jacket sufficed instead of the torn wolfskin.

That spring revelled in freak conditions. Mid-March had seen record low temperatures, yet by mid-April records were being set in the opposite direction. The sea ice was slowly but surely breaking up a month earlier than usual. We could probably cope for a while, but once the magic point of minus 9.4 degrees Fahrenheit was reached, our troubles would really begin. There could be weeks or only days to go.

When seawater is cooled a touch beyond its freezing point, ice forms in thin discs or platelets known as frazil ice. This growth takes place anywhere within the top few inches of the surface. The frazil crystals duly open up to form a slush and the water takes on the oily look of grease ice. This in turn consolidates into rind, a flexible surface coating about an inch thick within which the frazil crystals grow with the action of seeds. Each little crystal is made up of platelets of pure ice separated by brine cells. Their growth rate depends on the temperature. At around minus 9.4 degrees Fahrenheit the whole character of sea ice alters, becoming far stronger in terms of its weight-bearing capacity.

By Easter Day, 'summer' fogs were stopping aircraft activity and at Alert, Geoff reported *plus* 2 degrees Centigrade. The difference between this temperature and that experienced during a so-called normal year was considerable. For instance, during exactly the same week of the year of Ralph Plaisted's first expedition, the temperature sixty miles farther south than Alert but also along the coast was minus 40 degrees Centigrade. Another side effect of this early warmth would be soft drifts to trap and spin the tracks of our Skidoos.

None of this overall picture seemed to worry the others. Both were cheerful as ever, and I should have been grateful for this. I well remember journeys in deserts, on glaciers, down foaming rivers when overall dejection had struck at the team and I'd said to myself, 'Now's the time to cheer them up, to act positively and to push harder.' It had never been difficult and usually worked well. But now, faced with a team who didn't need cheering up, who seemed unable or unwilling to grasp the full weight of the elements ahead, I found myself wanting to bludgeon their spirits to a level of realism.

It is easy to see in retrospect how unnecessary and dampening my resulting actions were. Oliver's diary recorded: 'Ran is very pessimistic and argumentative. He won't listen to advice.' He was right. It was a lesson well learned and a further example of the excellence of the Arctic Ocean as a testing ground. My desire to push harder, to go north as fast and as far as possible, was unaffected by my certainty that we would not reach the Pole. But two days out of every four it was a frustrated desire.

Perhaps I have overstressed the few things that went wrong between the three of us. There were, throughout our five months in the Arctic, only two brief evenings in our tent when a genuinely bad atmosphere hung heavy. But the silent, largely hidden feelings existed along with the physical stresses. A man wrapped up in his moods may well know that his ability is unimpaired, that the mood is only his own protective reaction to extreme conditions experienced and anticipated. But he is risking the danger that outsiders will misinterpret his behaviour. During Wally Herbert's Arctic expedition the press used the term 'winteritis' – calling it 'an Arctic condition which clouds the judgement and can become a danger'. 'What effect' asked the *Daily Sketch*, alluding to Wally's imagined behaviour, 'can such appalling conditions have on the mind and morale of a man?' Cherry Garrard, describing Scott's 'winter party', wrote: 'The loss of a biscuit crumb left a sense of injury which lasted for weeks. The greatest friends were so much on one another's nerves that they did not speak for days for fear of quarrelling.'

Our group was no exception. One day a wide river of undulating grey nilas ice barred our way. I decided to try out for the first time the rubber boat we had brought with us. After inflating it Charlie and I clambered aboard.

Ol stayed on the bank, holding one end of a nylon coil that played off a drum inside the boat. Charlie pushed us off, one of his boots sinking through the pancake as he did so. The rind broke under the boat's weight, and we were afloat.

For ten yards we made progress. In the front I smacked the rind;

at the rear Charles provided the propulsion. Then abruptly she would go no farther. The rind had become nilas. My paddle slashed down on the thicker substance but instead of splintering, it simply accepted the blade the way porridge closes over a spoon. And the boat refused to plough through the porridge, strain as we mightily did at the paddles.

Glancing back, I saw the nilas forming behind us. Soon we would be jammed in the quagmire. Seconds counted. Without hesitation, or explanation, I shouted above the hiss of the jellied river, 'Pull her in, Ol. *Quick.*'

'Why? She's doing fine.'

'Don't argue, just pull.'

I could see Ol shrug with irritation. My sudden change of mind within minutes of the boat's launching was beyond him. He was obviously thinking ... Ran's panicking or has gone round the twist. Either way his judgement must be badly impaired ...

If I was misunderstood, the fault was mine. My companions, after all, weren't Arabs who blindly accepted orders they didn't understand. Nor were they, like the navy men with Scott and Shackleton, trained to obey without question. They wanted explanations, especially when apparently unnecessary changes of plan were involved. After two years with thirty Arab soldiers and ten years of leading expeditions in various lands, I'd become far too insulated. I felt there was a time and a place to explain decisions and actions, and that that time was not during moments of potential hazard to the expedition's equipment or members. At least as I saw it.

When involved with the more dangerous activities of nature, I'd always felt reactions needed to be instantaneous. There is no time for the powwows and reasoned discussions of the military mind. With Arab soldiers, who accepted my instant changes of mind to suit a changing situation, I had been at peace with myself and results had never suffered. In the British army, where there is little room, especially in peacetime, for impulse and instinct, I had always felt crabbed and ill at ease.

Charlie and Ol were both strong individualists, both leaders, who disliked being told what to do in the best of times. Being human, they appreciated personal involvement. Normally I respected this and many a democratic discussion took place over the years between the three of us, but when instant action was required I reverted to the one-man bandism I was accustomed to. Not only was it instinctive with me; it also, I rationalised, saved time.

But, as with the boat and the nilas, it naturally did not work with us as well as it would have had I selected yes-men for companions. Their pride sparked automatically when told to do something that they considered unreasonable, over which they had not been consulted and which they considered inadvisable in any case.

But there was another factor which stirred the chemicals between the three of us. Urgency. They avoided any outward show of haste at all costs, as though it were a sign of fear, as though to hurry in the face of adversity was both unseemly and somehow ungentlemanly. Both were army-trained and loved the army way of life – especially Oliver. The steel rules of behaviour instilled in them were deep-rooted, undiluted by too much reality. Both had participated in military exercises in various lands but always within the framework of regular infantry Standard Operational Procedures. When the bullets fly an officer, commissioned or otherwise, can demonstrate his guts by ignoring them, or appearing to. I had learned that such outward shows did not always help the outcome of an operation. A boat stranded in the nilas would cause as great a delay to our journey as a dead or wounded officer to an advance.

Fortunately, however insane or terrified the others may have thought me at the time, they at least continued to fall in with the suggested course of action, even if not at top gear . . .

Back to the case at issue. Ol tugged. He weighed 185 in his furs and had oxlike power. But the boat seemed glued to the nilas, and unable to close with the bank we floated at two miles an hour away from Oliver's belaying point.

I put one leg overboard and rocked the boat. Charles did likewise on the far side. Finally we broke the grip of the sludge and Ol began to win the tug-of-war. A near-disaster, and I had learned that boats are not the answer to rivers of sludge.

But after each new incident relief was short-lived. As in Geoff's case, the Arctic Ocean was no place to learn one's lessons – by the time one's learned them it's often too late to take advantage of the hard-won knowledge ... When Wally Herbert set out with two friends to circumnavigate Greenland they ran into bad weather between Thule and Alert. One of the men, a tough New Zealander, later described the experience in the *Sunday Times:* 'I was travelling across a pan of ice which suddenly fractured. Seawater flooded across it, soaking my boots. I couldn't dry, and got frostbite in three of my toes.' The following day the poor fellow had to be evacuated, leaving the yearlong expedition only two-strong.

Any day now *we* feared an accident. Every day involved a succession of decisions. Was it safe to cross? How and where? How long to delay, waiting until two inches of new ice became four inches? One wrong decision could lose a man together with all his equipment. If the radio and beacon went out, we would end our days slowly starving.

There were leads that moved fast and unevenly, humming like bees or hissing with a sibilant whisper that warned of too-new slush. Others ground together with the sound of chomping horse teeth, spewing green blocks from between their closing jaws. In this region of fragmentation, an accident was likely. The anxiety this caused Ginnie was sometimes evident in her voice. Her job was difficult. In addition to informing England of our progress and fielding requests from sponsors, which she did through our friends Jack

Willies, Phil Birkett and Graham Standing at RAE Cove Radio Station, she had to keep her radios, antennae and masts in working order despite the conditions. There were constant problems and a great deal of tension at the base ... the aircraft, its crew, its rising costs and its many breakdowns ... Many times the Otter would not find the ice group and the farther north this happened, the worse were Ginnie's nightmares. Geoff and Mary were very close to one another, and Ginnie's radio duties cut her off from them. She had little enough time to sleep, let alone to have a friendly natter.

The extra flights of the chartered Twin Otter to resupply us had incurred more bills than we could meet. Now Ginnie had to raise £40,000 over her radio knowing that, if the money did not arrive, all our efforts would come to an abrupt end. All administration, correspondence and planning for the immediate future lay in her court. She had no one's shoulder to cry on, nowhere to seek advice. Our three United Kingdom supporters were often impossible to contact. Mike Wingate-Gray was often in Arabia, Andrew Croft seriously ill in the hospital and Peter Booth on an army assignment. She sometimes felt cut off, even desperate. There were days when she knew the ice group was on unstable ice and the aircraft she sent out came back reporting no sign of us, yet she had to be seen to be calm, not to overreact.

Throughout the last two weeks of April success truly hung in the balance. We worked hard, spoke scarcely at all except inside the tent, slept little, lost a great deal of weight and strength and lived in a dream world. It was so long since we had seen land or anything normal. Every new view was different but it was always ice, snow, water and sky. No night and no day. The sun circled roughly the same height above the horizon now, so the available light varied little from midnight to midday. When the weather and Skidoos allowed, we travelled twelve hours and camped for six, so many of our days were made up of eighteen, not twenty-four, hours. Twice we managed over twenty miles in a twenty-four-hour period. The muddle-headed, dry-mouthed uncertainty caused by our constantly changing timetable induced a sensation of floating, of acting in slow motion in another world totally disconnected from reality.

The only certainty was north. We must go north. Every minute spent gaining northerly paces produced satisfaction, every delay frustrated. Ollie had scribbled out a table showing the most northerly point reached by previous attempts. This was eagerly referred to – giving a fine edge to the competitive urge that helped to drive us on. At 86°00′ N we knew we had beaten Bjorn Staib, the Swedish explorer who narrowly escaped the breakup of 1963 by finding T2, a massive ice island manned by American scientists (since deserted). At 86°14′ we passed the farthest north of the great Norwegian explorer Nansen, who used a ship and dog teams but was turned back by a chaos of ice blocks on April 14, eighty-four years before. At 86°34′ we passed the record of the Italian Lieutenant Cagni, who seventy-seven years before reached his limit on April 24.

Each day or night merged into a whirling nightmare race, a steeplechase along the course that Wally Herbert had called a 'horizontal Everest'. All memories I have of the time are confused if vivid scenes in no special sequence. Only my diary, a tatty notebook with ninety-six pages of almost illegible scribble, gives shape to the events and the feelings. Here are some excerpts:

> The mists are down again. All day white-out. I wasted time this morning. Set out into the Great White Nothing on what I thought must be a due north bearing because yesterday's tracks led due north – I checked by the sun last night. After twenty minutes good going (using Charlie out ahead and Ol behind as continuing reference points) we got muddled up in some rubble. I checked on the compass, which although it's not always

trustworthy indicated that we were heading south. That was surely not possible even in this crazy part of the world. Much against my instincts I did a complete about-turn and went back the way we'd come, feeling totally confused. Not far past where we must have camped last night – couldn't tell for sure since all tracks were gone – we came to wide fresh crack-up. Went along the floe edge and found a crossing place. Quite good after that except for deep drifts and lots of heaving at overturns. I suppose the crack-up caused my error: the floe we camped on must have revolved 180 degrees overnight so our Skidoos ended up pointing south whereas I presumed the opposite. In future I'll ignore anything but the compasses when it's like this . . . Even when the wind's at its worst, our camp drill's pretty slick now. Each bloke knows his own action back to front, eyes closed, mitts on. Even loo drill has been got to a fine art, though it's still a low point of the day. What with no solid meals except supper we all go just after the tent's taken down but the chute's still over the Skidoos. If you do it slick and quick you can avoid getting a frozen Aristotle, to use Ol's terminology. This evening Charlie's timing went wrong and the urge caught him unawares in the middle of a two-mile foot reconnaissance. Fortunately for him no wind at the time. But of course no paper either so he cut off the long tail of his wool Hobson shirt and used it as well as his silk balaclava, sadly burying them afterward. (Funny how convention sticks with us even out here: Charlie trudged at least two hundred yards through drifts and got behind a big berg well away from me.) . . . Last night I woke at 0230 to find the others sitting tense and bolt upright. Charlie muttered, 'My God, they're field-firing.' It turned out to be a noisy bout of new fracturing in our immediate area . . . April 20. Low on fuel again but must keep going. The Otter came out and our beacon was on at the agreed time. But they could not find us. Let's hope it's not my navigation. I'll check the noon sun tomorrow if it is fine. These foot reconnaissances day after day are doing me in. Ol keeps giving me bombs which I use. They're some help but the everlasting trudging up to my knees, the slithering and falling on ice bits, the dampness are making the piles worse ... Today, out of sight of the others, they just got too bad and I lay on the ice and cursed. But self-pity doesn't do any good. I think the banging about on the Skidoo does them less harm than the walks ... This afternoon I was a mile or so ahead in a place of wide paddocks and high walls. Found one that looked fine for a strip, and deciding to camp there since we were almost out of fuel, I wandered all over it to test for a bump-free runway. Soon my tracks were everywhere. For two hours I waited for the others. No one came so I set out back. Confused by all the tracks I somehow missed the outward one leading back the way I'd come. It's quite a place, this, when you realise the consequences of being lost with no tent and no radio. You've got to keep a hold on yourself and think slowly. In a while I found the route out secured on a patch of trackless hard ice and soon reached the others – delayed by a breakdown ... Last night I was awakened by Charlie being violently sick at the tent door. This morning they were both feeling weak but got up on time nonetheless. Charles has swollen areas of poison on his chin. Ol's giving him penicillin pills. Could our diet be wrong? ... Crossed eighteen leads today and a wall of newly broken ice some thirty-two to thirty-five feet high. We let the sledges down the far side on ropes after heaving them up manually ... April 24. Lost communications tonight. The radio sent sparks flying all over the place. Charlie reckons some damp has crept down between the high-power and the low-power circuits causing a short. He's shoving loo paper into the burned part of the casing on a wire to dry it. Hope it's okay for tomorrow's call ... May 1. By night the tent shook to the thunder of a new breakup. Sleep was difficult because of the menacing rumble all around and the metallic whine of the ice half an inch from our ears.

The imagination, try as one might to count (black) sheep jumping pressure ridges or a five-star meal by a log fire, kept dwelling on ... What will happen if a fracture opens up under the tent? Will I get out of the sleeping bag in time? Will the tent collapse on us in the water? Will they find us if the radio is lost? ... and other equally fruitless worries. A fracture *did* open under one of Wally Herbert's store tents during his Arctic crossing, but none of his team was inside the tent at the time.

On May 7, at 87°11.5′N, some 167 miles from the Pole, we finally came to a halt in a region of swirling mush. We waited but it did not solidify, and on May 16 the Twin Otter came down on the only unbroken ice pan we could find. We loaded our equipment and headed south for Tanquary Fjord en route to Alert. We had failed.

The unaccustomed warmth and comfort brought a yearning to sleep. Below the miles flashed by, 130 of them every hour. The floes were smooth as ivory, the fractures thin as writing on a page of vellum seen from afar. They floated by in a dream of half-formed memories, the cutting cold and the tension so quickly erased by the healing veil of the mind.

I thought I would never write about this place. What could I say? There is nothing to describe. No history, no buildings, no animals, no people, no real scenery even. Just the ice, the water and the sky.

People read of places where they might like to go one day. But no one wants to travel on these semi-frozen wastes. Why should they? It has nothing to offer but pain and frustration.

At Tanquary Fjord, a long-empty research base, Ginnie was waiting by herself in one of the three huts. We sat on a crate. Her hands seemed small and cold at the ends of her wolfskin sleeves. The sun had faded the blue of her eyes. She gave me two messages. One from Wally Herbert: 'You beat the farthest north of Simpson, Staib and even Nansen and should feel rightly proud of your achievement. Warmest congratulations. It was a truly great effort. Wally.'

The other, from Mike Wingate-Gray, informed us that His Royal Highness the Prince of Wales had agreed to become patron of the main circumpolar expedition.

This brought home to my weary brain that everything we had just suffered, the whole painful nightmare, must be *repeated* as a mere fraction of a far greater whole.

From Alert to the Pole and over to Spitsbergen is about one thousand miles as the crow flies. We had just logged over nine hundred miles, but if only our distance *toward* the Pole, ignoring detours, were considered, we had completed a mere 263 miles. Not impressive stuff by way of convincing sceptics as to our potential.

We had set out to learn lessons as polar apprentices. We had done just that. But was it enough?

How would the key people feel? The Royal Geographical Society, the sponsors, the governments? Would they now lend their support to the main venture?

Chapter Three

> If you have hoped and your expectation was not fulfilled, then go on hoping.
>
> TALMUD

In London the autumn months of 1977 were full ones. One day the great desert traveler Wilfred Thesiger lunched with me at the barracks. I had long found him a fascinating character – his will is of Damascus steel. Just to think of his accomplishments and against what odds inspired me. And I needed inspiring just then. The list of what we had not got but needed to obtain if the main journey was to take place was overwhelming.

Thanks to our Omani friends we were not in debt but once again had no funds. We needed an icebreaker costing at least £350,000 together with a crew of professional seamen who had to agree to give up their careers for at least three years. Also there were side aspects to owning a ship, such as spare parts and servicing, which could soon create large bills.

We needed to find a Twin Otter aircraft for polar resupply. Because srmy support with a Hercules C-130 was out and because chartering a Twin Otter for so long would be unthinkably costly, we had to operate our own Twin Otter with our own crew. Such an aircraft costs upward of £1 million.

Ship, aircraft and crew, if ever found, had to be fully insured. And insurers just might feel there was an element of undue risk to our venture.

The land team, which had appeared our only solid asset, was now wavering. Geoff and Mary had shown signs of romantic attachment over the past two years. When needled, both denied it hotly, but faced with at least another year of office work before any chance of further travel, both of them decided to leave. For a while they carried on with us, then Geoff departed to film green turtles in Bermuda and Mary returned to her publishing company in time to join ex-Prime Minister Heath promote his book around Britain.

I was sad to see them go. Both Ol and Charlie believed Geoff's hands would never withstand extreme cold again: they also thought that, tough though he was in normal circumstances, he was not the right person for polar winter work. I was less sure about this, but Geoff left anyway, so my feeling was academic. The other two seemed fine for the team, but Ginnie would need a replacement for Mary; someone who could ideally double as an emergency reserve for the ice group. It would need to be a man this time, but, being of a jealous nature, I certainly did not want someone tall, dark and handsome.

In the Arctic Ginnie had found our London friends difficult to contact when she needed them. For the main journey – which we agreed to call simply the Transglobe Expedition – we needed to have a much more solid organisation back in England, a full-time staff of executive secretary with volunteer helpers.

Also, much as I had always hated the idea, it seemed inevitable that a committee of experts be set up to encourage the different sides of the venture and, after our departure, to keep it rolling; ideally at no cost.

Through George Greenfield, I approached Sir Vivian Fuchs. He agreed to be a member but not the chairman of our main committee. He approached Rear Admiral Sir Edmund Irving for that post, retired hydrographer of the Royal Navy and past president of the Royal Geographical Society. Sir Edmund kindly accepted and over the months ten other eminent individuals joined as well.

For Mary's successor and for office help I advertised whenever free newspaper space was available. A young civil engineer, Simon Grimes, was hooked in this way. 'While drunk and eating chips at 1 A.M. in a friend's flat,' he wrote in his diary, 'my eye caught an advert, "Wanted, sixth person to join ... With impending unemployment and no better ideas, it seemed like a good idea at the time. Interested in polar regions, have itchy feet and am mad enough.'

Simon was a Cumbrian, an experienced climber, a member of past expeditions to Norway, Greenland and Ghana and obviously intelligent despite his recent downward trend in jobs. After getting his degree he was a trainee engineer on road construction sites, then outdoor-pursuits instructor at Brathe Hall. This led somehow to office cleaning and then us.

He was neat and self-assured. I sat him down for the normal black talk: '... and I must be honest. I'm not the easiest of people.' I paused. 'If you're looking for a democratic outfit, you're in the wrong place. I believe the leader should be just that.'

He was thin and small in stature only. 'You don't need to give me all that guff. I've been warned you're a ruthless bastard.'

That shut me up. Simon moved into the office soon afterwards and began to learn the ropes. I gave him all food and polar hut responsibilities, since these had been Mary's.

Despite his gruff, assertive ways and his apparent scorn of our way of doing things, I liked him in a funny sort of way and felt he would be just right for the base camp with Ginnie. The other three did not share my opinion; indeed they nagged at me constantly to get rid of him.

At the time there were two other contenders but one was pudgy and incapable of even the lowest level of self-inspiration. The other contracted hepatitis.

After five months I was still the only one in favour of Simon, so reluctantly I had to tell him it was no good. He was quietly emotional but in a controlled voice asked if he could stay on to help us for a while nonetheless. Of course he could; I was only too grateful.

Simon's diary: 'R. told me I had not been accepted. I never knew but suspected I was blackballed by Charlie.'

Charlie, never one to disguise his likes and dislikes, was openly rude to Simon by trying to ignore him completely, very difficult in our tiny office with its phone shortage.

Six months later, in the absence of anyone else, the other three grudgingly agreed to reaccept Simon – Charlie on the firm condition that I never asked Simon to be third man if Ollie or I became injured or sick.

This did not seem an idyllic arrangement with which to begin a long period of togetherness, but I was sure time would convince the others of Simon's obvious good points.

Colonel Paul Clark told me privately that he was to be posted as full colonel to the missile defence headquarters inside Boulder Mountain, Colorado. But above all else he wanted to join the Transglobe Expedition. As a yachtsman, a position on our ship's crew would be wonderful. He knew we had no ship but had no doubts one would turn up. Could I put him on the short list as an unpaid deckhand? I could and did.

Poul Andersson, a Danish sea cadet who had sailed in Antarctic waters, joined us that Christmas. He had no money so we got him an evening job with the Youth Hostel Association and he slept on the office floor alongside Oliver. He set up an old table beside Charlie's and called it the Marine Desk. At twenty-one, he was several years younger than the rest of us, with a wonderful quiet sense of humour; everyone liked Poul.

Early in 1978 two rural characters from Suffolk appeared in jeans and motheaten tweed coats. The taller one with salty blue eyes and fuzzy black beard impressed me at once; possibly a subliminal reaction to the many films I had seen of heroic destroyer captains who, minus their sea caps and guernsey sweaters, resembled Anton Bowring. He had a Russian grandmother, six years of seagoing experience on iron-ore carriers, shrimp boats to Chittagong and more recently Greenland Sea ice protection vessels. His buddy, Mick Hart, was a fellow seaman. Poul made tea in tin mugs and my interview of the two began.

'There's no pay with us, you know,' I said.

'No, that's fine. I'm interested in any form of seafaring job, even cook,' Anton replied.

Mick, it seemed, also was not fussy. What, they asked, would their duties be and when would they begin?

'Right now –' I hesitated; I did not want to lose these two – 'right now we haven't actually got the ship we want. In fact we have no ship at all yet. Poul here has been looking into alternatives, haven't you, Poul?' He nodded wisely over his tin mug.

Both visitors looked unconcerned so I took the plunge. 'Really your first job can be to get the ship, along with Poul, and you can start right away at the Marine Desk here.'

The Marine Desk was toppling under the weight of four of us and a heap of Arctic Pilot books. Anton eyed it and the general confusion around the office with enthusiasm.

'How much is the expedition prepared to pay? I mean, what type of vessel are we after?' I noticed the *we*. Encouraging.

'An icebreaker. Catch is, it mustn't cost anything. That's one of our rules. It applies to the phone and the stationery too. We have *no* funds.'

The talk took quite a while. Next day we borrowed a second desk from the nearby office of the RAF Escaping Society, whose staff were absent.

As the Marine Desk became the Marine Office and grew in numbers, so Charlie, the only 'land' person in that half of our room, was squashed further up against the wall.

Anton's diary at the time read: 'When I heard of the expedition I wrote to Mr Ran Fiennes, some obscure gent I'd never heard of, to ask for a position on his ship. I was thinking in terms of being a deckhand. His reply implied that the expedition hadn't quite left the country so, with a friend, I went for an interview. They were pretty well organised but they had *no* ship. So Ran said yes. Very happy to have you on the ship but first you must find one and a crew for it. Also all the stores and equipment you think it will need, free berths and port facilities at all likely ports of call on the route, etc. He said all this must not cost a penny. Not a penny. If I was prepared to take this on, then yes he was happy to take me on and immediately.' A little later Anton wrote: 'It all seemed like a nice idea at the time. The more I got involved in it, the more I was obsessed. It's like a germ, this expedition, or a disease.'

Anton, Poul and Mick somehow slotted themselves around the Marine Desk. The only phone was on Charlie's desk. There was much yattering and needling between them.

Charlie worked well when watched. He was still the biggest of us and the most powerfully built. He was, however, idle by nature and took an evil delight in avoiding any task that could possibly be done by someone else. If, on the other hand, there was an important task which could not wait and there was categorically no one but him available, he would set to with a will and enjoy it.

His evasions, plottings, and deceptions were always aimed at one end – to avoid hard, or even gentle, work. When there was no escape he would knuckle down to it. But he knew that I knew that once my back was turned he would take a quick smoke break which would become a well-earned five minutes that in turn would develop into a brief siesta which might well last through the afternoon. So there was continual war between us until the real travel began and Charlie was on the move. Then he was transformed, his sullen moods became rare and he worked at least as hard as the next man.

It had been his frustrated love of travel, of a fight against the elements, that had brought about his black moods at Thule. Cooped up with two girls, both of whom he felt were nagging him unnecessarily, he had thought of us up on the ice cap and felt he was missing out. That and his natural idleness which the girls resented had kindled sparks of hostility.

I once noticed two enormous sheets of paper on Charlie's desk completely covered with several hours' work of elaborate doodling. On asking him what he was busy with he replied evenly, 'A great many things,' took one of my cigarettes and settled down to write a letter to the chairman of a potential sponsor company. The letter began, 'Dear Sir Arthur.' An hour later I found the letter still on his desk and this time it said, 'Dear Sir Arthur. We would be extremely grateful . . .'

For a long time afterward whenever someone caught him staring into space they would call out 'Dear Sir Arthur.' Which at least would have the desired effect of bringing him back to earth. Charlie had, I felt, untapped potential, but in London it was necessary to set him specific tasks and keep badgering him until they were done.

Oliver, intelligent, full of charm and immediately attractive to all but a very few females, possessed a most generous nature. Unfortunately for him he could not indulge this happy trait because he was penniless. By night he slept in our storehouse within the barracks. He ate the leftover food from our training journey. In the evenings Charlie and he worked as barmen at the Admiral Codrington pub close to the barracks. This earned each of them enough money for cigarettes as well as a good square meal at the end of the day.

Life in the little office was bedlam. Simon and Ollie, Ginnie and I shared a phone. Typing was done by two very kind volunteers who managed to keep up with the flow of correspondence. There were over seven hundred sponsor companies by then: food and equipment were pouring into the barracks.

I needed above all a full-time secretary, someone who would handle everything, every complex side of the venture when we had all left the country. There might be a dozen part-time volunteers helping him but they would come and go. He would provide the permanent pivot in London. I found a company willing to pay a salary for such a job of £3,000 all inclusive per annum. Not very tempting for the sort of lively executive we needed but it would have to do.

I looked for someone likely to prove patient, honest and above all loyal.

A series of interviews followed:

There were three retired wing commanders, two youngish 'retired' captains and a professional fundraiser. None were any good. But this was incidental since all balked at the prospect of £3,000 with no expenses and unlinked to the cost of living.

A Royal Marine colonel, recently retired, appeared. *He* interviewed *me* and told me he liked the job but as soon as he'd gone, we both thought about it. He must have sensed that as far as the expedition was concerned he would in my eyes be secretary, not colonel. It wouldn't work.

In September 1977 Ant Preston wrote in. He had been a

National Service RAF pilot officer. For some twenty years, partly in Africa, he had done PR and export work. Now he wanted something different, something lively. He was to get more than he bargained for.

He began at once on a month's two-way approval. He was a gentle, quiet man with a wry sense of humour and endless patience: his idealism and loyalty, which were to be severely tested, were to prove critical when the troubled times came.

On December 15 our patron H.R.H. Prince Charles asked me to show him the film of our Arctic journeys and to introduce the team. We set up the projector in a drawing room at Buckingham Palace. Prince Charles flew back that evening from the United States, where among other things he had dined between Sophia Loren and Farrah Fawcett-Majors. This must have been a stunning experience which would have left lesser mortals comatose. As it was, in the drowsy light of the flickering projector and to the monotonous tones of my narration, I thought I saw our patron's head list slowly to starboard in his armchair. Whether or not this was so, he was charming to us and enthusiastic about the endeavour. If I ran into any problems I must not hesitate to approach him. He would help us if he could.

When, by my self-imposed deadline of Christmas 1977, there was still no aircraft or ship, I broke the news to the others and to our sponsors that still another year's delay was necessary. We would now leave England on September 1, 1979. Everyone took this philosophically; the work carried on.

The new year crystallised the long-standing Antarctic problem.

Anton Bowring dispelled my hopes that if we had our own icebreaker and our own Twin Otter we could mount our crossing attempt self-contained and needing *no* support from governments.

'Poul and I have now checked up on all ice-class ships on the market. Most are far beyond sponsorable price. But a few of the older steel-hulled ships just might do the job *and* are on offer at a reasonable cost. These are the types we're concentrating on. You tell me we must carry fifteen hundred 45-gallon drums to Antarctica for your fuel plus one hundred tons of mixed dry cargo. Well, any ship we can afford to get and to run will be likely to have space for only two-thirds of the fuel.'

Which meant getting some five hundred drums from Cape Town to Sanae coastal camp in Antarctica by other means. There are *no* other means except the South African ship that annually replenishes Sanae from Cape Town. So South African governmental approval remained critical.

Next problem. We might easily fail to cross the whole of Antarctica in one short summer season, the period when travel is possible. If so we would need evacuation to a coastal camp to spend a winter waiting to carry on where we left off the previous year.

The only practical camp for this contingency plan was Scott Base, which belonged to New Zealand. So the New Zealanders also remained on my critical list.

Lastly, even with our ship to bring fuel supplies in to both sides of Antarctica the ice crossing distance was so vast and our aircraft so small we would need a minimum of twenty-three fuel drums at the South Pole itself, roughly our halfway point and the only manned spot along the whole route. A dozen or so United States scientists work in heated huts there all year round. Only the Americans could provide us with fuel at the South Pole. Technically there was no problem since they stored considerable reserves there. But the United States State Department, like our Foreign Office, dreaded private expeditions in Antarctica. They did not need to be brilliant to appreciate that without assurance of fuel at the South Pole we would be foolish to set out at all.

In a nutshell I had to get these three governments to promise this specific support, or my plans were paper tigers . . .

I met New Zealand's top Antarctic administrator and polar expert, Bob Thompson, when he visited London. He seemed friendly but made four points very clear. In his experience there was no model of snowmobile 'capable of crossing the Antarctic continent let alone hauling a sledge over it'. A Twin Otter would lack the necessary range. There was no scientific value to our trip, and 'radio communication is known to be difficult if not impossible at most times between Antarctica and the United Kingdom.'

The South Africans and Americans appeared to concur with this bleak summary. All three countries put the ball in the court of our government by saying they would only consider our proposals if they had British government support.

Whitehall does have advisory committees on most things from nuclear weapons to garbage disposal but not on private polar expeditions. They could only be convinced by Britain's tiny polar clique. Sir Vivian Fuchs and our new Foreign Office friend, whose name I must omit, were the key figures, since both knew our hopes and our limitations and both were influential in those polar circles which could, if they felt it right to do so, provide us with the required backing.

But, within the narrow confines of the polar establishment, there were three gentlemen with a long history of blocking ventures of an apparently nonscientific nature. They had for instance attempted to stop Sir Vivian's own Trans Antarctic Expedition in the 1950s. Luckily Sir Anthony Eden's approval of the venture had made things difficult for them. All three were now, it appeared, at work to put wrenches in our spokes.

The president of the Royal Geographical Society, Lord Hunt, himself the leader of the first expedition to ascend Mount Everest, may or may not have been approached by them. At any rate

Andrew Croft, our most active and originally our only supporter within the polar establishment, wrote to Lord Hunt: '... It seems that the "Trio" are doing their best to ensure that on future RGS expeditions only science really matters. Therefore any mountaineering expeditions in the Himalayas and elsewhere will not be supported or approved. Fiennes has a reasonably good programme in science ... scientists are keen to cooperate, but I already suspect that some have been warned off by the Trio ... If science is to be the only important matter on expeditions henceforward, largely due to the Trio, what will happen to the youth of our country? I believe that the future of our society should continue to include adventure as well as science.'

Meanwhile Sir Vivian suggested to the RGS Expeditions Committee that they might set up a small group to look at my proposals. Since he himself was now on our own committee he would not participate. Lord Hunt was present and did not object to the scheme. At the same time Sir Vivian warned me of an aspect of my preparations which our own committee did not agree with. They were not convinced of my likely success in covering all our needs in kind rather than in cash. It was felt I should also be trying to raise funds. Nonetheless our chairman wrote to the relevant person in the Foreign Office asking how we should set about getting government endorsement of our plans.

The Foreign Office reply was rather helpful: 'The answer lies in finding an expert body that will give us independent advice about the expedition and whose judgement and status will be recognised by the foreign Antarctic authorities concerned. It seems to us that the Royal Society's British National Committee on Antarctic Research is the appropriate body ...' And the Royal Society in turn suggested that the advice of the British Antarctic Survey be sought to help them in the vetting process.

On October 30, 1978, a year after our return from the Arctic, the RGS Expeditions Committee approved of Transglobe officially, but much work had yet to be done to get government blessing. In November the Royal Society's list of criticisms arrived. The Skidoos were thought to be underpowered for the weight to be towed at high altitudes. The Twin Otter was inadequate in many basic respects. We were likely to need more assistance than might reasonably be expected from existing Antarctic resources. An accident to our Twin Otter could have dire consequences . . .

So, with ten months to go, we remained distinctly unblessed.

Both Ollie and Charlie would abscond from time to time – Ollie on 'bird-watching' sprees to Windsor Great Park and Charlie 'on business'. It was seldom necessary with any of the team to check up on them once I had given each a list of 'items required' at the beginning of each month. But from time to time things did go embarrassingly wrong in our dealings with sponsors. Some products like windproof jackets from competing manufacturers were similar but in certain small ways very different and we needed both types for different climates. Charlie, in a vague moment when posting off colour pictures of products being used in Greenland to the relevant sponsors, sent a slide of Bostik glue to Ciba Geigy (makers of Araldite glue) and a similar slide of Araldite glue in use to Bostik Ltd. Somehow we lost neither sponsor, but their feathers were ruffled for quite a while. Oliver once sent off a circular letter we used for prospective sponsors which said, 'In return for your sponsorship we will send you colour photos of your products in use against polar and tropical backgrounds and in extreme conditions, together with bimonthly reports on the equipment concerned.' Unfortunately what Oliver wanted in this case was three years' free supply of monthly items for the various female members of the expedition team. One of our volunteer secretaries noticed the untoward context and censored the letter in the nick of time.

That Christmas Ginnie and I wanted only to sleep. We passed the holiday at home quietly with Poul Andersson, who could not afford to go back to Denmark.

His life was the expedition: he had fallen in love with a pretty blond Danish girl, but he also never missed a day at the barracks chasing up strange spare ship parts such as zinc anodes which none of us had ever heard of. Poul did not seem too well that Christmas but we thought nothing of it at the time. We were all tired.

The lack of ready cash did not help. More and more we were busy in the evenings and at weekends now so there was less time to earn bread money. When Ollie had to fly to Vienna for Skidoo maintenance instruction he asked me for £5 pocket money. The Skidoo people were paying for his flight and accommodation but he didn't want to go with no cash at all. I lent him £5 and on his return a week later got it back again. For food those days Ollie ate expedition rations cooked on an expedition cooker on one side of the Marine Desk. Sometimes he saw his wife Rebecca but most of the time she lived in Paris, where she worked for the Chase Manhattan Bank. Whenever she could afford it she bought a weekend ticket and Ollie joined her in Paris. She worried about Ollie's safety and had tried to dissuade him from the Greenland and Arctic journeys. Each time she had given in, but she was increasingly unhappy. I should have worried more about that.

His Majesty Sultan Qaboos of Oman had deposed his father back in 1970 in a palace coup. It had been bloodless except that the old sultan had accidentally shot himself in the toe. It was in fact the father that I had worked for, but the new sultan was kindly disposed toward Transglobe and during a visit to London hosted a reception at Les Ambassadeurs restaurant in Park Lane. Our Omani friend, Dr Omar Zawawi, invited executives from the various United Kingdom companies with work contracts in the Oman, and His Majesty made it clear that he supported our venture and encouraged the company representatives to do likewise. Several of them responded generously.

At the time the only person authorised to sign Transglobe cheques was myself, and I resisted doing so. Of course this way everything took a lot longer. Money moves people; its absence leaves them notably apathetic. Nonetheless the original members of our team and the Marine Desk mob came to abide by this system and so, to some extent, did Ant Preston.

Barry Sheene, Britain's motorbike ace, helped us with two-stroke engine theory using the machines in his downstairs hall. Most weeks two or three of us were away on courses with the army or sponsors. Subjects included generators, polar huts, outboard engines, Land Rovers, parachuting equipment, rubber boats, petrol cookers and meteorological instruments. After a ten-day medical course Ollie wrote: 'I don't think Chas much liked the sight of blood but at least we've now got two medics, not one.' Until then Ollie must have wondered who would cope if something happened to *him*.

In the spring our committee met for the first time in an oak-panelled room in the barracks. Thereafter till our departure it met every two months. Subsidiary committees – also volunteers – were formed to look after the as-yet nonexistent ship and aircraft.

A director of the Chubb Fire company suggested to the Chubb chairman Lord Hayter that the group might purchase a secondhand Twin Otter, allow the expedition to use it for our polar crossings and at other times Chubb would charter it to recoup their outlay. Four times I met the Chubb directors. Not all of them were happy at first, but after some months deliberation it was agreed – Transglobe finally had the use of an aircraft.

Ant Preston, a considerable aerobatic flyer in his spare time, took on all aircraft details, including the obtaining from sponsors of a set of retractable skis, second propeller, charts, all spare parts and assorted items, the absence of which in Antarctica or the Arctic could ground the Twin Otter and cut off the ice group.

There are a handful of Twin Otter pilots in the world with Antarctic experience. The best was Giles Kershaw. By 1978 he had five seasons of Antarctic flying to his credit. He agreed to fly for us for no wages, but as his flight engineer he wanted one Sergeant Gerry Nicholson of the Royal Engineers whom he had worked with down south. Gerry, a quiet, good-natured man from Sussex, was a regular soldier. Mike Wingate-Gray and the SAS lobbied the army for six months before Gerry was eventually released to us for the duration of Transglobe.

With ten of us working in an office the size of half a squash court and queuing up to use one-and-a-half telephones (the second one was shared with a hospital unit along the corridor), the place looked, sounded and sometimes smelled like a chicken coop. The military exchange allowed no direct phoning and they were understaffed so even a local call could take three minutes to put through. Then Tarmac International lent us an office with three free phones in Baker Street, which made all the difference. The Marine mob were left at the barracks. The rest of us moved out to Baker Street, where things ran more smoothly, and just as well. Time was running short. Sponsors would not put up with still another year's postponement.

Prince Charles, whose appointment calendar gets booked up over a year in advance, agreed to launch the expedition from Greenwich on September 2, 1979, so with nine months to go I planned a work schedule for each person and held monthly meetings at the barracks to check that no one was lagging behind and all were keeping fit.

A typical meeting at the old office:

Loud complaints from the mariners (whose sole property the

room now was – in their opinion) at their half-dozen visitors drinking *their* tea, plonking track suits on *their* files and sitting on *their* tables.

At 9:30 A.M., the time set for the meeting, everyone seemed to have turned up.

'Okay, last month –' I started.

'Hold it, Ran, Ginnie's not here. She's taking Bothy for a pee.' Bothy was her long-haired Jack Russell terrier.

As she returned, the phone rang. Charlie answered. Two or three present interrupted with 'Dear Sir Arthur!' or 'Ah, Monica? No, sorry, Angela – or is it Jane?'

After placating the major up the passage who was phoning to ask for peace and quiet I was able to start. The subjects would sometimes appear disconnected:

Over the last month Simon had failed to progress with the rations lists I'd ask for. Why? He'd had to move his flat; it took up time. But, shouted someone, he still appeared to have time to wander round secondhand bookshops buying up bargains for subsequent sale. Much muttering but eventual promises that the ration lists would be finished in a week.

'Charlie ... another month's gone by and you still haven't got the Jockey underpants supply.'

'The bloke's been on leave.'

'Well, try his boss.'

'He's in Japan selling underpants.'

'Phone the first one at his home. We've got to have the underpants.'

'Never mind my underpants, Ran, what about more important things? Ginnie hasn't got the radios yet.'

A powerful kick from Ginnie landed on Charlie's back.

'Sneak. Mind your own items.'

'What *about* the radios, Ginnie?' I had to try to chase her in public, though of all of them she was the most difficult to pin down and the most fiery when chased.

'Never mind. They'll be ready and packed with all serial numbers at the customs well before we leave.'

Turning to Ollie, the golden boy whose sponsor-getting talents were unsurpassed, I gave him a typed list. 'Seventy more items this month, Ol. The only ones *you* seem to have outstanding are Chinese bamboo poles, skin calipers and the three-year lighter flints supply.' I knew Ollie had been disappearing for days at a time, usually when the weather was good, but since he always finished his lists in good time, what did it matter?

Ant Preston gave a succinct rundown on aircraft supplies. 'Gerry Nicholson, our engineer,' he added, 'will join us in the Tarmac office next week full-time.'

Anton followed with news of the latest ships he and Poul were looking at.

When the administrative matters were thrashed out, usually in two or three hours, we changed into running gear. There's a cinder track inside the barracks and everyone had to jog around it twenty times. Two of our volunteers with stopwatches shouted out the number of laps each person had done as he passed. During one run Poul was sick and went deadly white. I didn't worry too much, though, since Ollie and Simon had also been sick during the runs. Charlie and Anton invariably arrived last. Ginnie and her terrier Bothy lolloped along, tripping the others up and generally being a nuisance. Ginnie was a hopeless case anyway, being far too unfit to jog more than two circuits without stopping to lie down on the grass edge.

David Mason joined up as our ice team reserve and roving troubleshooter to sort out cargo problems in Antarctica, the Arctic and all points between. As a Welsh Guards captain he had received a medal for bravery in Arabia. A proud and strong personality. We clashed at our first press conference and exhibition at Farnborough one wintry day that February over a simple matter of where to place road signs to direct our guests. I told David that I wasn't interested in arguing the pros and cons, that there were probably several ways of doing it but I was a difficult cuss and on Transglobe matters my way would have to do. Or charming words to that effect. We had no more problems between us for the next four years, and David took over whole sides of the expedition and, with quiet efficiency, kept our complex resupply going free of transport costs between both polar regions, Africa, America, Canada, New Zealand, Australia and Europe.

It was also at the Farnborough conference that Anton finally got his ship. By chance his father Peter was then chairman of Britain's largest insurance brokers, C. T. Bowring. Anton had once worked for them but only lasted as a landlubber for a couple of months. Peter, realising the danger that any dealings with Anton would smack of nepotism and might hinder rather than help our chances, kept a low profile when Anton began to woo the company. Proud of their connection with Captain Scott, whose ship the *Terra Nova* they had provided, Bowring saw an excellent public relations opportunity in being identified with *our* polar vessel. Unfortunately, despite the Bowring board agreeing with the notion, the ship that Anton had decided we must have cost twice what they were prepared to pay. Timing intervened. That month Peter Bowring was engaged in negotiations with the huge New York insurance brokers, Marsh and MacLennan, and as a symbol of planned joint operations he suggested each company buy *half* the ship. This was agreed to and £700,000 was paid for a twenty-seven-year-old ice-strengthened research vessel, once the famous *Kista Dan* but, in 1979, just a very smelly Canadian sealer.

So at Farnborough Peter Bowring announced the news of the

purchase and Prince Charles flew the Twin Otter (which Chubb had recently painted with the Chubb Transglobe livery) onto the icy apron beside our exhibition hangar. Later that year a biography of Prince Charles was published. The author was on the plane that day.

> It was an icy blizzardy day in February and we are a thousand feet above snowclad Hampshire in a tiny twin-engined de Havilland Otter, the Prince of Wales at the controls. For thirty minutes our fragile aircraft has been buffeted by strong winds, rendering the prince's assistant private secretary a colour similar to that of the landscape beneath. In the cockpit our pilot's headphones sit incongruously above his pin-striped city suit; he resembles nothing so much as a hardened, if harassed, international businessman – which, in a way, is precisely what he is. This is the only time he has sat down all day.
>
> We are losing height. In the foothills just outside the airfield perimeter we pass over a squad of army personnel on tank exercise. They are also on discreet guard duty, we can tell, as they snap to a salute in our direction. Two minor bumps and the Otter is down. The passengers gird their loins for the ceremonies ahead but suddenly the engine note rises again.
>
> There is just time for a quick glance to the cockpit, where our pilot is pulling back hard on the throttle before we are airborne again. The Prince of Wales is enjoying himself.
>
> His private secretary is not. There is a low moan from his direction as we bank steeply to circle the Royal Aircraft Establishment. On the ground, outside hangar P-72, the expectant crowd radiates astonishment. The Prince looks down with a grin, then chats cheerfully with his co-pilot. A look at his watch tells him he is still five minutes ahead of his scheduled arrival time. He's going to do it again.

Back over the startled military detachment, who snap to attention again; down, this time rather more bumpily, and up again, even more sharply.

Before we took off, the Prince had been warned of icy runways at both ends of his journey. After he had climbed aboard, his head briefly reappeared through the hatch to assure his private secretary of the abundance of air-sickness bags. Now he is taking six icy risks for the price of two.

For the third time we are saluted, and (for the third time) we are down – this time, it seems, to stay.

An appreciative pat of the dashboard and the stopped Prince joins us, now the airline captain asking if we've enjoyed the flight. He braces himself to orient himself in where we are: at an exhibition of the Transglobe Expedition, of which he had graciously consented to be patron.

In the space of seventy-five minutes the Prince of Wales shakes some three hundred hands and talks to perhaps half their owners. The expedition, at least, is something which gets his adrenaline going again. It is the kind of thing he would like to have done himself if he were not a prince. He examines the tents, the water shoes, the prefabricated Tri-Wall huts, the skis, the Snowcats, the canoes, the maps and the tins of baked beans as closely as if he *were* going on the expedition.

He is supporting the expedition, he says, 'because it is a mad and splendidly British enterprise.' He will hope, he goes on in a fit of enthusiasm, to drop in on it 'somewhere in the world in the next three years – if it can be arranged.' His staff shoot each other morose glances.

The Prince left us; the hangar soon emptied of people. Ginnie's dream was nudging toward reality. It had taken long enough.

The office was still understaffed. I appealed on Radio London and twelve applicants phoned in. Within a week all had dropped out but two. One, Dorothy, was a great help with fast accurate typing. She also had a fiery temper. One day she stomped up to my desk, afghan coat and blond hair swinging, and glared at me. I forget what I'd done but I clearly remember her words: 'You are an evil toad and you stink of tomcat.' After coffee she calmed down but Ollie, Charlie and Ant Preston, who overheard, managed to repeat the epithet for months afterward and to wrinkle their noses whenever I entered the room.

Joan Cox had already worked with us for two years. Now her daughter Janet also joined us. Both stayed till the end and, between them, typed the manuscript for this book.

On certain obligatory weekends the territorial army still claimed our time. One such spring exercise took place in Norfolk. It was to be my last with the regiment. Charlie found an excuse to miss it . . . he said one of his fingers had been sprained when stuck in a pocket of a billiard table.

Since the entire regiment was to operate in twos, Ollie and I paired off. Cross-country distance to be covered during the Friday and Saturday nights was some fifty miles. Movement by day was stupid since other regiments patrolled all roads in the area.

At dawn on Friday we were spotted and chased by Gurkhas. We split up and crossed a river. Norfolk was quite cold that week, minus 16 degrees Centigrade. I got wet to the waist. On the other bank I met up with Ollie; still dry. He had found a sheet of ice over a deep pool and crossed over it. Army leather boots are not as warm as polar mukluks even when dry, so we moved as fast as possible and reached the final rendezvous an hour before it closed on the Sunday morning. Nobody else made it on time, not a single member of our much-vaunted unit.

It seemed our polar training had had some use after all – until I took my boots off and found one black and frostbitten little toe. I had survived Greenland and the Arctic Ocean but not Norfolk in spring.

Back in the office a body blow awaited me. ICI Petrochemicals, after 'careful consideration', had decided to withdraw their support of fuel supplies. I had only myself to blame. Back in 1975 my fuel estimates, the basis for ICI's original agreement, were based on a small fishing boat. Once Anton decided which ship we needed he gave me estimates far beyond my original ones. Gerry, the Twin Otter engineer, did likewise, and these new shockers convinced ICI to fade out of the picture sooner rather than later.

For me a nightmare hunt began. What good is a ship and aircraft with no fuel?

All British sources were exhausted. I got onto the French, Germans and Italians, even the Japanese. All said no thanks. Philips Petroleum took four months to say no. Six other major American companies obviously considered my request too ludicrous to deserve a reply. So I did what I had promised myself not to do and asked Prince Charles.

He saw me in his sitting room in the palace and listened intently. There was a twinkle in his eye as he said he would do his best.

A week later the prince's office telephoned. I was to phone one Dr Armand Hammer in Los Angeles.

Before I did so Ginnie found a brochure about the doctor.

'Good *God,*' she said, 'he's an old friend of Joe Stalin ... *and* Lenin.'

'But the palace intimated he hobnobs with President Carter.'

'Yes, it says here he's been in with most of the United States presidents. He started the Russian-American grain deals.'

Her voice rose several octaves. 'He owns a major oil company called Occidental. Clever Prince Charles.' And then she looked puzzled. 'But how come Prince Charles knows him?'

'Perhaps the doctor's an ace polo player,' I suggested.

'Rubbish,' she snorted, 'it says he's over eighty.'

I phoned the doctor that night, my bandaged black toe sticking out of a slipper's end.

'He may be over eighty, but he sounds razor-sharp,' I told Ginnie afterward. 'It's not his company Occidental that will help. They don't retail gasoline so they can't. Somehow he's persuaded another oil company, Mobil Oil, to agree.'

'I thought Mobil refused last month,' Ginnie said.

'They did, but that was Mobil Europe, not Mobil U.S.A., and that was before the doctor spoke to their boss man.'

We were talking of well over a million dollars' worth of fuel. Mobil Oil's support with fuel for all sides of the venture was a great relief. I thanked God and Prince Charles, Dr Hammer and the Mobil board with total sincerity.

The doctor then wrote to me: was there any other way he could help?

There was. I had asked both Britain's TV companies to send a film team to cover the journey. Both had declined. Could Dr Hammer possibly find an American-based company? Within a month he had found that no United States film company was interested: the journey was simply too long for them. So the doctor formed his own film company and started hiring a team to join us.

With five months to go Anton's search for the crew intensified. Since the Department of Trade would not allow our ship to sea without a full and professional crew, Anton could not simply sign on enthusiastic volunteers. Yet why *should* professional seamen, at a time of unemployment due to contracting merchant navies, want to give up their careers and future prospects? Certainly not for the glamour. If there was to be any of that, the land group was the more likely to reap it. The ship would enter the polar circles at both ends and both sides of the world, true enough, but only for a few months. For them most of the three-year voyage would involve calling at ports quite likely to be visited by any merchant seamen. We worked out it would cost Transglobe £420,000 at standard salaries to pay a crew. That Anton found volunteers to man the ship for nothing but a statutory queen's shilling per month was, I think, remarkable.

He advertised in free newspaper space and on the radio, and one of his earliest finds was Ken Cameron, an engineer. Anton was exuberant. 'If I can get a Scotsman for nothing, I'll get the lot.'

In Ken's words: 'I was on a half-million-ton tanker halfway to the Persian Gulf and ready for a change. I saw the advert in the *Telegraph* and wrote to the box number. Poul Andersson sent me impressive details in a blue folder. Expecting a well-monied and efficient organisation I visited the Duke of York's barracks and asked for the Transglobe Marine Office. I had put on my best suit and was prepared for a stiff and high-powered interview. When I reached the office I found the curtains drawn, Charlie asleep on the floor and Poul Andersson of the Marine Desk just emerging from his sleeping bag under a table.'

But Anton soon formed an interviewing committee which sat in the salubrious chambers of Trinity House by the Thames. Presiding was Captain Tom Woodfield, Elder Brother of Trinity House and retired skipper of an Antarctic vessel. I joined them to ensure that marine Transglobers did not escape the black talk.

A convinced and active trade unionist and shop steward of many years, Terry Kenchington applied as bosun. Cyrus Balaporia, an Indian from Bombay with several years P&O Line service as a ship's officer, appeared at about the same time. Both were individualists and experienced seamen. Two New Zealander engineers, longtime friends, were bored with standard voyages and were hoping to start up a garage in England when they heard about us. In Jimmy Young's words:

'We went to see this Transglobe outfit. It seemed they were desperate for one engineer. Mark and I reckoned we would call their tune a bit and said they could have both of us or neither. We considered ourselves macho, sporty types so it came as a bit of a shock later to find out the Transglobe people had decided we were a couple of pooftahs looking for a three-year marine love-in. My main reason for joining was . . . well, what a journey! I couldn't stand the thought of someone else doing it, knowing that I could have done it.'

A couple of natural comics also joined up that spring – Eddie Pike, ship's carpenter, and Martin Weymouth, deckhand. Martin had long golden hair – it really was golden – which fell in frizzy fashion down to his shoulders. Martin came from Leighton Buzzard and was at once nicknamed Buzzard. After a while it was difficult to remember his real name, and I found myself introducing him to Prince Charles as Buzzard.

And our friendly American colonel resigned his commission with the USAF and joined up as deckhand.

In May Anton and the crew he had chosen by then flew out to Halifax, Nova Scotia, to collect the ship. He had failed to find a skipper, so the Bowring Steamship Company lent us one of theirs, Captain Les Davis from Carlisle. The crew liked him at once.

The voyage from Canada was rough and helped knock the volunteers into a tight-knit group, so tight that subsequent crew were to find integration difficult; in some cases impossible. Two men Anton had chosen were quietly rejected by the others and left. A pretty auburn-haired girl with a small, slim body and large, almost feline eyes applied as cook. She was a civil servant working in the patents office. After much discussion the ship selection committee decided the benefits of a girl cook among a dozen hairy males outweighed the inherent dangers, so Jill MacNicol left her bureaucratic haven for three years at sea. She had no previous cooking experience.

Anton was given a free berth in Milwall Docks by the Port of London Authority, the same one used twenty years earlier by the Trans Antarctic Expedition of Vivian Fuchs and Edmund Hillary. Once the ship was berthed, work began in earnest. At weekends, with help from local cadets, there were up to thirty people working on board.

It was at a press conference that Ginnie, plus champagne bottle, officially renamed the ship the *Benjamin Bowring* in memory of the company's founder, who was himself a bit of an adventurer. The ship was full of atmosphere. It was easy to fall in love with her, and we called her the *Benji Bee.* In 1952 the famous shipbuilder J. Lauritzen, hearing that lead mines were to be developed in northeast Greenland, commissioned the building of the *Kista Dan,* as she then was, in Aalborg, Denmark. Specially designed for her role, she had an all-welded hull and strengthened bow and frame. In the northern summer she plied between Greenland and western Europe. Then in the Antarctic summer she would head south, often sealing. (One of her charters was to make the film *Hell Below Zero* based on the Hammond Innes novel *The White South*.) After many Antarctic visits she was sold to the Canadians and renamed *Martin Karlsen* as an eleven-hundred-ton trader and survey vessel.

With only two holds and sixty-four metres long she was just big enough for our purposes. Her twenty-seven-year-old Burmeister and Wain six-cylinder diesel engine gave us twelve-hundred-brake horsepower and, when she was in a good mood with a following sea, ten knots speed.

Anton had tried to get the vessel to London free of any charge. He failed by only £32.

He wrote of the voyage: 'Having worked for eighteen months with only Poul Andersson, I found it difficult to share the fruits of our labours with the newly recruited crew members, all of whom naturally wanted to display and use their own skills, which were far superior to our own. So, during the voyage, Poul and I often sat together in a cabin moaning about our apparent redundancy while our team of professionals seemed to do everything.'

Some weeks later Poul offered to help Ken and the engineers in the cramped confines of the engine room. Using a heavy hammer at an awkward angle, he began to feel a pain in his chest but, as was his way, he finished the job. When Poul complained of recurring pains, Anton took him to hospital. Within twenty-four hours Poul had a massive heart attack. Within a week he was dead. At twenty-two, Poul was a friend to us all. Especially to Ginnie and Anton.

Of his long struggle to get the ship, Anton wrote:

> There were times I was furious with Ran and his ice group colleagues . . . and times I was proud to be associated with them. At first Ran was very helpful and guided me through an instructive stage where I learned the attitudes and methods of Transglobe. After a few months I was then left to get on with it on my own and I remember being very irritated that thereafter until the expedition was under way Ran took little or no interest in my progress. That happened in such a way it seemed a deliberate disinterest, which worried me. Because we seldom had a chance to discuss these matters I was never really sure what was on his mind until he phoned one day to say that, having had a chat with Robin Knox Johnson and as there was no evidence of a ship and time was running out, I should consider a contingency plan which could involve a smaller vessel, a fishing boat, at a reduced cost. I insisted that without an ice-strengthened ship we would

have complications all along the route. To his credit he allowed me to continue my preparations and I realised from his conversation it was *entirely* up to me to find the ship and a buyer before September, 1979, if the expedition was to set out at all. I had a huge task and was not at all confident of success. On seeking professional advice I became even more confident of failure. I don't think Ran ever understood this or the moments of anguish I went through. Charlie used to annoy me because he never seemed at all interested in the office work and often sat with his feet on his desk seemingly doing absolutely nothing. I suppose I was jealous because he was destined to be fully involved in all the most exciting and personally challenging results of all our efforts with the least amount of preparatory work. However, such is Charlie's character that it's difficult to be angry with him for long before his guffaws of laughter and his good humour force a smile on the lips of his most vociferous critic.

Ollie too caused some irritation by his dedication and hard work to obtain what I considered to be the most trivial ornaments which were not entirely necessary to the success of the expedition. But he also did devote himself to the strenuous chores of his scientific, mechanical and medical studies. His good humour and permanent energy outweighed any criticism one may have had for his search for trinkets.

Ginnie always had my respect. She was always fighting for fair deals. Like Ran, she worked much harder than anyone else to get Transglobe recognised. At the same time her charm was engaging and she was always sincere, which made her bad moods all the worse if one was the cause of them.

Life in the office was very intense and I was part of that intensity. In such a situation it is difficult to look on colleagues with affection. Instead rivalry and irritations develop when one person crosses the territorial boundary of another by doing

> something it's not supposed to be their job to do . . . For me the nerve-wracking sense of urgency of those days was challenge enough to compensate for the ship's lack of physical challenge. Ran's ability to organise us and his meticulous planning kept most of us on our toes, and I came to think of the others as good friends . . .

That March Giles Kershaw, our pilot-to-be, and I met in Cambridge for a meeting with the executives of the British Antarctic Survey to try to sort out the remaining criticisms of our Antarctic plans. Our lack of a second plane in case the first crashed was at the top of the list.

It was finally agreed we would get an insurance policy to cover any mishaps to a BAS plane should one be called on to rescue our ice group. We had also to agree that the whole expedition would be aborted if at any time we did need to ask for such BAS help.

This seemed hard but as Giles said: 'You can see their point of view. A few years back an *official* French scientific group needed help and the Americans put three Hercules out of action attempting to rescue them. Unofficial private expeditions, if ill-equipped or conceived, are a menace in areas like Antarctica where there simply is no room for error.'

Sir Vivian Fuchs had put together a legitimate scientific programme for us that mostly consisted of magnetospheric and glaciological research work. But we also had other tasks involving meteorology, high frequency propagation, cardiology and blood analysis.

On April 9, nearly six years after my first approach to his predecessor, our Foreign Office friend wrote to the relevant representatives of New Zealand, South Africa and the United States. He stressed that 'nothing in this letter is to be taken as implying that the British government sponsors or is in any way responsible for this expedition.' Nonetheless, he said, the government's appointed vetting bodies had judged us scientifically and logistically and were prepared at least to recommend that I should visit the letter's addressees.

British Airways sponsored the necessary flights. I flew to Pretoria and Cape Town, and the South Africans agreed to assist with fuel transport from the Cape to Sanae base. In Washington I met a representative of the State Department and the United States overall Antarctic decision-maker, Dr Todd of the National Science Foundation. The doctor was guarded. The Japanese explorer Naomi Uemura had, he said, also appealed for NSF blessing for a journey to Antarctica. This had been turned down only the previous month. Knowing what good connections Uemura had with the *National Geographic* organisation, I realised the implications. But Dr Todd did not give an outright no. Indeed he seemed friendly; my request would be considered, he said.

I returned to Britain and, with only eight weeks left before our own D-Day, received Dr Todd's decision. The United States could not assist us in any way because all its resources were already fully committed and none could be diverted from the United States programme.

I replied that we would set out soon and, with luck, would be at the South Pole by January 24, 1981. I cut down my South Pole fuel request from forty to twenty-three drums and mentioned that the lack of this small amount might dangerously stretch our lines of communication.

Dr Todd stood firm.

Sir Vivian wrote, 'the situation is uncomfortable but can be solved in the time available.'

I think we all accepted that only direct intervention by the British government to the United States State Department could perhaps now alter things.

So we carried on as planned. If, when we were ready to begin the crossing attempt, the United States still refused fuel at the Pole, then Giles would somehow have to establish fuel depots on the way across and in the middle of nowhere.

Sir Vivian estimated that for Giles to take twenty-three drums to the Pole himself he would have to use up eight hundred extra drums worth of fuel en route – far more than we would have available.

On previous expeditions I had repaid sponsors by holding exhibitions of their products. On a hovercraft trip up the Nile, shows in Khartoum and Kampala produced export orders worth £12 million. I decided to hold ten exhibitions at centres along the Transglobe route with the help of local British commercial attachés. Two proved impossible, but the majority were to take place on various set dates.

As a rehearsal we set one up a few weeks before departure at the World Trade Centre in London. It took nineteen of us three days to erect and H.R.H. the Duke of Kent, vice-chairman of the Overseas Trade Board, opened it to the public in early June.

In Britain the public tends to show a good deal of interest in expeditions that challenge mountains and oceans. Other ventures of a non-specialist nature seldom catch on and I was having a devil of a job trying to get media coverage for Transglobe. To the rescue again came George Greenfield, who eventually managed to arouse the interest of the *Observer* newspaper, then owned by Atlantic Richfield.

One Tuesday lunch the American owner of Atlantic Richfield and the *Observer* executives asked George and myself to explain the plans. This was clearly crucial to any decision they might make. The voyage I described that lunchtime made Ulysses and his adventures appear like a Ronald Reagan cowboy film viewed in the eighties.

The next day I again had to give a persuasive lunchtime presentation, this time to a group of top London insurance brokers.

Would they feel it safe to sponsor Transglobe's aircraft and ship with free insurance policies? On this occasion the voyage came over as about as risky as a Tupperware tea party.

The *Observer* gave us an excellent contract for the rights to Transglobe feature stories, and the London insurance market covered all sides of Transglobe, comprehensively and at no cost.

Anton Bowring was worried. With two weeks to go, he had no volunteer skipper with or without ice experience whom he considered acceptable.

The Bowrings were prepared to let Les Davis skipper for us again, but we could not meet his salary. At an emergency ship meeting Tom Woodfield of Trinity House said a friend of his, a retired admiral, was prepared to take the *Benji Bee* at least on the first leg to Antarctica.

Anton's diary read:

> I first met Admiral Otto Steiner (who, despite his name, had helped sink German ships in the last war) when I entered Tom Woodfield's office. The admiral was sitting at a desk. He looked around at me with a monocle in position and his bearded face somewhat regal. We shook hands, and he said, 'So you are the young commissar!' Not quite understanding the application of the word, I thought this was flattery, looked bashful and muttered, 'No, I'm really just the office boy.'
>
> The other committee members gathered to discuss a list of anxieties about the ship and crew which Otto had produced. His main concerns included oilskins, personal insurance, master's reports and, above all, 'the clap'. I began to get anxious about him. He seemed out of touch with the requirements of a Merchant Navy skipper. I could see problems arising from having a Royal Navy master and a wholly Merchant Navy crew.

Anyway, while the committee bravely tried to put the admiral's mind at rest that the crew would not all get the clap and what to do if, by chance, they did, I wondered just how my carefully selected and good-natured crew members would take to the barking discipline of a much older man ... After the meeting I hurried to the barracks where I saw Ran and told him my misgivings about the new appointment and my fear that all our plans would be ruined if the crew left because they couldn't get on with the skipper ... My own panic may have been a bit of overreacting, but I was concerned about the ship's personnel being harmonious. At the same time I had my own position to worry about. Ran wanted me to be wholly responsible for the ship and marine side of the venture, except for the master's role on board. But at the committee meeting it was agreed I should be the purser, with the responsibility of being a sort of secretary to the master. However, Ran and the crew seemed to be reasonably satisfied with the admiral so my anxieties were halved. For the last few days before departure he took up residence on board and got the ship into order. I kept a fairly low profile and remained in the office where I had much work to do if we were to leave on time.

Back in the barracks, most nights we toiled till midnight. It was hot and dusty through July and August. I packed, numbered and listed over one thousand cardboard boxes bound for eighteen different bases around the world over the next three years. Ollie had special responsibility for mechanical gear, Ginnie radio gear and Simon food. Only Charlie represented the team back in the office during the last two months and I phoned him daily with new action lists, items to obtain, kit to modify, extra food to order. Now that the chips were truly on the table he worked as hard as anyone and I inwardly forgave him all his previous reticence in the field of labour. Ollie herded us all into a Land Rover for dental checks and assorted injections. By night with two others I drove endless van-loads down to the docks and dumped them on the quay beside the *Benji Bee*.

My mother lived alone in the country, and I now went to say good-bye. She was and is the best of all possible mothers. I took away a pair of warm socks she had knitted.

The day before we left, September 1, there appeared in the editorial column of the New York *Times* under the heading 'Glory': 'The British aren't so weary as they're sometimes said to be. The Transglobe Expedition, seven years in the planning, is scheduled to leave Greenwich, England, tomorrow on a journey of such daring that it makes one wonder how the sun ever set on the empire.'

Before our departure I was meant to introduce Prince Charles to our advisors and sponsors in the Great Hall of the Queen's House within the grounds of the National Maritime Museum. But I overslept and arrived late. Down at the quay by the *Benji Bee* Antony Preston marshalled the crowds with a loudspeaker. Overhead I saw a red helicopter; the royal taxi. I ran up the street and saw it land on a lawn behind a tall iron fence. Prince Charles got out and headed for the Great Hall. I scaled the railings, disentangled my coat from the spikes and, hoping his armed detective wouldn't get the wrong idea, headed across the lawn at the double.

His Royal Highness was wearing a black tie. He was in court mourning because the IRA had killed his great-uncle and friend, Lord Mountbatten, only a few days earlier. Prince Charles had cancelled all engagements but the launching of Transglobe. For us he made an exception because he believed the earl would have wished him to help an enterprise in which Lord Mountbatten himself would have taken an interest.

Many of our families, friends and helpers joined the thousands of well-wishers who came to see us off. Geoff and Mary were there too, side by side.

'When's the wedding?' I asked Geoff.

'Wedding? What wedding?'

The only times I had seen Mary cry in the Arctic were when she was furious with me. Now it was otherwise. A month later they did become engaged; the first but by no means the last of our expedition's love stories.

Prince Charles skippered the *Benji Bee* away from Greenwich Pier and the gay bunting on the *Cutty Sark*. If ships have hearts, that once-proud schooner may have sighed to see us go.

The ripple of flags among the fading crowds, the blare of horns and the wash of white from smaller craft behind us, veterans of Dunkerque with proud old men at their helms, held the echo of Prince Charles's words:

> One of the expedition's achievements has already been the creation of a unique spirit of cooperation among industrial undertakings in Britain and overseas. This cooperation during the seven important years of planning and preparation has made it possible for the expedition to fulfil its every need from the goods and services provided by more than six hundred sponsors. Transglobe is certainly one of the most ambitious undertakings of its kind ever attempted, and the scope of its requirements is monumental.
>
> ... Although so much has changed in the world since explorers first attempted to reach the Poles at the beginning of the century, the challenges of nature and the environment are still very much the same
>
> ... Above all, the human risks are still the same. They're all there today, the frostbite, the loss of body fat because of the cold and the protracted bouts of shivering, especially at night, the unsuspected crevasses and traps for the unwary, the thin ice.

... Even though a decade has passed since man first set foot on the moon, polar exploration and research remain as important as ever.

... As this great journey unfolds and people from many nations become involved with the Transglobe Expedition, I am confident that this ambitious and courageous undertaking will do much to provide interest and inspiration to old and young alike throughout the world.

Chapter Four

> The sun's rim dips; the stars rush out: at one stride comes the dark.
>
> SAMUEL TAYLOR COLERIDGE

The Board of Trade sent surveyors to the *Benji Bee* two weeks before our official departure, and their report produced major setbacks. Much was to be done, especially to the tons of concrete ballast in the holds, before the ship could leave the Thames.

So when Prince Charles left the ship down-river at Tilbury the land group did likewise and a WRAC in a minivan drove us to the barracks. We loaded everything for Africa into it and onto two Land Rovers, a Range Rover and three trailers.

In driving rain we set out separately in the early evening, but Ollie and Charlie came to a sudden halt in Parliament Square. Our trailer sponsors, it turned out, had forgotten a split pin in the retaining hub of one of the trailer wheels. We'd hoped to catch the midnight ferry from Folkestone to Dunkerque, but the trailer and other delays meant catching a later one from Dover to Calais.

I had told Anton we would drive to Paris, where our first trade exhibition was to be held, then down to Barcelona for a second show. The piper had to be paid. When the Ministry of Transport allowed the ship to leave she was to head straight for Barcelona to collect us, the vehicles and the exhibition crates and sail south to Algiers.

Anton's troubles soon began. The land group had all signed an expedition legal contract, but our lawyers didn't produce copies for the crew until just before they were ready to leave. They objected strongly to the clauses, as did Admiral Otto Steiner. I was in France. Anton in London was confronted and Sir Vivian Fuchs and George Greenfield rustled up a newly worded contract based on the one signed by members of Sir Vivian's own expedition of the 1950s. This one was signed without fuss by everyone, but then a new fracas arose about who should control the ship's purse strings. From Paris I tried to persuade the committee to give full financial authority to Anton but was overruled. I was to stick to expedition work and let the admiral worry about ship matters. It began to sink in that I would do well to forget previous journeys when my hand was the only one at the expedition tiller. Anton was not the only one learning to be second string to the fiddle.

Our Paris export show was in the heart of Montmartre on the first floor of a lovely old house with a circular marble staircase, ornate ceilings and extravagant chandeliers.

The passersby passed us by. The British commercial attaché said he'd seen it all a hundred times at British trade fairs. 'They've never liked us or our products. You'd have done well to have left France off your exhibition list altogether.'

Charlie drove off alone in the Range Rover toward St Tropez. A recent girlfriend of his was to meet him there for a few days' holiday. Simon, Ollie and I somehow managed to get the repacked exhibition crates loaded back on four railcars bound for Barcelona. No sooner was this done than French railways announced a strike which effectively stranded our exhibition. Since the railways' shop stewards were unlikely to respond to appeals to their better nature, we left Paris and at Perpignan near the Spanish border met Charlie, who announced his intention to marry Twink, a most shapely and attractive lady who was also an executive of Berlei – one of our sponsors. The wedding, he said, would take place in Sydney after we had crossed Antarctica. I noticed, however, that thoughts of impending marriage did not dull his perception on the beach that afternoon when a small English girl with gigantic breasts and nothing over them parked herself beside us. Simon, sunbathing, developed a squint.

Barcelona had suffered severe storms, ten people were dead and the roof of the hall where our exhibition was to be had partially collapsed. The show was off, to my great relief.

In the sprawl of Barcelona's outskirts we found an exotic campground called the Torro Bravo. Mosquitoes adored it and proliferated in its scenic pinewoods with a ready diet of international campers.

Simon, who slept in a Land Rover, not a tent, was badly bitten. Good training, as Charlie remarked, for Africa. Luckily, though, the *Benji Bee* hove to at Barcelona's prime berth, right opposite the port's main bar. Eddie Pike and the Buzzard expertly winched the vehicles and trailers on board and lashed them to the decks. The atmosphere on board was tense. The admiral took me up to his cabin. He seemed hurt and testy.

'That man must go before we leave Barcelona.' He sucked furiously at an ancient pipe, one from a rack of four. It soon became clear what had raised Otto's hackles. At first he had remained non-dictatorial and very long-suffering. He had let the bosun, Terry Kenchington, lay down a system of deck watches, but felt the chosen system of one man on for a week at a time was ridiculous. He had finally been forced to clamp down when, soon after arrival here in Barcelona, he found no one at all on watch when a gyro alarm in the neighbourhood of the bridge went off. Had he not noticed it himself the gyro would certainly have burned out.

The final straw for Otto had been when he gave the first officer, a Canadian, some orders for the bosun. Terry stormed up to the skipper's cabin. The admiral, he said, should not interfere with his, the bosun's, warps and winches. His powerful fingers stubbed the skipper's desk, sacred font of authority on the *Benji Bee*. Everyone concerned, he added, must in the future be consulted before any edicts were doled out.

This was, of course, too much for Otto: indeed, it probably went far beyond any parallel experience of his long Royal Navy career. He summoned people to his cabin in groups and issued a series of instructions, all of them basically sensible, indeed, probably overdue, given normal circumstances. Except the *Benji Bee* and the hierarchy of her crew were in no way even vaguely normal. Any skipper with a tidy mind was sooner or later bound to be driven bonkers by the situation and in particular by some of the personal traits of Terry, the bosun.

Otto added that Terry was, he believed, drinking heavily. He was worried about the young wife he had married only a week or so before leaving Britain. The Canadian officer had only the previous day told Otto that if Terry did not leave then *he* would because 'that man will *not* do what he is asked. He is totally out of control.'

I asked Anton for his opinion. As always, he counselled patience and understanding. His view of the crew he had put together was that they were neither Royal nor Merchant Navy, they were purely unpaid-travellers and would respond, given time, to the dictates of common sense. In his opinion they were a remarkably fine and professional group of *individuals,* but it would take time to weld them 'into an integrated crew' because of their many different backgrounds, religions, opinions. 'There won't be instant harmony,' Anton said. 'We must work at it.'

I went to Terry's room, which was an unbelievable mess. In England he had had a mass of curly fair hair. Now he resembled Kojak minus the lollipop. One of Otto's recent suggestions had been haircuts so Terry had gone the whole hog by way of a protest. Before entering equatorial waters it seemed to me a pretty sensible move, quite apart from the protest value, though a bald Terry did make a fairly evil-looking pirate. I had a long talk with him. Whatever his defects, one thing was clear. He *loved* the ship, was totally loyal to the expedition and worked as hard or harder than the next man. I thought I should try to get to know him better before agreeing to his firing. Otto, who had a forgiving nature, agreed to allow the bosun another chance and all appeared rosy. By way of insurance and bearing in mind that I would soon be chucked off the ship for three months in Africa, I held a general meeting on deck. Apart from talking of future plans I outlined the likely problems we could all face through living together during the years ahead. I suggested some guidelines but admitted they might not work. Time would tell …

The four French railcars appeared as though by magic on the siding alongside the ship, but no official was available to break the customs seals. Finally the Canadian officer helped me open up the cars with wire cutters and a crowbar. (Later the British consul would pass us a message with accusations of piratical behaviour but by then we were gone, with the exhibition in one hold.)

We nosed out at night and headed for Africa. The Mediterranean was dead calm beneath a cloudless sky. On board Jill served baked mackerel. I *hate* fish. All fish. But knowing that normal people like fish I had jumped at the chance when a sponsor offered us five tons of fresh mackerel. One freezer was full of the stuff. By the time the crew reached Barcelona they'd had a surfeit of it and also of ravioli, another commodity I somehow seemed to have overordered.

Dave Peck, the second mate, seemed to be making all the time with our pretty cook but I noticed other eyes cast in her direction. No problems, though ... there were plenty of ports to call at, probably too many for the admiral's peace of mind, remembering his dread of 'the clap'.

The second day we came to Algiers, where a clutch of officers came aboard. All had gold pips or stripes on their uniformed shoulders. Customs, port officials, police, sanitation and other unguessable authorities.

Otto now came into his own with white uniform and sea hat. The monocle and conquistador beard fascinated our acquisitive visitors and put them off what was doubtless their normal custom of demanding goods for favours; or rather it almost did. An hour later with Anton's voluminous wads of forms signed and stamped, Otto saw the port junta off his ship with a mere half-dozen bottles of whisky and some passé boxes of tea bags.

'You'd better disembark before their brethren come for a second visit,' said Otto.

While Jill saw us off with a delicious lamb joint uncontaminated by mackerel or ravioli, Terry and his deck crew winched the vehicles onto the quay. Ken Cameron informed Otto that the variable pitch control for the propeller was jammed in reverse. In his determination to avoid another Arab boarding party, Otto ordered immediate withdrawal backward since they could not go forward.

A British attaché arrived and took Ginnie, Simon and Charlie away in his car. Ollie and I were to sleep in the vehicles as light fingers, the attaché warned, were everywhere. From the end of the pier we watched the *Benji Bee* depart backward into the clammy darkness.

To ensure security for all three vehicles and the trailers Ollie spun a web of cotton around our lineup and attached tins at intervals. I slept in the cab of the front Land Rover, but Ollie decided he could only guard the rear from outside, so he set up his lilo and mosquito net in the gutter.

Around dawn the local foxhounds arrived without warning in full cry. I shot out of the cab, cut my ear on one of Ollie's tins and was almost garroted by a cotton line. Ollie struggled out of his sleeping bag and mosquito net wide-eyed.

'God,' he muttered, 'the hounds of the Baskerville at full moon.'

There were no dogs, but overlooking the harbour security fence was an impressive mosque from which issued the muezzin's dawn chorus to the faithful. The local verger must have set his loudspeakers on full volume. An awful noise, unlike any ever heard in Arabia, beat the humid air. Even the mosquitoes took off.

'Just as well,' said Oliver, pointing at a wave of black sludge advancing along the gutter in which he had slept, complete with fish bones, half a bowler hat and the remains of a cat.

For two full days I struggled with customs formalities and a complex of bureaucrats. I got nowhere fast until I met the chief of the port authority himself. For the sum of 1,000 dinars, some 250 dollars, he cleared the wall away with three phone calls, which left me with exactly £80 worth of dinars for the rest of our stay in Algeria.

We drove south on good tarmac with heavy oil tankers for company. Flat-topped mesas straggled away through the roadside haze. One hundred and ten degrees Fahrenheit at noon. First Simon and I in one Land Rover, then Ginnie with her car full of radio gear, and the others behind in the Range Rover. At dusk we made camp beside the rolling sand-dunes of El Golea. I stopped there because of our instructions from the British Natural History Museum. The sand lizards or skinks which they wanted would be found in the sands of Khanem a few miles north of El Golea. Ollie, our trained skink-catcher, approved the site and immediately set his traps, baiting them with corned beef.

The next day the sun rose huge and orange and all the traps were empty. Clouds of large flies which tickled and little flies which bit attended us all day as the sweat ran down in rivulets. We wore next to nothing. Ollie recorded 122 degrees Fahrenheit in the afternoon. We could not decide whether it was worse inside or outside the tents.

After two skinkless days Ollie decided we must be more aggressive. Perhaps this particular sandbowl was bad news for skinks, so we trooped out into the dunes with water bags, compass and skink traps. Two hours of dune-trudging later, Ollie had picked up no tracks (he assured us that the five-inch lizards did leave identifiable tracks) and decided to call it a day.

'Are you sure you can track them?' I pressed.

Ol's confidence was undaunted. 'These things always require perseverance. Skinks don't grow on trees, you know.' Spoken like a true scientist.

Everyone was touchy by dusk when, almost to order, the flies and the mosquitoes began their familiar whine.

Next day I joined Simon in our Land Rover to hunt skink-catchers. In fly-blown El Golea they speak French and/or Arabic. Simon spoke French and I spoke Arabic.

'What do we want?' I asked him.

'Un homme qui pent attraper les poissons-de-sable,' said Simon without thinking. 'What about in Arabic?'

'Ah.' I did not want to be outdone. 'The Latin form is *Scincus scincus cucullatus.'*

'These Arabs may not learn Latin at school,' he said evenly as we passed by a row of mud-and-brick hovels.

I was ready for him. 'The colloquial term for lizard is *dhub* or *zelgaag*. Since skinks are lizards that should do.'

Much investigation led us to the mud home of one Hamou, the local guide. Inside there was a freezer full of Coca-Cola beside a colour TV set. Hamou assured us he was *the* skink-catcher of the region but he must warn us it was a dangerous and therefore expensive business. Did we realise that sand vipers and scorpions, which lived under the same sand where skinks must be sought, were in abundance? During the last year alone, he assured us, 128 people in town had been treated for scorpion stings and three of them had died. Sand vipers were deadly poisonous.

'Twice,' he added, 'when hunting skins I have plunged my hand into the sand and brought out sand vipers gorging skinks.'

That afternoon, with Ollie watching closely and three bedu boys to help him, Hamou led us into high dune country, not a mile from our camp, and within minutes had captured two prime skinks. By evening he had a third and we took him home to enjoy the tinned fruit and tomato purée we paid him with. For two days Ollie applied Hamou's tactics and added to his collection of pickled lizards, and each time he popped a new catch into his formaldehyde bottle he swore he would never again become involved in anything so cruel. The British Museum was less delicate.

Pleased to leave the El Golea sauna, we went south to Ain Salah, which means Salty Well, where we replenished our water supply with salty water. Warm winds from the western dunes fanned our camp that night in the Jebel Moujdier. Mice called jerboas hopped about, and overhead a lammer falcon wheeled on dusk patrol.

Next, on to Tamanrasset, self-styled tourist centre of the Hoggar Mountains. South of the ugly sprawling town we drove off the gravel track at the Ain Tahadat or Jo-jo Spring, as generations of hippies had dubbed it. The proprietor, who looked more Italian than Arab, was introduced as Spaghetti by a German tourist already camped by the rocks around the spring.

'Three dinars for each jerry can of my water,' said Spaghetti in passable French. We filled all our cans and paid with marmite and honey. Below the spring was a dry wadi that the German told us had been a roaring vent one hundred and sixty feet across only a week before. So we camped beside it instead of in it.

Our next move was southwest across the dry wastes of the Tanezrouft for our second task – bat-collecting on either side of the Mali border. Papers for such a journey had to be signed by the wali of Tamanrasset and the police chief. I visited the hotel with Charlie, who discovered to his horror that one beer cost the equivalent of £1.50, and a shot of gin £2.50. (Double the figure to get the approximate dollar amount.)

The chef de dairah, or chief functionary, at the wali's fort found my Arabic quaint and chatted for an hour about my former employer, the Sultan of Muscat, whom he cheerfully described as an evil reactionary whose son was an enemy of the people.

Remembering that my papers needed signatures I refrained from protest, but once my papers were safely signed and pocketed I told him about the torture wounds I had seen on Muslims from the hands of the Marxists. Which must have convinced him I was a CIA agent, because he promptly took me to the police chief. Another hour of politics and depletion of my western cigarettes gained another set of stamps and signatures on our papers. The customs officer was asleep in his office and signed without a word when awakened.

I then located a desert guide who spoke French. 'Due west to Bordj-Moktar. The track has not been crossed for five years. Much bad sand, no piste.' My Michelin map indicated a good piste to Bordj-Moktar but perhaps the guide was more up to date. After all, sand does shift about.

'You better go Gao by way of Timeiaouine,' said the guide, 'then I will take you.'

I explained we had only food to pay him with. This disgusted him; obviously an urbanised bedu who dealt only in dinars. 'You go without a guide. It is possible. You may not get lost.' These encouraging words seemed to absolve him of all feelings of responsibility. I then asked where we might find colonies of bats.

He sat up at that and frowned. *'Les chauves-souris?'* He pondered a while. 'Ah, those are west. Maybe you look in the wells of Silet.'

I was dismissed.

For fifty miles we drove along rocky track into the Hoggar peaks, and at eight thousand feet we came to the pass of Assekrem and walked up a well-worn mountain track to the little rock chapel with its sole guardian, an elderly French friar, Petit Frere, to whom, as was customary, we carried water and food.

On the plateau above the chapel was a set of meteorological instruments with which he took meticulous daily records. The view from that lonely chapel was an experience. A cool breeze plucked at mountain flowers rare and tiny on our perch while beyond the silent hanging void great mountains soared to spires and pinnacles of dizzying height.

The rock road took us back to Tamanrasset through another pass as dusk fell about us with clutching fingers of indigo gloom. Back at camp Simon lit a fire of roots, and Charlie gave a shout to 'Come and have some curry, it's still warm.' Ginnie and Simon preferred to wait for their own stew but I went over to the Range Rover – no harm in seconds.

Ollie spooned out some curry.

'How was the bat hunting?' I asked him.

'Not a sausage all day. There was a storm in the afternoon that knocked the tents down.'

I thanked him for putting ours up again and took a mouthful of curry. Without a doubt it was the hottest I have ever tasted either side of Shiraz. Ollie passed me a glass of what looked like water. I gulped it down. It was gin. My eyes and tongue bulged out. The world seemed to come to an end, red-hot sandpaper rasping my throat as I gasped for air.

I threatened vengeance through watering eyes, but of course only increased the genial merriment.

From Tamanrasset we drove west on worsening tracks to a place called Tit. Here there was a fork not shown on my map. There was no sign at the fork, but I found one three hundred yards from the current track. Abalesa and Silet lay to the left. The vehicles rattled like peas on a drum as the track leapt from scarred black basalt steps to sand-filled ruts. Dark storm clouds massed behind in the unseen Hoggar.

We sped over wadis green with *gai'sh, kfeeter* and the ubiquitous *ghadaf* dwarf palm, rousing clouds of dust so fine it reflected the very sheen of the sun, an orb of spectral orange.

Dusty as ghouls, we emerged to slake our thirst at the well of Silet. Simon, master of water, flung our roped canvas bucket down the stone-rimmed hole and drew up a gallon or so that he poured into a jerry can through a filter. 'Little bastards,' he muttered, blowing at the filter's gauze.

I peered over his shoulder – not difficult, since Simon is Ginnie's size. A dozen miniature hook-tailed tadpoles writhed in alarm as the warm air struck their ugly little forms.

'Hookworms, liver worms, toe worms, every sort of nasty design and those are just the visible ones.' Simon seemed delighted. 'Imagine what a drop of that water would look like under the microscope.'

I watched Simon apply sterilization and purification tablets to our bottles once he had pumped the water into them through lime candles; but even then I wouldn't have drunk any except for my parching thirst.

One of the vehicle starters then gave up the ghost. For five hours at 105 degrees Fahrenheit Simon struggled to fix it, burning his fingers on the hot metal. No luck. Ollie, disapproving of Simon's fault-finding methods, ended up shouting at him. His diary that night recorded: 'S. very set in his ways. He never wants to listen.'

Despite the lassitude we all felt, Ollie decided Silet looked good for bats, and I went along with him to interpret. We found the village elder who spoke French of sorts. At the mention of bats he stiffened. 'Not in this village. We have no bats. But outside in the wells . . . maybe many.'

He tried to explain the location of the wells but without a local map it was useless. Reluctantly he agreed to come, and four miles from Silet showed us some gravel pits where shafts had been sunk between twenty and fifty feet down. We lowered Ollie on a rope, tried four but found nothing except pigeon feathers and the odour of dead animals. In one well, though, where there was water and slime, we watched fascinated as a thin green water viper over five feet long surfaced and raised its head to stare at us. As Ollie approached, it submerged with startling speed.

We found no bats here but to the west, across the wasteland, there would be countless bats in the wells of Tim-Missao, or so the elder told us. We gave him at least a year's supply of tomato purée for his pains.

Weeks later I discovered from a Frenchman that bats were thought to be sons of the devil, whose main desire was to steal the souls of young Saharan villagers. No one wanted to annoy the local bats by giving their presence away to foreign bat-catchers, so the best policy was to keep us moving on to ever-new bat pastures.

*

For three days Simon rationed our water as we edged south and west over featureless wastes. The sun did not burnish a clear desert sky – violent dust storms raged throughout the land and often blotted out the trail.

On October 15 in a shallow wadi far from any track, we happened on three lonely camel saddles. Close by to burial mounds of black rock the three lay in the dust, each with a neat pile of utensils beside it – cast-iron cooking pots, carved wood spoons, metal fire tongs, heavy clay gourds. Why?

I went off on foot with Ginnie and picked up the long-ago piste of twin camel trails which led south and west, and by evening we rejoined clearly defined vehicle tracks from the north. The wind stirred sandstorms all night that lashed at our tents like driven sleet. Then driving hour on hour through a yellow gloom with our lights on, it was necessary to get out and verify that we were still following tracks.

Crossing wadis, the vehicles bogged down in the soft, loose sand. Once we came on a scene that might have been straight out of a surrealist film. Two great trucks overloaded with goods and people appeared fleetingly between surges of the storm. They sank to their axles as we had. A giant of a man, turbanned and robed in white, gestured kinglike as figures swarmed down from the loads to push and pull. Blue-clad touaregs from Mali and nomads bent in two long lines under the will of this great bearded Moses. All had their robes whipped and billowed in the screaming dustclouds as we watched from our cabs. We made camp only one hundred miles north of the Mali border, sticky with dust and our own salt, tired and thirsty.

Next day we took on a guide at Timeiaouine and crossed the unmarked border soon after dusk: our guide left us there without a word.

Trailer springs fractured, tow bolts snapped and tyres punctured, but we made our way south from the Adrar and down the lovely vale of Tilemsi. The life became more interesting: scorpions, spiders, the nocturnal music of frogs, crickets and nightjars; insects of fascinating shapes and hues, rabbits, foxes, lizards and gazelle. In places the valley was as green as an English spring and spattered with purple where tents of nomads sprawled by herds of grazing camel. But there were also skeletons, some still furnished with rags of dried and hairy skin; they lay about the trail, especially where zones of sand caused mini-deserts. In one such arid place a wizened nomad waited. He offered us camel milk from a brass bowl, and when we had drunk he proffered his empty goatskin for water. Another, searching the sands for a lost camel, was obviously parched. He drank deeply, his dust-caked eyes closed tight. I could only guess how wonderful that moment of relief must be to him; the feel of the water in his throat, a satisfaction urban peoples, in their sufficiency, can rarely savour.

At Gao we reached the Niger and followed its westerly curve four hundred miles to Timbuktu. This was a paradise for Ollie, always a keen ornithologist, and we stopped many times for him to identify this or that species from his bird book. From the Camargue to our camp at the Torro Bravo, from Algiers to Timbuktu, he noted everything with feathers. His entries included the Egyptian vulture, the shirka, the mouse-bird and the bee-eater, the brubru shrike, the cut-throat weaver, the white-rumped blackchat and the hoopoe. The bird I remember most vividly was a Timbuktu chicken. We arrived in Timbuktu, famous for epitomising the back end of beyond, at dusk and discovered a 'restaurant' whose menu for that evening (and every evening) was 'Sardine, beer and dead hen'. The beer was cold if you drank it quickly, and the sardines, if you got them down before the indigenous flies did, were excellent. Our chef, a man with indescribably dirty hands, entered the dark room with a proud air of 'now for the *pièce de resistance*'. The *pièce* was, in fact, one of the scrawny chickens harmlessly cleaning up our crumbs, and it put up a great deal of *resistance* when Cookie grabbed it by the neck and plucked it bare. Only then was the pitifully squawking bird put out of its misery by having its neck wrung. Our appetites dispersed more quickly than the feathers. Timbuktu is the end of the desert here, where flood plains and regional lakes of the Niger take over. Camping in the forest of Timbuktu is not recommended. The sand is soft and, once stopped there, vehicles and trailers are tricky to get going again. The dry grass conceals a bedding of marble-size burrs, sticky and itchy.

We woke wet from a clammy sleep to the maddening call of the vinaceous doves and multicoloured hoopoes in the pango-pango trees about our tents. Whether the trees were really pango-pangos I couldn't tell, but Simon, our only member to have travelled in West Africa before, called them that and we went along.

In Timbuktu Ollie learned, as expected, that there were no bats but, at Goundam, we would find them in the thousands. Goundam is a village of hilly bumps around which snakes a Niger tributary fringed with gardens and palms. We camped on the southern side of the river four miles from the village, a spot from which Ollie made a series of bat-hunting forays and, in our foldaway canvas boat, a journey upstream to a great reed-covered lake rich in bird life. Close by the camp, in some ruins, Ollie at last found his bats.

With bird-catching nets stretched across all exit points, he and Charlie and Simon roused the dormant bats and trapped six, none bigger than a sparrow. Ollie's initial delight at this long-delayed success soon turned to gloom when he had to pickle the little things. Charlie, the morale officer, made an especially hot curry to cheer him up.

I was sorry to leave the river camp, a happy place of chattering fire finches, hovering hawks and lunging kingfishers. Skulls and carcasses of cows littered the brush around us, probably the site of an abandoned charnel house. Ginnie took the opportunity to wash clothes on the riverbank, and I began the detailed plans for unloading in Antarctica. By the time we reached Cape Town some two hundred pages of equipment lists had to be checked and allotted priority groupings.

Leaving the river we passed a troupe of long-tailed monkeys on a watermelon trail. Secluded pools flashed with bird colour. (By now Simon was incubating malaria, but didn't know it.)

In Niafunke we learned that the floods were up and our route south was barred, the ferries unable to cross the swollen river. Another track was west from Niafunke, skirting the flood country through nomad lands, and we decided to follow it. This westerly loop of seven hundred kilometres should get us back on our original route at Koutiala, we believed.

My recollections of our journey between the desert and the lakes are fractured ... A camp with a new moon outlining giant anthills and cicadas that chirped through the silver night ... A once-great forest of dead and dying trees where no birds sang and too many cattle had for too long churned the undergrowth into pigpen mire ... A pueblo village where it seemed every inhabitant came out and followed us, jogging and clapping along their only 'street' until the last child and yapping dog dropped away in a dusty halo ... A nomad encampment where black Arab-speaking Mauritanians sang at sunset, the men with spears, shields and knobkerries, the women with proud banana-end breasts and rings of coloured beads. Soft orange light wrote the scene on my mind, dug-out canoes pulled high in the reeds, groups of smiling girls stomping and chanting in time as they flayed heaps of millet to flour dust. And, like regiments on the move, lowing herds of African longhorns jostling behind thorn corrals, each with a series of long-branded scars on its flank ...

For three days we drove southwest through damp forests and the irrigated rice lands of Kouruma. At Markala, by the thundering Niger barrage, we reached tarmac again. Now camps were made in forest, not savannah, under coconut palms and baobab trees. One moonless night I heard Ginnie moaning outside our camp area. She was lying on her back. There were ants on her legs, but she ignored them. For some years she had had slowly worsening stomach pains. Tests indicated a spastic colon but all the normal pills she tried gave no relief. I gave her pain-killers and by morning she felt well enough to drive.

Simon's eyes were badly bloodshot. The dust and irritation of the past few weeks together with his contact lenses were causing him pain. In Loulouni, close to the Ivory Coast border, he bought yams and guavas and cooked a delicious meal over a log fire. We dined in an elephant-grass clearing while lightning forked and thunder burst in the rain forests all around.

At the Mali border we filled our cans with fresh water and drove south to the Ivorian frontier post of Ouangolodougou. On November 4 we reached Tiassale. We were soaked from recent showers and a bit high from the weeks without baths. I hoped to find a camp beside the Bandama Rouge River where we could swim as well as hunt for water snails – Ollie's last official task in Africa.

That night we set up camp in a space cleared of bamboo and undergrowth, and Charlie found a nine-inch black scorpion, which Ollie promptly pickled 'in case it's interesting to the museum'. Simon cooked with a slow log fire of mahogany and managed to get a chicken from the village a mile down-river. Using a Land Rover starting handle for a spit he fried the bird with yams, stewed onions and eggplant. A true feast.

I felt more and more sure that Simon's selection had been a good one, and that the others would soon accept him completely. Part of the early trouble may have been his refusal at one time to join the

SAS. A Quaker, he would only join a nonfighting unit. He had ended up with the 144th Parachute Field Ambulance Regiment, a tough bunch whose training turned out to be as warlike as the SAS exercises, and on the Welsh training weekends I'd found Simon as tough and fit as the best of us – if not fitter.

Ollie the intrepid proceeded to lead us on a snail-hunting foray into the nearby forest, but fifty yards from the camp we came across an apparently endless file of black ants, some half an inch long. They packed a shocking bite, as Ollie discovered when a couple became lodged between his shirttail and pants. There were also black-and-yellow spiders of great beauty, and everywhere dappled light fell in laser beams from the black canopy far above us. Tree boles were massive, the vegetation underfoot deep and rich with decayed matter. Butterflies, moths and dragonflies graced the speckled gloom until dark when gyrating fireflies took over.

Happy with his slimy plunder, Ollie took us back to camp. Ginnie was bathing on the sandspit, her towel and soap at the ready on the end of a mahogany canoe. As I joined her by the dusk-lit river a native man, silent as the current, arrived in a second dugout and beached on the spit. Ginnie whipped around and grabbed her towel, all two-foot square, and confronted the visitor. He stared back, not at all embarrassed, and after a while smiled and went into the jungle. Ginnie did not share his aplomb.

Finally Ollie was satisfied with his haul and we left the forest, driving three hours to the south and the Ivorian coast and the capital city of Abidjan. Our ship the *Benji Bee* was already at berth in the harbour. In the northern suburbs of the city we met Anton Bowring, who guided us to a villa owned by a British building company. Two of our crew were in bed there with malaria, being nursed by Jill the cook. Simon with swollen glands and heat exhaustion soon joined them.

*

On November 20 the *Benji Bee* moved out of Abidjan's wide lagoon into the Atlantic. We were at once in a heavy swell. Eddie and Dave were still weak from malaria but back on duty. Simon, nauseous and vomiting intermittently, felt alternately hot and cold, and Paul Clark, appointed ship's doctor, looked after him.

Next day just off the Greenwich Meridian we crossed the equator, and Admiral Otto, dressed as King Neptune with pitchfork and crown, presided over the crossing-the-line ceremonies. The golden-haired Buzzard, with two footballs under his T-shirt, was Neptune's bride Aphrodite. Terry the bosun, with a firehose and tins of green detergent, thoroughly soused those crew members unlucky enough not to have crossed the line previously.

The clocks kept going backward as the coast we followed veered east. Sperm whales were spotted, and flying fish died on the hot decks. Up in the fo'c'sle sorting out cargo, the cloying odour of bad mackerel clung to my shirt and hair, but I saw no ghosts in the fo'c'sle despite tales from Terry of the Danish seaman thought to haunt that part of the ship.

We moved into the Benguela Current, and the weather closed in. Down in number two hold our forklift truck broke loose and slammed down on its side, crushing a generator and other cargo. Battery acid ran free and poured down through the floor slats onto the Antarctic cargo below. (Anton received a message at this time from Ant Preston in London saying that Giles and Gerry had left Farnborough in the Twin Otter plane on their long journey to meet us in Antarctica. We wondered if we'd ever live to see it.) And the weather deteriorated. The wind stayed around Force 7 for days. Sometimes the watch officer kept headway at a mere three knots in the plunging seas, and the order went out for safety lines on deck as waves crashed over the bows. The *Benji Bee* rolled to 27 degrees and more. In my diary I wrote:

> Down below at nights our porthole leaks – each time we roll to port it submerges with a buffeting crash, a stream of sea water running down to soak the bench and the carpeting. Last night Charlie screamed as a specially violent wave knocked us sideways. A heavy glass ashtray careened off his bedside table into his face. Ken Cameron, chief engineer, has a double bunk. Each time the ship rolls beyond 30° he shoots out sideways like a cuckoo on a platform, and a moment later he returns up against the wall with a splat. All night as we plunge and heave, I hear strange noises. Our cabin is just above my stores hold and I lie wondering what such and such a crash, thud or metallic grind might mean. Has a vital steel sled come loose? Or a box of delicate radio gear? What's that smell of gasoline? Has an ice spear punctured a fuel drum?
>
> The imagination tends to run riot for landlubbers like me …

In her early days, the *Kista Dan* made sufficient headway to face the South Atlantic with confidence. Now her engines were twenty-seven years old and her pistons scaled. In itself this was neither dangerous nor remarkable, but bearing in mind her ice-resistant shape was not designed to cleave smoothly through heavy seas, the loss of power caused by scaling was a factor that couldn't be ignored when planning a heavy-laden voyage through the biggest seas in the world.

With no landmass to break them, the huge waves of the southern seas can spin around the world maintaining their size and their motion. Icebergs and hidden 'growlers' can nowadays be spotted on the radar, but a ship like the *Benji Bee* is no safer from the sheer power of freak waves than, say, Shackleton's or Scott's wooden ships.

Our old engines which, on our way to Cape Town were slowed down by mere Force 7 headwinds to less than six knots, might well not produce enough power to keep steerage in the foaming conditions of an all-too-common Force 10 gale south of latitude forty-five degrees south. The moment of truth, given such conditions, would come if the skipper decided it was safer to turn tail. The action of turning the ship between waves might temporarily put her in imminent danger of broaching through the vertical force of water hitting her hull. And even after a safe turn the danger of pooping would remain so long as such conditions prevailed ... Slowly we edged down the parallel to the Skeleton Coast, and slowly the seas grew less boisterous. Of the crew I wrote: 'Things may well alter but, touch wood, I've not heard a cross word nor a grumble between any of those on board except two of the officers who rub each other up a touch. They are a great bunch but obviously have a hard job with this old ship. It's as well they seem almost to love her.'

On December 3, a touch dazed and very happy to see land, we reached Saldanha Bay, a few hours north of Cape Town. Flocks of seagulls, thousands of them, rose and fell over shoals of fish. Colonies of jackass penguins squawked and squinted from their rocky homes along the shoreline. Terry and the Buzzard ran to the chain locker, and the anchor rattled away at a touch to attach us to the South African seabed. Five days later, December 8, we arrived in Cape Town harbour under the gaunt bulk of Table Mountain, and set up one of our promotion exhibitions. A press conference followed. Ginnie was asked by a feminist reporter whether her role as base camp leader and radio operator proved that the sexes are equal even in the most extreme physical conditions. Her reply: 'I'm not going on this journey to prove a woman can do anything a man can, as some people seem to think. Women are not as suited or better at doing anything that is normally done by men. There's a role for women and a role for men, and they should complement each other and not create a feeling of competition. I'm not a women's libber nor out to prove myself in a man's field. I came because I love my husband and he's here, not back at home. I have helped with the planning and organisation from the start but I'm not brave. If I thought about it in depth at a personal emotional level, I probably wouldn't be here now.'

Ollie's wife Rebecca came out from England. Ollie told me, 'It's like a second honeymoon,' and it seemed to me that she had accepted his staying with us for the next three years. I was to be proved wrong.

Sir Vivian Fuchs visited for a week and I was able to get last-minute advice from the only man in the world to have led a trans-Antarctic expedition.

Until Cape Town whatever filming there was of our journey was done by Anton Bowring and me, but now Dr Armand Hammer sent a four-man professional crew to take over all the filming. Bad relations between photographers and the others have actually stopped expeditions from time to time and had, from my point of view, ruined one of my own previous ventures. I was determined to get on well with Dr Hammer's men and was sorry when things began on a bad footing. Among other things, I refused to promise them the exclusive use of a Skidoo, sledge and tent in Antarctica. Their sound man, Tony Dutton, later wrote: 'Our first real contact with Ran Fiennes was not a happy one, and indeed left us confused and rather angry. We could see no real justification for what seemed to be the obsessive secrecy of a radio call with Prince Charles, and the refusal to commit tents or Skidoo to us nearly caused us to abandon the shoot. I now count myself fortunate to have been able to spend time getting to know the team members. This contact gave me not explanations but a growing insight into what made the expedition the remarkable cohesive force, the family, it undoubtedly became.'

*

It was on a burning hot day that David Mason arrived with his polar gear and Ginnie's terrier dog Bothy. Both were to join the ship down to Antarctica. A third member of Transglobe, Anto Birkbeck, who was to join us in Antarctica only, turned up in baggy World War I khaki shorts, a faded drill shirt and battered trilby. I had hoped that the majority of the land team – Ginnie, Ollie, Charlie, Bothy and I – would spend the coming winter about three hundred miles inland from Sanae coastal base. But most of our equipment and fuel would have to stay close to wherever we unloaded the *Benji Bee*. To look after it and avoid its disappearance under snow-drifts as well as to maintain an airstrip and camp for our aircrew, Simon was to winter there. And since he could not be alone I'd asked Birkbeck, of the battered trilby, to join him. It was to be a two-man Antarctic base with neither man experienced in Antarctic conditions. On the other hand, who was?

We left South Africa on December 22. On board were twenty-eight men, one woman, one dog and a number of mice.

Most of our crew members possessed a good deal of charm and more than one had kissed the blarney stone, so they left a number of heaving breasts and tearful cheeks on the quayside.

Since our holds were laden to the seams, much of the decking was crammed tight with drums of gasoline. No Smoking signs proliferated and, when the skipper was around, no one smoked.

The mayor and crowds of well-wishers saw us off. A kilted piper played 'Auld Lang Syne' as the *Benji Bee* sounded her own salty dirge on the ship's horn and moved slowly out of the Duncan Dock into the Southern Ocean.

Ollie wrote at the time: 'I found great difficulty in not showing my feelings as I waved good-bye to civilisation. The sea was rough and I think most of us felt miserable and a bit frightened of the future.'

I know what he meant. It would have been different if just one of us had some actual knowledge of what we were shortly to face.

At 7:00 P.M. we passed Cape Agulhas, the last land for twenty-four hundred miles, and set a course south toward the pack ice.

Chapter Five

> We must select the illusion which appeals to our temperament and embrace it with passion, if we want to be happy.
>
> CYRIL CONNOLLY

Admiral Otto Steiner addressed the crew.

'Initially we anticipate Force 8 gales rising to Force 9. West of the Agulhas Basin are found some of the worst seas anywhere. It will be rough, but worse still in the Roaring Forties which we enter on Christmas Day. The direct route to Sanae is twenty-four hundred miles but we must add a dog-leg in order to approach it from the east. Last year the South African ice-breaker *Agulhas* tried a direct approach and was forced back with damage from dense Weddell Sea ice. Don't forget, it was in the Weddell Sea sixty or so years ago that Shackleton's ship was crushed and sunk. Our first icebergs can be expected after forty-five degrees south and from the end of December there'll be permanent daylight. We will *not* make way in whiteout conditions and all bergs will be passed to the windward – growlers lurk to their leeward. We have sufficient food for twenty-nine men for two months and I'm pleased everyone including the ice team, the scientists and the film crew have agreed to take their turn at watches and, in the event of an ice build-up on deck, work with shovels and axes.' Otto also laid down a number of rules, stressing the dangers of the southern seas in a boat heavily laden with high-octane fuel.

Quite apart from individual icebergs, some up to fifty miles long and two hundred feet high, pack ice creates a formidable barrier around the frozen continent. The annual freeze-up which creates the pack grows in depth at a rate of two to three feet per year and extends outward from Antarctica for as much as a thousand miles. Average summers tend to break the pack into a mass of fractured floes that form a wide protective belt off the coast but often leave a narrow navigable shore lead. Although the main pack is from two to nine feet thick, there is a short period during December and January, the summer months, when ice-breakers and ice-strengthened vessels like ours can hope to shove and manoeuvre their way through it. But not every summer – sometimes it's impenetrable, and sometimes, although a vessel may find loose pack on entering, she may be in trouble from an early freeze-up or simply a local wind change that contracts the pack and any object caught in its clutches.

Briefed on the dangers, we all wished devoutly for speed, but the old *Benji Bee* cruised at a mere nine knots with favourable conditions. And some on board had more immediate worries. For example, Simon wrote: 'Queasy all day. Slept a lot. Not sure if the Stugeron pills are helping.' And Bothy soon proved that house-trained dogs are not automatically ship-trained dogs. Uncertain where to go, he spread his blessings all over the ship and usually in dark shadowy gangways. Not a day passed without some new victim trodding fair and square on his latest deposit. Anyone who left their cabin door open was fair game until the day he discovered the 'lawn', situated on the boat deck at the stern. Further north in warmer climes this green mat with grass stems of rubber was used by sunbathing crew members off watch. Bothy took it over. His favourites on board were the Londoner engineer Howard and Terry the bosun, whose head was now hedgehog- rather than Kojak-style.

Two days out the ship tossed and rolled on a grey-black sea. Wandering albatross and white-chinned petrel beat the wind between the masts and over the crashing spray. A Christmas tree, lashed by the crew to the mast, was torn away by powerful gusts. In the rolling chaos of the galley, little Jill and big Dave Hicks strove to prepare Christmas fare for the hungry. Walls of green water curled over the down-plunging prow, then buried the bows and foc's'le with shuddering blows felt by everyone aboard ...

At this same time Transglobe's little aircraft moved high above the jungles of Brazil. Giles and Gerry flew from England via Iceland and Ottawa to Toronto, where a set of retractable skis were fitted. From Toronto they hopped to Miami, South Caicos Island and Trinidad. On December 24 Giles took off early to miss the cloud build-up over the jungle. They landed at Manaus on the banks of the Brazilian Amazon, the town where people can eat piranha and chips and get their own back on the little monster fish. Christmas Day Gerry wrote: 'Up at 6:30 A.M. and on to Ascencion in Paraguay. The longest leg of the whole flight; 1,330 miles in nine hours. Then to Mar del Plata for Christmas in shirt sleeves. Down the coast to Comodoro Rivadavia, also in Argentina, our stepping-off point for Port Stanley in the Falkland Islands. We spent an extra day for our clearance to be checked – there's a dispute here at the moment about who should own the islands, Britain or Argentina.' An inadvertent brush with history ...

Christmas Day found us well into the Roaring Forties – the tempestuous area between forty and fifty degrees south latitudes. Our little saloon, tolerable enough for fourteen at table, was ready to burst with twenty-four. At all times five were on the bridge or down below or sleeping between watches. Constant radar surveillance was kept for hidden growlers – semi-submerged bergs such as had sunk the *Titanic.*

Amidships and close by the skipper's cabin Anton had hung a brass inclinometer, the same simple instrument Captain Scott carried on H.M.S. *Discovery* and our only relic from that earlier southern voyage. Cyrus was at the helm that day as a giant roller forced the *Benji Bee* to tilt forty-seven degrees each way. Christmas goodies bit the dust, Bothy slid on his side a good six yards and Admiral Otto nearly swallowed his pipe.

It seemed to me the ship could not much longer last such treatment. She would surely be shaken to pieces. Could her thirty-year-old hull really survive the twin strains of the enormous weight of our fuel and cargo within and the hideous battering from without? As a poor and seldom sailor secretly in need of reassurance from an old salt, I sought out Anton.

'Sit down,' he said, 'have a dram.'

I refused, deeply regretting the quantities of Christmas food and booze I'd already put down. 'Everything okay?' I asked.

'How do you mean?'

'The ship. The hull . . . you know.'

Anton's black eyes glinted, 'That is not a thing anyone would predict. Perhaps. Perhaps not. This is not *rough,* you know. We'll be lucky if we get away with no worse than this.'

And then he told me the story of another British expedition that had set sail for Antarctica the previous year via Rio de Janeiro in a converted wartime tug named the *En Avant.* She was eight years older than the *Benji Bee.* Her hull had been strengthened to cope with ice, and she set out in the southern summer as we had, bound for the Falkland Islands. She was never seen again. Her crew included a well-known polar sailor and mountaineer, Major Bill Tillman, then in his eightieth year. 'It's my bet they were knocked down by a wave in heavy weather.'

Feeling even worse, I went below and held a Christmas church service.

We crossed the 50th parallel late on December 28 and the first iceberg passed abeam. Up in the darkened foc's'le at 1:00 A.M. the graveyard watch stood by silently. Ahead little could be seen but the glint of wild foam.

One man hunched over the radar console, his features long and gaunt in its reflected orange light. Now and again he would pass some brief information to the figure behind the oaken wheel. Our course was 220 degrees magnetic.

From dark onward Ollie in a dark donkey jacket could be found out on the bridge wing, binoculars at the ready.

Each day, with Terry operating the winch gear, two oceanographers who had joined the expedition in Cape Town trawled for plankton. With bathythermographs they obtained depth-to-temperature profiles. Side by side with salinity measurements they used these to identify large-scale water bodies. Their purpose was to study current patterns and the interaction of the water bodies at subtropical and Antarctic convergences. The behaviour and condition of these currents influence the existence of tiny phytoplankton and thus their predators, the zooplankton, including krill. Dr Chris McQuaid, chief oceanographer and Irishman, showed me a jar of seawater solid with tiny crustaceans after only a ten-minute trawl. 'This,' he said, waving his hand at the great grey mass, 'is the most productive ocean in the world. For a scientist its richness and diversity are irresistible. Krill may well prove to be an important source of food, so abundant that it can be harvested in thousands of tons. Commercial krill fisheries already have been established by several countries.' He dabbed a finger in the jar of slimy sea-life. 'Unfortunately there are plenty of examples in recent history of what happens when commercial interests go on a spree and ignore the simple laws of nature. Here we have a source of protein valuable and by modern methods quite easy to harvest. It may take only a few years to be culled to the point of scarcity, even extinction.' He warmed to his subject.

'Krill is the central link in the vast and complex food webs that form the ecology of the Southern Ocean. Remove too many krill and you endanger whales, seals, seabirds and fish. In order to cull a new source of food for man and exploit it profitably, commercial interests may cause havoc.' Chris's Irish brogue grew stronger with emphasis: 'Unless we, the searchers, know all the facts we can't present a convincing argument for control. But our resources are limited in manpower, money and opportunity, unlike those of the krill fishermen whose backers feed on their own profit and mankind's necessity. That's why the voyage of the *Benji Bee* is such a godsend.'

On January 2 the pack closed about the ship, and the battle was joined. The hull shuddered each time we struck a solid chunk, and our bow rode high to mount the ice. With luck our laden weight would split the obstruction and sunder it in two, and often this happened. When it didn't, though, the skipper repeated the run until it did.

The wind still blew, a lot colder now; but the sea was calm beneath its weighty mantle. For two days we averaged three knots within the pack ice. Only once did the skipper retreat and search for a new route rather than batter a way along the selected one.

The crow's nest was big enough for one man to sit in slightly cramped comfort. Ginnie, who hated heights, refused to scale the ladder to the nest, thereby missing a great view of the pack, especially in the eerie pastels of evening. Two hours was the normal stint for a crow's nest watch. The occupant used binoculars to ensure his route choice was not simply the next most inviting lead but the general direction of least ice for as far as he could see. Directions were passed down an antique intercom system to the bridge. Dave Hicks, who being steward was in charge of the ship's drink supplies, took his own central heating up to the nest with him. His course through the pack was noticeably more zigzag than other people's. When not passing directions he would hum, whistle, belch and generally carry on a bizarre conversation with himself, all of which came through the loudspeaker on the bridge.

On January 4 we entered the coastal lead and, back to nine knots, moved west with the high cliffs of Antarctica to our south and the rim of the pack to starboard.

Ginnie made contact with the South Africans at Sanae base, and their leader promised to send flares up from the ice bay at which it would be safest for us to unload – he called it by the Norwegian name Polarbjorn Buchte. His base was only ten miles inland from this bight, and the weather, he said, was good.

We passed many indents in the ice cliffs but none where the ship might anchor, let alone unload, since the cliffs were at least forty feet high.

Finally, though, the South African flares were spotted around midday and we moved into a bay half a mile wide at the mouth. Hemmed in by high cliffs it tapered V-like for a mile and a half to its apex where the cliffs fell away to a snow ramp, which gave access to the interior.

The winter sea ice had not yet left the bay and its surface looked solid enough. But Sir Vivian Fuchs had warned me not to trust such bay ice. It only needs a strong northerly wind to start new fracturing, which of course begins along the seaward edge, where unloading must take place. Sir Vivian's team had lost a great quantity of stores in this way.

The paperwork I had worked on through Africa and the South Atlantic was designed to enable all unloading to finish in eleven days, using all crew members despite their ignorance of snow vehicles and cold-weather hazards.

Antarctic unloading is traditionally handled by tractors and Snowcat vehicles. We had one little groundhog from our Greenland run in 1976 and five Skidoos. With this minifleet, hundreds of drums of fuel, each weighing 450 pounds, and over a hundred tons of mixed cargo had to be moved some two miles to the ramp at the bay's apex.

It was important that the ship leave Antarctica as soon as possible – each day that she lingered for unloading increased the risks to her.

Giles and Gerry were now in the Falkland Islands. When they reached Sanae our cargo had to be ready beside an airstrip. Their task would be to ferry close to 100,000 pounds inland some three hundred miles to the edge of the Antarctic plateau. At six thousand feet above sea level, a forward base had to be established near an abandoned South African base on the edge of the 'known world'. This base nestled in the outer rim of a mountain range, the Borga Massif, south of which no man had ever ventured.

For nine hundred miles toward the South Pole a vast tract of land, over ten thousand feet above sea level, awaited us. As far south as Borga we would be travellers – thereafter we would be explorers of one of earth's last untrodden regions.

It took Sir Vivian Fuchs a hundred days to cross the continent by a far shorter route and using closed cab vehicles which cut down the risk of exposure to his men. We obviously needed to count on at least that long, but the Antarctic summer, the period when it is possible to travel, is only one hundred and twenty days. Amundsen tried to challenge nature by starting his South Pole attempt a month early. He regretted his rashness when extreme cold forced his team back to their base for a further month's wait. Captain Scott failed to return from his own South Pole journey by early February and was caught out in an 'autumn' blizzard that, sadly, sealed his fate.

To be isolated from a base on the polar plateau outside the narrow confines of summer is to invite a speedy demise.

Otto rammed the edge of the bay ice to make a nest for the ship in its outline. The South African boss and some of his men appeared in snow vehicles.

They had seen nobody for a year. I would not have liked to bump into them on a dark night – most wore oil-ragged clothes with headbands around hippie hair which fell to their shoulders, and most were tall, rangy men with unkempt beards.

The *Benji Bee* crew, looking tame beside the locals, lost no time in disembarking down a ladder to feel Antarctica under their mukluks.

Looking down from the foc's'le with Simon I noticed two groups had formed. The first was a dozen Transglobers, all armed with cameras, in a ring around a single Adelie penguin that stared back at them with an arrogant expression.

The second circle was of hairy South Africans bunched around Jill, the cook. Each group in its fashion was mesmerised.

The boss took me up the snow ramp, and a mile beyond it paced out a relatively flat six hundred metres. 'The prevailing wind goes this way. You can tell by the direction of the *sastrugi,* the ridges of snow, so your Twin Otter can use this as an airstrip and you can lay out your cargo alongside it.'

Thereafter we proceeded to flag out a route from ship to ramp to inland cargo site. And the unloading commenced. Gradually the mountain of stores subsided. During this unloading period the wind rose to fifty knots, spray surged high as mounting waves crashed against the rim of the bay ice. Great icebergs began to shift ominously to our north and soon the mooring stakes for the *Benji Bee* snapped. There was no choice for Otto but to ride out the storm a safe distance from the coast. Up on the bridge, when the ice broke in the storm, Ginnie and I watched whole segments of the Buchte Bay ice ride out to sea, and on one I counted eight drums of Twin Otter fuel, over three hundred precious gallons, float past us into the wind-whipped whiteout. One of the ice sections carried Ken's motorbike, and it occurred to me that if some future southern sailing skipper, after dinner and a dram, were to spot an ice floe bearing a motorbike past his ship, he would probably go cold-sober the rest of his life.

The weather cleared as quickly as it had deteriorated, and the sun shone from a cloudless sky when the Twin Otter arrived, roaring over the *Benji Bee* at mast height. After a faultless display of hedge-hopping Giles landed beside our painfully prepared airstrip. But not *on* it. After all the hours of working to clear this and other strips for Giles, we learned that he took a special delight in virgin landing sites untouched by axe and shovel.

For the first time all elements of Transglobe were together. In a short while the ship would have to leave, and in less than a month including bad weather Giles had to ferry enough fuel and rations to the Borga site for our eight-months' stay there. We too would then have to make a fast disappearance from Antarctica before the oncoming days of winter – the long dark months when no plane can possibly fly anywhere over the frozen continent.

A prefabricated hut was erected at Sanae. Giles flew Ginnie and me inland over black mountains and the glinting scars of crevasse fields, to the east a moving river of ice, the Jutulstraumen Glacier, then beyond the peaks of Giaeverryggen and Borga Massif and down close by the mountain Huldreslottet. A horned peak named

Ryvingen reared from the snowfield eleven miles east of the mountain. Just below it Giles settled the Twin Otter, leaving us to plan the siting of our base, which had to be as sheltered as possible from the blast of the coming winter storms. And for this we took note of the sastrugi, which told us that the prevailing winds blew from the south. Our huts, made of simple cardboard, needed to take advantage of such information and natural cover if we were to survive.

Antarctica is by far the coldest place on earth. Temperatures on the plateau plunge in winter to minus 120 degrees Fahrenheit. At such temperatures a steel rod dropped on a rock is likely to shatter like glass; tin disintegrates into loose granules; and the mercury in thermometers freezes into solid metal. But it is the wind that affects humans most by scouring the skin of those vestiges of warmth trapped by pores and hairs. Minus 40 degrees in still air is not bad, but minus 20 degrees with a sixty-knot wind is lethal ...

Ginnie concentrated on the siting of her radio antennae, needing to have contact with Cove Radio Station in England. Cove lay to the north but she also needed to have High Frequency and Very High Frequency contact to the south back to the ice group and the Twin Otter crew during the coming crossing attempt.

I wanted to shelter on the northern leeward side of the Ryvingen feature, but after a heated discussion in our tent – hundreds of miles from the nearest person so we could happily vent our opinions as loud as we liked – we agreed to compromise. Poles to make the antennae sites were placed west of Ryvingen's 'wind-shadow', where there was a clear line of sight toward the Pole. Then we paced the cable distance back to the east and flagged the site for Ginnie's radio hut; from there, a fifty-metre gap to the generator hut site and another twenty-five meters to the living hut site. We finally paced eight hundred metres east up the hill and sited the Very Low Frequency research hut with a further eight hundred metres to its antenna site. The VLF recording equipment had to be at least this distance away from our generators on account of its sensitivity. Actually the compromise resulted in excellent sites for the various antennae and partial shelter for the huts.

The next day Giles brought Simon and Anto up together with all materials needed for the radio hut, which we put up in twelve hours, and on the next flight David came up to begin logging cargo into the new numbered and flagged lanes beside the main hut site.

Leaving the three others to get on with the thirty-six-foot-long main hut, Ginnie and I flew back to Sanae and the ship. All the drums had now been moved to the Sanae lines, and the ship was ready to depart. That night we held a farewell party on board, and next day, January 17, sitting on our rucksacks by the fractured edge of the bay ice, we watched our friends sail away, the mournful hoots of the *Benji Bee* reaching back to the bight long after she had disappeared.

The weather had changed up at Borga. Intermittent gusts of wind lashed at the one finished hut. The three men were joined by Ginnie during a six-hour lull, enough for Giles to fit in the six-hundred-mile round flight. The team had to work without pause during such lulls, afraid that the next blow would undo any half-finished work. Fortunately the huts were light to move about and easy to erect. The heaviest bits, wooden floorboards, could be dragged into place even by Ginnie.

It seemed Simon and Anto worked well together, a good omen, perhaps, for their coming winter confinement down at Sanae. Simon wrote in his diary:

> On January 18th we began the main hut, the longest, and worked through the night and the next day in bitter cold, stiff mitts and icy balaclavas. There was a fire in the radio hut

because the stove was left on too high a setting. David discovered it just in time – a warning to us all. Blowing snow and misty all day. No ferry flights. The camp looks habitable and occupied. Nice to have started it from scratch. I think Ran credits Anto and myself with the bulk of it. The surrounding *nunataks,* especially Ryvingen which overhangs us, never cease to catch the eye. The ever-changing sun and clouds bring a new view every day. Sanae will seem dull and sordid after the clear crisp air here.

On January 25 the ice team left Sanae. Each Skidoo towed two laden sleds. The journey to Borga would zigzag between mountain ranges and crevasse fields. Although the magnetic compass was usable – the local error was only eighteen degrees – it had to be treated with care because the alcohol, cold and thick, made the needle sluggish. I soon developed the habit of double-checking its final lie and tapping it gently in case it had yet to settle true.

Each sled carried more than we would need for the 370-km journey – I planned to use the run as a rehearsal for the next year's crossing attempt. Not including the five full cans on the rear of our Skidoos, we towed twelve hundred pounds each.

Thirty-foot double ropes linked Skidoo to the lead sledge with a similar gap to the rear sledge. In principle any one of the three units could plunge into a crevasse but would soon be arrested by the halted weight of the other two. Of course going downhill or on slippery ice the principle might not work out too well if the Skidoo were to fall through first. There would be little benefit to a driver whose Skidoo dangled in an abyss anchored by its sledges if he himself carried on downward. So we each wore a mountaineer's harness with a line attached either to the Skidoo or to the lead sledge, depending on personal preference.

In the beginning there was only a flat, featureless whiteness; a good firm surface, and the machines ran well over the ice shelf. It was difficult to accept that all this ice *floated* on the ocean. Somewhere not far south we would have to cross the dreaded Hinge Zone, where this floating shelf became the Antarctic ice sheet – and then we would, for the first time, be truly on the Antarctic continent with rock beneath the ice under our feet.

This ice sheet covers all the land of Antarctica except for a few so-called dry valleys. Its size is 5,500,000 square miles, which dwarfs the United States. Seen from outer space it radiates light 'like a great white lantern across the bottom of the world', according to astronauts. The average depth of the sheet is six thousand feet. Were it to melt, every second person on earth would drown. These statistics, of course, did not occupy my thoughts as we approached the rim of the sheet – I concentrated on the nature of the Hinge Zone, its location and its crevasses.

Ninety kilometres from Sanae, whiteout conditions clamped down as we descended gently from the wide mound called Eskimo Icerise. We camped until two days later there was again brilliant sunshine in a robin's-egg-blue sky.

Back at Sanae, crevasses were opening. 'At night,' wrote our visiting cameraman, Bryn Campbell, 'we hear the bay ice breaking with the noise of a tank battle. A long fissure spreads from the western cliffs, still very narrow but hundreds of feet deep. Across the top of the bay a pencil-thin line breathes in and out. We agreed not to wander around on our own.'

That day we set out to cross the Hinge Zone using the South African map route. (A year later a group of twelve South African scientists did likewise. They lost two machines forever and a young scientist fell ninety feet and broke his neck. In 1981 at a British base further round the coast two scientists were killed in crevasses using Skidoos like our own. In 1982 three scientists from

Geoff Newman in our initial wolfskin clothing at minus 45°c

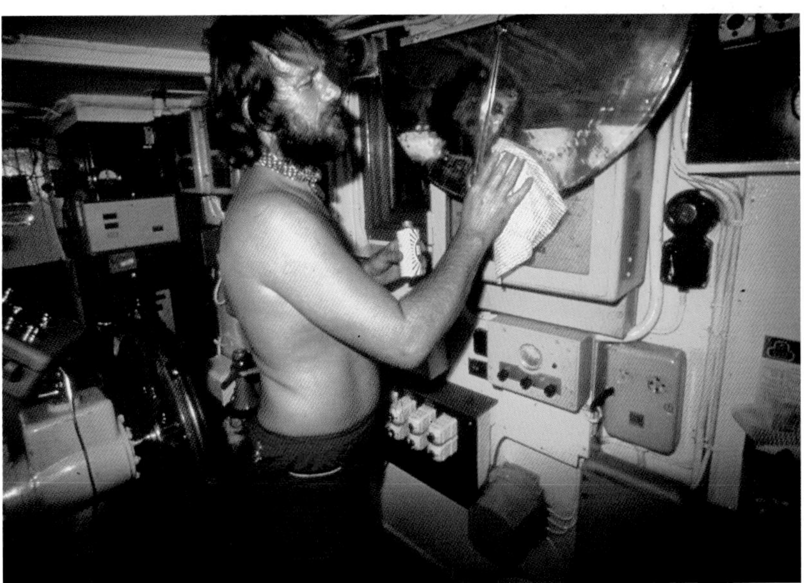

Dave Hicks polishes the inclinometer which was borrowed from Scott's ship *Discovery*. It tells the amount of roll from side to side in heavy seas

Oliver and Simon at a fuel stop in the Sahara

From L to R – Simon, Charlie and Oliver at a jungle camp in the Ivory Coast

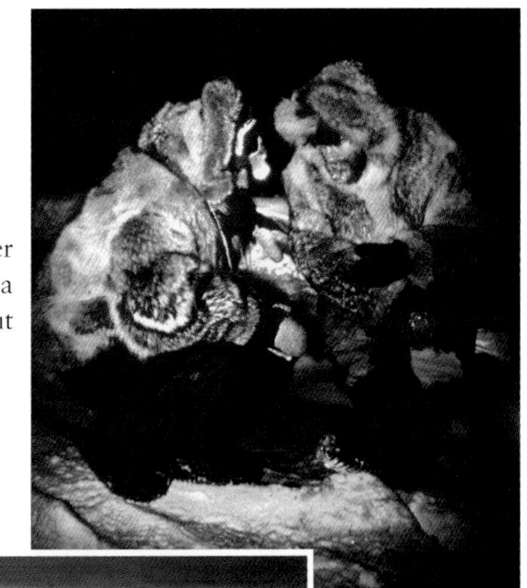

Oliver and Ran confer about food storage in a deep snow dugout

The *Benjamin Bowing* arrives at Sanae near the Greenwich Meridian

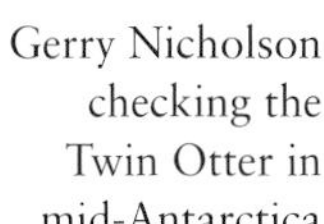

Gerry Nicholson checking the Twin Otter in mid-Antarctica

Simon erecting one of our cardboard Triwall huts. In the background is Ryvingen, the last known feature for hundreds of miles of unexplored polar plateau

The last mountains before the polar plateau

Simon and Ginny erect the 80 foot radio mast near Ryvingen

Charlie and his skidoo on the edge of a crevasse we located close to our camp

Oliver and Charlie check our sledge runners

Oliver and Bothie check out our improvised crevasse

Charlie watches Giles and Gerry leave Ryvingen for their long flight back to the UK

Bothie does not like his monthly wash

Soon after we begin the crossing of the polar plateau. We navigate by the sun and our local time

Pitching the tent in the polar gloom

Ginny's Morse code was incredibly fast

Oliver in the food tunnel at Ryvingen

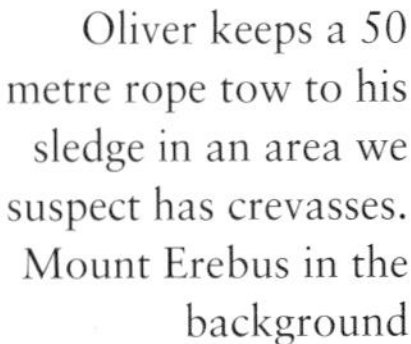

Oliver keeps a 50 metre rope tow to his sledge in an area we suspect has crevasses. Mount Erebus in the background

Our Nansen sledge being hauled over a sastrugi

Oliver in a field of mini sastrugi

Giles flies low after a supply drop of fuel and food

another British base disappeared along the coastal ice on a local patrol. The little expeditions of the eighties are studded with tragedies, as were those longer journeys of Shackleton, Mawson and Scott. Radios and aircraft do not, as modern armchair scoffers would have us believe, provide some magic safety screen.) I lined up the bearings of successful features, at first mere floating mirages, weird and distended but growing to distinctive shapes as we approached. All had Afrikaans names – Draaipunt, Valken and Dassielkop, or head of the rabbit – and each was isolated by many miles of moving ice.

Crevasses in this zone average six to nine metres wide and four to five kilometres long from north to south. Summer was well advanced and we could expect the drifted snow cover hiding the crevasses to be rotten and weak. But our Skidoos, unladen, weighed only seven hundred pounds and their rubber tracks spread the ground pressure to a mere .028 pounds per square inch, less than the foot of a dog or a man. The narrow runners of the heavy sledges were a different kettle of fish; they would break through more easily. To prevent this, speed seemed the best answer.

Warily we edged east toward the black mount of Marsteinen.

With no warning the Hinge was before us and beside us. A glint of undershadow a few yards ahead, green and sinister in its suddenness.

I accelerated, felt a lurch beneath me, then solid ice once more. More green lines left and right now. Head for the white. Forget what's happening to the sledges. Worry only about the Skidoo and yourself. Four or five within a hundred yards ... sweating as you tug the steering bars left, and left again, spot a new chasm and veer right, flinging the body weight sideway and forward to give more cutting edge to the steering ski.

Then a patch of firmness. I stopped and looked back, breathing hard.

My sledges had opened up craters. The worst place for the others would be in my tracks. Watching is worse than doing it yourself, I thought, any moment expecting to see one of the little jinking machines and its muffled human cargo disappear.

They stopped before reaching me. I had crossed to the solid place over a spit of snow, and I saw now that my sledge had broken the spit and a two-foot-wide green scar cut the others off from further progress. It seemed narrow enough to jump. Remembering my duty as cameraman I unloaded a 16-mm Bolex cine camera and moved to the edge of the crevasse. Ollie and Charlie watched from their side but did not stop me. (It was a foolish action – eleven months later a young man was to die in the same area through moving unroped over this spider's web of hidden cliffs.)

Only luck stopped me from plunging the height of St Paul's Cathedral. I was at first quite unaware of any danger, because I could see that the far lip of the crevasse was a sheer drop. Had I stopped to think, memories of crevasse photographs and diagrams would have warned me that my own side of the divide was likely to be no clean-cut right angle but a tapering overhang liable to collapse under pressure.

It was the monopod of the Bolex that probably saved me. I placed it a yard from the edge, and it sank unopposed through half a dozen inches of granular snow crust into thin air. My blood froze. I found myself shouting at the others, 'Why didn't you warn me, you bums?'

Their reply was a quantity of laughter muffled only by their face masks. How much they understood the seriousness of my predicament I never did find out. With the feeling I remembered so well from Arabia, treading where antipersonnel mines were suspected, I retreated as though barefoot on hot bricks. Once, one leg went down to the calf; I remained rigid, then picked it up and placed it with slow pressure elsewhere.

Sweating, I got back to firmer cover, and cursed myself as well as the others under my breath . . .

I did film their wild charge over the rift, but from a safe distance, which made for a boring film but a live cameraman. A matter of priorities.

That morning kept the adrenaline pumping and the eyes behind our goggles shifting rapidly as we advanced over the most broken of ice fields, and it was with a sense of relief that I swung southeast up the last steep climb to Marsteinen nunatak.

We were over the Hinge Zone, the first known obstacle behind us.

By sticking with care to the old South African route and travelling for fourteen hours we then reached the black-and-orange cliffs of Nalegga with their ridgelike needles; high sentinels of the horizon. All day the temperature remained around minus 28 degrees Centigrade, and with little wind, not at all unpleasant for travel. As new scenery unpeeled to the south and west great ranges hovered in mirage, pulsating images of levitated cathedrals and castles in the air. Jekeselen, Grunehogna, Sletfjellnutana and many an unnamed pinnacle. Deep windscoops like immense polished amphitheatres fell away to our flanks and hillocks of blue mirror-ice crowned fields of sastrugi in the katabatic wind lanes. Rocks of crazy shape lounged lone and menacing like druid megaliths, spawn of long-ago rockfalls on their willy-nilly way to the north and the sea.

We made camp under the shadow of Nalegga. Morale was high, the sledges handled with ease. The unspoken feeling was one of relief. Antarctica, it seemed, was an easy touch compared with the Arctic.

The first main climb was behind us . . . the ice sheet was five thousand feet above sea level at this point. A series of chunky nunataks guided us south and east out of the Sellkopffjella range;

then wide-open snowfields between flanking escarpments to the rocks of Skoddemedet, our penultimate goal.

As we rounded its southern wall the distant bulk of Ryvingen Mountain rose peak then shoulders into view until the whole impressive feature reared above the snows of the eastern horizon.

With binoculars we could see the little smudge of shadow at its base, our home for the coming winter.

Ginnie and Simon were hard at work; the huts were finished but a great deal remained to be done before the long months of darkness began.

Simon had been taught to erect radio masts. Using Charlie and me as his labour gang he mounted the ten-inch triangular sections one by one until he was eighty feet up tightening the last bolt. Ginnie then made up antennae, which we hoisted to the top.

Simon joined one of Giles's ferry flights down to Sanae so that he and Anto could settle in to their own winter camp. But the film crew, Bryn and David, were there too as the South African ship had delayed her departure back to Cape Town. On February 1, the day he returned to Sanae, Simon wrote:

> A great feeling of elation when we took off from Ryvingen but this subsided on getting back to our hut at Sanae. Damp, windy and despondent. Met by David Mason in a black mood and a silent Gerry. David painted a grey picture of what I would find and for once was not far wrong. Whole place in a shambles, squalid and depressing. The cargo lines broken up by odd ragged bits of kit scattered about and sticking up out of the ice. The hut, which the cameraman once described as 'your cosy little home' in a filthy condition. Dark and smelly inside, all the film crew on their bunks from which they apparently rarely stir, apart from Tony, who is embarrassed by it all. Just outside it's

like a battlefield; burned pots mark the site of our loo with muck, loo paper and slops all around the entrance. Anto is in a silent rage. I try to remain cheerful . . .

Two days later the crew, Bryn and David, left with the South African ice-breaker. So Simon and Anto began to clean up. 'When I lifted the stove,' Simon wrote, 'I found a deep-charred hole beneath. The drip valve and flue sections were also damaged. Very angry. If I see the crew again, they won't be welcome.'

Giles and Gerry finished the last of seventy-eight ferry flights on February 10. After a hot meal with us they took off and soon disappeared into the gathering dusk above the southern ice sheet. Next day the weather clamped down; whiteout and zero visibility. From now on we were alone. Should anyone be ill during the next eight months there could be no evacuation, no rescue in any shape or form and no medical assistance.

We had to handle batteries daily but also beware of acid in the eye. Extreme-cold burns, fuel burns, deep electrical burns, appendix rumbles, serious tooth trouble – all such hazards had to be avoided.

Temperatures would plunge to minus 50 degrees and below. Winds would exceed ninety miles per hour. The absolute wind-chill factor would reach minus 120 degrees Fahrenheit. For two hundred and forty days we had to live with these conditions, or not live at all.

Chapter Six

Silence is a great peacemaker.

HENRY WADSWORTH LONGFELLOW

This is not a geographical treatise, but a few impressive facts about Antarctica are worth mentioning. It is bigger than Europe or India and China together, than the USA and Mexico combined, far larger than Australia. Yet 99 percent of this huge tract of land is buried unseen beneath an ice sheet with an average depth of 1½ kilometres; in places, well over 4 kilometres. This massive weight of ice actually crushes the landmass downward by some two thousand feet so that it is largely *below* sea level. If all the ice were to melt, the world's sea level would rise by three hundred feet. Mountain peaks rise to 16,000 feet above sea level; those along the Antarctic peninsula are linked under the Atlantic to the Andes.

Although our winter was to pass in a world as lifeless and alien as a dead planet, Antarctica was not always so. Three hundred and fifty million years ago there was life of a sort, worms and scorpions for instance, on the polar plateau. Then the temperature dropped and an ice cap closed over the land. Some eighty million years later this ice cap receded leaving a marshy terrain with meandering rivers and peatbeds that later became coal seams ... Two hundred and twenty-five million years ago there were forests of giant horsetails and shrublike ferns roamed by reptiles that grazed on the luxuriant foliage and provided meat for smaller fish-eating reptiles. A jolly society ... Two hundred million years ago Australasia, Antarctica and India were all joined up and formed Gondwanaland – named after the Gonds, an Indian tribe. The Continental Drift theory reckons that one hundred and ninety million years ago Gondwanaland broke up and the bits drifted apart. For fifty million years the Antarctic 'bit' was riven by volcanic eruptions. Geological information then becomes scarce, but there was probably no major change. Because it is so cold the air holds little moisture – Antarctica can be called the largest cold desert in the world.

The very coldness and remoteness make exploitation of minerals unrealistically costly. Neither Sir Vivian Fuchs nor Dr Armand Hammer feel there is much chance of oil or mining companies showing more than superficial interest in the foreseeable future. This is excellent, since Antarctica is surely the last untainted wilderness which man has yet to despoil.

We were quickly impressed by the power of the wind. The long lines of fuel, equipment, food and Skidoos were soon hidden by drifts. Marker flags blew away, and I decided everything but the fuel must come inside. The huts were already too cramped to use for storage so I excavated tunnels. Hut doors unprotected by foyers were quickly blocked up and 'leaked' at the edges, where a spray of superfine snow blasted through; to stop this, sticky tape was applied to all cracks and only one door per hut was used, not for direct access to the elements but into ice tunnels.

Ginnie's radio-hut foyer was a circular yard covered with a parachute. This was never satisfactory for long since snow weighed the material down and tore it. I had to replace the chutes once every two or three months. Ginnie refused my offers of a snow-tunnel foyer on the grounds it would be claustrophobic in her daily workplace. (This was to prove extremely fortunate.) Her remote VLF hut, however, had a small ice foyer that could only be entered via an empty forty-five-gallon drum with top and bottom sawn off and a removable hatch; a short ladder leaned against the drum's bottom but access was awkward, especially carrying heavy twelve-volt acid batteries.

Ollie built a thirty-foot-long tunnel down to his garage door. This turned corners, was narrow, low and furnished with metal struts which caught you on the cranium unless you kneeled downward with great caution. The pharaohs would have paid Ollie a princely sum as a pyramid entry-system engineer.

The tunnels leading to the only door of our main hut had three escape hatches, two of which were ice staircases with canvas trapdoors and one a high drum with a stepladder dangling from it. It was sensible to learn how to negotiate these tunnels in the dark and in a hurry. We all knew what had happened to eight Russians the previous year whose hut had caught fire. Their bodies were found in an egress tunnel; all had died from asphyxiation. Presumably they'd failed to find their escape hatches in the dark ... I remembered a three-week BBC-sponsored expedition through London's underground sewers when our navigator, a seventy-year-old sewer officer named Alf, led us down brickwork tunnels of magnificent Gothic arches. All walls were peppered gorgonzola-wise with pipes which periodically gushed effluent into the main artery. Alf knew every bend: once a pipe by a tunnel Y-junction produced a brief but pretty waterfall and Alf stopped to glance at his watch. 'Eleven-thirty sharp,' he announced, 'that'll be the French ambassador.' He had been down there on and off since the Second World War, and many a time his intimate knowledge of the network allowed him to escape alive from sudden flash floods . . . After three or four months we too were able to move through the tunnels and locate our hatches in the dark. But fire remained an ever-present fear.

The main tunnels took me two months to excavate. They included a lavatory cubicle that stayed around minus 31 degrees Fahrenheit throughout the winter. It was good to get away from the others and to meditate for a while; a fairly short while since although your backside freezes far more slowly than your extremities, it does still freeze if you expose it for long enough. By the end of March the tunnels were two hundred yards long, and every item we possessed was in them. By pouring kerosene into a small hole in the middle of the tunnel system and igniting it with burning rags I ended up after three days with a thirty-foot-deep slop pit. Cleaner slops, like dishwashing water, I threw over the snow platforms, steps and walkways in the tunnels to turn them to ice: we called the result 'permaslop'.

One day, running short of nails, we decided to visit the old South African base below Huldreslottet Mountain some eleven miles west of our camp. Bothy could not be left alone, Ginnie said, so she put him in a rucksack. I had an old photo of the buried entrance shaft but an hour's fruitless digging revealed only a box-hut. We retrieved some nails, mostly bent, and as it was late in the day, headed back east. On the way Charlie took a steep hill at a sharp angle; his sledge overtook his Skidoo and overturned. Rolling it back he noticed on each side that five out of eight upright steel tubes, the supports between runners and platform, had fractured. I checked mine and found it similarly broken. Ollie's was not. Further inspection revealed that the platforms themselves were slightly buckled.

The unpleasant truth slowly dawned that the crossing journey to the Pole was now at risk. I had consigned two spare wooden sledges to Borga purely as camp workhorses, but no spare steel sledges because after their success during our Arctic training I considered them unbreakable. My error was in concluding that the twelve-foot nine-inch Antarctic models, being exactly similar in every respect but length to the eight-foot six-inch Arctic models, would prove equally tough. In normal circumstances perhaps they would have, but I had foolishly allowed the ship's unloading team to use them for transporting fuel drums inland, often three at a time. There were bigger wooden sledges for that purpose but I had thought to speed things up. There was no point in crying over spilled milk, though, so I resolved to repair the bars later in the winter . . .

With the tunnels finished we began to train in the valleys around the camp, which seemed to be crevasse-free.

Ollie unpacked his ice drill and excavated core samples from the surface to a depth of ten metres. He was to do this at each degree of latitude during our crossing.

Since neither he nor Charlie were practised in cross-country skiing I laid out a half-mile ski-track circuit, and after some initial instruction they trained on it daily and later around the Ryvingen plateau.

In early March we started towing Pulka man-hauled sledges (pulks) for increasing distances. If we ever crossed Antarctica the day would come when we would have to pull our own sledges over mountains where no Skidoo could go. Our last chance to master the art was here in Borga before the sun disappeared.

Human beings are not ideally designed for getting on with each other – especially in close quarters. Shut two of them up together for any length of time in a situation of stress and, more often than not, you have fireworks. They react by wanting to escape. On many expeditions there is no way out, no means of transport, so a situation of forced togetherness exists that breeds dissension and often hatred between individuals or groups.

Although the four of us had worked together on and off for four years, the relationships between us were undergoing constant changes. New sets of physical circumstances bring on different reactions. A personal fear of crevasses, for example, might simmer for many months in one person and not in the others. The introduction of third parties from time to time to our company could cause upsets between us, but of course this did not happen during the Borga winter. Temporary illnesses or passing moods might make one of us sensitive and morose while another might experience a temporary high. Enough to make sparks fly.

There was a clean divergence within our little team. Ollie said, 'Charlie is similar to myself. I am much closer to Charlie than Ran. Ran leads the expedition and as a leader has to be slightly offset. Charlie is like myself, likes enjoying himself.' Ginnie and I, since the tantrums of honeymoon and early marriage, had grown into an easy relationship that gave us both the invaluable knowledge that we each had one totally loyal ally who would *never* be disparaging behind the other's back. Charlie and Ollie were good enough friends to trust one another similarly, which tended to produce two units that understood and respected each other's strengths and peculiarities.

In this way we avoided the unspoken fear of betrayal that makes for suspicion and aggressive isolation. If you didn't have to worry whether *your* friend was working behind your back or moving his or her allegiance to the other camp you could stay free and easy, and the general atmosphere reflected this. Very important in such close confines where any slight shift in the atmosphere was felt without a word being spoken. During that winter word was spread among some of Ollie's and Charlie's acquaintances in

London that we were all engaged in hostilities, even 'knife fights' in our cardboard camp. Luckily, far from physical punch-ups, we actually experienced less verbal hostility than most marriages contend with in a similar time period with far less cramped conditions.

Apprehension of what lay ahead may well have affected us without our knowing it. The strain was there and every now and again it burst to the surface. Our grouping was a great help. When I felt positive hatred for Charlie or Ollie for some petty reason I could either wax virulent to Ginnie or else spit out vicious prose in my diary. The next day or even hour I might feel quite different about the earlier object of my loathing and wonder how on earth I could have put such abuse on paper. Ollie and Charlie doubtless used the same vent-holes for their dislikes and frustrations.

Sometimes minor injuries affected our moods. For a while Ollie could not lift his left arm above shoulder level without shooting pains. One morning, after a bad night, when approached by Ginnie to start up a generator he reacted with unaccustomed spleen, asking her why Charlie, who had less to do, could not do it.

And down at the Sanae camp our two friends had their own moods to cope with. Simon's diary recorded:

> Working silently in a temper. Every movement Anto makes is a desperate irritation when I'm mad. I suppose because there's nothing else to vent my feelings on. Grit my teeth and work on in angry silence. Good mood and good relations return if nothing said. – And again: – We visit the South Africans on the Skidoos. Anto would not keep level despite the bad visibility. Infuriated but I kept quiet ... he was very cold with painful hands and groggy on arrival. I left him in their power-shed to dry. One topic which is taboo here is apartheid. There is a mixture of two types – the extreme left-wing British commies (as the others

call them) and the extreme right-wing Dutch farmer types . . . I wouldn't choose to winter in isolation with one person again . . .

Bothy's presence, I suspect, was a helpful diversion, despite the fact that he continued to leave his signature where it was not wanted and, as camp cleaner, it was my daily job to remove these frozen offerings. To teach him that 'outside' did not mean the tunnels but the open air outside the tunnels proved beyond me, and Barbara Woodhouse was not available for advice. Ginnie didn't want him in her radio shack while there were bare electric wires all over the place. Later, when the shed was ready she took him there daily except during blizzards when she needed both hands free for the safety line to reach the hut. Bothy could not, in such conditions, be allowed out unless on a lead. He would quickly get disoriented and die within minutes, as we would if it wasn't for the safety lines from hut to hut.

Much of the time Bothy had to be left in the warmth of the main hut. Ollie, with meteorological reports to make every six hours (the job of three men in most polar bases) and three generators to maintain, was usually at work in the garage. My own time was largely spent in the tunnels and around the camp with shovel and hand sledge. So Charlie, whose main job was cooking, was often alone except for Bothy. In his diary he complained that Ginnie had brought the dog all the way out and that now he had to look after him. Actually I think he liked the dog's companionship. They certainly spent hours playing together, mainly with rubber balls, which Bothy was adept at catching and 'throwing' back.

I had erected the pyramid tent we would use for the crossing and found two guy-ropes broken and one of the four ten-foot metal legs buckled. The tent was the finest available, used by the British

Antarctic Survey as well as other governments operating scientific field parties in the south, but the BAS had warned me that katabatic winds could tear away even a three-man pyramid tent; indeed, over the past few years they had lost whole field survey teams through this alone.

The weather closed in along with the fast-fading sunlight. By May 2 the temperature had dropped to minus 41.6 degrees with a thirty knot wind. The wind chill factor – in other words, the temperature experienced by our skin – was minus 110 degrees Fahrenheit.

Oliver had set up an anemometer that recorded wind speed and direction. The mast was beside the garage, and cables ran beneath the snow to read out instruments in Ollie's end of our shack. Knife-cold katabatic winds poured off the polar plateau, gaining velocity as the land dropped through five thousand feet, until they slammed against the very first obstruction, our little cardboard camp beside Ryvingen Mountain. We were partially protected from the southeast winds but not from the southwesterlies. With the latter, our cardboard life became a distinct problem. I found it difficult to do any job over and above keeping the camp running safely. Ollie had a similar struggle with his generators as the carbon monoxide exhaust fumes blew back into his hut. At such times Ginnie, however busy she was, had no help from me or the others.

The gusts would hit us with no warning. One minute Ollie's anemometer would read absolute zero and there would be a deathly silence. The next, the hut shuddered as though from a bomb blast as eighty-mile-an-hour winds from the high ice fields struck us.

Visiting the VLF hut one morning I was knocked flat by a gust although a second earlier there was not a zephyr of wind. A moment later, trying to get up, I was struck on the back by the plastic windshield from my parked Skidoo. Ripped off from the cowling, I never found it again. An empty forty-five-gallon drum that Ginnie had placed at the base of the eighty-foot mast disappeared altogether, and the camp haulage sledge which weighed three hundred pounds, was blown sixty yards and deposited upside-down. Ginnie's parachute 'porch' also tore apart, and two tons of snow blocked her doorway. Safety lines were vital in these conditions, even between huts fifty yards from each other.

I once went out from the tunnel end with Charlie intending to help him with some job along the outer wall of the main hut. We got separated. Once clear of the tunnel there was nothing but the wind. The whole world was the wind. Only by concentrating every faculty could I move against it in the right direction. Whiteout conditions were complete. I lost the safety line and was at once totally lost, totally confused. There was no point in opening my eyes to windward – sharp spicules of blown snow blew horizontally at eighto knots. I tripped over and felt a fuel drum. By the angle at which it and those beside it were stacked I at least knew the direction of the hut some thirty paces away. I aimed at the middle of the hut, and with huge relief walked right into it at a point where the snow had not yet drifted over the roof. Carefully I edged along the hut until I bumped into Charlie. He had only just reached the snow hatchway after a similar experience. Had either of us walked a touch further left or right and missed the fuel drums we might well have wandered about disoriented for as long as it took to freeze; not very long, I suspect.

At other times spirals of snow, some forty feet high like sand devils, whirled across our plateau, struck the camp briefly then raced on to disappear down distant valleys. These spirals sometimes united into great moving fronts of whiteness that bore down upon us to claw at the huts, shriek hideously through the radio masts and suck away any item left unanchored on the surface. When it was black and moonless these plateau storms were truly unnerving.

Even inside the hut conversation died when the heavy roar shook our fragile walls and the floor panels creaked as though about to take off. Even the tiniest hole or crack was sought out by the fine powder snow blown by such winds. A keyhole left untaped would permit a pencil-thin jet which, given time, could fill a room to its own level.

I spent hours each day shovelling entrances and porches clear, ensuring that escape hatches were free and burning rubbish in pits from which it could not blow away. My first tunnel slop-pit was close to the entrance and beneath a drum escape hatch. One evening a bad storm half-blocked the entrance. Ollie emerged through the howling gloom and found me shovelling at the entry hole. He made off toward the drum hatch intending to climb down from it on the dangling ladder. Just in time I remembered there was a kerosene fire raging inside the ten-foot-deep slop-pit immediately below the drum hatch. I rushed out into the blizzard, hurried along the relevant safety line and got to Ollie just as he had lowered himself half into the drum – in his duvet jacket, he would have fried like an unplucked chicken . . .

The worst risk we faced was from fires. Our stoves worked simply on a gravity drip-feed system. The amount of heat radiated depended on the amount of kerosene you allowed to flow into the 'burning bowl' at the stove's base. Any sudden down-draft entering the stove's metal chimney could put out the flame, and within minutes the hut's temperature would be down in the minus twenties, at which time work, especially in the radio shack, became, to put it mildly, difficult.

I spent hours modifying chimney stacks and vents with little success. One forty-five-gallon drum screwed into a stove's drip-feed pipe gave it fuel for only eleven days. The drum tops became iced over as they lay in the fuel lines. Each week I dug three or four out – diesel and petrol for Ollie's shack; kerosene for the radio and main huts. In poor conditions with no light I made an occasional error, once screwing a gasoline drum into Ginnie's kerosene drip-feed system. The results were spectacular, but luckily Ginnie was inside at the time and applied a fire extinguisher before the whole hut went up in a ball of flame. We also used smaller wick heaters, but these had their own hazards – not fire but soot. If the wick was not trimmed correctly or was left burning after the fuel ran out, black soot was deposited in layers over every item in the hut, greasy soot which smeared and contaminated.

When southwesterly winds prevailed at the same time that Ginnie needed Ollie's biggest generator, a ten-kva diesel, to power her one-kilowatt radio, then his worst problems began. With wind from that quarter he could not open either door, because the garage would fill with snow. The diesel generator put out a great deal of heat and had to be closely watched while operating since it was faulty. With temperatures of minus 50 degrees Fahrenheit outside Ollie would sit naked in his shack with sweat pouring off him, counting every minute until Ginnie's call was over and he could stop the generator.

We all slept on boards along the apex of the roof. At night we turned our stove low to save fuel. At floor level the temperatures dropped to minus 15 degrees Centigrade, and at bed level, eighty feet up, about 2 degrees Centigrade. On nights the wind blew our stoves out, it was quite nippy in bed.

On their separate bed-platform Ollie and Charlie had room for clothes, books and a mug of coffee. Ginnie and I had no spare room but we did have the advantage of each other's company. The other two never openly objected to their lack of female companionship but it may, I suppose, have become an unspoken source of friction had not the four of us worked together as a group for so long beforehand.

Since early April many nights were lit by a carnival of aurorae, ribbons of iridescent green or white that snaked in subtle patterns from horizon to horizon. On moonless nights the stars were close and brilliant.

I talk of night or day but in reality there was only moonlight or pitch darkness. None of us seemed to mind this any more than, in summer, the equal oddity of permanent daylight.

At minus 40 degrees Fahrenheit with no wind, navigation practice was a pleasure. Normally I shot Nunki, the lead star of Sagittarius which trailed behind the seahorse shape of Scorpius. Also Syrius or Canopus and Spica, an old favourite from the Northern Hemisphere . . .

Before the last few hours of sunlight left the plateau we set out for a peak named Brapiggen. The journey was to be the last of our ski-training runs some eight kilometres either way. We carried between us a seventy-pound rucksack and two pulk sledges with two hundred-pound loads. There was no wind as we left. Our breath rose in personal haloes lit through by orange autumn sun.

At the foot of Brapiggen we stopped to eat chocolate, shift rope traces from bruised shoulders and generally savour the personal pleasure of a hard struggle well-won. I did notice that Ollie lagged far behind Charlie but thought nothing of it; Charlie was usually able to plod faster than Ol when carrying or towing heavy weights.

We all wore cross-country skis with sealskin strips for uphill grip. On the return journey the leather thongs began to work loose and our hands were too numb with the cold to readjust the skins tightly. Progress slowed. A snow scurry I'd noticed at the base of Ryvingen developed into a local windstorm. The sledges by now felt heavy as millstones. I also felt frostnip cracking at my wrists, neck and hips where gaps between garments allowed the wind to rip away my body heat. Windburn blisters would, I knew, grow in these places.

With four miles to go I entered the storm belt and at once lost sight of the others. Although I could see nothing at all ahead, not even the tips of my skis, the disembodied peak of Ryvingen, pink from the sun, remained visible above the surface storm. A steep brow lay ahead – and at its base I bumped into Charlie. One of his cheeks was blistered, his hands were numb. Together we hauled my sledge with its tent, stove and safety gear to the ridge of the rise as dusk fell. Another hour or so would see us both as rigid as deep-frozen meat. Ollie, who carried a tent and cooker, would have to look after himself.

By the time we saw the beam of a powerful lantern Ginnie had placed by the tunnel entrance, neither of us was talking clearly. Ginnie looked worried but said nothing and gave us hot soup . . . Ollie appeared forty-five minutes later, his face bloated with frost-nip. Realising his danger he had abandoned his sledge at the foot of Brapiggen and struggled back with lifeless hands. The last hour of dark groping had worried him as much as it did the rest of us.

For a week or two we wandered about blistered like boxers feeling tender after a rough bout. Ollie and Charlie, who had the most unpleasant blisters, took Batrim broad-spectrum antibiotics for a week, after which their sores stopped weeping and more or less settled down.

But the experience made it obvious that clothes acceptable for use on Skidoos were not ideal for man-hauling. My own homemade balaclava had a small mouth-hole that was adequate for Skidoo use. Skiing in the storm I breathed hungrily and, unable to suck in enough air through the small frozen hole, I had to tear the balaclava's face flap down and in the process got frostnipped lips. Also, despite my windproof neck extension, skiing caused movement and allowed wind to enter above the jacket top. A seven-inch long, one-inch wide band of frostnip, red and tender, rose below my Adam's apple. Goggles misted quickly. Since as navigator I badly needed to see clearly, I removed the goggles, but the liquid in my windward eye started to congeal. When I closed it, the eyelashes quickly became sealed with ice. Fortunately we had time to alter our face-masks to cope with these problems of man-hauling in such conditions.

Now the polar darkness closed in for good and we made no more sorties.

After weeks of work laying cables, cutting antennae and trying them out at different frequencies, Ginnie achieved clear communication with Cove Radio Station and with Portishead Marine Radio Station in the southwest of England. They were able to connect her with any telephone subscriber in the world, given a period when the ionosphere suited a given frequency. Since no one who knew our whereabouts would expect us to telephone them we decided to use this to our advantage for April 1.

I phoned Andrew Croft using a German accent (the operator kindly announced a long-distance call from Hamburg) and greeted him as an ex-Wehrmacht colonel who had been involved in the same work but on the other side during the Second World War. I invited him to lunch at London's Savoy Hotel on April 1. He accepted ... George Greenfield and the foreign editor of the *Observer* were both phoned from Kabul in Afghanistan by a Scottish journalist with a scoop about the Russian campaign there. They separately agreed to meet him at the Savoy ... Ant Preston was offered an attractive job by a London magnate, and Ollie, as a Greek shipowner, invited two others along ... At 12:30 P.M. on April Fool's Day the various guests turned up in the lobby of the Savoy to meet their unknown hosts. They ended up well and truly fooled but mollified by lunch together as the guests of Ollie's elder brother, who happened to be the managing director of the hotel. Back in Borga, with homemade raisin beer, we drank a toast to the longest distance April Fools in history.

*

All communications at Borga involved basic cooperation between Ollie providing the power from his little generators and Ginnie the transceivers and know-how. Ginnie's technical expertise was nil, on a par with that of any normal housewife. But necessity, and a few visits to Racal, the manufacturers of all her radio gear, plus an above-average helping of common sense and determination, allowed her to cope when things went wrong. She was modest about her ability, but the chief at Cove was not. He described her as an 'amazing communicator'.

As winter set in, coatings of ice built up on the various antennae increasing their diameter from one-eighth of an inch to well over one inch and their weight correspondingly. This broke loose terminals, and the eighty- to ninety-knot winds tore two-foot metal screws from their snow beds, allowing the antennae to blow free, wrap themselves around the mast and its guys and in places become buried in new snowdrifts.

With a torch in her mouth Ginnie struggled around in the blizzards unravelling wires, soldering connections and carefully digging up ice-caked antennae that tended to break easily. Since more snow flew in as she dug, she took two days to excavate a twenty-foot-long, four-foot-deep trench in which to bury cable. To improve the transmission of her main V-antenna she cut sixteen twenty-one-foot copper radials and laid them out at the two ends of the V and connected by resistors to create a false earth. How effective the ice sheet itself was for an earth remained open to debate.

Ginnie was often overtired. Her work involved long hours outside in the dark after storms, and she began to get nervous. And with it suggestible ... In late May Ollie mentioned casually that he'd heard footsteps following him from the generator hut to the tunnel entrance. He called it his imagination. Not long afterward I noted in my diary, 'Last night Ginnie's stomach pains were bad and she went down the tunnel to the loo with a torch. When she came back shivering she said, "There's something there." I remonstrated but she insisted. "I don't mean a danger but ... a *strong* presence." "Nobody ever lived here before," I said. "Giles has stories of Hitler's air force dropping metal swastikas on the rock features to claim the terrain, but even that's probably baloney."

For a while there were no further 'happenings', but during a June storm she felt 'it' again. 'This time it came round behind the radio shack and followed me back down the tunnel,' Ginnie said. But she saw and heard nothing ...

Meanwhile down at Sanae ... Simon was to record:

> This morning we failed to start the Skidoo despite two hours' work in a growing windstorm. The South Africans contacted the American radio operator at South Pole base and mentioned the proposed Transglobe crossing. It seems none of the Americans knew anything about us. Now they do. No idea what political repercussions there will be. The shit is stirred and we are in a temporarily safe backwater. The enormity of what we are all trying to do still hasn't sunk in.

Ginnie also wrote up a little broadsheet called the Ryvingen *Observer,* which summarised the BBC world news. On May 6, bodies of U.S. airmen were flown out of Iran following an abortive attempt to rescue the hostages. Tito's funeral was discussed. One hundred demonstrating Afghanis were shot by helicopters over Kabul. SAS soldiers killed half a dozen terrorists at the Iranian embassy in London. The food in British motorway cafés was summed up as greasy and tasteless.

*

Early in June my back began to pain me, as though bruised at the base of the spine. Very few positions were easy other than lying down. Ollie as medic was naturally concerned, and at breakfast one morning he told me his usual weekly fuel needs but added, 'Since your back's bad you can hardly roll drums around. Let me collect the drums for you.'

'Rubbish,' I snapped. 'I'm quite capable of moving the drums myself.' As I left the room I regretted my senseless pride and rudeness. It was to Ollie's credit that he didn't blow a gasket at my behaviour. In his diary that night he simply wrote: 'Ran's back is bad so I offered to help him with fuel. He is so stubborn he won't accept any help over his drums. As far as I am concerned he can look after his own medical and dental problems from now on.' One could hardly take exception to his annoyance.

There were, of course, good and bad days as the endless roar of the wind, the lash of the driven snow and, above all, the uninterrupted polar night ensnared us all in our pettiness, making mountains out of the smallest molehills. Gradually our focus became more introverted, more tied up with our separate egos and reactions to the most trivial matters.

Here is a mixed bag of excerpts from my diary at the time:

> My lumbago pains were worse today, can't even bend without pain in the leg. Slightly late for breakfast. As the eggs have gone off I added horseradish and salt to them. Ugh! The fried bread is full of the filthy taste of the bad fat we nicked from the old Borga base. Still, the cup of tea and Charlie's bread is great, even though the margarine is ten years old . . . Ollie cut Charlie's hair today. He also poured warm oil down his own ears to clean them out. He thinks he's going deaf. At supper he wears a red pile suit streaked with oil smears. Bothy gets randy and clasps Ollie's legs. Ollie tries to shake him off but Charlie guffaws and encourages

the dog ... Tonight Charlie began the Hobbit books for the third time round. His cheese and ham flans are excellent but Ollie's home-fermented apple-flake beer is disgusting ... Ginnie says Ol has been behaving oddly of late and is easily irritable. I took some piping to his garage this morning to crush it in his vice. When I came out I felt lightheaded and a touch sick. The CO fumes are strong down there on days like today when the wind's from 110 degrees. I went down again an hour ago to see if Ol was okay. He seemed fine. But perhaps the continued inhalations are affecting his mood. If so, it should clear up when we depart ... Today Ollie passed out in the garage but luckily came to and groped his way out. He has a filthy headache. As a result of the shock, he has given us all a tour of the garage and generator workings so we can cope if he should come to grief ... This evening I ran into Ol staggering down the tunnel. His face was pale and he slurred his words. He told me he'd sat down for a bit in the garage to have a smoke and noticed that his hands were twitching. Getting up with difficulty, his legs felt leaden and he nearly collapsed in the garage tunnel ... Ginnie is cross and says Ol is rude and pompous. She feels he doesn't appreciate how hard she tries to make contact with Portishead radio to get telephone contact with Rebecca for him.

And that same day Ollie wrote: 'Everyone, except Charles, is very bad-tempered so I'll just stop talking.'

Down at Sanae, Simon and Anto coexisted. To meet them and listen to them you would think all was idyllic. But, as with our own problems, they let off some steam on paper. Simon did, anyway:

March 18th. Am increasingly annoyed by the existence of Anto. Grit my teeth and curse silently. Went out alone for solitude.

Then back to absorb myself in cooking and once more to accept Anto's presence ... April 17th: Anto getting on my nerves, just sits at his desk reading. I sat in the lee of the garage skylight drum in a filthy temper. It passed ... May 10th: My emotions going from one extreme to another. Anto's presence, his teeth chomping as he eats, his silent book-bound presence exasperates me at times, the symptoms of cabin fever ... His current maddening trick is to put pans of water on and being deaf, which he admits to, to leave them boiling. He's got the idea, though, because I slam them onto the floor if I have to cross the hut and take them off. Watching him fiddle with tape recorder leads, it dawned on me that he is big, brawny and thick. A philosopher maybe but nearly as impractical as the Borga crew. Maybe the world needs people who aren't as practical and efficient but a few of them help things tick over ... Anto's annoying habits are getting to me again. Cabin fever symptoms. I see them, diagnose them and hope I can keep them under control. I *know* my reactions to trivia are irrational, I know *why*, yet I can see how they could drive me to verbal or physical violence. Like nitrogen narcosis, once it's arrived you know it but can't back out without a sudden change of environment or shock stimulus. I think the anti-Borga attitude that prevails is a good thing, a temporary *bête noire* to give us an external focus for irritation.

Anto kept no diary but noted his feelings – for the most part not recognisable, I suspect, to Simon – toward the end of the winter:

The base is small with no space to escape to. So we live at close quarters which is bound to be slightly testing with just two of us. When cut off with only one companion there is a tendency to share everything or to maintain extreme reserve and keep the option of developing a relationship. We opted for the latter course by tacit agreement. The base worked well and we lived our own lives in our own areas of the hut. Strong demarcation developed over jobs and spaces and we rarely met except over supper, a radio schedule or a job that required both of us. This was a successful and amicable arrangement but would probably have been very different but for the South African base ten miles away. We went there about once a month and the extra dimension of living space and human contact helped greatly in enabling us to lead such independent lives within the same hut. Our relations were never more than momentarily strained.

The anti-Borga attitude that Simon mentioned does not come over strongly with Anto although he did once mention in a letter home: 'We are fortunately far enough away from Ran's reach to be having a delightfully peaceful time by the sea.'

Reading Simon's diary I wonder how on earth we, the Borga gang, ever managed to reach Antarctica, let alone spend a winter there. His comments at random during 'the dark period':

I told Ollie on the radio how to make up a honey-whisky-lemon drink for Ginnie's birthday but he says they only have honey left. Lack of self-control, lack of stock-taking, lack of interest or lack of competence. Whatever it is the mind boggles . . . It is hard to believe they have finished all their frozen meat but knowing the improvidence of that lot, anything is possible . . . Borga has nothing for us which is good . . . I am glad I am not at Borga. I think the inefficiency would drive me mad. They are planning to send such things as meteorological items on the critical transpolar flight next spring. I tried to suggest that if weight was critical things like the meteorological records should not be included. Ollie threw one of his got-to tantrums so I didn't argue. My general impressions are at Borga the Gang of Four, à la Mao, is

> grossly inefficient with Ran doing three men's work, half of it unnecessary ... Spoke to Ol and told him the various things we've done to the Skidoo here which he said only needed a new drive axle. It's like talking to a brick wall; he's obtuse and incurably dog-in-the-manger over tools ... Up at Borga they appear to spend the winter breaking stuff while we spend it repairing and making things ... Trying to teach Ol the basics of pressure/height variations for use during the crossing journey is very frustrating. He hasn't the slightest grasp of the fundamentals. I've stopped thinking how to help and just verbally agree that his method is okay. I despair of Ol even establishing a decent arbitrary datum on rock at Ryvingen ... Am reading a polar book by Paul-Emile Victor. He summarises Nansen's equipment as chosen and designed for lightness, simplicity and efficiency. Shackleton I respect but Nansen is a man after my own heart. Our ice group could learn a lot from him but I'm sure they won't ...

Simon and Anto often held long discussions with the South Africans. All agreed that the Land Group of the Transglobers could be split up into officer types, NCOs/good troops and those that didn't give a damn for rank. Simon wrote:

> Ran and David fall into the first lot; Ollie, Charlie and Gerry into the second and the rest of us into the third. Ginnie's personal relationship with Ran makes it impossible to categorise her so simply. David took a rather cavalier attitude to camp life before he left. He certainly worked hard but on things he wanted to do. Such things as washing-up didn't enter his mind. This went down badly with Gerry, who was very domesticated. Anto and I, had we worried about it, would have told David he was an idle bugger. Gerry seemed inhibited by David's 'rank', treated him

> with the reserve that he would have given a serving officer. We anticipate trouble if David and Gerry have to spend much time together next summer . . .

The dark days flew by. I began to cherish our crude but relatively peaceful existence with its beguiling simplicity. At the same time I felt subtle tremors of apprehension when on moonlit days the bald white scars of the Penck escarpment rose livid through the silvered distance to the south. With each month that slipped past, my stomach turned as it once used to during school holidays when the next dreaded term-time approached . . .

In Antarctica Christmas is no great feast day. Instead, Midwinter's Day, July 21, is celebrated fiercely in every lonely base camp by the seven hundred and fifty men and handful of women from a dozen nations who form the transitory population of the vast continent. Radio messages of fraternal greetings zing back and forth, the state of the ionosphere permitting, between the multinational scientists, all of whom feel the same joy that the longest night is over and the sun is on its way back. Most bases were ignorant of our existence, but those with wide-eared radio operators knew and sent us greetings – the Japanese, the South Africans, the British.

Ollie laid the table with our SAS flag, made napkins from meteorological report paper and produced a secret bottle of white wine with which we toasted our patron and the crew of the *Benji Bee*. Harmony ruled at Borga. But not for long.

Benjamin Franklin once said, 'Anger is never without a reason but seldom with a good one.' The mini-euphoria of Midwinter was soon dispersed. Reality was, after all, another three months of darkness and blizzard even if the sun was slowly, imperceptibly, climbing our way.

Raging snowstorms ripped through the camp one after another, week after week. Continued shovelling kept the entrances free and, in Ol's case, the generators operating. Then the diesel generator, our main workhorse, went out, and Ol found a hole the size of a silver dollar in the crankcase. This was beyond his means of repair so he moved it to one side to make more room. Charlie and I helped him tug the heavy machine over the plywood floorboards. Suddenly he said he felt uneasy and went outside.

We heard a shout. I rushed out. Ol shined a flashlight under the hut, and gaping at us was a cavity some fifteen feet deep, and wide as one-third of the hut itself. The exhaust pipe from the diesel had for months eaten away at the snow, and now the garage foundations were shaky. Perhaps it was as well the diesel machine would no longer vibrate and wriggle about, but with less power at his disposal Ollie's servicing work on the smaller machines doubled. He began to look very tired and blotchy.

The next day I groped my way along the safety line to Ginnie's VLF hut with a man-hauled sledge. Opening the hatch cover of the drum entrance, I dangled both feet down to feel for the ladder's top. Carrying a fully charged twelve-volt battery, I had no spare hand so when the ladder slipped I couldn't steady myself. I fell only seven feet into the ice lobby, but acid spilled over my gloves, clothes and boots, and the battery fractured.

Ginny joined me in the hut. Soon her VLF work would begin and there was much preparation still to be done. The hut's heater caught fire on ignition and in dousing the flames Ginnie's hand was burnt. Surface burns, but a nuisance in a place where things heal slowly. She had also placed her Zippo lighter in the hip pocket of her trousers, and laying cables that afternoon, she forgot to remove it until she received a cold burn on her thigh in the shape of the Zippo. Not, she felt, a mark of distinction.

That night I couldn't sleep and at dawn felt queasy, almost seasick. There was a sharp, ragged pain from that part of my stomach where I consider my appendix hangs out. This did not go away, so

I eased myself down the homemade ladder from our bed platform. Once erect, I felt faint and nauseous. I stumbled to Ollie's area and woke him. He looked down. 'Probably fumes from the heaters; get some fresh air.'

I went out into the tunnel. Hot and sick, I lay down on the ice floor in my longjohns and tried to breathe deeply. Then the cold got to me and I moved back into our room. I may have blacked out for an instant. I don't know, but I found myself on the floor, head spinning. I called for Ginnie. She had only been asleep for three hours after night VLF work but she woke up and dragged me to a cardboard couch we'd made. The pain came suddenly and surprised me in its intensity – like a knife grinding deep in my gut – and stretched around from the gut to the small of my back. With it there was numbness and tingling in both hands and up the arms to the elbows.

Ollie took my temperature and felt my appendix with an uncommonly cold hand. He wrote: 'Ran got ill this morning and thought he had appendicitis. He certainly looked very sick. I took his temperature and pulse every hour and gave him paracetamol.'

By midday the pain had gone, by evening I felt normal. What caused it, I've no idea. Fumes? Nervous anticipation? Who knows? I do know Ollie must have been as relieved as I was that he had no appendix to cut out . . . it had been two full years since he'd watched an appendectomy . . .

Next day with minus 45 degrees Fahrenheit, a thirty-knot wind and no moon I found Ginnie crawling across the floor of the radio hut filthy and choking. At first I couldn't even see her as black smoke belched from the hut into the ice lobby. She couldn't talk but pointed at the fire. Acrid fumes and an empty extinguisher told their own story. Within minutes it was freezing cold in the hut. There was nothing to be done; the fire was out and frostbite was an ever-present hazard in such conditions. So we went back to the main tunnel as fast as we could fight our way against the wind and hand-over-hand it along the safety line.

In the tunnel we met Ol, and I could see in the flashlight that he was recovering from another dose of carbon monoxide. We did our utmost to sort out our heater and fume problems but, in times of the big winds from certain directions, nothing worked. It may seem as though Ollie and Ginnie did all the work and Charlie and I could have helped them out more. Not so; we all had our hands full. Yet anyone who wished for help had only to ask.

Next morning Bothy had yet again utilised Charlie: this time right inside one of Charlie's fur boots. I removed the mess, smacked Bothy with a ruler and agreed that he should thereafter sleep in my end of the hut locked away from Charlie's boots by two doors. But we were all tender-nerved by that time. The atmosphere crackled for a while. Everybody felt it and nobody spoke. To speak would be like dragging a wire brush over raw skin.

In his biography *Scott and Amundsen,* Roland Huntford wrote: 'In polar expeditions, as in most tight-knit groups, there is usually a process of selecting a natural or psychological leader. It is a conflict akin to a fight for domination within a wolf pack or a dog team; a more or less overt challenge to the established, formal leadership. How he deals with this threat to his authority is one of the tests through which most commanders have to go and upon the outcome of which depends the cohesion of the group.'

I never consciously engaged in such a struggle with Ollie or Charlie, but I suspect on all expeditions and during my army days I held no brief for split command. And as a great believer in the thin end of the wedge, I tended to steer clear of asking for advice or suggestions from those in my current group – to do otherwise mostly encouraged them to offer further advice when it wasn't wanted . . .

At the end of this month of July Ollie went skiing in the moonlight. Five minutes out from the huts he discovered his trouser zipper was undone. His hands were too cold to handle the metal tab effectively so he just left it undone. On returning he found his family jewels were frozen assets and hastily used a saucepan full of warm water to improve the situation. He was lucky. That day was our coldest. The wind held steady around forty-two knots, the temperature at minus 45 degrees Centigrade. The chill factor was therefore minus 131 degrees Fahrenheit, at which temperature any exposed flesh freezes in under fifteen seconds. Ollie had exposed his for a good fifteen minutes. Very lucky.

At this time the crew of the *Benji Bee* was earning money through charter work to keep the ship a going concern. The only charter available was passenger and cargo work between the coral islands of the Tuvalu group and Western Samoa, a hot and humid region, so Anton Bowring and the rest of our family sweated and nursed their prickly heat in the damp oven of the *Benji Bee* while we shivered to their south.

Back in London David Mason, Ant Preston and a group of volunteers tried to get things ready for the second half of the expedition. Every week Ginnie sent back lists of equipment needed at one or more of our Arctic bases. Each time that I thought the lists were closed, new items occurred to me.

While David handled the barracks work, Ant Preston slaved away in the office with three or four volunteers. The executive committee, especially our chairman, naturally liked to keep tabs on how he ran things and looked in fairly often. Sometimes Ant found that what the committee wanted was not the same as what I wanted, and he felt that his loyalty lay with me before the committee, although I was now a long way away. This, of course, made things difficult for him, since he was legally employed by the committee. For a number of reasons the committee felt he ought to resign, in spite of the years of hard work he had put in and the fact that nobody could replace his knowledge of Transglobe's workings. This was not something reflecting badly on the committee or on Ant Preston. Both were doing their best for the cause. Ant drove down to Cove Radio Station and radioed us the facts. All four of us promptly wrote letters to support him, which Ginnie read over the radio to the Cove operator. Ant, I'm glad to say, was not sacked and carried on his excellent work at our nerve centre. The committee, especially chairman Sir Vivian Fuchs and our Foreign Office friend were still trying to gain American approval for our twenty-three vitally needed fuel drums at the South Pole. As yet they'd had no success. And another problem: Ant Preston warned me that Giles Kershaw would not now be able to fly the Twin Otter up in the Arctic and so we must find another pilot. For three weeks Ginnie chased radio frequencies hour after hour to make telephone contact with the only three Arctic Ocean pilots we knew to have sufficient experience to do the job up north. The best, Dick de Blicquy, now worked in Saudi Arabia but our second choice, Karl Zberg, the pilot who had flown for us back in 1977 when we failed to reach the North Pole, was available and said he would fly for us for a hundred dollars per day. I agreed since there was no option and contacted my old friend from the Omani army to ask whether he and Dr Omar Zawawi might meet this unforeseen wage bill. They did.

There were two other temporary hitches throughout the winter, but the worst news involved a problem no radio call could solve. On July 26 Charlie warned me that Ollie's wife, Rebecca, was urging him to go back to her once we crossed Antarctica. Charlie had seen some paper that made him believe that Ollie might well have to acquiesce or face the possibility of divorce. Ol, he felt, would leave the expedition rather than his wife.

'But that choice won't have to be faced,' I said, trying to convince myself. 'Ollie had always told Rebecca he would only do one more sector of the expedition. He told her that back in seventy-six regarding Greenland. He's still with us. She always lets him carry on when the time comes. There'll be no problem . . .'

Charlie, who knew Ol better than I did, was not convinced. A few days later I talked to Ol about it, suggesting we ought at least to warn the committee about the faint possibility of his disappearance. Ollie was adamant. 'It's none of their business, it's a personal matter and anyway nothing may come of it . . .'

So we left it until September, hoping it would just go away. It didn't. Rebecca had a nervous breakdown and went to a hospital. Ollie, not surprisingly, managed a radio call to her there and assured her he would leave Transglobe after Antarctica.

We immediately began to discuss the situation if he did leave. I was determined that no untried replacement be thrust on us. Charlie agreed but wasn't as determined as I was to resist pressure the committee might exert should they feel three was a minimum number for safety.

Using a pressproof code Ginnie devised we informed London of the Ollie problem and of our intention to carry on as two if he did leave us. Our chairman's reply was not a surprise:

> Accepting the fact that Ollie's resignation is one hundred ninety-five-per cent certain we are very concerned with your proposal to proceed northward to the Pole and complete the journey with a two-man team. We would ask you to give deep thought to your decision. There are many factors which militate against a thirty-three-per cent reduction in the team during what is probably the most hazardous part of the entire journey. I need hardly list them in full but the following are salient. It would be contrary to the conditions laid down by the Royal Geographical Society which agreed to not less than three after the original recommendation

> that there should be four men. The question of safety is uppermost in our minds, and there is no doubt that Sir Vivian and Colonel Andrew Croft are adamant that it would be foolhardy. To have to set up an emergency rescue operation in the north would bring down a heap of coals, not so much on you as on the committee, which ultimately is responsible for your well-being, for which we are all anxious. I cannot be too emphatic on this point, which is the unanimous opinion of the committee, which will continue to resist the idea of a two-man team.

Still, whatever might happen in the north, we had Ollie with us for the more immediate crossing attempt, so tomorrow would have to look after itself.

On August 5, a memorably cold day, the sun reappeared for precisely four minutes. Down at Sanae, Simon reported a hundred mile-an-hour wind and foul conditions, but the irrepressible Ol produced some 'beer' he had fermented from old vegetables of an indeterminate type and we toasted the sun.

Over the previous three months Ginnie's work had doubled because her VLF programme, after initial experiments during the first half of the winter, started again in earnest. She had to record at precisely the same time as two other Antarctic coastal stations involved in the same programme. The experiment was known as the International Whistler Programme.

Ginnie now discovered that her time-code generator was faulty, which meant abandoning the project or else completing it manually. And manual operation involved her pressing a recording button every fourth minute and every fifth minute for twenty-four-hour periods without a break. Night after night she sat in the little hut buffeted by the wind. Wrapped in blankets, she kept awake with flasks of black coffee. There was no fixed heater in the VLF hut so

I kept a mobile kerosene burner going for her. The fumes gave her headaches, but she felt that was better than working in an icebox. Some nights I took a sleeping bag up to the hut and slept there to keep her company. I have weird memories of that little cardboard room vibrating in the storm, the wind a solid roar all about us pierced only by the unearthly sounds of the whistlers. Sometimes the whistlers did stop, and there was utter silence. Then, exactly like the frenetic dawn chorus of the Borneo jungle, a mad jumble of electronic chirps, shrieks and animal cries came from the speaker.

By October Ginnie was absolutely dog-tired, and hallucinating. Once I found her asleep on the cold floorboards with a livid red weal between a swollen eye and cheek. The last of her candles was flickering and almost out. She had been outside checking the antenna and had forgotten to close the visor of her face mask.

Her journeys to the VLF hut were often in pitch darkness and blizzard with no possible means of navigating the half-mile stretch from our tunnel hole except hand-over-hand along the safety line. From time to time she said she heard babies crying in the darkness and someone whispering incoherently from close behind her. When my work allowed I went with her to the hut and collected her again the next morning.

By early October we had several hours of sunlight each day. All winter the moonlit summit of Ryvingen had irritated me. I felt a powerful urge to climb it. Since the others did not share this, I tried alone. I failed to get beyond the scree walls of loose rock debris on my first go and on my second and last attempt, by way of a steep nine-hundred-foot ice wall, broke a crampon – the iron spike attached to each shoe – halfway up and came down inch by inch in a sweat and shaking with fear. I never tried again.

A neighbouring peak was unnamed on our map, so Ollie agreed to record its height with his aneroid barometer. There was one remaining pair of crampons, so we each wore one on our right mukluk, or Eskimo boot. Ollie was even more afraid of heights than I was, so our attempt to scale the peak (which he intended to call Prince Charles Mountain) was doomed to be a dismal failure.

Sitting on a rocky shoulder of the mountain some seven hundred feet up, unnaturally close together and chatting in tenor voices, we tried to avert our gaze from the horrific white void below.

'Look,' said Ol, 'a hole in the ski slope.' Sure enough a wide blue fissure gaped at us from the very middle of our old ski- and sledge-training slope, where we had so often fallen heavily and unroped.

'When did that happen?'

'I don't know,' Ol said, 'but there have been explosions around and about these last few days.'

We descended using ropes, ice axes and finally our backsides.

When we got back I drank some of Ollie's so-called beer for the first time. He relieved himself some by writing a ditty that went:

Holes like that on yonder hill
Really make me feel quite ill,
Reminding me of Charlie's mouth,
I hope there are none to the South.

As the sun climbed higher day by day sudden explosions sounded in the valleys and rebounded as echoes from the mountain walls about the camp. Avalanches or imploding crevasses? We didn't know . . .

'I wish you weren't leaving me,' Ginnie said.

We expected to set out during the second half of October, once we knew Giles and Gerry had safely crossed the Antarctic from the Falklands. On October 17 Ginnie contacted Buckingham Palace, but a minute after Prince Charles started to speak to us the communications closed down. All I heard was that he had entered a steeplechase and was placed fourth out of five riders. He had completed the course and received £40. The palace organised a second call on October 20, which came through clearly, and Prince Charles wished us godspeed on the crossing attempt.

A week before our departure date the temperature was minus 50 degrees Centigrade. To the south, high winds raised snowstorms that obscured our intended route up the wall of the Penck escarpment. With four days to go, Ginnie received via London a copy of a news release from New Zealand:

> British explorers planning to traverse the Antarctic Continent are ill-equipped for so hazardous a venture. The Transglobe Expedition Skidoos are underpowered for such a journey, insists Bob Thompson, superintendent of the Antarctic Division. The expedition was initially warned in Washington that the United States would not respond in the event of an emergency.
>
> The Americans have since modified this hardline position, saying they would mount a rescue mission in a crisis but would get the explorers right out of the place, thus aborting the traverse attempt.
>
> 'The Skidoos used by the British have been found by New Zealand ice teams to be underpowered and requiring modification to become effective in Antarctic conditions. They are also far smaller than the covered machines used by Sir Edmund Hillary when "hell bent" for the Pole in 1956 while their traverse route is twice as far,' says Mr Thompson.
>
> He also has reservations about the range of the twin-engined Otter aircraft the British will use for liaison and supply missions . . . In London Mr Thompson met Transglobe Expedition leader Ranulph Fiennes and told him the mission was ill-equipped and foolhardy.

In the offices of Mr Bob Thompson's Antarctic Division in Christchurch, New Zealand, a sweepstake took place. A map of the Southern Continent was pinned with flags along our proposed route, with such comments as 'First crevasse accident'; 'First Skidoo breakdown'; and 'Pulled out by U.S. rescue Hercules.' Their Scott Base field commander, Roger Clark, was a lone voice saying that although he admitted our aircraft was a weak link he thought we'd make it. Others laughed, knowing Clark was a British expatriate. The general view was 'too far, too high and too cold'.

Such sombre predictions weren't easily laughed away as we sat in our cardboard hut contemplating the immediate future. They were, after all, the voice of those who knew Antarctica. Wally Herbert, whose travels include pioneer Antarctic journeys as well as his unique crossing of the Arctic Ocean, said, 'So it [the Antarctic crossing] is really up to him. It is perhaps a challenge to him he would love to take on to prove [the odds] wrong and to succeed, but he will be doing it against all the massive evidence of history.'

Whether we were to succeed or not, at least we had weathered the eight-month polar winter and managed to remain friends. I remembered Thor Heyerdahls's words: 'The most insidious danger on any expedition where men have to rub shoulders for weeks is a mental sickness which might be called "expedition fever" – a psychological condition which makes even the most peaceful person irritable, angry, furious, absolutely desperate, because his perceptive capacity gradually shrinks until he sees only his companions' faults while their good qualities are no longer recorded by his grey matter.'

We had come close to disruptions, but as Charlie put it in his summary of the winter: 'We had worked closely in preparation for the trip. We knew each other's moods and when to lay off. Therefore the strains were negligible.' Well, more or less . . .

On October 28 Giles landed heavily on our homemade strip. He brought mail and Simon and returned to Sanae while the weather held.

We slept for four hours, and then, at 2045 hours, said goodbye to Ginnie, Simon and Bothy, and left Borga for ever.

The temperature was minus 50 degrees Centigrade, the wind a steady twenty knots.

Chapter Seven

> I suppose the one quality in an astronaut more powerful than any other is curiosity. They have to get someplace nobody's ever been before.
>
> JOHN GLENN

I only occasionally keep a diary but on the way toward the South Pole I was more faithful. Much of what follows is culled from it. It gives as automatic and immediate an account as I'm capable of, and I only hope it serves well.

For sixty-four kilometres over blue-white steppes and clinging to 187 degrees magnetic we move across the Penck glacier to that high wall of ice called the Kirwan escarpment.

We wear five layers of clothing and footwear. The coldness cuts through as though we were naked. Fingers numb but still alive enough to hurt, which is good. Toes and nose likewise. The others wear the Eskimo wolfskin parkas which still smell of bad mackerel we had inside the tent. I have a large duvet jacket of duck down; perhaps not so warm but much easier to move about in and see out of. It smells of damp dog.

Dead ahead, each time we crest successive ice dunes we see the black pointer rock of Stignabben, the very last feature for a thousand miles.

Nearing the escarpment I noticed it is grey, not white, and realise this means sheet ice, honed to marble consistency by centuries of wind. Still darker veins lace the great slope; gravity cracks. I look back once. The others are black specks on the rolling dunes of the Penck.

To the east, streamers of blown snow crest the escarpment but right now beside the Stignabben cliffs visibility is good and I spot the curve of a slight reentrant. With adrenaline pumping away all feeling of coldness, I tug the hand throttle to full bore and begin the climb.

Will the rubber tracks grip on this incline of ice? There was nothing like it in Greenland or the Arctic Ocean. If they don't, we're in trouble. I try to will the Skidoo upward, to force every ounce of power from the little engine. Twelve hundred pounds weigh down my two bouncing, leaping sledges, a hell of a load for a 6450-cc engine at seven thousand feet above sea level.

Twice I wince inwardly as the tracks fail to grip. Flinging my weight forward, then rocking to and fro, I pray aloud.

So far an uneven patch always saves the situation, allowing renewed grip, another surge of speed which carries the Skidoo – just – up the next too-smooth section.

The climb seems to go on forever. Then at last an easing of the gradient, two final rises and, wonderful moment, the ridge-line. Fifteen hundred feet above Ryvingen camp and forty-five miles from it I stop and climb off.

Such moments of pure elation are fleeting and rare. I savour the feeling. To the north the peaks of Borga Massif seem now like mere pimples in the vast snow sea, Ryvingen itself just a shadow along our back bearing.

Within the hour the others are up and chatting excitedly. We may yet prove our detractors wrong.

The immediate vicinity of the escarpment is no place to linger, so we take a last look at the distant mountains, then press on south. By dusk there is nothing to see in any direction but endless fields of snow. Now I have only clouds to navigate by. In a few days they too will be gone.

October 30, the third day out. An unpleasant day. A thirty-knot wind stirs the snow and soon sets up pea-soup conditions. We climb gradually: the true plateau is still four thousand feet above us.

Hard ice bumps, not visible in the gloom, upset our Skidoos. As they roll over, the riders must jump well clear to ensure their legs are not crushed between the ice and the seven-hundred-pound machines.

Charlie's goggles split this morning and allow the bitter wind to nip the bridge of his nose. He cannot see at all well and needs to concentrate hard to spot my tracks. We must not lose each other.

When we packed up the tent Ollie told me he felt very tired. This was unusual from someone who never complains about his sufferings. After four hours' travel he staggered off his Skidoo and lurched over unroped. His speech was slurred.

'I'm getting exposure. Must stop a bit.' He was shivering. As medic he knew exactly what symptoms to expect.

In these conditions it would take us two hours to make camp so Charlie and I unpacked the vehicle tarpaulin, and struggling against the wind, secured it around a sledge in such a way as to provide a small windproof shelter. We boiled water from snow and gave Ollie two mugs of tea and some chocolate.

He is physically the toughest of us and wears full polar gear, five layers plus a wolfskin. This indicates the hazards we must face in attempting the crossing with open vehicles. Still there is no point in wishing for closed-cab Snowcats. They would use far too much fuel for the Twin Otter to cope with. We must just carry on day by day; mile by mile and be careful.

Ollie looks grey but says he feels better. We put on our face-masks again, tie up hoods and reluctantly emerge into the elements. It has got worse. Now I can see no shadow, no cloud, nothing but my Skidoo. Even my sledge is a mere blur in the howling murk. After eighteen miles of frozen creeping I give up and we make camp.

Ol's diary for the day says: 'Very bad weather. I think we should have stayed in the tent.' I saw his point, but Greenland in 1976 had taught us we *could* travel in whiteout and high winds. Every hour of progress, however slow and painful, *might* help tip the scales in favour of eventual success. It is so easy when the winds roar outside and your eyes sting with the hissing spicules of flying ice to stay tentbound. When you look out of the tent and cannot see the nearest sledge, let alone the sun's source, it is easy to think how pointless it is to try to travel in the certain knowledge that twelve hours of frustration may at best produce a mile or two of progress.

Poor Charlie has spilled his full pint-mug of coffee over his sleeping gear. His only comfort is the sight of Ollie's fingers and mine, which are badly split at the tips and down from the cuticles. For some reason we have always been more susceptible to this than Charlie.

I check the map and tell the others we are now at nine thousand feet above sea level. The Skidoos are pulling the loads effectively. If this is still true another two thousand feet up we will have one less worry – the altitude power-loss predictions of the New Zealanders.

To set against this, I notice that Ollie's steel sledge uprights have now also cracked, so we have between us three as yet undamaged wooden sledges and three possibly dicey steel ones. During the winter I had drilled the broken tubes until they accommodated metal rods down their middles. I secured these with split pins. As yet these splints seemed to be preventing further damage. But we are only two days out.

Now that the sun is up full time, ultraviolet rays gnaw at the snow bridges over crevasses which we must sooner or later cross.

The sooner we do so the less rotten each will be, the less likely we will end up plunging to a speedy demise.

To avoid the harsh glare of driving into the sun I had opted for travelling during the twelve-hour period which, on the Greenwich time-scale, is called night. However, following the scare Ollie's condition has given me, I now switch to 'daytime' travel, when it is slightly warmer as the sun is higher. The switchover gives us all twelve hours' extra rest, which we can well afford. Now I find navigation, especially around midday when the sun is dead ahead, a real problem. It is more difficult to spot some imperfection or oddity in the snowfields ahead at which to aim my compass. Since I like to take sun altitude shots at midday, not midnight, yet do not wish to interrupt our travel hours by a prolonged halt, the new schedule means less position-fixing shots. I decide to use the millimeters for approximate latitude progress and the theodolite only when we stop for Oliver to drill.

On October 31 we broke camp at 0530 hours (Zulu or Greenwich time) and travelled until 1730 hours. Ginnie, Simon and the aircrew had to switch their 'day' and 'night' times accordingly. That day I did stop for a noonday sunshot which gave us a position of 74°32′ South, 02°26′ West. This put our heading only one degree out from the intended course, despite the conditions.

We are all finding travel an effort. The cold is intense. Especially uncomfortable are fingers and toes, nose, forehead and cheeks. Charlie still has troubles with vision and now a swollen knee after a heavy overturn this morning. I have painful piles and the back of my left hand is swollen egglike. I caught it between the chassis and a sastrugi when my Skidoo went over this evening. But as yet no serious injuries. All very tired. Charlie and I a bit queasy tonight. Ollie's aneroid barometers confirm we are climbing steadily. Good sharp clouds today.

On the average I stop every ten minutes for a bearing, still 187 degrees magnetic, against the clouds. As they are moving slowly and thus maintaining their silhouettes for quite a while, this seems to work well enough. But the midday glare is so harsh I am experiencing liver spots on my retina, and when I squeeze my eyes tight shut I 'see' a deep red colour full of floating black dots.

The snow is deeper and softer. We are in a shallow valley, I think, but perhaps this is an illusion. Charlie commented this morning that 'Everywhere is uphill.' I looked all around and saw what he meant. The terrain does indeed appear to rise away from us on every side.

At about midday, after a compass halt, I try to move off but can't. Ollie checks over my Skidoo.

'The drive axle's gone.'

'Can you fix it?'

'I can, yes, but in these conditions it may lose us a day. As we are only ninety-six miles from base could we not get Giles in? It seems flat enough here. He could bring in a reserve Skidoo.' My natural reaction is to refuse. It seems pointless carrying a spare drive axle if when a replacement is due the job is not done in the field. And again the aviation fuel we have at Sanae and Borga is strictly limited. The plan is for replenishment every three hundred nautical miles. A few unscheduled flights could scupper the whole trip. We have allowed a 20 per cent additional supply for unforeseen emergencies, but this is no emergency, I decide.

Whether or not the Twin Otter comes, we must unload and erect the tent. The cooker is then lit and the radio warmed up beside it for an hour until it is usable. I talk to Ginnie. Giles is ready in Borga and happy to come out. He would like to check on our position before we get too far away. That decides it. Within three hours the Twin Otter appears and we swap Skidoos. Before he goes, Giles confirms our position. He also warns us that extra flights like this one once we are far from Borga can only be for the most extreme reasons. The fuel stocks must be strictly budgeted. Also, every flight involves considerable risk, as Giles would later sum up: 'My greatest fear is the ignominy of a forced landing in the middle of nowhere and the possibility of requiring assistance from the only two other aircraft sources in Antarctica: both hundreds of miles away from our route. Of course I am aware of the more immediate physical dangers but any pilot, like a climber, gets used to the natural hazards and accepts them. Out here I am flying blind most of the time, being too far away from the Omega beacon transmitters for our direction-finding kit to give me our position. A fairly small error in navigation could mean the loss of aircraft or crossing team.'

He told me to build high snow-block cairns every time we camped. Given clear conditions, these might help him trace our route visually because the sun would glint on the vertical snow piles in terrain where everything else is horizontal.

The temperature as we camp is minus 53 degrees Centigrade. We don't seem to get acclimatised to the cold: life is still evil up here. Ollie says we are now higher than ten thousand feet above sea level. I tell him that future drive-shaft changes will have to be done in situ. 'Well' – he is squinting badly, a sure sign he is overtired – 'I only carry one spare and the way you stop and start every few minutes for a compass check we are going to break a good many drive shafts. They've got plastic teeth, don't forget. Each time you pull away with a jerk-start to drag your sledges out of the soft snow, you put tremendous strain onto those teeth, not to mention the torque elsewhere. You've got to stop less often or we'll get nowhere fast.'

I can see his point but can't resist making mine: 'We'll get nowhere even faster if we get lost. I need to keep checking. It's not as if there were any features to use.'

He does not reply, but we both know that I will have to work out some other means of navigating that entails fewer halts.

As we head further south away from the mountains and away

from the sea we will enter a climate where there are no storms and no clouds, only surface winds and mists. Without clouds the vista will be utterly featureless. At times when whiteouts hide the sun my only means of progress will be the compass aimed at imperfections in the snow up ahead. But when the sun does shine I can use a sun compass such as was mounted on my Land Rover out in Oman. There is no sun compass here, but they are simple to make. The next day I scratch a series of lines around my plastic windscreen. It is useless at protecting me from the wind so I might as well give it some purpose in life. Then another set of scratches on the flat fibreglass cowling just in front of the handlebars.

To check on our accuracy and to get some life back into our frozen limbs, I stop for five minutes every hour. Charlie keeps at least one mile behind me and Ollie a mile behind him. So when I stop and take a compass bearing on the two specks back along the trail, I have an immediate check on our angle of advance during the last hour. If this has been two degrees too far west, I overcompensate by two degrees to the east the following hour.

There are no more broken drive shafts.

For four days and nights the temperature hovers around the minus fifties. This makes for weird and wonderful light effects, halos, sun pillars, mock suns and parhelia, but we are in no state to appreciate them.

Three upright bars are missing from Ollie's sledge: further cracks in the welding of Charlie's and mine are spotted most evenings.

At one halt Ollie was smoking a cigarette while we stamped about in small circles attempting to force the blood back into our toes. With no warning a deep belly-rumble sounded from somewhere under our feet – a sinister reminder that nowhere out here in these seemingly innocent snowfields should we move about unroped and off our guard.

Will we spot crevasses in time to avoid them? Almost certainly not. This early in the season there will still be a fair covering of drift hiding their presence. Even if an open fissure approaches dead ahead I doubt we will see it in time. It's quite possible all three of us would drive straight down it. After all, I spend my time staring up at distant clouds or down at the scratches on my cowling. Charlie's vision is hardly good enough to follow my tracks, let alone spot holes, and Ollie, well, he's half-asleep most of the time.

Each day is a repeat of the last. Up at 5:30 and work fast to get warm. One mug of coffee each from the flask but no food. Temperature between minus 42 degrees and minus 51 degrees Centigrade. Tent and everything in it coated with hoarfrost. I exit first, followed by Ollie, and start to pull out the tent pegs. This unsettles showers of hoarfrost inside, so Charlie curses me silently. Sometimes not so silently.

Outside we each pack our particular items of responsibility. Nobody talks. Just before we are ready to go we do up each other's facemasks and check there are no chinks at all for our number one enemy, the wind, to seek out and bite through. Once goggles, facemasks and hoods of wolfskin or duck down are in place, vision is restricted to dead-ahead and the only hole is a penny-sized breather vent over the mouth.

To fix safety harness around crotch and hips involves taking outer mitts off and so must be done in a few seconds. If you don't get it right the first time, and it has to be done by touch since you can't see below your voluminous jacket, then mitts go on again and minutes are wasted banging arms up and down violently to force the blood back into freezing fingers. When the harness is on, you clip it to a twenty-foot coil behind your Skidoo seat. Then the task of starting the engine at a temperature which engines do not like starting in. Make one wrong move or an out-of-sequence action and long delays are caused. Try to engage gear too soon and your drive belt will split into so many pieces of brittle rubber. Turn the ignition key a touch too hard and it will break off in the lock. Get the choke setting wrong or out for too long and the plugs will foul up. Changing plugs at minus 50 degrees with any sort of wind makes your fingers cold again and that makes the first hour en route purgatory.

My first compass check is done with care. If the sun is visible, even though only as an approximate light source in a wan light sky, I absorb myself in its positioning and the angle of existing shadows, however faint they are, vis-à-vis our desired azimuth for the day.

We set out at our one-mile intervals. Sometimes the whole day might pass without a word spoken between me and the others.

For ten unspeakably long hours we head south. By November 5 the snow surface is still reasonable so there is little to divert the mind from the nag of feet and hands and face. As you travel you are forever kicking one foot or the other against the chassis, or booting the air hard to keep the blood down.

Without your right hand on the throttle grip the Skidoo stops just as a car does if you take your foot off the accelerator. So when you want to swing your freezing throttle hand about in windmill motions you have to use your left hand across your chest on the right handlebar where the throttle grip is. To steer like this is not too effective and, on a rough surface, not feasible. When it is rough going, therefore, your throttle hand, especially the thumb, goes through a good deal of unpleasantness.

I am lucky. Fifty per cent of my mind is at all times concentrating on the exact direction of our heading against either the clouds or, when as from November 6 onward there were none, the shadow play on my cowling scratches.

The other two have no such diversions. Only their private thoughts and the bitter vicious cold. That we have managed to cover half the distance from coast to pole on open vehicles at such temperatures speaks well for the clothing and footwear which protects us.

When at length the ten hours are over we are more than ready for sleep. But there is much to be done. Ollie tends to the Skidoos and covers them in an orange tarpaulin. Then, if we have crossed a degree of latitude since his last site, he drills for ice-core samples. I build an eight-foot snow cairn as a marker, erect the tent and lay out all our bedding gear. Then I start the cooker and shout for Charlie, who brings in his radio gear. He begins to prepare the day's only meal by melting snow blocks. If we are at a drill site I take sun shots to establish the sun's altitude, then go into the tent to compute our position. Charlie melts the ice-core samples in a steel pot, carefully bottles the results for Ollie to label. Before each man enters the tent he brushes as much ice and snow off as possible. If you want to make yourself unpopular quickly, bring snow into the tent.

Wet clothes and footwear are hung around the tent roof on string lines, where they soon begin to steam. Life while the cooker is on is heavenly. The evening meal takes 1½ hours to rehydrate. When ready the food pot is placed on Ollie's sleeping bag . . . he traditionally sleeps in the middle. Charlie makes a noise of a certain sort which signals the chef's come-and-get-it. As one, three spoons dip into the pot. Each spoon is precisely the same size and should not be dipped too often as compared to the other spoons. I am exceptionally greedy, and since both the others know this, any attempt to get more than my fair share is normally a failure. But I keep trying. The meal consists of rice or dehydrated vegetables mixed with one of four varieties of dehydrated meat. This meat is in reality soya beans but we conveniently forget that fact. We do not wash our pot because the residue is either scraped clean or left to be mixed with the following day's menu. After a cup of hot chocolate comes the evening radio schedule – which includes a full weather report for the World Meteorological Organization, and the taking of urine samples for use with our calorific intake programme. Then sleep by 10:30 P.M., trying not to think of tomorrow's travel. (Despite having 6,500 calories per man per day Ollie loses twenty-six pounds during the journey. Charlie loses sixteen pounds and I lose three pounds.)

On November 6 we come to 77°30′ South and converge with the Greenwich Meridian. Two hundred miles into unknown terrain, with eight hundred to the Pole, we stop for Ollie to complete one of three specially selected drilling sites. The cores are not melted, simply bagged and by a tortuous route will be sent still frozen to laboratories in Copenhagen.

Up to this point we have been travelling twice as fast as my schedule predicted. This might soon make our resupply impossible. As Simon wrote: 'Ran's rapid progress is now our major problem.' Giles and Gerry now fly a great deal and sleep little, having to race against time to carry the fuel south. As a result Simon and Ginnie are alone a lot at Borga, where their relationship is a mixture of mutual respect alternating with periods of hostility. Some examples from Simon's diary:

> I do all the physical work but Ginnie spends her time coping with sheaves of admin problems and messages for the U.K. I know only one person who could cope with such pressure, but possibly not in this environment ... We are relaxed, eating and chatting for two hours, despite urgent need for sleep. As Ginnie says, we would soon turn into morons if we just crashed out after work. Nearly all the London office people are absent, which infuriates Ginnie, who does not tell Ran so's not to give him unnecessary headaches. She only relaxes when out of her hut and never before lunchtime. I have a reasonable working relationship

with her . . . 7th November. Left in peace. Ginnie and Bothy and me running the smallest base in Antarctica. Had an acrimonious exchange with her today about protecting kit from snowdrifts down at Sanae – but this didn't leave ill feelings . . . Hectic work while Giles is airborne, because we must keep the radios and generators working into the small hours. Peaceful here when only Ginnie, Bothy and myself remain. Ginnie very relaxed and friendly, a total contrast to back in London, although, like me, she's not much good before midday. She carries a lot of responsibility for admin, kicking London and keeping worries off Ran's shoulders.

November 8. The surface has begun to change. At first mere outcrops of isolated hummocks like African anthills. From time to time these are connected in ribbons across our front and crossing them is a bone-shaking process. At noon Charlie hands me three steel struts he has retrieved en route. Checking my front sledge I find six uprights are gone and one runner is no longer held rigid. Repair is out of the question. We must just hope the sledges last out and these bumps disappear. Perhaps they are just a local phenomenon.

We have done fifty miles today. In ten days we have covered 444 nautical miles from Borga. Our camp tonight is halfway from the coast to the Pole, but the major suspected crevasse fields are still ahead.

Since Giles's Omega system does not work this far south we must hope that snow cairns lead him to within beacon range of our location tomorrow night when we will need fuel. We will be at near-maximum range for him so he must find us on the first attempt. If the Americans allow him to fuel at the Pole he can start basing his flights from there, as we may be nearer the Pole than Borga in a week or so.

Tonight's radio call brought news that the U.S. authorities have confirmed their 'no help' position. I can understand their attitude – most official government groups take a dim view of freelancing private expeditions – but I can't like it. Now we must plan to complete the whole crossing with no outside fuel support, which will doubtless be a nightmare for Giles, though he has always believed it possible despite outside opinion to the contrary. I've told Ginnie to go ahead with any plans Giles can work out for a self-contained air-support plan to the Pole and beyond. Meanwhile we'll carry on to 80 degrees and wait there until a flight plan is agreed on.

Today, November 9, saw the worst terrain yet. To reach this camp at 80°04′ involved us in a tortuous journey over ever-worsening ridges of sastrugi – they average eighteen inches to two feet high and are often perpendicular so we can't climb them. This means a tortuous course, precious fuel used in detours and many stops for Ol to replace broken springs and buckled bogey wheels. Still we *are* at 80 degrees a whole month ahead of schedule.

Tonight Ginnie passed us Giles's 'beat the fuel shortage' plan. He will bring enough aviation fuel to this camp to enable him to set up a further fuel depot at 85 degrees. Once *this* camp is stocked to that level we will set out to 85 degrees while Giles, Gerry and Anto Birkbeck from Sanae remain camped here with the Twin Otter. When we get to 85 degrees Giles will ferry all the fuel from 80 to 85 degrees. Then he and the others will stay there until we reach the Pole. This 'one leg on the ground' approach is necessary because Giles would never be able to find a fuel cache out here unless someone with a radio beacon were left there too.

To add to our problems, a warning from the London committee has reached us ... 'To emphasise the dangers of arriving prematurely at South Pole without adequate resources to proceed immediately from that vicinity, we have been informed quite firmly that you will be *evacuated* by the Americans at the expedition's expense.'

So we lie in the little tent while Giles flies in with fuel drums whenever the weather allows. Every day we delay is for me an almost physical hurt. The terrain shows every sign of deteriorating to the south as do our Skidoos and sledges. But my main concern is the southern crevasse fields. Every day we delay, the snow bridges which might see us safely over the danger zones become weaker and more rotten.

Nobody knows what lies ahead because nobody has been here before. But unmanned balloons have passed above, and analysis of their instrumental data indicates that great coastal glaciers are fed from this part of the ice sheet. At around 81 to 82 degrees south to either side of the Greenwich Meridian the presence of a high valley is suspected. This is thought to drain ice from the plateau down to the giant Recovery Glacier. Huge crevasse systems as far inland as 83 degrees south, 15 degrees east suggest a deeply penetrating ice stream.

Before leaving England we had inquired about the crevasse dangers and Dr Doke at the British Antarctic Survey told us that 'previous traverses into the area have been turned back by crevassing, so it seems possible that a lot of the way between, say, 79 degrees south and 83 degrees south may be badly crevassed.'

The uncertainty of the hazards ahead makes waiting difficult. For days the weather is filthy and Giles can't fly. Communications are also difficult, at times impossible.

Simon visited the lonely VLF hut by himself at this period, and wrote:

> No sign of Ginnie's ghost, a presence which she and Bothy felt during the winter, despite ragging from R, C and O. A youngish man, I gather. Scandinavian? Not malevolent, just *there*. Bothy

was sometimes scared, but that may just have been ice movement. But I believe Ginnie. The long solo nights in the hut must have enhanced her perception. I went up to the VLF hut today to scavenge wood for sled repairs. It's an empty hut with an aura. I sealed it up, as I knew I would not want to go back up there. The graffiti on the wall, written by Ginnie in three different pens, presumably in stages, was apt and rather scaring in a way.

As whistlers and gibbons cries
Screech in the ears
The ghost of Ryvingen
bursts into tears.

'Why have you come to disturb me
after these many years?
I will haunt and will taunt you
and drive you away.'

With the wood from the hut Simon strengthened a camp sledge, and Giles has brought this out to replace Ollie's steel sledge, which had begun to look decidedly dicey.

It's difficult to maintain good relations between the three of us. We are cramped up, damp, dirty, cold and, above all, frustrated. The days pass so slowly. The sound of the wind gnaws into your brain: it never stops. An intended joke meant as banter at the expense of someone feeling low can cause the blood to rise very quickly. At such times the offender had better recognise the danger signals in time and back away if the atmosphere is to remain reasonably healthy. Again this is no time nor place to maintain, openly at least, any rigid viewpoints or position if three men, all strong individualists, are to tolerate each other's company.

*

After seventeen days Giles has completed his tenth flight to our camp. To stock up the cache to the minimum needed for the next phase he has, in dubious weather, had to fly twelve thousand nautical miles in ninety-two hours and use up six thousand precious gallons of aviation fuel. Only tenty-five drums now remain at Ryvingen. It's difficult to fully appreciate the risks Giles has taken. Especially on take off from Ryvingen. In his words: 'I had to take off in the mountains from the terrible surface of hard, crisscrossed sastrugi and carrying an enormous weight. I couldn't spread the load over more flights because we didn't have the fuel.'

There has, though, been one advantage in the long delay. Ollie has completed three test drills and calibrated the aneroid barometers against the one we left at Sanae at sea level. Dr Gordon Robin, the director of the Scott Polar Research Institute, for whom Ollie's work is carried out, once summed up the reasons for our drilling assignment this way:

'We are interested in how the Antarctic ice sheet works. We want to know whether there is a faster outflow of ice than the snow falling on top. There are many things you can't learn from flying over the ice sheet, and this is where the Transglobe Expedition comes in: what the snowfall is, what the temperature is and various other records of climate. The ice sheet stores an incredible record of past climate. People have drilled down to two thousand metres into the ice sheet: that tells a history of climate over a hundred thousand years or more through the study of two types of oxygen atom. To understand this you need to know what the snowfall on the top surface was like at first. So we asked Transglobe to collect a sample every degree of latitude on the whole crossing down to about two metres, melt it down and bring a sample back from each spot so we can see how the ratio of oxygen of one sort to the other varies. Additionally we need to know the accumulation of snow. This is difficult to measure for a small rapidly moving group but they will try to take very detailed samples down to about ten metres. We will eventually get these samples back and put them in a sort of nuclear counter device. This will tell us exactly where the 1955 deposit from the H-bomb explosion was at that time in the ice sheet, and by measuring how deep that is you can work out how much snowfall has accumulated during the following twenty-five years.'

After Depot 80 I became more sporadic in my recording, reverting to type, and no longer kept a daily diary.

The day we left the 80 degree cache the Americans did give permission for Giles to refuel from South Pole stocks. This was the result of direct contact between the Foreign Office and the State Department, which in turn culminated seven years of approaches, proposals and disappointments. The delay in its arrival, though, cost us seventeen precious days of travel ...

Now the polar summer was with us, and life was positively comfortable in terms of temperature, as we were well into the minus thirties. But the sastrugi did not improve. Day by day they increased in size and number. By the end of November, entering the theoretical crevasse fields draining to the Recovery Glacier, we noticed long rounded spur features descending from higher ground to the east.

The sastrugi ridges now resembled a ploughed field with the ridges running directly across our line of advance. For two hundred miles these ridges averaged two to three feet. With the four-inch raised blade at the front of our skis it was only possible to mount a sheer-sided obstacle of twelve inches or so. Progress was therefore painfully slow and involved much axe work, many overturns and wasted fuel on account of the eternal detours. We could not progress at all with our standard fifty-foot-long tow ropes, since the sledges got caught up between ice furrows and jammed, so we changed to five-foot tow ropes, which in the event of a crevasse fall would probably cause both sledges to follow a Skidoo downward. Once, for twenty-nine miles with hardly a break, the sastrugi walls stood three to five feet high and our progress, tortoise slow, was a series of broken springs, sheared-off steel sledge struts and futile cursing.

I didn't dare to glance at my sundial . . . only by keeping total concentration on the maze of ice walls ahead was any progress possible without frequent overturning of Skidoo and sledges.

On the last day of November we entered a series of rolling valleys free of sastrugi and began to feel elated, although none of us dared hope the ridges were all behind us.

I stopped as usual at the end of an hour and, without noticing any irregularity, on a slight incline to the south. I leaned back, enjoying the sensation of resting my back muscles against my bedding bag. In a little while Charlie came up beside me, stood up astride his seat, stretched and said, 'Well!' which was what he normally said at halts. Intending no doubt to check his sledge for any new damage, he stepped off his Skidoo toward me and no more than four yards away.

As though a trapdoor opened up beneath him, he was suddenly foreshortened, disappearing right up to his thighs. One hand never left his handlebar, and as he fell he hung on for dear life. Slowly he withdrew his hips and legs and pulled himself back onto his seat . . . 'Gawd,' he breathed, looking down at the blue-green hole into which he had so nearly disappeared.

Seen from the security of my Skidoo seat, the incident was pretty funny, and there was no way, on seeing the expression on his face, that I could stop myself from breaking into a kind of manic laughter, laced, no doubt, with the old 'there but for the grace of . . .'

Charlie watched me in silence. He looked at the thin rotten ice around the periphery of the hole and then at my Skidoo.

As my laughter died a bit he said evenly, 'You think that funny? In a minute or so it'll be a whole lot funnier because there must be a good two inches of snow bridge, maybe less, right under you at this moment. Any movement you make pulling your starter cord is going to send you on a long drop to nowhere. And is Charlie Burton going to shed tears? No. He is not. He is going to laugh himself sick.'

The realisation that he was absolutely correct, that I *was* in imminent danger of collapsing the fragile skin of granular snow sitting over God knew how deep an abyss, wiped the smile off my face. Gingerly I started up and engaged the gear. With sweat breaking out, hardly daring to breathe, I pulled away. Nothing happened, the air hissed out between my teeth. The others also crossed safely, we carried on. We'd been lucky, and we knew it.

That night we camped at 82°50′ and a degree or so to the east of the Greenwich Meridian. This placed us at the northern limits of a suspected crevasse field some sixty miles in depth and forty miles wide. I prodded the surface with special care before erecting the tent.

At about this time there was also bad news from Ginnie. Giles, in landing by the Ryvingen camp, had run into a bank of sastrugi. The Twin Otter had bounced over the ridges but the tail of the aircraft rudder was damaged ... 'It didn't hurt the aircraft,' Giles recorded, 'nearly as much as it hurt me. I lay awake all night thinking. Since my first flight aged sixteen I had never scratched an aeroplane. Of all my flights, seven seasons and four thousand flying hours in Antarctica, never mind all the other hours in other countries, it had to happen here. If things had been a bit different, if there'd been a cargo on board, the whole tail might easily have been a write-off.'

Gerry managed to repair the damage overnight, and they

returned to the depot. With the Twin Otter, its crew and Anto now sitting it out at the 80-degree cache and all fuel rationed, I knew we had to reach 85 degrees before requesting another flight.

But the first few days of December saw us in worse conditions than I had thought existed in Antarctica. Bogey wheels, ski attachments and springs snapped and buckled. Ollie ran out of certain spare parts and had to improvise. In places the iron-hard ridges were separated by ditches less than the length of a Skidoo and negotiation of the successive walls involved axe work and manhandling, just as on Arctic Ocean pack ice.

Our progress slowed to a painful crawl. With breaks of one or two kilometres between them, these forbidding sastrugi fields carried on for three hundred miles, sometimes almost impassable, sometimes mere serried waves of ice bric-à-brac. With increasing frequency whiteout conditions clamped down. To negotiate even the lesser sastrugi belts without a clear idea of where the bumps were would be asking for trouble, so we stopped until the light improved . . .

Cannoning off a wall of ice in a medium-size sastrugi belt, I felt resistance and found that a sledge box had dropped through the steel mesh platform of my lead sledge. So much of the tubing had snapped and disappeared that there were now areas of no tubing at all. Using canvas straps I hitched up the loose boxes and carried on. The principal criticism of our steel sledges was always their rigidity: their lack of 'give' when crossing rough ice. Now I noticed that so many connector tubes were missing that the twelve-foot-long runners were in fact bending and snaking to conform with the ice surface below. So long as a few upright tubes held the runners to the platform, they might yet survive the journey, I thought.

But my sledge was of oak and hickory, an adaptation of an Eskimo design. On December 4, in the centre of a particularly rough ridge belt, one of its oaken runners split right along its two-inch-thick length. There was nothing to be done but abandon it, together with its load. We shared out the vital fuel cans between us but left behind the crevasse ladders, tent heater and all noncritical gear.

Then limped on.

Life had become a succession of monstrous sastrugi fields. The pole seemed unattainable. It was better to forget everything but the next horizon.

Charlie's ski leaf-spring broke, and Ollie had no spare. Still, with tape and wire he managed a temporary repair but this would last only hours. Some twenty-eight miles short of 85 degrees the ski became irreparable so we scouted about for an airstrip. A four-hour search revealed a narrow sastrugi-free lane just long enough for a runway after a lot of ax work. On December 5 we set up camp at this bald vein amid the sastrugi fields ...

Only five days previously a group of twelve South Africans had set out on a sixty-mile journey from a geological field base back to Sanae. Their activities were to impinge on our own. Led by their boss Hannes, a tough Afrikaaner with previous field experience in the region, they were home-bound by the same route over the Hinge Zone that we had ourselves used to reach Ryvingen.

One of their heavy snow tractors plunged sixty feet into a crevasse and was jammed still further down by its one-ton fuel sledge. The three men in the cab were rescued with only a few bruises but the machines could not be retrieved. Now there were now only two cramped cabs for nine people. Three of the group decided it would be best to return the remaining distance, about a day's ride over flattish terrain, to Sanae base. The weather was fine so they set out on a Skidoo with no tent and minimal rations. The remainder carried on and camped on the edges of the Hinge Zone. At some point Jed Bell, a young scientist we had spoken often to by radio during the winter, fell ninety feet down a hole and broke his neck. The five survivors, after recovering his body, pressed on northward and made radio contact with Sanae – and learned that the Skidoo group had not materialised. Worried, Hannes himself set out on a second Skidoo to find them and soon picked up their tracks. He failed to notice, though, that the spare fuel can he carried scuffed up against the Skidoo's chassis and started leaking. He ran out of fuel and also lost radio contact with both Sanae and the tractors.

By the time we were established at our 85-degree cache there was a good deal of understandable upset among the Sanae scientists. Anywhere else they would simply call for search and rescue, but Antarctica is not normal. There is no systematic search and rescue apparatus. The British bases four or five hundred miles away had no operational aircraft at the time. The only other aircraft, American ski-equipped Herculeses, were over two thousand miles away at McMurdo Base and would be unlikely to be able to land anywhere in or near the search area. Obviously the Transglobe Twin Otter provided the answer, but how embarrassing for Pretoria and, indirectly, Washington if we were officially requested to provide a search and rescue for employees of the same polar establishment who for so long had resisted our presence on the grounds that we would ourselves require search and rescue from their resources. This may have had a bearing on the delay before we were asked to help out.

The situation for Ginnie was complex. She was above all keen to prevent further loss of life. She tried contacting the London office and eventually reached David Mason. Simon gives an impression in his diary:

> Giles drives Ginnie to rage with his revised plans. The two of them seem to brush each other up the wrong way. Ginnie says Giles does nothing but argue and Giles says she is only happy when

> she's moaning ... The bureaucratic inertia is shocking: it seems Ginnie and David Mason are the only ones even trying to do something. I have no constructive suggestions to make other than stuff Pretoria. The Sanae team are a shell-shocked rabble ... they are intelligent but totally inexperienced in search and rescue. They are tired, shocked, leaderless and under the thumb of a —— in Pretoria. God help them because they can't help themselves ...

Soon after the three South Africans set out by Skidoo the weather closed in on them. They mistook the faint hump of one ice-rise named Blaskumen for another called Esquimo. Close by the seafront they weaved their way between crevasses along the tide crack, but uncertain whether they were east or west of Sanae base, decided to stay put. Within hours the two sleeping bags they owned between them were soaking wet, they had only eight packets of dried biscuits and no cooker to melt snow and so began to dehydrate as they shivered away the days ...

Within hours of our arrival at the 85-degree cache, Giles left the 80-degree camp manned by Gerry and Anto and brought us our first fuel load. A second flight would be necessary before we could press on so Giles flew back to 80 degrees. On his way there he received a radio message from Ginnie saying that Pretoria might shortly ask for our Twin Otter to carry out a search and rescue flight near the coast. But at 80 degrees Giles was some seven hundred miles from the likely search area and six hundred miles from the South Pole. Should anything happen to the Twin Otter at this stage with our own lines of communication so stretched, our fuel at bare minimum without allowing for any problems of our own and two major crevasse fields still between us and the Pole, we could quickly end up in a trickier situation than our South African friends. Their débâcle had after all occurred within only ninety miles of their permanent base camp.

Not having anticipated the need to wait at 80 degrees before flying the second fuel flight out to 85 degrees, Giles had dropped off our only portable generator during the first flight. Which left nothing at 80 degrees to power the aircraft's vital engine heater and battery ... For two hours Giles waited at 80 degrees for confirmation of the rescue mission. When he heard nothing he opted to start the aircraft engines at once before they became too cold and fly down to Ryvingen, where there was a generator and he would be closer for possible rescue work. I told Giles we would wait at 85 degrees for as long as necessary.

Gerry and Anto climbed out of the little tent to see Giles off. Anto's diary describes the scene of Giles's takeoff attempt:

> Giles had a good charge reading, 15 per cent r.p.m. (well above the requisite 12.5 per cent), active ignition ... the lot. But she wouldn't start. Our hearts sunk. We took the battery into the tent and warmed it up over a Primus. Then we covered the starboard with a parachute and warmed up the oil sump while the engine oil temperature rose to 20 degrees C, which was good. Again Giles tried. Again 15 per cent r.p.m., yet the engines still would not fire. Now we resorted to the spare battery. Gerry had assumed this was an exchange unit and so had not checked its charge. The truth was not long in coming. It had *never* been charged. We were stuck at 80 degrees south. The very middle of nowhere. It was an evening of despondency as the full realisation of the disaster hit home. Four men might die. Also the critics would now have their predictions confirmed. We would have to be rescued. A restless night followed as we tried to keep the Primuses going to warm the battery. We also had to keep our little solar panel lined up with the sun to get the full benefit of its trickle charge.
>
> Next morning. There is just enough charge left in the main

battery to merit another attempt at starting off it. Again we used a draped parachute and the Primuses to warm the engine to 20 degrees C. and then again attempted to start up. As before the propeller turned, over and over, but wouldn't fire. Giles could only keep his ignition on and watch the battery life drain away. Suddenly she fired! We broke into a carnival and rushed to dismantle the camp. We contacted Ginnie and she said Hannes, the boss, had at that point just reported picking up the tracks of the three missing men. Our final takeoff from 80 degrees was hair-raising due to the heavy load, high altitude and short strip. We lurched heavily to beyond the airstrip we had cleared and clipped the first sastrugi as we lifted off. But we made it.

Late on December 6 Giles brought in the remainder of our fuel; enough, we hoped, to see us to within sixty miles of the South Pole, for without too many detours, we could make three hundred miles with full sledge loads and with no replenishment depots. Giles, understandably worried about his engines, flew straight off for the pole, hoping to pick up its radio beacon at a hundred miles out.

When he reached the Pole another message came in from Ginnie. Now Hannes himself was missing. The other three had been out with no shelter for six days and their outlook was grim.

Giles flew direct to the fifty-square-mile coastal zone, where he felt the lost men must be. The Twin Otter's official range is about one thousand miles. The straight line distance from the pole to Sanae is thirteen hundred miles, so when Giles reached the search zone he was on his 'last drop'.

By the uncanny nose he had developed after seven seasons down south, Giles picked up some tracks several miles southwest of Sanae base camp, and soon afterward overflew the black huddle of the lost group. He landed close by. All three men were still alive. A blizzard had blown snow into their clothing and sleeping bags. This was melted by their remaining body heat and then turned to ice as they became colder. One of them was the base doctor. The men were soaked through, utterly dehydrated. The doctor had lost twenty-six pounds, the other two sixteen each. Giles flew them back to Sanae, refuelled and, an hour later, located and brought in Hannes as well.

Up at Ryvingen, Ginnie received the good news, and as Simon wrote: 'Ginnie gave up the radio shack for the first time in twenty-nine hours and went for a wash.'

Two days of hard, slow toil saw us out of the last sastrugi field. By 85°30′ the dreaded dragon's-teeth bands had disappeared and the surface began to improve. The weather, though, deteriorated, and twice we struck camp in total whiteout conditions ... For three days I followed an easterly deflection to avoid the crevasse zone a hundred and ten miles before the Pole, and then, on December 13, began the final run in along 201 degrees magnetic. For the last eighty miles we were enveloped in mist. Two of our sledges were falling to bits, their structure bearing no resemblance to the sleek units of a month before. Yet the runners were undamaged and the platforms, attached now by only four-corner uprights out of sixteen, still supported the full loads with a little help from makeshift cross-straps.

On December 14, after nine hours' travel through the mist, I stopped with sixty-one miles on the mileometer. This *must* be the South Pole. There was nothing to be seen.

Ollie came up, all excited. 'We passed the huts about a mile back on the left.' Elated, Charlie and I followed him back. He stopped and pointed. Sure enough three black shapes could be seen in the gloom.

Closer inspection revealed merely a group of flags some six

inches high; probably ice-markers. Initial disappointment soon turned to anticipation. After all, these were the first local 'features' of any sort that we had seen since leaving Ryvingen a thousand miles to the north. And where there were flags there were likely to be people. We quartered the area for about an hour, but found nothing. We camped and contacted the South Pole operator.

'You are three and a half miles from us. We have you on the camp radar. Come on in.'

He gave us a bearing and, an hour later, a dark silhouette loomed through the thick mist directly ahead.

At 0435 hours on the fifteenth of December, some seven weeks ahead of our schedule, we arrived at the bottom end of the Earth.

Chapter Eight

Nature is often hidden, sometimes overcome, seldom extinguished.

FRANCIS BACON

The base at the South Pole, unlike any other in Antarctica, is protected from the elements by a metal dome. There are eight prefabricated huts within the dome, and in winter when the temperature plunges to minus 110 degrees Fahrenheit its outer doors are closed. The dome is designed for the wintering of a dozen scientists and six or seven administrative workers.

The base commander is not normally a scientist, and Tom Plyler was no exception. An ex-Marine lieutenant with Vietnam experience, he was a strict disciplinarian. His methods of running things were precisely the opposite to those of Hannes back at Sanae. Mine were, I suppose, somewhat in between, or perhaps they just changed according to the people I was involved with at the time.

Not willing to set out for the second half of the journey, which included a potentially unpleasant descent of the Scott Glacier, until Ginnie had set up a radio base at the Pole, I asked Tom if we could stay at his place for a week or so.

By chance it had just been discovered that the dome's sewer outlet was not far enough away. For a number of years the effluent, sinking into the ice, had opened up a cavern beneath the dome over a hundred feet deep, the bottom thirty of which consisted of chemicals and sewage. As a result the dome was slowly tilting one way and stress on its nuts and bolts had already caused some to shear off. Given further strain and extreme temperatures the situation could easily become serious. The wintering scientists would not enjoy the twin threats of being crushed by falling girders or of suddenly descending into a lake of sewage.

Tom Plyler held a karate black belt. I'd never been particularly impressed by the activity, but in a little makeshift gymnasium at the base he gave me a demonstration, with me as his 'opponent'. Fortunately his blows, a vicious blur of palm, fist and foot, fell short of my nose, crotch and knees by, so to speak, a hair's breadth – as intended.

'Do you rassle?' Tom asked, as I let out my breath. 'Arm-rassling, Turkish rassling. We use these judo mats.'

'No, I never have. Except with my wife to get the car keys.'

'Well,' said Tom, 'you're a good size, so come along tonight after you've done the evening dishes.'

It was an interesting experience. I did manage to extract a howl of pain from Tom with a standard British army lock which put his forearm out of commission for the evening, but not before he had almost squeezed the guts out of me with a California scissors, and my neck was all but dislocated. I was beginning to think life in the polar dome was more hazardous than out on the ice sheet. At least you could fall down crevasses out there and not drown in your own sewage.

'We have to watch germs here,' Tom warned me.

'But surely the cold kills all germs.'

'It does outside, but some of the scientists spend their entire

Antarctic year in centrally heated huts either up here or down at McMurdo. You say your wife will be bringing a dog here. It will have to stay outside in your tents. *No* pets at the Pole.'

'He'll be fine in our tents. He's very long-haired.'

'Good,' said Tom, 'and another thing. Be careful of cold germs. They are really virulent up here and we can't afford, especially during the summer season, to lose a scientist's working hours. It costs one million dollars to keep just one scientist here for a year.'

He explained one of the cold-prevention methods. When new arrivals entered McMurdo they were given iodine-impregnated handkerchiefs in sets of three: one to blow the nose, one to wipe the nose and one to wipe the hands. At one dollar per handkerchief it costs three dollars to blow one's nose . . .

Ice-sheet neighbours to the Pole station are the Russians at Vostok. They hold the world's record temperature, minus 128 degrees Centigrade. Some of the U.S. scientists, about to fly there by Hercules for an exchange visit, took orders for a 'shopping list'. They had an agreed barter system, and prevailing rates were:

1 bottle of US vodka = 1 bottle USSR vodka
1 Russian leather hat or leather boots = 1 cassette radio
1 complete leather outfit = 1 pair jeans or a calculator

Not having vodka, jeans or calculators, we missed out on the deal.

Back at Ryvingen Ginnie and Simon packed up the instruments and gear we would need in the northern hemisphere. Giles flew it down to Sanae, where Anto boxed and listed it together with kit from his own base.

Later that spring the South African ship would come to replace Hannes and the others at Sanae. David Mason was due on the ship too in order to help Anto pack and load. The two of them would then return to London with the gear and in a few short months have it serviced and repaired and repack it to various Arctic outposts.

On December 21 Ginnie bade a sad farewell to the cardboard camp at Ryvingen. Soon it would disappear beneath the snow forever. It had been her home for eleven months.

Jamming herself in the fuselage with Simon and Bothy she must have wondered if Giles would ever take off, the load being well over the recommended maximum figure. The takeoff was a nail-biting affair, but it worked and brought us the last cargo we needed at South Pole. The mathematics of what Giles had achieved were startling. Every pound of cargo that he flew from the coast to the South Pole used up 13 pounds of fuel. My requirement list for the Pole, mainly fuel and rations, totalled 7,500 pounds and to get it there cost us 230 drums of fuel from Sanae.

For five years I had tried to gain information about our descent route, the Scott Glacier. Even the Scott Polar Research Institute had no details. It seemed no one had experience of its nature; certainly not in the last decade and, like the rapids on rivers, crevasse hazards change over the years. The aerial map of the glacier indicates extensive crevassing at its crest some 9,000 feet up, crevassing in belts along its 140-mile course and crevassing at its foot some 500 feet above sea level. It looked generally unhealthy, to be treated with great caution. I planned to take ten days over its descent.

One private worry was the question of actually locating the glacier's crest some 180 miles from the Pole. It is one thing using sun and compass for 1,200 miles to reach the South Pole, quite another to pinpoint mountain or glacier features travelling *from* the Pole when moving obliquely across the direction of the South Magnetic Pole. No problem when you have experience, but confusing when you don't.

As Ollie said: 'I was staggered that we had managed to navigate so accurately that when we got to the Pole and despite the white-out we were only three and a half miles away from it. If we'd had clear visibility we would have easily seen it. But I was slightly worried about the next stage. From South Pole to Scott Base would be more difficult and a lot more hazardous.'

I made up my mind to leave the Pole as soon as Ginnie's radio arrangements were made, since each day we lingered increased the dangers ahead. Summer was already well advanced. Crevasse bridges, already weakened, would soon be rotten and in places non-existent.

Inside the dome colourful preparations were going on – Christmas was only two days away. Charlie and Ollie were enjoying themselves and had made many friends. It was good to be with Ginnie again and undeniably tempting to stay just two more days to enjoy a proper Christmas.

Ginnie did not try to stop me, although like the rest of us, she was nervous about the Scott Glacier ... 'Besides,' she said with a weak smile, 'the Christmas dishwashing is probably well worth avoiding.'

So we made ready to set out the next day, December 23. I felt a twinge of sympathy for Captain Scott. He had left the Pole sixty-nine years before on January 17, too late to be sure of a safe return. 'All the daydreams must go,' he had written. 'It will be a wearisome return.' And of course neither he nor his companions ever did return.

Next morning, with unexpected radio calls and messages to write I was late in getting my kit packed. One result was I committed a cardinal navigator's error, one which I had learned before many an army operation ... I failed to rehearse my navigational intentions for the day, to obtain a mental picture of direction through sun and wristwatch. I also had no excuse, as the sun was clear and visibility unlimited.

Tom Plyler and a chilly band of amateur photographers were stomping up and down by the international flags which mark the exact spot of the geographical South Pole. I lashed my kit down quickly, kissed Ginnie and set out due north. *Every* direction was due north, and I aimed for the airstrip forgetting that we had actually *arrived* via the airstrip seven days previously. Soon realising my predicament, I determined to make a bold front of it and complete a wide left circle onto the correct bearing once out of sight of the dome. Unfortunately, the terrain being flat as a pancake, my only hope was that none of the polar scientists would have any idea which direction I *should* be heading in, and anyway they would rush back to the warm dome to unfreeze their camera fingers as soon as we were out of photographic range.

I had forgotten Giles. Catching a lift on a snowtrack, he rushed after us and long before we even reached the airstrip overtook me with the news that I was heading back to Sanae. Having flown in and out of the Pole during five long seasons and in all weathers, there was no way Giles was going to be taken in.

I thanked him but kept to the circular correction. Some three miles out I stopped and checked the charts. About 180 miles away a single jagged peak, Mount Howe, marked the upper rim of Scott Glacier. This, my mathematics suggested, was on 261 degrees magnetic, so my true 'meridian of advance' should be 147 degrees west and this should lie directly beneath the sun at 2100 hours, 44 minutes Greenwich time. But the sun in fact passed over what my compass indicated to be this meridian almost an hour too early. So I must be heading along 132 degrees west. I put all this to Ollie and Charlie who were quite happy to follow in more or less any direction, just as they had en route for the Pole. Not even Ollie, who is mathematically brilliant, could see any discrepancy, so I continued to follow 261 degrees magnetic. Whatever error I might be making would be to the left and west of Mount Howe, so if, when we reached the edge of the plateau the mountain was not visible, a sharp right turn would in theory take us straight to it.

Uneasily and with frequent accusing glances at the sun, as though it were personally to blame for my uncertainties, I carried on along 261 degrees.

At 5:00 P.M. on Christmas Day I stopped on a small rise and noticed a black speck dead ahead, the summit of Mount Howe: the first natural feature for over a thousand miles and as good a Christmas present as anyone could wish for.

We began the descent in fine weather, but there was an air of nervousness. I could feel this as I suspect the others could, despite our habitual silence on the move. Our aerial map showed the crevasse fields plainly, a regular rash of them dotted all over the glacial valley like smallpox scars. There was little point in plotting a careful zigzag course that on the map avoided the chasm belts, since there were bound to be countless unmapped crevasses just as lethal which the photogammetric interpreter had decided were unworthy of his map if indeed they had showed up on the photograph in the first place. Better to steer for an obvious feature on a simple downhill route and to keep checking its gearing in readiness for sudden whiteouts. A series of great east-west swells heralded the first ice disturbance. Huge bridged crevasses passed under us. We held our breath but there was no need to worry – these monsters had solid enough lids to take light weights. It was the narrower fissures from four to twenty feet wide yet potentially as deep that were the more likely killers. And these we came to around noon.

That day we learned that sweat comes easily at minus 30 degrees Centigrade when fear sits in your stomach and creeps down your back. Oliver counted forty crevasses crossed in twenty minutes. He travelled last and still had two sledges. Our second wooden sledges, broken and useless, had long since been abandoned. Each time I crossed a relatively weak snow bridge my sledge broke through and made my route impassable for the others. Charlie, knowing this, naturally veered off my tracks each time a green scar showed up what he called a bomb crater. He then caused further cave-ins beside my own craters and left Ollie with a good deal less choice, especially at those crevasses with only a narrow causeway of remaining snow. Often weird snow hummocks or boils went side by side with the most cut-up zones and served as sinister markers. But not always . . . some of the most rotten slopes had the most innocent appearance. By evening a mist crept dark and sinuous from low lacunas to the east. The La Gorse mountain range to which we were headed on 244 degrees magnetic disappeared. Soon I could see nothing at all, and being in the very middle of a belt of boils and cracks to the east of Mount Early, felt it best to stop. Everywhere we trod first had to be prodded with an ice axe. Charlie let me out on a long rope until I had cleared a short airstrip and tent-spot. Cracks like veins ran everywhere, and each of us on occasion stumbled into them, usually to knee-depth. We called them ankle-crackers, and there were several across the airstrip. Since the mist stayed wrapped about us all night Giles never came.

In the morning a steady wind cut down off the plateau averaging thirty knots. Anxious to find a safer spot for Giles to bring us fuel, I decided to move on despite the total lack of visibility. This proved not very sensible. To move through a highly volatile zone unable to spot the hazards ahead or underfoot could, in fact, be described as stupid. My motivation, though, was purely a desire for progress . . . it was well known that these glaciers could trap mist conditions for days, even weeks on end. To wait for good visibility might write off much precious time.

When my decisions were obviously wrong, Charlie proved an excellent weather vane. He showed his disapproval without a word through his mood – by what he did *not* say. He would tell Ollie his feelings, not me, but he knew that I knew he disapproved. Ollie's diary reflects this: 'Charlie very shirty, as he thought we should have stayed in the tent and not travelled in the whiteout through the crevasse field. Ran wanted to get to a better strip.'

By chance, the whiteout cleared an hour or so after we set out, which was just as well, since our nightmare trail led down through a long blue corridor that twisted and fell and then ended in a cul-de-sac caused by a twenty-foot ice bubble. Now we were surrounded by seemingly bottomless cracks, so we retraced the corridor to an offshoot and tried again. A maze of sunken lanes laced with traps finally released us, shaken but unhurt, five miles from Gardner Ridge. Through binoculars the snow slopes south of this rock ridge seemed gentle and solid.

By early afternoon we reached its foot and made camp beside a good strip. The view to the east and north was impressive. Dizzy cliffs shrouded in frozen gloom were capped with that golden light seen only in far polar places where the air is pure in the vast white fields which have drowned all lower land.

There is of course no life in these parts unless you count the rare sparse lichens, southernmost plants in the world, which incredibly survive on the polar granite. Great dikes of pegmatite, of fine-grained igneous rock, reflect the sun's fire in ochre splendour. The upper sediments of sandstone and shale are interspaced with seams of lignite coal and many fossil stems and leaves of ancient plants. Lower down, in the shadowed moraines, are fossil tree sections up to eighteen inches in diameter, evidence of warmer times.

What if we succeeded or failed in our transitory aim? I thought. It means so much to us, but *reality* is here in this wild forgotten place, witness to millennia ... My thoughts wandered and I let them. It was good to relax after the pent-up strain of the upper icefall. Another six thousand feet of nastiness lay ahead.

*

Giles arrived with Ginnie from the South Pole. We took twenty-four full jerry cans in exchange for empty ones, then they flew down the glacier to spot trouble zones. Giles was casual yet precise in his description of the obstacles and in his route advice.

As the glacier narrowed, flowing north between successive mountain ranges, so tributary rivers of ice poured into it from flanking valleys. The junction points where the separate ice currents met were zones of greatly disturbed ice and for us areas of extreme hazard. Likewise, wherever the ice was confined by sheer rock faces and squeezed through narrow passes, there would be trouble. One such defile, five miles long, was, in Giles's opinion, impassable. He suggested a detour up a side valley and back via a hump-back pass which he said 'looks possible'. I later learned that Giles, wishing neither to worry Ginnie nor to paint too realistic a picture, since there was nothing to be gained by discouraging us, had not gone as luridly as he might have into his description of what he saw . . .

Early on December 28, in a whiteout and a wind gusting to forty knots, we skirted the east side of Gardner Ridge and followed the Klein Glacier for a dozen miles to the mist-blurred outline of the Davis Hills. These nondescript rocks swim almost submerged at the point where the twin frozen rivers of Scott and Klein clash with silent but ferocious force.

Both at this chaotic junction and for some miles downstream of it, the ice was in turmoil . . . 'It doesn't know whether it's coming or going,' was Ollie's immediate reaction to the impressive vista of nature showing off what we glimpsed from a gravel spur north of Davis Hills.

We sneaked gingerly along a finger of good ice beside the gravel spit until the region of hummocks and splits to our immediate east met up with the monoclinal pressure ridges and chasm belts from the main Scott Glacier flow.

By way of an excuse to delay the moment of truth, I stopped a few yards short of the first snow bridge, an eight-foot stretch of yellow sagging snow, and took my map out. Every detail of the crevasse zones for the next ninety miles as passed over the radio by Giles was marked on this map. My leather mitts were old and shiny with use. The wind, powerful all morning, sliced through the gulley and tore the map away. Briefly it caught against a hummock and I ran after it. My safety rope jerked taut and I fell flat on my back. The precious map scuttered away like an autumn leaf. I tried to start up in a hurry, which with our Skidoos was usually a mistake. The plugs fouled.

The map was gone. Now the recommended route was only in my head. I'd always taken a spare map and navigation kit and packed it onto another sledge. Now Charlie produced it and we entered the crevasse field. Giles's route ran along a curly spine, the impact line between the two converging ice lanes, and we followed it, grateful that we were neither to the left nor to the right because the deep shadows of great caverns marked each flank like the random stripes of a tiger.

In a mile or so the crevasse field ended. Then quite gradually our route veered north-northeast and the Scott Glacier fell away before us to reveal a breathtaking panorama of mountain and glacier, ice field and sky. The world seemed to start at our feet, dropping six hundred metres to the far horizon, where our highway disappeared between the cliffs of Mount Walshe and the Organ Pipe Peaks.

For thirty miles keeping to the centre of the glacier, we made good time until, close to Mount Denauro, a rash of rotten snow bridges collapsed beneath us. We all suffered shocks, and as usual Ollie at the back was the worst off. I spared him no time for sympathy, because I knew that I must soon locate the valley which gave access to Giles's detour.

Four miles short of the defile between Mount Gardiner and

Mount Russell I stopped and checked with binoculars. The ice between the forbidding cliffs ahead was shadowed but nonetheless visible as a line of even disturbances . . . the sight of it reminded me of rapids spotting from upriver in British Columbia. The difference was that there no detour was possible, whereas we hoped to cheat the icy jaws ahead by a sideways jink into the mountains.

No sooner had we veered to the western flank of the glacier than Charlie's sledge collapsed a wide snow bridge. I saw Ollie struggling to help extricate the dangling load but was not going back over one step of the perilous route unless needed, so I sat and watched and in due course they were again en route. We climbed over a thousand feet to a high, wild pass where the wind bit through our clothes and whipped up spirals of snow from the granite fortress of Mount Ruth and its senior twin Mount Gardiner.

To the west a ragged company of primordial peaks speared the sky, mere reminders of the vastness of their ice-buried bulk. And faintly, too, the ice rivers themselves, many bearing names from the 'heroic age' of polar exploration – the Amundsen, Alex Heiberg and Devil's glaciers.

From the pass we climbed still higher to the north until the steep valley fell away between the cliffs of Mounts Ruth and Gardiner. Charlie, careful never to sound excited about anything, described the subsequent downhill journey: 'The descent was hair-raising, too steep for sledges which ran down ahead of the Skidoos sometimes wrenching them sideways and even backwards over wide droopy snow bridges. Some of the bridges had fracture lines on *both* sides and were obviously ready to drop at the first excuse, like overripe apples. How we made the bottom, God only knows. We camped on blue ice.'

I had not wanted to stop but a wall of pressure hummocks and crevasse scars blocked off the bottom end of the valley from one cliff face to the other. We had travelled some fourteen hours and covered five days' worth of scheduled progress. The only way out of the valley was forward to rejoin the Scott Glacier. If we were going to sleep somewhere solid it had to be here on the deep blue polished ice above the pressure wall. The spoil of rockfalls lay all about, embedded in the ice, and the wind shrieked down the natural air funnel all night, but we were tired and slept well.

Next morning there was no talk over coffee. We were all apprehensive. The wind had gone and it was warmer than at any time for a year. From the flat lip of our blue-ice campsite another steep slope saw us once more sliding downward, sledges out of control, brakes fully applied.

Below the last incline I headed for the northern foot of Mount Gardiner, hoping for an exit lane around the pressure wall. There was none. The Mount Ruth side looked impassable, so we nudged at the wall itself and ran along a narrow corridor at its foot. In one place, rotten as a worm-eaten plank, the wall was split and a branch corridor led through to the main flow beyond. One by one we passed cautiously over the sagging divide, and the fun began. What a day. At the end of it Ol wrote: 'Thank God it's over and done with, as it was quite the nastiest and most dangerous experience of my life.'

Much of the surface was glare ice, smooth as glass and difficult for the rubber tracks to grip. One time Ollie's two sledges both fell into separate crevasses bringing his Skidoo to an abrupt halt just short of a third. One disturbed region averaged a crevasse every two yards, and two-thirds of these were unbridged, the rest too rotten to support more than one sledge crossing at speed.

As Charlie's diary put it:

> The descent was a nightmare I don't care to recall. Some people will think it must have been easy simply because we descended so quickly. All I can say is let them try. Ran and Ol were as

> frightened as I was even if they don't admit it. That's why Ran kept going hour after hour without stopping. He zigzagged in every direction trying to avoid the worst areas. He didn't have much success and on one of the upper ledges, we found ourselves right in the middle of a major pressure zone. Great ice bubbles and blue domes reared above us as we slithered along a maze of craked corridors, totally lost. My sledge took an eight-foot-wide fissure diagonally and broke through the bridge. My Skidoo's rubber tracks clawed at the blue ice, slipped sideways and the sledge began to disappear. I was lucky. A patch of grainy white ice gave the tracks just enough forward purchase to heave forward again. The sledge wallowed up and over the forward lip of the crevasse. Nobody who wasn't there hasn't felt the deadly lurch of snow giving way under his seat and hasn't seen the line upon line of white and blue telltale shadows in a major crevasse field and been forced to carry on, going over more and more for hour after hour, can imagine the sweaty apprehension we experienced.

At one point it was necessary to cross from the west to the east side of the glacier because the west had become impossible. This involved moving parallel with the crack lines and, unless extremely quick and wary, ending up with both Skidoo and sledge travelling along the top of a delicate snow bridge. In such circumstances there would be no escape from a cave-in. We completed this crossing along an imaginary line drawn between Cox Peak and the western end of Organ Pipe Peaks.

The last concentrated nightmare, southwest of Mount Zanuck, was a series of swollen ice waves similar to swell in the southern ocean. In between each rounded crest were furrows pocked with treacherous seams. Ollie had a particularly bad time here ... The hours crept by but so did the features, weird isolated boulders borne by the flow many miles from the original rockfalls that spawned them, the powerful inflow of Albanus Glacier, the sastrugi slopes below Mount Staneman and finally Durham Point beyond which there was nothing but ice and the Pacific.

We had arrived on the Ross Shelf.

Dog-tired we camped a mere five hundred feet above sea level, and there spent a day repairing, repacking and, in Ol's case, drilling.

On the last day of 1980 we moved due north for fifty miles and away from the crevasses that shifted about the foot of the glaciers. The snow thrown up by our Skidoo skis landed on our clothes, and the sun then melted it because the temperature was plus 1 degree Centigrade.

The surface was excellent once on the move, though its slushy texture made it hard to tug out the sledges from a standing start. There was no longer any need for facemasks or sweaters. Indeed, life was indescribably comfortable, easy, carefree. Following the northerly push I switched half-left onto 183 degrees magnetic, confident we would miss the great complex of disturbances called the Steershead Crevasses. Gradually now the mountains to the left tapered away until, as on the plateau, there was nothing but ice and us.

For nine days we kept to this heading. Once a whiteout stopped us for eight hours and Giles flew out since we were low on fuel. The fifth day out we completed seventy-nine nautical miles. The glare was intense. I navigated by storm clouds to the west. After ten hours of steady and slightly damp progress we camped. Ollie fell asleep while drilling and Charlie while cooking the stew.

On the seventh day we crossed the 180-degree meridian, which at this point is also the International Date Line. We increased our mileage for the day to ninety-one nautical miles and used only a gallon for each eight miles.

On the ninth day, despite a semi-whiteout, we drove a hundred nautical miles and likewise on the tenth when at noon a high white mushroom cloud first became visible on the horizon ahead and to the right – the volcanic steam cloud of Mount Erebus.

I thought of the recent DC-10 crash on Fang Ridge, Mount Erebus. Erebus in Greek mythology is the son of Chaos or the Great Abyss. He signifies darkness. At 1:48 P.M. on November 28, some six weeks before, Erebus son of Chaos had sired death. To us, as the 13,000-foot volcano loomed slowly larger, Erebus was just a pure white mountain beneath which nestled our long-aspired goal – Scott Base. By dusk two other features made famous through the expeditions of Scott and Shackleton appeared far away but distinct – Mina Bluff and Black Island.

On January 10, after eighty-one nautical miles and some unpleasant crevasses, large and small, we camped at the tip of White Island. But two hours from Scott Base, Charlie's Skidoo developed piston trouble. Ollie had carried a spare engine all the way from Ryvingen, worked late and completed the engine change by midnight.

Next day at 6:00 P.M. the commander of Scott Base came out to meet us with a sledge drawn by huskies. He led us over the sea ice, scattering docile seals and screaming skuas, to Pram Point, where the wooden huts of his base huddled by the edge of the sea. Above on the rocks some sixty New Zealanders looked down at us and a lone kilted piper struck up the haunting tune of 'Amazing Grace'. Ginnie came down with Bothy on a lead to prevent his quick demise at the jaws of the huskies.

In sixty-seven days we had crossed Antarctica, but as yet the total expedition was halfway neither in time nor distance.

But this was no time to think of that.

Chapter Nine

> Confidence is simply that assured feeling you have before you fall flat on your face.
>
> L. BINDER

Many kind folk around the world sent messages to say they were pleased we had made it. Our patron, His Royal Highness Prince Charles, and President Reagan were among them. A note from our SAS regiment simply said: 'Just in case you are not getting your copy of the *Red Star* regularly. With best wishes.' Enclosed was a cutting from the relevant Soviet newspaper, *Krasnaya Zvezda,* commenting on our journey.

The British mountaineer Joe Tasker wrote asking for my comments on polar survival in winter. He had just attempted to climb Mount Everest in winter. 'It seems,' he wrote, 'that we are involved in similarly grim struggles ... you will be aware that we did not unfortunately make it to the top. In the end the mountain, with its war of attrition, won the day ... But we will return in the winter of 1983.' Sadly Joe was killed in 1982 on the northeast ridge of Everest.

*

Scott Base owned some twenty husky dogs. Each summer a dog trainer/driver ensured they were kept fit and regularly used. They were the last such dog team on that side of the continent and were not immunised against diseases likely to be carried by Bothy despite his long stint in the south. The trainer, called Doggo by all, made it clear to Ginnie that Bothy should keep well clear of the huskies at all times.

A donation from our friends at the South Pole arrived and enabled us to hold a party with the New Zealanders. We expected to stay at Scott Base for a month. They let us eat with them and sleep in the base. We shared camp duties and gave them our remaining rations, though these were not all in good condition, being, after all, three or four years old.

Simon joined their three instructors, whose job was to train the McMurdo Americans in polar survival. Giles took many of the New Zealanders flying but soon had to leave Antarctica for the long flight to New Zealand. The first five hundred miles were over ice mountains and the remainder over the sea, an anxious flight for both Gerry and Giles.

Of us all they were the only professionals in terms of experience and skill. They had worked in Antarctica during previous years with many different governmental organisations. Giles had a critical nature, vital to a good polar pilot. When later asked what he though about the amateur nature of the expedition . . . 'I think the great thing is that our ice group are not professionals at anything. I mean, they have learned how to cook in the case of Charlie; how to be a mechanic in Ol's case; and Ginnie, how to be a radio operator. Ran is a good leader, probably a great leader, but he had to learn about navigation. The great thing about these four people is their *persistence* in getting across, not their individual abilities.'

I think Giles knew that much of our strength, despite our lack of experience, lay in our collective ability. Remove any one of us and the other three became a far less capable entity. And unfortunately it was now clear that Ollie would leave us, determined as he was not to give up his marriage and feeling that he could no longer stay with us *and* keep Rebecca.

When interviewed about his decision, Ollie was not evasive: 'The time has come,' he said, 'when I must try to lead a normal life. My wife was never keen on my doing the expedition, but somehow she has accepted it for the last seven years. Although she has not pushed the point, I think the time has come when I have got to give it up. I have more or less been neglecting her these last few years and now, not in a year's time, I have got to stop it and get a job and make our marriage work. I have spent a lot of time away from home and that's not the best basis for a marriage ... I hoped that I might, if you like, be able to get away with it for as long as possible. I've done it stage by stage and Rebecca has said, "Fine, fair enough, carry on." I think I have got to go back.'

Back in England there seemed to be a lingering suspicion that the Rebecca situation was merely an excuse, that Ol had some other deeper reason for leaving. Some even suggested Ollie might be frightened of the Arctic Ocean. So what? Who wasn't? Anyway, if true, he would never leave on account of it, any more than Charlie or I would. I was full of only partially suppressed fear about the Arctic Ocean but this was no reason for giving up, not after having just completed the Antarctic crossing. Not for any of us. Another suggested motive was some alleged deep rift between Ollie and the rest of us, most likely between him and me. Such rumours tend to mature slowly over the years. Ollie's interview with an American film team at Scott Base went this way: 'Has the team individually gotten more happy as the expedition has progressed?' Ollie: 'I don't think we have got more happy but we certainly haven't got less happy. Ran and Ginnie tend to keep themselves to themselves. Back in 1976 and 1977 was the time Charlie and I got to know them.

Since then we have worked with implicit trust between us. No, it hasn't got *happier.* It's always been happy.' 'Both you and Charlie have a pronounced sense of humour. How do you feel about Ran? Does he have a sense of humour?' Ollie: 'Charlie and I joke a lot the whole time and I think we reflect the lighter aspect of the expedition. Ran has more worries. I think his sense of humour isn't as warped as Charlie's and mine. He is, I think, the finest expedition leader one can come across. He plans things to the most minute detail and he's very easy to work with – there is no, if you like, leader-others atmosphere. We are very much like a family. I certainly wouldn't have gone across with anyone else.' 'And now you are going?' Ollie: 'I think two is the best number. With two you have less equipment and two can generally do things quicker than three.'

A message came from our executive committee that a delegation of three, the chairman, Sir Vivian Fuchs and Mike Wingate-Gray, would fly to New Zealand to make certain that the question of a replacement for Ollie was thoroughly discussed. They were solidly against Charlie and me attempting the Arctic alone.

On January 19 the *Benjamin Bowring* broke through on Ginnie's radio. She was seven miles out in heavy pack.

The American icebreaker, U.S.C.G. *Polar Star,* arrived and began her duties keeping a sea line clear through the ice. At 13,000 tons she could steam continuously through six feet of ice at three knots and ram her way through ice up to twenty-one feet thick. Her crew were unusually animated that day . . . the U.S. hostages held for so long in Teheran were released.

Simon climbed up Observation Hill with his camera and the four of us walked out past Captain Scott's wooden shack to Hut Point. It was not difficult to imagine the feeling of the pioneers in the early days when their masted ships appeared on that same horizon. As our own little ship entered the bay I wondered whether our friends would all be there after their year of hard grind and charter work in the Samoan isles.

The *Benji Bee* finally slid between the ice floes below Scott's Hut and the strident strains of 'Land of Hope and Glory' came over the ship loudspeakers. After a parting of a year and many miles the two parts of the expedition family were meeting up. Not all eyes were dry, nor, in a short while, were many throats. Several strangers could be seen on board, mostly New Zealand scientists and also Bryn, the *Observer* photographer, come back to catch up on a year of missed photographs. Dr Armand Hammer had sent in a three-man film crew with the same intention, one of whom we recognised, Tony Dutton, the amiable sound recordist. The other two were Americans from Wyoming, Mike Hoover and his wife Beverly Johnson, a top rock-climber.

Because the ice team had arrived at Scott Base six weeks ahead of schedule the ship had yet to complete a local charter journey so, having dropped off Bryn, the film crew and Jimmy Young, a *Benji Bee* engineer who wanted a spell at Scott Base with his countrymen, she set off for a two-week voyage of scientific research in the Ross Sea.

On February 12 the *Benji Bee* returned, having ventured further south than any other ship for many years. The entire crew then took to the ice fields to experience sledge work with dogs and Skidoos, cooking and eating ice rations and sleeping out in pyramid tents.

Three days later we left our good friends from the New Zealand and American bases and sailed north.

Anton prevailed on Les Davis, the current skipper, to anchor off Cape Evans, the site of Captain Scott's main base. Anton then took all of us ashore in a dinghy and the hut was unlocked by its keeper, Roger Clark, ex-base commander of Scott Base. He had elected to return to New Zealand with us rather than on the official aircraft.

This was the hut from which Scott and his four chosen companions made their last journey. The Kiwi caretakers had preserved the hut well. It was just as it must have been seventy years back: pony harnesses hung on hooks; Victorian chemical bottles lay about in the 'laboratory' and seal's blubber spread over the lobby floor. On the granite hillock above the hut a rookery of penguins flapped and strutted in their dinner jackets, and the two dozen Transglobers strolled about more quietly than was their custom. We felt, I think, a silent affinity with our dead countrymen, their journeys long done, ours only half completed.

Beyond the lie of land and ice the great Pacific rollers once more toyed with the *Benji Bee*. On February 23, we were rolling violently when the cloud-hung mass of Campbell Island was sighted. Soon we entered the protection of its long natural harbour between *green* hills.

After fourteen months without a blade of grass, this remote but fertile land was a wonderful sight, not unlike a western Scottish isle. A dozen New Zealand scientists who worked at a base beside the entry fjord made us very welcome. We were the first British-registered ship to call since records began in 1945, according to the base leader.

He had his men show us the island on foot. First a colony of sea lions playing in a rock-girt bay, then elephant seals wallowing in noisome pits from which they reared their ugly heads to mouth foul-breathed roars. All around were bogs of peat and beds of kelp and on a high hill flanked by cliffs we listened to the hollow clap of beaks where rare Royal Albatross hens sat on eggs as big as cricket balls.

We left Campbell Island the same day, bound for Lyttleton, New

Zealand. And once more grew accustomed to the nonstop rollers and the broken crockery. Plates and cups went back and forth. A wooden parrot, hung from the ceiling, gyrated above the saloon table, and Bothy played endlessly with rubber balls which needed no throwing since now they rolled about with a life of their own. From time to time a dark wall of water struck the plate-glass saloon window, then hissed away down the scuppers. I listened to the crew's tropical memories of the year in Samoa, a part of Transglobe I had missed of necessity but with regret.

As February passed by, the weather slowly improved, and by the time we reached the green hills of New Zealand, life was back on an even keel.

As we entered Lyttleton harbour it was raining from a dull grey sky and the dockworkers had just gone out on strike in sympathy with the national airline. We British felt very much at home.

With three weeks to spare until our exhibition in Auckland at the opposite end of New Zealand, skipper Les Davis put the ship into dry dock for inspection and careening. Fortunately, there were no expensive surprises and we were able to sail north to Auckland on March 23.

The chairman, Sir Vivian Fuchs and Mike Wingate-Gray met us at a private house, where we sat for an hour to discuss the thorny issue caused by Oliver's imminent departure.

In a nutshell the committee was determined Ollie should be replaced. I was equally determined that he should not be replaced until such time as I found two of us alone were unable to cope. Charlie was not particularly adamant about the matter either way but if there was to be no showdown he was inclined to favour two. Ollie himself spoke strongly in favour of our being allowed to do as we saw best since we had as much Arctic Ocean experience as our committee advisers.

The chairman, Sir Edmund Irving, pointed out that at meetings already held in London with the full committee it had become clear that all the committee were in favour of three. One view had been that, logically, two men set out and one was lost, the other was left in a serious predicament. If three men set out and one was lost, there remained two to render immediate aid. Our old friend and supporter Colonel Andrew Croft had said categorically that there was no question of two for the North. He considered the alternative to three men would be suicide. Mike Wingate-Gray had confirmed to all present that prior to the forming of the committee he had obtained my agreement to abide by decisions made by the committee. He had also pointed out that I must be aware of the need for the three-man team – it was clear SAS policy for teams to comprise four members; hence my initial four-man team and dismay at the loss of Geoff Newman. Dr Geoffrey Hattersley-Smith's view had been that the Northwest Passage could safely be executed by two, although probably not in one season.

In view of this it had been agreed as a compromise that in the event of intransigence on my part two could be accepted through the passage and as far north as Alert but *not* thereafter. It had been decided that my threat (if I were not permitted to continue with Charlie alone I would pull out together with Ginnie) was mere bluff. This was a correct assessment. The final consensus of opinion had been that the expedition must proceed as a three-man team, since failure caused through taking a two-man team would be worse than abandonment of the venture.

I thanked Sir Edmund for passing on the views of those back home and tried to make my own points sound as reasonable as theirs. I quoted Wally Herbert, the only man to cross the Arctic Ocean before. During his crossing he wrote: 'As a two-man party we would travel harder, faster and more efficiently than as a three-man unit.'

'But not more safely,' Sir Edmund pointed out.

I could not argue this point except in a roundabout fashion. 'Naomi Uemura,' I said, 'a five-foot-tall Japanese, reached the North Pole alone. I can see no reason why two hulking great Brits can't do likewise *and* carry on down the other side of the Arctic.'

There was silence at this so I quickly pressed on. 'The two of us have now spent six years together, including travel in Greenland, the Arctic Ocean and Antarctica. We know each other's limitations and strong points. We have worked out a modus vivendi. However well we may know some third person in normal circumstances, he may turn out very different given the unique strains of Arctic Ocean conditions. Quite apart from character interaction between us and such a third man, his very presence could easily undermine our own mutual compatibility.'

Mike Wingate-Gray's answer was to ask Charlie what *he* thought about another man. Charlie, difficult to pin down when he doesn't want to be, answered only part of the question. 'For the overwintering at Alert I think I would prefer no one else but the three of us, including Ginnie. I do know another member of the team whom I could put up with but I don't think he would fit in with Ginnie and Ran. Equally I know that Ran has someone in mind who wouldn't suit me. So we are in a predicament where it would be better to keep to just the three of us.'

At this time I learned that our chairman, without my knowledge, had written to our patron, His Royal Highness Prince Charles, stating his concern about my plans to proceed with only Charlie.

I decided I'd put my side of the situation to Prince Charles when he visited the *Benji Bee* in Sydney during his coming Australian visit. The fact that Prince Charles was prepared to become involved in such discussions of expedition politics filled me with admiration. It would have been so easy for him to have suggested we sort out our own problems. Because he *did* act as final arbitrator for the expedition we were able to sort out such matters by passing the buck upward to someone whose judgement we all respected.

The meeting in Auckland, then, was frank and friendly, but it ended inconclusively. A month later Sir Edmund called a meeting at the Royal Geographical Society consisting of Arctic experts, including Wally Herbert and representatives of the British Antarctic Survey and the Scott Polar Institute. Andrew Croft remained strongly against a two-man attempt. Later that spring Mike Wingate-Gray said that 'the final decision should be made by the commander in the field.' Sir Vivian said that speed was of the essence and that two men, given no trouble, were faster. Nevertheless, a third man was a wise precaution. It was summed up . . . 'Conventional wisdom based on tradition and experience argues for three men but the need for speed and the question of comparability/suitability provide a case for two. The committee leaves it to the leader's judgement and will back him up.'

The differences were not totally forgotten. Andrew Croft wrote: 'The fact that you have no one adequately trained to be the third man has forced the committee to compromise with you against their better judgement.' And five months later Sir Vivian made it quite clear that if I did set out with no third man the blame should things go wrong would be entirely mine.

George Greenfield, who has been a part of Britain's major expeditions for over twenty years, once summed up committees in a letter to me: 'Having lived through several expedition crises, I thoroughly appreciate the many problems that are bound to arise when you have a fairly elderly if distinguished committee in London and a team of younger people at the "sharp edge". These problems are further compounded by the difficulties of communication.'

In fairness, I could not forget that without the backing of our committee we would not have set foot in Antarctica, that their time, advice and support were given free and in good will and that, were they to agree to everything the field leader proposed, there would, after all, be no point in their existence.

After the Auckland exhibition, where the Right Honourable Robert Muldoon, prime minister of New Zealand, in his opening speech likened the Transglobers to old English merchant adventurers whose exploits struck responsive chords with New Zealanders, the passage to Australia was calm and warm. I had crated off for the Arctic a great deal of Antarctic equipment in two containers. The work for the Yukon River and Northwest Passage journeys could be done on the long voyage from Sydney to Los Angeles, so apart from the fifty-two thank-you letters to Christchurch and Auckland, I tried to relax and get rid of my Antarctic pallor.

In Sydney the *Benji Bee* was moored to the harbour's passenger terminal directly opposite the city's opera house. On April 14 Prince Charles visited us. On the boat deck we gave him three cheers and a miniature silver globe marked with our route by way of congratulations on his engagement to Lady Diana Spencer. Bothy joined the cheering with an aggressive yapping session, which he stopped only when Prince Charles patted and spoke to him.

In the skipper's cabin I explained to our patron the likely Arctic problems. He appreciated that things were unlikely to go as well as they had in the Antarctic. Afterward he toured the exhibition, as did Dr Armand Hammer, who reaffirmed his support for our venture and said he would send further film teams to the Arctic.

Later in the day Charlie was married to Twink. Their honeymoon would be the voyage to Los Angeles. Next day Anton Bowring married Jill; the *Benji Bee* was becoming quite a family ship.

On April 17 we left Sydney. Ginnie was to fly back to England to go through her Antarctic tapes with the analysts at Sheffield University Space Physics Department. She would rejoin the ship in Los Angeles. Paul Clark stayed behind to organise merchandise after-sales, and Ollie to tidy up the aftermath of the exhibition. After that he would return to London and begin a new life with Rebecca.

The original group of Geoff and Mary, Ollie and Charlie had dwindled somewhat, but, I told myself, there was still a chance Rebecca might later sanction Ollie's return to the Arctic.

On the way from Sydney to Los Angeles I worked in my old hold, now comparatively empty, to prepare kit for the Yukon River and the Northwest Passage. Once, in sweltering hot weather and close to the equator, the skipper stopped the ship. Everyone including Bothy went swimming in the wonderfully cool Pacific swell.

Nigel showed me a copy of telex traffic between our London office and a U.S. telex operator. President Reagan had agreed to open our Los Angeles exhibition if his commitments made it possible. As it turned out, of course, the president was nearly assassinated. But he sent us a message:

> My warmest congratulations to you all on your magnificent achievement of completing the 2,200-mile crossing of Antarctica on open snowmobiles. Now that you are halfway through your 52,000-mile polar circumnavigation of the earth we welcome you to the United States and pray that your luck and skill during the next half of your trip, which promises to be even more harsh and hazardous, will keep you from harm's way. You are attempting something which has never been done before which takes tremendous courage and dedication. The 'can do' your expedition so perfectly exemplifies is still alive in the free world. We wish you godspeed and clear sailing.

The Los Angeles exhibition went smoothly, although the site was in old deserted dockland and difficult for visitors to find. People on board, however, were unsettled. The excitement of the Antarctic success had faded. For the crew the future looked dreary; soon they would drop off the land group again and face another period of charter work or laying up. For the land group a journey of great uncertainty lay ahead.

It was a time of squabbles and barely muted ill-feeling. A chance visitor would have noted nothing ... all seemed fine on the face of it, but underneath the uncertainties were making currents and cross-currents. Even though I saw little of Charlie – Twink naturally took up his time – he too was on tenterhooks and found my presence irritating. A brief look at the diary of Anto – a friend – indicates the state of things:

> One of the problems of being together for so long is that some feel there are plots against them. I noticed the ASA setting on my camera had been adjusted and at once thought someone had done it out of spite. Ran is, I believe, using 'crew opinion' as an excuse for not having outsiders on board. I am sure he is also using me in a most dishonest way to this end but I cannot think why. It has me most depressed. I am amazed at Ran for being so devious. I discussed this with Charlie who showed me his diary. It is full of incidences where Ran and Ginnie have played such 'games'. Charlie said there is only one thing he is out for and that is to complete the voyage for himself, not for Ran. That should be my attitude, too. What an 'up and down' life this is. It is to be avoided in the future.

Back in London things were also none too good, according to a letter from Ollie:

> The Skidoos from Borga have just sat in the barracks unprotected. None of the work I asked Simon to do was done in the

Antarctic. Just ensure that Charlie does take the heads off and checks the pistons before use. The setup back here is very depressing. The barracks are a shambles and I don't feel the office or committees are really pulling their weight ... London is cripplingly expensive even if you do nothing. I intend working for six months and seeing how the land lies then. At the moment Rebecca seems to be even encouraging me to do the North Pole so if all goes well I could come out to Alert in the winter: that is, if the committee allows it, which at present seems unlikely. All the best and keep your chin up. You are better off than I am here. I only wish I was with you.

Luv, OLIVER

I wrote back wishing him well at finding a job and expressing my hope that he would be back with us in the winter.

There was little that could be done to raise individual morale. One could only hope the promise of renewed action would buck up the land group, and the ship's crew would settle down once details of the future became clearer. As far as Charlie's seeming dislike of me was concerned, there seemed little I could do about it since I was unsure of its reasons. He was always friendly and jovial to my face and when the two of us were together, so it did not affect our efficiency. I only learned about his feelings secondhand through his conversations elsewhere and, from the little detail I gleaned, his dislike was on general grounds rather than for specific reasons. Rather like father/son or mother/daughter relationships when the two simply grate on each other and can't get on together however hard they try. The only difference in our case was that I had no objections to Charlie and found his presence no problem at all.

I suspect that part of the trouble may have been his desire, a very human one, to see his own point of view acted on, especially with regard to practical land group activities. There were numerous examples of this after our arrival at Vancouver, site of our last exhibition. They weren't earthshaking and will hardly be of interest to most readers, but they counted, had their effect ... I was packing in oilpaper a selection of spare outboard parts and asked Charlie to carry them since he would travel in the rear boat. A few ready spares, such as propellers, pins and plugs, I stacked for each boat. Charlie said I should also carry some of the maintenance spares. 'Why?' I asked. 'Because,' he said, 'you might capsize and lose them all.' 'Rubbish,' I said, 'nobody will capsize and even if you did everything is lashed on.' I was to be proved at least partially wrong. Part of Charlie's feelings may also have come from his natural dislike of being told to do things. On our way up the Pacific the skipper Les Davis once asked me, 'What's up with Charlie?' 'Nothing,' I said, 'why?' 'He was really irritable this morning when I suggested Dave Peck had given him the idea of a two A.M. ship's party. He rounded on me and said, "*Nobody* gave me the idea. *I* decided on it.' I told the skipper not to worry, everyone got irritable from time to time.' I also remembered Charlie's words on one occasion near Scott Base: 'Nobody *orders* me to do *anything.*'

I felt the fact that Charlie had a proud and independent spirit could only be beneficial on a journey such as we were soon to make together, but it must also have made it difficult to act as second string to any bow. I often asked Charlie to complain openly when he had objections but that was just not his way. He tended to bottle things up. I spent seven long years with him and never got to know him. Strangely enough, I am not convinced that this was a bad thing. The fact that we had never been friends meant that we also needed never fear losing a valued relationship through too much enforced proximity. For success in our venture there was no need for individuals to be friends – just equable companions.

Simon Grimes once told me: 'The best way for two good friends to bust up their relationship is to go climbing together for a month.'

On June 19 we left Vancouver and passed through the mist-clad Aleutian Islands with nothing but distant Midway Island to our south.

From the moment we left Vancouver, a race against time had begun.

Less than a dozen expeditions have successfully navigated the Northwest Passage in either direction. Those who have done so used craft with some protection from the elements and took an average of two years to get through. This is because of the pack ice which besets the narrow coastal sea-lane and most years makes any navigation impossible. The ice could not be expected to break up, even if 1981 was a good ice year, until mid-July. It was likely to re-form over the sea (should it have broken up in the first place) by early September. To navigate three thousand miles of ice-strewn, mist-covered ocean in six weeks meant really moving, and, above all, being ready to set out into the passage from the mouth of the Mackenzie River by mid-July.

I had figured on sixteen days to cover the eleven hundred miles of the Yukon River – our preparation for the Northwest Passage – with six days set aside to drive up the newly opened dust road from the Yukon Bridge at Dawson City to Inuvik on the Mackenzie River, the end of the road. This, working backward, meant a start up the Yukon by June 27, when the skipper aimed to drop us overboard in the boats.

Research in England intimated that the ship might approach to within nine miles of the Yukon River mouth. Shallows caused by silt would make further progress impossible. This research proved inaccurate, possibly due to changing silt conditions. Even before we came near to the Yukon mouth things began to go wrong.

First came a storm in the Bering Sea with a headwind that slowed the *Benji Bee* to a crawl for precious days. 'On June 29,' Anton wrote, 'we bounced about with a Force 6 from the north and pitched heavily in shallow water of twelve fathoms. Passed Nuniwak Island covered with snow. Still breeze and only 5 degrees C. By midnight there were 112 miles to go but we could make only four knots. We stopped for thirty minutes to fix a fuel leak.'

By the evening of June 30 the wind steadied to ten knots and we were steaming inshore. The echo-sounder showed there were only between eight and ten feet of water under us. We anchored at eight P.M. with six feet of water under the ship. I checked with the lead line. During the night the wind calmed down, but as soon as we launched the boats it increased to twenty knots and lashed up a nasty sea. We launched a lifeboat from which to film them with the ship in the background. When they disappeared in the swell we slowly made way back to the ship to hook the boat to the winch lines. It was a hell of a job to hook up. Nearly pulled the bottom out of the boat on the down slams and we parted a strand on the winch line.

Bryn Campbell had been assigned by the *Observer* newspaper to cover the Yukon journey and so had rejoined the ship in Vancouver.

Because my boat loads were originally planned for three people in three inflatables the absence of Ollie meant carrying more stores in only two boats. With Bryn and his personal gear as well as the extra weight of foam buoyancy, both craft hung menacingly low in the water but rode the breaking waves better than the ship's lifeboat.

Soon the ship was a faraway speck, visible only from the surge top of waves. No land was visible ... we were still fourteen miles off and the marshes of the Yukon mouth were low and featureless.

An hour out from the ship I noticed the swirl of white breakers ahead and thought back to the very first day of the Canadian river expedition some ten years earlier. Bryn Campbell had been on board my boat and within an hour of our setting out was very nearly drowned after being knocked overboard by a branch and caught in a swirling logjam.

History, they say, has a habit of repeating itself.

Chapter Ten

No! There's the land. Have you seen it?
It's the cussedest land that I know,
From the big dizzy mountains that screen it
To the deep, deathless valleys below.

ROBERT SERVICE

Bryn began the journey with me but navigation was difficult with the two of us on board. I manoeuvred close to Charlie, and Bryn crawled across to join him. Of the next few minutes he wrote:

> The waves began to break over us, hitting us hard from behind. Often we were completely awash and I marvelled at our buoyancy – a stubborn muscular resilience you could actually feel. But as we watched Ran's boat pounded by the sea and disappearing into the ten-foot-deep troughs, we had all too vivid an image of how vulnerable we were. I turned to talk to Charlie and saw him lifted bodily by a surge of water and thrown clean over my head. As the boat capsized I tugged my feet free of the fuel lines and jumped as far away from the propeller as I could. Then the hull crashed down beside me …

As I moved into the white-topped wave line it became obvious this was no sudden squall. The surface turbulence, like most river rapids, was caused by the bedrock conditions over which the water moved. The combination of Yukon floodwater from prolonged rains and the annual thaw, the uneven and unseen silt banks beneath and the eastward set of the Bering Sea against these banks, had combined to produce a local cauldron. A wave of silt-laden sea-water crashed down on my boat from behind. Another surged in from the side. For a long moment I could see nothing but foam and spray. I rubbed my eyes which stung from the salt and at the top of a new breaker glanced behind.

A momentary flash of orange movement, then nothing as I slammed down into a furrow. The next upswing was a big one and gave me a clear view of the turmoil behind ... Charlie's boat was upside down five hundred yards back. No sign of either occupant.

It was a while before I could even begin to turn around. The secret of survival in these shallow, riotous waters was to remain totally alert and keep the bows at all times into the next breaker. It was a matter of aim and balance. After another big one I whipped the tiller around, and the game little boat sped through 180 degrees in time to face the next attack head on.

Now the wind was more ahead than behind, which was safer. On each upsurge I crept closer to the upturned inflatable, my mouth dry – I still could see no bodies. Then an orange-clad Charlie dragged himself slowly onto the boat's bottom. I had asked Dunlop to sew handholds along the hull for this sort of incident, but in wet mitts I knew it was difficult to keep a grip on them. Next time I saw them Charlie had grasped Bryn's hood and was helping him up.

A wave deposited me close to the others – almost too close, since my propeller sliced the water beside their rubber hull. I needed more control. Unlashing my cargo tarpaulin I began to chuck full jerry cans overboard. With six gone and some three hundred pounds lighter, there was more response to the tiller, but since everything had to be done with one hand, time had passed by. The others looked blue with cold. Using their hull handgrips they were trying to reright the boat with their weight. It did not work.

I coiled up a safety line and tried to come alongside. Both craft were flung violently about. Twice I almost was washed over them, then I tossed the wet rope.

'Got it,' Charlie shouted. 'Keep it slack while I fix it.'

With the boats secured, I left my engine on idle and jumped across and together we heaved to reright the boat.

But she continued to wallow with little response. A wall of water rushed by, tearing the rope from its fixture point on Charlie's boat. My boat was adrift and rapidly moving away from us. I watched with my mouth open.

Charlie's voice interrupted my mental void. 'What a bloody silly time and place to get drowned.' He was about to leap off our little patch of safety. Released from my reveries I jumped clumsily as far as I could toward my boat, but now some twenty yards away. Each new wave increased the gap. My survival suit made every movement heavy. I felt futile, but an edge of desperation and a burst of effort saw me beside the hull and clear of the propeller.

On board again, I prepared a second rope. Our luck was good ... a brief lull between waves, no more than a minute but enough for Charlie to attach the line to the centre of one side. Staying on my boat I reversed away until the line was taut with elasticity. Charlie and Bryn bent their backs and on the next upsurge their boat flipped over like a reluctant limpet pried by a fisherman's blade.

Naturally the outboard defied all attempts to restart it so we made fast a long tow-line. If at that point my own outboard had stalled, our lives would probably have been lost and the expedition brought to an abrupt halt. True, we carried in Charlie's boat a spare engine that, although wet, had not ingested water. But the chances were slim.

As it was, the one engine plodded on, and tortoiselike we approached the ship, our only haven. In her lee the seas were calmer and the crew soon had us all aboard. We said hello again to the friends who three short hours before had waved us off for a likely three-year absence. I asked Bryn if he would mind handling a third boat for the Yukon stage. He said nothing, obviously unhappy at the prospect. He did not see how he could cover things photographically if he was having to look after a boat, one hand on the tiller at all times. He could plainly see that my motives were selfish . . . All I wanted was to get from A to B as quickly as possible and catch up on the precious time we had lost. To hell with photographs. A week could easily lose us the race to get through the passage, and we were already a week behind schedule. We *must* set out from the Mackenzie River mouth by the end of July at the latest. And this was already looking unlikely.

I knew we could ascend the Yukon with three inflatables. All my load plans had been prepared for it. Weight is critical to small inflatables – a few pounds can mean the difference between their planing, almost gliding, and their failure to get off the hump and thus dragging through the water using too much fuel. With only two boats, three heavy people and the necessary equipment, we would probably double the time needed for the Yukon. I couldn't afford this simply to maintain a long-standing friendship with Bryn, a man whom I greatly admired. So, despite his obvious dislike of the idea, I pressed him and he made no open complaints. But his mood toward me underwent a subtle change. Luckily he shared two great loves in life with Charlie – rugby and cards – and during the expedition the two had become great friends.

Anton owned an ancient inflatable, patched all over from past wounds, which he donated for use as a third boat. Ollie's own craft I had dispatched from Vancouver as a spare for the north. Now we needed to find a less hazardous approach route to the Yukon's mouth. The skipper took the *Benji Bee* south some thirty miles to the Black River mouth, which is connected to the Yukon. Again we nudged inshore as close as Les dared. With twenty-four feet beneath the hull we waited for good weather. But it worsened, with ugly skies and driving waves. We knew the breakers closer to land would be as bad as before. Although we were but nine miles from the coastline a Force 5 gale blew from the northwest, and overnight this increased to Force 7. The ship began to strike the sea floor when pitching in the heavy swell as Les weighed anchor and we moved away west to deeper water.

That night we made radio contact with a barging company that advised us to try another mouth of the Yukon much farther north. On my maps this northern mouth did not appear to connect with the main river but to merge instead with inland swamps. Our radio contact assured us this was not so, that we should head for this mouth called the Apoon Pass to the north of Norton Sound. The skipper, Anton and I pored over the charts. How to close with the Apoon Pass? A glance at the soundings off its mouth indicated the best course would be to go sixty miles east of the pass and anchor off Whale Islet in thirty-two feet of water. The inflatables would have only four miles of protected water to negotiate to the harbour of St Michael Village, the original Russian settlement in Alaska. There we could seek advice about the coastal journey to enter the Apoon.

With a hundred and twenty miles to go and off a dangerous lee-shore, one of the tie bolts that held the ship's engine in place sheared. This had happened before and the engineer Ken Cameron had only one spare bolt, which he fitted as we floated slowly toward the Alaskan coast. After eight hours of work down below the engineers were satisfied, although anxious that another bolt might shear with no replacement.

Early on July 3 we reached Whale Islet and after brief farewells – the second time around is seldom as emotional as the first – we again went overboard.

The inhabitants of St Michael were Eskimos with mostly Russian names. It was a sunny windswept place of wooden houses connected by paths of duckboards laid over the sodden turf. There was a ghost-town air about the settlement where once a lively Russian hamlet had thrived until the czars sold the fur-rich state to the Americans, an act over which their Soviet successors must froth at the mouth even to contemplate. Wyatt Earp had retired from his gun-toting to become the local pub keeper; presumably to avoid the likelihood of being shot in the back anywhere less remote. The local fuel agent was an adventurous sort who knew the Eskimos of many outlying settlements along the coast and up the Yukon to the village of Kotlik, a short distance up the Apoon Pass. He said he would guide us there in his own fibreglass boat, a Boston Whaler. This was four or five feet longer than the inflatables and about the same width. Like them it was open, but its great advantage was a more robust transom that would take two outboards and so allowed twice the thrust. The disadvantage was its weight, which made it impossible for two men to beach, let along portage, over shallows or rocks.

The coastal journey was slow, wet and cold. West of the sheltering promontory of St Michael the full surge of the Bering Sea again struck the shore and we moved broadside to it through barren Pastol Bay. Despite the shortness of the journey, some seventy miles, we took from midnight on July 3 until well into the next day to reach Kotlik and, on arrival, were soaked through, stiff and cold. In itself this didn't matter, but it worried me for the future . . . here the water and the air were comparatively warm, but up in the passage both would be near freezing. I made up my mind to change from inflatables to a Boston Whaler, such as our guide to Kotlik owned, once the Yukon preparatory journey was finished.

Our two boats had worked well, but Anton's old Zodiac was not fit for further use without major repairs so I left it with the Kotlik state trooper, a policeman with sheriff-like powers. In return I obtained an old and dented aluminium dinghy with a flattish bottom and so light I could lift it with one hand. On flat river water it was adequate, but if we were to run into rapids ... the state trooper clicked his teeth together: 'Not so good. A couple of waves and she'll go straight down.'

The state trooper let me use his radiotelephone, and late that evening I made contact with Ginnie and asked her to find an open Boston Whaler with two outboards to power it. She was to have it ready in twenty days at Inuvik where the northern road ran out and the Mackenzie River began. Obviously she had to find full sponsorship for the boat and the transporting of it to northern Canada. We certainly could not afford to buy it.

Ginnie took it in stride. Her Land Rover and trailer were in good repair, but Bothy was suffering from mosquitoes that favoured his nose and eyes. She was staying at the Klondike Lodge just east of Dawson City – a small truck-repair garage-cum-hotel. In exchange for the use of their telephone Ginnie made beds, washed up and waited at table in the tearoom.

That night the state trooper allowed us to sleep in the Kotlik jail. There were three little cells, dark but protected from rain and mosquitoes, and we laid our bags out gratefully. Unfortunately a drunken Eskimo ran amok and Charlie was thrown out of his cell. This was acceptable, since by squeezing up we still had sleeping room. But an hour later another Eskimo threatened to shoot our state trooper, who naturally conducted a preemptive strike with his

Eskimo deputy and hauled the would-be assassin into the second jail cell. We were homeless again.

But fortune was with us. The Yukon salmon run happened to be in progress that very week, the annual event which makes more money than anything else for those Eskimos and, further east, Indians, who own nets and a boat or a fishwheel trap. So the ramshackle Kotlik fish station was open. A private company paid cash to the locals for their fresh salmon, prepared and boxed them and flew them out once a day by small plane from a strip of muddy grass nearby. The fish folk let us sleep on their floor and fed us waffles and coffee.

We got up early. The rain had stopped and I went to thank the state trooper. 'Be careful,' he said. 'Most of the year there are no rapids for a thousand miles upstream from here, but this is the time of the summer winds. I've seen waves big as houses out on the river. No river man will operate on certain stretches during the winds. You get the wrong conditions, man, and you'll sure as hell drown.' 'But you say there are no rapids,' I protested. 'Sure I do. This is something different but just as bad for a boat. Mebbe worse. Lookit, the winds power down the river canyon and strike the water. All you need is a strong south wind hitting a north-south canyon with the water running *into* the wind.' He drew a diagram in the dust of his hut floor. His wife was an attractive Eskimo girl. 'The down-flowing ripples get whipped up till you've got line after line of standing waves real close together. You get caught in that lot, fellah, and you'll get to Dawson like I'll see heaven and that means you won't see Dawson.'

I thanked him. 'When you say waves as big as houses, how big's that?' 'Twelve feet high, friend. Twelve feet high.'

We left around midday. The boats moved well despite full loads of fuel past the deserted hamlets of Naguchik and Hamilton to the

Nunachik Pass. Deep forest closed in on either bank, until by the hut called Kravaksarak we joined a major arm of the Yukon, the Kwikpak. This in turn, after five hours, led to a place of many forested islands and the river, brown and immensely powerful so soon after the breakup spate, widened to two miles or more. It would be easy to go wrong in the maze of winding channels but our maps were accurate.

The river wound through wild, largely uninhabited forest country. Alaska is mountainous, and in winter temperatures plummet to minus 70 degrees Fahrenheit. Wolves and bears survive, but there are valleys and mountains where white men have probably never travelled.

There were many sandbanks and floating snags but the journey was quiet, even lovely. We glimpsed foxes, bears and many river birds. The miles passed by until we came to the village of Marshall.

Although we had progressed through the twilit night without sleep and covered a hundred and fifty miles, we were still over a week behind schedule, with little hope of gaining time. Every hour lost on the so-far balmy Yukon could represent a day of painful progress up north; we were already operating within the narrow eight-week time corridor of the Arctic summer.

One of our outboards had developed troubles which Charlie had been unable to solve, so I bargained with a Marshall Eskimo called Simeon. He owned three outboards and said he might sell me one. He was a proud man and wanted to show he would not be rushed into a deal. I followed him about the village awaiting his reply. He went shopping in the single store and smiled at me from time to time. He was considering it. Then down to the riverbank to an odd low shack like a chicken coop. Steam seeped through the rafters; it was the village sauna. He crawled through the single low entry hole and must have stripped inside. I could see several pairs of bony legs in a row. I paced about outside, swatting at the mosquitoes for twenty minutes. When the old man emerged, his skin shining, he looked at me and nodded. The deal was on.

Next day we set out again, but three hours out the thin wooden slat on the transom of my boat split and the engine jumped clear of the boat and sank, breaking its safety cord. I carried a light 18-h.p. model and clipped this on instead. We progressed, but slowly … Slowly. I gnashed my teeth with frustration. I told myself all about Solomon and the lilies of the field but it did no good. After seemingly endless hours we passed the lonely village of Russian Mission below a forest-clad hill. The church and the graveside crucifixes were after the style of the Russian Orthodox Church. The Eskimo villagers, already more Indian-looking, still had mostly Russian family names – the local outboard mechanic, for instance, was called Pete Pederoff.

I hadn't planned to stop at Russian Mission, but half an hour after passing it I looked back to see Charlie's boat drifting around in circles in midriver. His engine had given up the ghost and he couldn't restart it, so we floated back to Russian Mission, which did not take long since the river had lately narrowed considerably and raced at seven or eight knots through steeper valleys, rock-girt in places like canyons.

A friendly builder in Russian Mission heard about our problems and let us use the construction workers' caravan for rest and for our equipment. Bryn seemed rather despondent, and that evening as Pete Pederoff took Charlie's outboard to bits said he would like to spend an extra day in Russian Mission – a scenic spot highlighted by the Balkan silhouette of the Orthodox church in the hill above the village. I sensed Bryn was in a delicate mood and increasingly uptight about the trip. His job was photography and he was not getting the results he'd anticipated. The blame for this he quite probably and quite correctly laid at my doorstep, so I went along but seethed inwardly as more precious time slipped by.

I also found myself silently annoyed with Charlie for his apparent inadequacy with the outboards. Yet this, too, I knew was my fault since there had been plenty of time during the expedition to have Charlie given extra instruction by local outboard service centres. I just had failed to do it. In my diary I ranted about this mechanical ineptness and complained that we needed an Eskimo for the outboards – hardly fair, since Charlie could equally well write reams of abuse about my inadequacies as a radio operator when I used the local radiophone to contact Ginnie in Dawson City.

I spoke to her again that night. Through friends in London and New York, she had located a Manhattan concern called Stanley Morgan that had agreed to buy an eighteen-foot Boston Whaler for us. Evinrude's boss, whom Ginnie finally located in Hong Kong, agreed to let us have two 60-h.p. outboards. In Vancouver Simon began to work in a local boatyard to modify an existing whaler for our use in icy water. Now Ginnie had quickly to fix free transport for the boat to reach Inuvik.

By this time the *Benji Bee* had returned to Vancouver and was berthed in the city harbour. When Anton heard I was planning to use a whaler he was unimpressed. 'I personally,' he wrote, 'think that a Boston Whaler is not a clever move. Its use to Ran is going to be very limited as it will only be useful as far as the open water allows. It weighs 1,500 pounds plus 40 gallons of fuel and two 60-h.p. engines at 260 pounds each. It will be quite impossible to pull across ice. It cannot be flown anywhere in the Twin Otter so they will have to ditch it before they've got halfway. Also the engines use up 8 gallons of fuel per hour. Even if they can do 30 m.p.h., should there be any rough sea they will be reduced to a crawl or risk breaking its back with all the fuel weight. Nothing to do with me, but the inflatables without the polystyrene filling would definitely have been the best bet.'

Nonetheless, with the outboards repaired and Bryn looking happier we set out from Russian Mission on a blustery morning. By chance, our day's delay saw us heading into a series of north-south valleys on the very day of the first big southerly blow of the year. Winds recorded that afternoon at Holy Cross, the village where we were headed, exceeded seventy knots and raised dust into a fine haze that paled the sun. I noticed with surprise that no boats were out as we left Russian Mission, nor, as we progressed for the first twenty miles to the northeast, was there any other sign of life. This was especially strange since it was the middle of the salmon run, the short annual period when a healthy income could be made on the river. Later I would think mad dogs and Englishmen . . .

I received some nasty little shocks during the morning and took quite a bit of water in the aluminium boat. The inflatables could fill to the brim with water and carry on floating high, but any water in my dinghy had to be removed at once. Draining was only possible when moving fast enough to tip the bows up and when a clumsy wooden bung was removed from a hole near the base of the transom. Unless the plug was replaced after draining, this hole could cause the boat to leak rapidly as soon as she slowed down and returned to a level plane. Lose the bung and things could get tricky.

Until noon the confused state of the river made me cautious but not alarmed. The dust clouds seen upriver never materialised. When we reached the area where we thought we had seen them they were not there. Just a trick of the light, it seemed.

But some fifteen miles short of Holy Cross we entered a long, narrow valley heavily forested on either side. Here the dust-cloud effect was even more marked than before. At the entrance to the valley an Eskimo fishing village nestled on one bank. The riverboats were, I noticed, drawn up above the shingle bank. Two men watched us pass. I waved. There was no response but a slight shaking of the head from the older of the two men.

Now the water began to careen about and strike with miniature breakers against the rock walls on the rim of each minor curve, but I still felt no threat beyond the normal swell and undulation of the great river's forces. As I nosed further out into the north-bearing valley, though, an unseen surge moved against the right side of my boat and almost tipped me off my plank seat by the tiller. Little warning waves unlike any I had seen except in rapids seemed to grow out of the water like boils erupting from the riverbed. Breaking into a sweat – I have a healthy fear of rough water – I steered quickly for the nearest bank. This was unfortunately the cut bank, the side of the river where the faster current ran.

Dust clouds rose from the cut bank as I tried to escape the central turmoil. It was as though a dragon breathed there. As I closed with the bank, a pine tree toppled over and crashed into the river. Then another, and with it a whole section of the bank itself collapsed. The roar of my outboard drowned all other sounds. The forces of destruction that gnawed at the river's banks operated in silence as far as I was concerned. This added to the sinister, almost slow-motion appearance of the phenomenon. At the time I couldn't grasp what was happening. I had, after all, boated up or down thousands of miles of wild rivers in North America and never once experienced this. Also, my private, long-nurtured idea of the Yukon was of a slow wide river as gentle as the Thames.

Above the collapse of the bank I saw that the forest, from undergrowth to the very tops of the giant pines, was bent over and alive with movement. A great wind was at work although in my hooded suit on the boat I could feel nothing. For a moment I hovered there in indecision. The waves in the middle of the river, some six hundred yards wide at this point, were surely uninviting, yet any minute my boat was liable to disappear under a falling pine if I stayed close in. There was no question of landing. No question of trying to turn broadside and then head back downstream. My boat climbed and fell like a wild thing, was shaken as though in a bulldog's teeth, then veered in response to invisible suction toward the crumbling cut bank.

Ahead the river narrowed still further, the bank grew steeper and the chaos of the central waves extended almost clear across the river. At this bottleneck I glimpsed between standing waves and crumbling bank a hump in the water. It was fleetingly possible to see the river actually mounting in height the further away it was from the bank. I had often heard that the centre of a river can be several feet higher than at the edges, given sufficient flow and force. But I'd never before clearly viewed the effect. It was distinctly off-putting.

I pushed with both hands on the tiller and the boat, reluctantly, edged away from the cut bank and began to head obliquely across the river. The only hope lay on the far side. Perhaps things were better there ... Somewhere in the middle of the river, where the turbulence was greatest and the hydraulic waves so close together that the boat no sooner fell down the face of one than the next raced curling above me, I knew I could sink within minutes. It needed just one brief error on the tiller and I would add critically to the ten inches of silt-laden water already swilling around my feet.

From the corner of my eye I noticed Bryn had seen my dilemma and moved his inflatable as close as the turmoil allowed. When I sink, I thought, Bryn's boat will be my only chance. 'As big as houses,' I remembered the state trooper's warning. I could well understand the exaggeration. The waves were no more than four or five feet high, yet their configuration, violence and closeness would make any local riverboat a deathtrap for its inmates.

Before another wave could swamp my wallowing craft I turned broadside onto the hydraulics, applied full throttle and headed straight into the maelstrom of the centre of the river. Whether sheer luck or the shape of the waves saved me I don't know, but no more water came inboard. Much of the time it was like surf-riding along the forward face of a breaker, then a violent incline and sideways surge as the old wave passed beneath and the next one thrust at the little tin hull.

An edge of exhilaration broke through the sticky fear that till then had held me in thrall. For the first time I realised there was a chance of survival and began to experience the old thrill of rapids-riding from the days long past when we tackled far greater waves from the comparative safety of unsinkable inflatables.

How long it took to cross the river was impossible to gauge, but gradually the waves grew less fierce and less close and then there was quiet water except for the outwash from the rough stuff. Ahead I could see, between waves and the quieter lee bank, a lane of smooth water edged by sandbanks.

Bryn and then Charlie emerged from the waves like bucking broncos. Both were smiling ... my narrow escape had not gone unnoticed.

That night we stopped in Holy Cross and the keeper of the travellers' lodge, Luke Demientieff, told us we were lucky to be alive ... Even paddle steamers, he said, would not, in the old days, venture out in such conditions. We had covered the worst stretch of the river in the worst possible conditions and, as far as the riverside folk were concerned, we were quite mad. When I asked him how anyone should know or care that we had passed, Luke said: 'It only needs one pair of eyes from one riverside shack to see you go by for the radiophones all along the river to start buzzing. When you passed the old huts at Paimiut and entered the slough by Great Paimiut Island the word was about you were goners.' He paused and added with a chuckle, 'Still, we're pleased you made it to the lodge. After all, business has been poor lately.'

For days we travelled the river, across the face of Alaska toward

Yukon Territory and the Canadian border. Deserted shacks, long overgrown yet still named on the maps, were often the only sign of life for fifty miles or more. Evocative names such as Debauch Mountain and Old Woman Cabin marked hundreds of miles of otherwise unchristened land. On one short stretch we passed by Old Andreafsky, Wilburs Place, Konolunuk and Kwikloaklol, but all we saw were a few empty huts in the trees and a wilderness of wooded hills and tangled creeks. At other times sheer cliffs hung down from racing storm clouds, as when the 4,000-foot-high mountains of the Kokrines reared to a halt at the very edge of the river.

By travelling long hours we sometimes began to catch up the lost time, but some new mechanical delay always held us up again. Galena passed by and Tanana and still we lagged back. Since the Yukon journey was to give us boating experience, not to provide a separate challenge in itself, theoretically we could stop anywhere and carry on by Land Rover as far as the Mackenzie River. But in practice, once committed to the river, we had to get ourselves to some point attainable by road from Dawson City, where Ginnie was based.

From Tanana I contacted her again and she agreed to drive south to Fairbanks, then north to the Yukon Bridge, the only bridge to our east and her west. We might reach the bridge late on July 15. If Ginnie did likewise we might yet make it back to Dawson City by July 16. If so we stood a good chance of entering the Northwest Passage on time and at little cost in lost experience because we would still have covered a thousand miles – the Yukon River journey would be shortened by only three hundred miles out of thirteen hundred.

Ginnie's extra drive would be long and tedious, but she had once spent five months driving a Land Rover and trailer about British Columbia and the Yukon – she thrived on long journeys ... This pickup went ahead as planned, and we sold the old aluminium boat to a local lad at the Yukon Bridge for two hundred dollars. I was almost sad to see her go.

The inflatables were loaded aboard and Ginnie drove us on the long haul to Dawson City. We arrived at the Dawson ferry shortly before midnight on July 16 and reported our presence to the local Royal Canadian Mounted Police. The head mountie said we were lucky. 'The bad winds have caused seven drownings 'round here during the past three weeks. Mostly canoeists. They just fill up and sink. They don't take lifejackets because they spoil their suntans.'

There was room for us all at the Klondike Lodge, where Ginnie had been staying, but my plan to move on north at once was frustrated and a further four days' delay followed because of a storm that destroyed part of the dirt road running the last three hundred miles from the Klondike to Inuvik. While we waited at the Klondike Lodge we completed arrangements for the transport by air of the whaler from Vancouver. An old friend, Bob Engel of Northwest Territorial Airways, agreed to provide a Hercules C-130, since no smaller aircraft would take the chunky craft.

Down in Vancouver the crew of the *Benji Bee* were making themselves at home, since Anton had found no charter work yet. Dave Hicks, always original, had discovered a local nudist camp with no beer vendors. This, he decided, was a crying shame and must be put right, so he purchased beer, obtained ice from an ice machine in a hotel beside the *Benji Bee* and spent the summer naked, dispensing ice-cold beer cans on the beach.

Finally news came that the road was reopened and we set out, joined by Jackie McConnell, a Scottish expatriate who ten years earlier had been a British soldier involved in our Canadian river journey. He so loved the country that he left the army and emigrated. On all my previous travels I had met no one as mentally tough or as easy to get along with as Jackie. It was good to see him again, although he was only to stay until Tuktoyaktuk.

The road wound north through a virgin land of rolling forest, tumbling creeks and very little else. There can be few roads anywhere so desolate and unspoiled, and long may it remain that way. We crossed the Eagle River, where fifty years earlier the 'Mad Trapper of Rat River' was hunted for weeks by posses of mounties after he had killed one of them. A gun battle beside the river proved that the mounties did indeed, at least in this case, get their man . . . Long hours of rain made the road as slippery as an ice rink, and the hours and the miles passed by with hardly a vehicle. We crossed the Mackenzie River fairly early on the second day.

Inuvik clings to the river's east bank about one hundred miles from the sea and not far north of the ferry. The whaler arrived a day later, and we trucked it to the riverside, where Simon began to fit the engines, steerage linkage and fuel system as he had been instructed in Vancouver. By nightfall he was finished. 'Bitten and sunburnt,' he wrote. 'It's hot and dusty up here. Too hot for long sleeves, too many mosquitoes for short.' Next day he explained the boat's layout and driving controls to Charlie. Then, with a ferryman's forklift truck, they launched the boat in the Mackenzie.

Simon travelled to Tuktoyaktuk on the daily river ferry guarding our equipment. Jackie took Bryn in an inflatable, and Ginnie came with Charlie and me in the whaler. The Mackenzie was wide and slow and full of mud flats, many of which we rammed – no problem, since we could always reverse out of trouble.

On the afternoon of July 24, back on schedule, we turned east at the mouth of the river and entered the harbour of Tuktoyaktuk in the Northwest Passage.

Bryn and Jackie left us in Tuktoyaktuk. There was no way Bryn would be able to photograph the journey through the passage – logistically we would be too remote for too long.

Back in 1977 Dr George Hobson of the Polar Continental Shelf Project, a Canadian government research department operating in northern Canada, allowed us to use his huts at Alert for our training journey. Now he gave us facilities at his three main northern bases at Tuktoyaktuk, Resolute and again at Alert. In exchange for our completing certain glaciological research tasks on the Arctic Ocean, Ginnie and Simon could use the Polar Continental Shelf Project's radio frequency and accommodations. They also agreed to drop off fuel caches in remote spots, providing these were within Twin Otter-reach of their base.

For a thousand miles we would be out of their range, but then there were the scattered outposts of the Distant Early Warning lines – manned radar posts set up along the barren coastline to detect a missile attack. For four years I had written to Canadian and American forces for permission to obtain minimal fuel supplies at these stations. Finally they had agreed to hold fuel and ration boxes for us, providing we got the kit up to them. Which prompted a further year's work finding an airline sponsor to do this free of charge. (Nordair did so the month before we reached Tuktoyaktuk.)

The difficulty of any form of resupply *between* such outposts meant carrying carefully selected spare parts, exactly the right amount of fuel for each stretch and enough rations to cope with long periods stranded somewhere with a radio failure.

I spent a day checking all spare parts and spare fuel outside the Polar Continental Shelf Project Parcol hut where Ginnie and Simon were to live and operate their radio base. Assured that I had too many rather than too few spares of everything, I handed the lists over to Simon and forgot about them.

For three thousand miles from Tuktoyaktuk I would have to navigate with my magnetic hand compass, my watch and the sun. I knew nothing of the Canadian Archipelago, as the Arctic islands off Canada's northern shore are collectively called, except the long history of expeditions attempting to force the archipelago passage and, in hundreds of cases, paying with their lives.

Great icebreakers could crash through the sea ice between the islands of the archipelago or even to the north of them, but in our boat class of non-icebreakers only a dozen or less expeditions have navigated the passage in either direction, and those that have, all using boats with some form of protection from the elements, averaged two summer seasons to complete the journey.

We had no wish to hang around for three years, and so my original plan to use fast light inflatables which could be man-hauled over floes. The whaler was a compromise. It was fairly shallow-draughted, so we could keep close to the shoreline and perhaps sneak between grounded icebergs and the coast, but too heavy to manhandle.

The company, whose flat-bottomed barges ply between Inuvik, Tuktoyaktuk and, when the ice allows, Eskimo settlements further east, have an office in Tuktoyaktuk harbour. I went there to pick up some advice. A barge skipper with sixteen years of experience in the region agreed to speak to me. His accent was Scandinavian, a large hairy man with a harsh voice. I shook his big hand. 'We're going east along the coast to Spence Bay and then up to Resolute. I wonder if you could give me advice on navigation.'

He looked at me with hard eyes. 'You're mad,' he said.

'No.' I showed him my compass and chart. 'I have the latest charts and an excellent compass.'

'You're mad, man. Throw it away.'

I began to get annoyed but took care not to show it. 'What do *you* use to navigate?' I asked. He moved to the window and pointed at a sturdy barge-towing tug. There was pride in his eyes.

'She has everything. She goes in the dark. Radar-beacon responders, MF and DF and we stay out in the deep channels. You' – he shook his head – 'you must hug the coastline to escape the storm winds so you will hit the shoals. There are thousands of shoals.' He began to sound as though he were enjoying himself. 'Also you can't cross the hundreds of deep bays for fear of the wind and big waves so you must hug the coastline, which is like the graph of a heartbeat. Up, down, in, out. Like crazy pavement. So you go much further and use much more gas. And most of the time it will be fog. No sun so you must use your compass. Yes?'

He showed me his chart of Cambridge Bay, a few hundred miles east. One strong finger indicated the words: 'Magnetic compass useless in this area.' 'You are too near the Magnetic Pole. You stay in Tuk. Have a holiday.'

I thanked him.

As I left he shouted, 'Maybe you can navigate by the wrecks of the other madmen who tried. There's plenty of them.'

On July 26 we said good-bye to Ginnie and Simon. Bothy was out chasing gophers. Ginnie said she would move north to Resolute as soon as my radio signal began to weaken.

In thirty-five days we had to complete the three thousand miles of the passage, which traditionally takes three seasons. But since our aim was not purely to travel the passage but to complete our circumpolar journey, there would be another five hundred miles still farther to the north, which we also had to leave behind us in the same short period before new ice began to close over the sea.

The sun hid in an orange haze as we left Tuktoyaktuk and turned east into a restless swell.

Chapter Eleven

> No man really knows about other human beings. The best he can do is suppose they are like himself.
>
> JOHN STEINBECK

Many tried to pass through the Northwest Passage over the last two centuries and hundreds died in the attempt. The stories are legion of misery and starvation, cannibalism, and death by bears or Eskimos; of shipwrecks caused by hidden shoals, violent storms and invading ice. Such tales are apt to encourage the adventure-seeker, until such time as he or she actually sets out along this loneliest of coastlines.

John Buchan described the passage as 'a part of the globe having no care for human life, not built to man's scale; a remnant of the Ice Age which long ago withered the world.'

This sounds a touch flowery, but even the down-to-earth *Encyclopaedia Britannica* is unusually descriptive:

> The hostile Arctic makes the Northwest Passage one of the world's severest maritime challenges. It is 500 miles north of the Arctic Circle and less than 1,200 miles from the North Pole. . . .

> Thick pack ice, moving at speeds up to ten miles per day, closes nearly half the passage all the year round. Arctic water can freeze a man to death in two minutes. Frigid polar northeasterly winds blow almost constantly and can howl to hurricane force. Temperatures rise above freezing only in July and August ... Visibility is often obscured by whiteouts of blowing snow ... Thick fog usually shrouds the channels during the brief summer ... There are unchartered shoals ... little is known about currents and tides. ... Navigation is difficult even with the most modern devices. The compass is useless because the magnetic North Pole lies within the passage ... the bleak featureless Arctic islands provide few distinguishing landmarks. Arctic blackouts can frustrate all communications for periods from a few hours to nearly a month.

Our first problem was the coastline; flat as a board and invisible whenever shallow water forced us out to sea, and the treeless tundra of the Tuktoyaktuk Peninsula might just as well not have been there. But the sun was out, so we maintained a due east heading until the glint of the breakers off Cape Dalhousie showed like silver froth on the horizon. We closed to the south with caution, for there were many shoals and breakers around.

Char Point was the next name on my charts, but it could have been one of many flat headlands so I set out across the ten-mile gap of Liverpool Bay not knowing quite where we were. Halfway across a hill stood proud from the otherwise invisible coastline ahead. At a hundred and eighty feet high it was a veritable mountain beside these coastal steppes. For me it indicated the whereabouts of Nicholson Peninsula, our immediate goal.

A low sandspit stuck out like a heron's beak on the east side of the peninsula and provided some shelter from all but southerly winds. Shallow draft vessels could enter with caution, which we did not long before dusk. There was nothing and no one in the little bay, so I called up the DEW line station, somewhere on the hilltop above, on their standby frequency.

'Cape Nicholson, this is Transglobe, d'you read?' The answer came back as though our progress into the bay had been monitored. 'You must be the English guys. We'll be down right away.'

A jeep arrived in minutes with the station commander, a cheery man, at the wheel. Yes, our fuel and rations had arrived and were ready for us but, no, he would not let us disappear from his little kingdom without at least a cup of Cape Nicholson coffee. After all, we were the only visitors he had ever had except those who arrived by air.

As it turned out Cape Nicholson provided more than coffee. I also caught a glimpse of the rare Barren Ground grizzly. Up at the little camp no more than a scattering of caravan-shaped huts clustered around the DEW radar dish; the nine inhabitants were jumpy. A grizzly had taken to prowling about the huts and the refuse dump. Careful not to be electrocuted, I climbed a couple of radar masts and slung one end of the radio antenna over each. Communications were clear. As I knelt on the tundra below the masts the station boss shouted, 'Bear,' and I found myself ten feet up the mast. 'Get your camera,' he said with a grin, 'someone's seen it up by the dump.'

We climbed into the jeep and soon spotted the great tan animal, although it blended remarkably well with the tundra. I urged the driver to get close. The bear was inside the track and a mere two hundred metres ahead. He accelerated, but the bear took off down the trail. With 30 m.p.h. on the speedometer we failed to catch the ungainly beast. For a full minute it matched our speed, then moved away from the track and disappeared into dead marshy ground where the jeep could not follow.

Back at the radio I passed Ginnie a message for the committee in London, a note deliberately discouraging about our chances of making Alert in the short time-span left to us. This was not because I *believed* we would not make it. My mind was quite open about our chances. But I did want London to start thinking hard *now* about the realities of our being delayed for a whole year. Seven years before I had decided on Gjoa Haven as being our halfway aiming point because it was well situated as a wintering base if we should fail to make the whole passage in one season. I had packed enough kit for three of us to spend the time there. Now all that remained was to start bringing the key figures in London to the idea that failure to get through in one season did not mean overall failure. After all, the handful of people who had beaten the passage in the past nearly all took three seasons to do so. What I worried about most was the less placid members of our committee getting the wind up through a sudden realisation that things for the first time were not going by the book. I wanted it to sink in well in advance that in my book, at least, delays were acceptable because they were planned for and, unwelcome as an extra polar winter at a lonely Eskimo outpost might be, it need not cast doubts on our eventual ability to succeed.

I reminded them of the words of Dr Hattersley-Smith, an expert on the passage: 'While I would not doubt that this journey can be done piecemeal, I think it unrealistic to suppose it can be done in *one* season. At least, you would have to have the most phenomenal luck to do it.' Unfortunately my personal policy of openly committing myself to less than I inwardly hoped to achieve had an unfavourable side effect on Charlie. He could not differentiate between a calculated outward show of pessimism and inward determination, which can hardly exist without a basis of optimism, however well hidden.

'You are too pessimistic, Ran,' Charlie would say.

'You're wrong, I'm not pessimistic.'

'Well, negative, then. You're overnegative.'

'What do you mean? When am I negative? When have I been negative on this expedition?'

Charlie thought for a bit. 'Not in the boat, no. And maybe not from day to day. But you give the others in London a generally negative impression. And that must be bad because you'll make them negative too. You're infectious that way.'

I never did manage to explain my philosophy on the subject to Charlie, but Ollie, certainly by the time we left Scott Base, had at least partially understood it. He told the camera crew: 'Ran treats life on the pessimistic angle which I think is very good because if you expect the worst and you get it you aren't disappointed. If you don't then you feel very pleased with things. So he always looks at the rate of progress or the way the expedition is running in a pessimistic light and always tends to treat things as if they were going badly whereas they might, in fact, be going rather well or on schedule.'

A strong easterly wind began to lift the bay swell as Cape Nicholson disappeared behind us. The next DEW station was more sea miles away than could be covered with a maximum fuel load unless we travelled in straight lines well away from the coastline. Somewhat ahead was Franklin Bay, with a mouth far too wide to cross and be sure of making an accurate landfall the other side with only a hand compass to steer by. Safer by far to hug the shoreline of the bay despite its deep incursion to the south and away from our easterly course. To do this we would need two extra drums of fuel, which some time ago the Polar Continental Shelf Project's Twin Otter had dropped off on a narrow spit of shingle south of Baillie Island.

For forty miles we bucked and tossed through a rising sea,

soaked in spray at every wave crest. With the floor bungs out the whaler drained herself dry as quickly as the waves washed inboard. A clammy mist hid the land to our east, but we moved with caution and eventually spotted the spit through the crash of waves against it. Trying to land from the east – which was the side where our drums were – was not possible. The boat would have been battered and swamped in minutes, so we edged down the long shingle finger to its tip; conditions on the lee side were slightly better.

It proved too rough to beach opposite the drum cache so Charlie slung out our light anchor. I lowered myself overboard into the surf with two empty jerry cans, a drum opener and a fuel pump. Charlie kept the boat hovering just beyond the breakers and threw another twelve jerry cans at me. Some fell short but soon came in with the surf. Three hours later we managed, to the accompaniment of much sweating and swearing, to get them all back on board filled with gasoline, the correct amount of oil and not too much blown sand.

Between Baillie Island and Cape Bathurst the narrow channel of Snowgoose Passage rips through shoals and bars. At first relieved to get through unscathed and into Franklin Bay, we very soon wished ourselves back again, for now the full force of wind and wave struck the little whaler. The lie of the coast was south-south-west and we had no alternative but to follow it with the waves curling at us from the port beam. We had to travel down the line of the wave troughs and hope to avoid a swamping. For forty-five miles any mechanical breakdowns would be likely to scupper us for good, since a rampart of unbroken cliffs from forty to ninety feet high formed the shoreline. Sometimes the waves crashed into a narrow shingle beach at the foot of the cliffs but mostly against the black rock itself to spin great curtains of spume that were whipped away by the wind.

The sky darkened and the waves grew higher, smashing inboard with increasing regularity. We were both soaked and our teeth chattered. It would be so good to stop and light a fire, but this could not be until the cliffs receded. Each time a wave broke over us, salt water poured through the face holes in our survival suits, running down back and chest and legs to collect in slowly rising pools inside our waterproof boots. Our eyes stung with the salt and my map grew soggy.

Progress became slower as the waves grew in size. We tried moving further away from the cliffs but conditions only worsened. Fifteen-foot walls of water raced up from the east and time and again forced us to face into the bigger ones. Often the boat hung almost on its side as these waves surged by in a rush of power.

As the day grew darker I saw a fire ahead, glowing through the gloom. For an hour it came no closer, then to our astonishment we saw that the cliffs themselves were burning and an acrid smell of chemicals was discernible in the wind lulls. Dante's Inferno. Sulphur deposits glowing red and orange, forever on fire. Yellow-grey fingers of smoke curled from deep crevices. All that was missing were devils with pitchforks and screams from the burning damned.

For forty minutes the cliffs smouldered and smoked above the angry surf. The wind worsened, and four endless hours later I spotted what appeared as a tiny beachside lagoon on my chart. The cliffs towered up higher than ever, then at last moved away from the sea's edge where a river disgorged itself. Years of silt deposits had built up a reef of shinglebars against which the surf roared in heavy, pebble-sucking breakers. Wiping water from my map and eyes I verified a tiny break in the barrier reef. If we could find this gap the safety of the lagoon would be ours to wait out the storm ... providing that new silt deposited over the nine years since my chart was made had not blocked up the original channel.

I climbed onto the front railing of the boat with the help of a jerry can and scanned the ring of breakers. There was a place of lesser fury in the boiling white water, and I indicated its direction to Charlie.

'Seen,' he yelled above the din of outboards, wind and waves.

For a moment there was chaos as we bucked corklike in the breakers. Then we were over and into a channel hardly wider than the boat's own width.

The propellers bit into silt almost at once. Charlie cut the motors and I poled in with an oar. The comparative silence was blissful. Now only the roar of the pounding sea against the narrow walls of our haven. We could only advance some fifteen yards into the lagoon, thanks to the shallows, so we made camp at once on the shingle. Rain fell in a thin drizzle, but we managed to make a fire of driftwood and climbed thankfully out of our sodden suits.

Turned upside down, seawater poured out of the leggings.

Our feet were white with the trenchfoot skin of a soggy corpse.

Not a good spot for communications to Ginnie, but I raised a DEW station somewhere to the east and told the operator we were fine and close to the cliffs of Malloch. At dawn a mournful mist shrouded our tent and the sodden beach. We climbed with clenched teeth into the wetsuits and plodded up and down the shingle for an hour to warm up.

I estimated a journey of some thirty miles to the far side of Franklin Bay, quite a bit farther than from England to France. Since we would not see the far side even in fine weather from here I saw disadvantage to leaving our own side in fog. The wind had abated overnight to a mere breeze and only the swell of the storm remained. After an hour on what I believed to be an easterly bearing there was no sign of land in any direction.

'Surely we should head further right,' Charlie shouted in my ear.

'I know what you mean,' I yelled back, 'but the compass says this way so just keep straight ahead at the dark patch of clouds.'

I had a local error of 43 degrees set on the compass and added five more for the effect of the boat's engines and metal fittings. How great the influence of the Magnetic Pole was I did not as yet know. But over twenty years I had developed an implicit faith in the compass compared with most people's instinctive 'sense' of direction.

Two hours later faint splotches of darkness nicked the misty horizon ahead. Fragments of ice, none larger than a football pitch, lined the eastern flanks of Franklin Bay but only in pockets. This was ice that had grounded on shallows and so would spend the next four weeks slowly melting until winter arrived with a further skin of ice over all the sea lanes of the passage . . .

The foreland which finally emerged through the mist was an unnamed cape south of Diamond Rock. The shoal of Rabbit Island passed to starboard, and we nosed with caution between Booth and Fiji islands. Ahead lay Cow Cove under the high hills of Cape Perry. As we closed with the cove a wan sun opened a shaft through the mist and, above the semicircular bay, the radar dome and masts of Cape Perry DEW station glimmered briefly, then vanished like a half-suspected dream.

The station boss insisted we stay for a meal and a night's sleep. Knowing what lay ahead I hastened to thank him and accept. Cape Perry would be our last 'safe' stopping place for close to four hundred miles. We left the whaler with its anchor holding the stern out and a bowline painter tied to a rock on the beach, slept well in the warm comfortable base, and were not worried when the wind boxed the compass overnight.

For eight hours the whaler was battered as a west wind, luckily a light one, sent surging surf onto our previously sheltered beach. The stern anchor soon tore loose, the whaler swung abeam to the beach, and as the gravel scoured her hull with each new breaking wave, water poured over her and onto the kit inside.

While we waited for equipment to dry out we got to know some of the eleven camp inmates. Some put up with the isolation because of high wages and the slow pace of life. One told me: 'I think my brain slows down up here. You only need a vocabulary of three hundred words to get by on.'

Each base comprises a large igloo-shaped radar dome and four radar dishes facing north toward the USSR. The whole network of thirty-one stations – twenty-one in Canada, six in Alaska and four in Greenland – was installed to give alarm of any sneak attack by bombers or missiles over the top of the world. They were built to last ten years but are still going strong twenty-five years later despite the deployment of satellites and over-the-horizon radar that can do the same job. The stations we called at were run by Canadians, but all daily weather information and radar readings were passed to North American Air Defense Command down in Colorado Springs.

On July 30, in a fog and a twenty-knot westerly wind, we headed east to the narrows of Dolphin and Union Strait. For thirty-six hours we ploughed east and saw very little ice but beach-grounded bergs. Our luck was holding. Being wet we were soon cold, but the mists cleared and stayed away all day and night and through the next day. We grew very tired and it was necessary from time to time to shout at each other to stave off drowsiness. Often, for hours on end, we would sing to ourselves. Past Clinton Point, Cape Young and a thousand nameless bays, we were determined not to stop on this barren north-facing coast with no stitch of cover from the elements. The evenings were soft and full of wild beauty which faded from red dusk to purple dawn with no nighttime between. But winter was poised on the balls of its feet. Already the sun at midnight caressed the silent surface of the sea.

For 340 miles we stood in the narrow space between the helm and fuel cans until at last, dodging between a rash of isles, we crossed the narrow channel to Victoria Island and left the Canadian mainland for the first time.

It was late on August 1 that we came to the DEW site at Lady Franklin Point and thankfully moored the whaler in a well-sheltered bay.

How did we react to the long cramped hours together? 'Well,' Charlie would say, 'team members were chosen for their temperament. We do lose our tempers occasionally but very, very seldom and mainly when under pressure. If something goes wrong, say an engine problem, and Ran tries to suggest what I should do, he may say, for instance, "Couldn't it be the water separator?" Then you turn around and say, "For God's sake, shut up, it can't be the separator because the other engine is running and they both work off the same separator." When you've been up for thirty hours you really can't put up with that sort of advice. What do I do to keep myself awake? Well, I'm always talking to myself. I'm the sort of person who listens to myself. Not really surprising. It's mainly about mechanical things. I think because I'm not a mechanic and need to chat the problems through in my head. Also you've got to amuse yourself because you can't hear what Ran is saying unless he yells, and he can't hear what you're saying unless you yell so you chatter away to yourself to keep going.'

At Lady Franklin everyone seemed asleep. It was well past midnight. I went behind the huts with my radio gear in a sack and, as at Cape Nicholson, scaled two radar masts to hang out my antenna.

I contacted Ginnie at once. She and Simon had been watching live television coverage of Prince Charles's wedding. At Tuktoyaktuk a severe storm had piled the tide up to three feet higher than normal.

Many Eskimo boats in the bay had sunk or broken up complete with outboard engines and fishing gear.

I gave Ginnie a fairly optimistic view of our chances at least as far as Gjoa Haven, under strict instructions that no hint of optimism should leak out.

I suddenly noticed that the station boss was lurking close behind me. Since I had my earphones on he need not have pussyfooted to get there. He glared at me. I smiled back politely – he was, after all, host and had a right to glare. I decided to close down to Ginnie. Perhaps I was unwittingly on a frequency that interfered with the base radio.

'Who are you communicating with?' he asked.

'With my wife.'

'Where is she?'

'In Tuktoyaktuk.'

'Do you have permission to use the radio up here?'

'Yes. On four-nine-eight-two megahertz.'

I opened my bag to stack away the headphones and antenna and he moved closer to peer inside. Deciding to seize the bull by the horns I laughed and said, 'We're all British, you know, not spies.' He gave me a severe look that clearly indicated that the second half of my observation was a non sequitur.

'Well,' I said, 'I'll be getting some sleep now. We must push on first thing tomorrow.' That did seem to please him.

A hundred and thirty miles to the east one outboard gave up the ghost and failed to respond to any known remedy. We limped back thirty miles to Byron Bay DEW site, where we spent three days replacing the crown pinion gear. Then on toward Cambridge Bay.

Wild storms lashed our passage over wide bay mouths and past forlorn capes of twisted red lava domes and fluted black pillars of cutaway bedrock. I looked for places of shelter but there were none, not even a shallow cave or leaning boulder. The rain drove down from a forbidding sky. I marvelled silently at our predecessors of a century past who had ventured along this coast under sail and with blank charts. More than a hundred of Sir John Franklin's men had died in this region. Many of the features which did have names reflected the unpleasant memories of those pioneers: Cape Storm, Starvation Harbour . . .

By the time we reached Cambridge Bay on August 6 the wind had steadied. As we entered the inner bay on a sunny if blustery afternoon I thought of one Colin Irwen, a young sailor from Bournemouth, who had managed to sail the entire passage to this point in a specially constructed yacht. But he got no further . . . sea ice closed in from the east. He was patient, but the two following summers saw no improvement. He cut his losses and married a local Eskimo girl.

It would not do to start counting our chickens. Not yet. We were less than halfway to Alert with only twenty days of safe sea travel left. John Bocstoce's 'Get out of the passage by the end of August or you'll be in trouble' was the warning word we took seriously.

An American DEW official collected us from the gravel spit where we anchored the whaler. Charlie began to sort out some wet kit while I set up the radio.

'Bring your firearms to the station commander's office,' the American said. 'No weapons while you're in town.'

I took my revolver and Charlie's .357 magnum bear rifle into the well-appointed office of the camp boss.

'Clear the guns, please, the commanding officer will be back soon.' I emptied the six bullets from my revolver and handed them over with some more from my pocket. Then I took Charlie's rifle and checked the built-in magazine. I cocked the unfamiliar bolt and a four-inch bullet fell to the floor. A brief look into the chamber.

Nothing there. So I pointed the rifle at the floor and squeezed the trigger.

It was a powerful weapon and the noise in that confined space was deafening. Blood spattered over the carpet as did glass from the fluorescent lights, plaster from the ceiling and parquet from the floor.

I had definitely cleared the gun, so I handed it to the American.

There were sounds of approaching feet in the corridor. The American poked his head out. 'No problem,' he shouted, 'just trouble with the lighting.' This seemed to satisfy the approaching feet. The American official found a brush and pan and with commendable speed brushed all the debris away. There was a gaping black hole, still smoking, in the floor in front of the base commander's desk. This he covered up neatly with a floor mat from another part of the room. The place looked as good as new.

The blood I traced to my chin, which appeared to have a small hole in it, to which I applied a handkerchief and stemmed the impressive red dribble. The American seemed to be enjoying himself. 'Hey,' he said, 'if the Arctic doesn't get you guys I guess you'll do a pretty good job on yourselves. Never a dull moment, eh?' He drove me to the local dispensary, where an Eskimo girl sewed me up with curved needle and dental floss.

That evening Charlie, seeing my half-naked, half-bearded chin, collapsed with laughter. He did not, however, get the satisfaction of finding out the story behind my problem for at least eighteen months. I had sworn the American to silence, and he was a man of his word.

Unfortunately, though, the Eskimo nurse did not check inside the hole before sewing it up, and to this day my chin swells up periodically as some mobile foreign matter – glass, concrete or parquet, perhaps – travels around the jawbone.

At Cambridge Bay, the first Eskimo settlement since Tuktoyaktuk, we learned that ice almost certainly blocked our way east. In a week or two, local boatmen said, it might shift, but in their opinion it was more likely to get worse. In fact, one good north wind would fill up the whole of Queen Maud Gulf with ice from Victoria Strait and in all likelihood stay there until the sea refroze in three or four weeks' time.

I radioed Ginnie that everything was packed up and a Polar Continental Shelf Project Twin Otter was due to fly her and Simon and the radio gear to Resolute Bay, her next intended base and many hundreds of sea miles to our north. En route they would be stopping to refuel at Cambridge Bay.

Could they take me, I asked, on a reconnaissance flight to the east of Cambridge Bay? It would not take long and would give me an idea of the ice situation. The Twin Otter pilot flying for PCSP was Karl Zberg, who was to fly for us up in the Arctic Ocean the following year. He agreed to help where he could and the next afternoon landed at Cambridge Bay. Ginnie, Simon and Bothy looked well, but now there was a second dog – a black Labrador puppy even smaller than Bothy.

'What,' I asked Ginnie, 'is that?'

'This is Tugaluk. Two months old and a good dog.'

'*Whose* is she?'

Ginnie thought quickly. 'She's a wedding present for Simon.'

Simon butted in that he wasn't getting married and even if he had been he wouldn't want Tugaluk.

'You can't keep her, Ginnie, you know that, don't you?'

Ginnie did. But, she explained, the puppy would have been shot if left as a stray in Tuktoyaktuk.

'Anyway,' she said with finality, 'Bothy has fallen in love with her. He'll probably get over it in Resolute so I'll find a kind owner and leave her there.'

The matter was closed.

I had a discussion with the pilot, Karl. Charlie and I had not seen him since somewhere near the North Pole four years before.

If the sea to the east of Cambridge Bay was blocked with ice we had only two alternatives: to wait, which I had no desire to do; or to skirt the mainland coast well to the south and, by adding a dogleg of some two hundred extra miles, creep *around* the ice along its southern and eastern limits. Obviously if the ice extended right up to the eastern coast of Queen Maud Gulf, even this plan would fail.

Such an extended route along a hazardous coastline with no settlements and no DEW sites would mean at least one extra fuel cache, and Karl advised the loading of three fuel drums for the reconnaissance flight. This done, we took off at once, because it was getting dark. Almost one hundred and fifty sea miles southeast of Cambridge Bay we flew over a nest of shoals and islets, one of which looked long, narrow and flat.

'Perry Island.' Karl prodded at his chart. 'It's supposed to be okay to land here except after recent heavy rain. If you have to come down this direction it will be on your way.' I nodded. After all, if we decided to come along this southern route, fuel right here would be ideal. If the ice up north proved penetrable, well, then, we'd go that way and someone else could use our fuel cache here if ever they found it. Looking down at the hostile mass of islands I found it hard to believe anyone would want to visit, let alone live in, so desolate a region. Yet until recently there had been a village on one of these islands, complete with a shop and mission post.

As Karl circled lower I began to appreciate that this was the very last place to choose for a boat journey. There were literally hundreds of islands, some pure rock platforms half-awash, and between them countless shoals broke the sea. Hostile though it undoubtedly was, this storm-bound coast, spattered with wrecked small boats, the Cambridge Eskimos informed me, would provide the only alternative to a year's delay if, further north, the sea proved ice-bound.

Karl buzzed the mud island, allowing his heavy rubber wheels to touch down briefly. Then with a surge of power he rose again and, circling, inspected the wheelmarks. How wet and deep was the mud? He had every reason to be careful. A little bit too much mud would prevent his taking off again from the tiny strip. Six laborious circuits and trial touchdowns later we landed and rolled the three drums to the edge of the island.

The sun had already disappeared when we left the islet with a perfectly timed liftoff. Karl skimmed northeast of Hat Island. Already there was ice. Two-thirds of the sea was ivory white, the rest a dusty ink. Jenny Lind Island, our cache point for this route, was cut off from the west. We needed to see no more. Either we went by the longer southern route or not at all.

I squeezed out of the cockpit and joined Ginnie in the darkness of the fuselage. We promised each other no more expeditions after this.

Back at Cambridge Bay Simon and the dogs joined Karl and Ginnie, and they flew off north to set up the radios at Resolute Bay.

We stacked the boat with as much fuel as possible and set out in a light breeze and low mist. Beyond the bay and the lie of the land the fog became dense. At this point our route lay south across Dease Strait and back to the uninhabited coastline of the Canadian mainland. Once again some of the shoalbanks on my map were blotted out by the grim words – 'MAGNETIC COMPASS USELESS IN THIS AREA.'

The white flash of broken water in the mist and the slight changes in the colour of the water warned us of underwater rocks. We carried two spare propellers, but with two hundred miles of shoal water ahead, could not afford to break off any blades too early on.

The wind rose to thirty knots. Dense fogbanks covered the islands and the mainland. It became impossible to tell which was which. I knew I must not lose our position against the chart since it would be extremely difficult to relocate once disorientated, even without a mist.

We nosed into a calm bay and waited for an hour. Briefly, a headland to the east cleared and we set out again. It was a difficult day to navigate in. For nine miles the coastline was flat and without a single feature. I told Charlie to hug it like glue or I would be unable to fix our position. We came to corridors of countless shoals where the sea boiled between gaunt stacks of dripping rock, and we layed off to plot a route through the obstacles before committing the whaler to running the gauntlet. Hour after hour I strained my eyes to recognise any coastal features, but there were hundreds of islands of all shapes and sizes and the coastline was so heavily indented with bays, fjords and islets that the mist made it all too easy to mistake a channel for a cul-de-sac.

A great deal of luck helped see us safely and accurately through a hundred and thirty sea miles of this nightmare passage, but in the evening a storm came from the west and threw great rolling seas over the shoals and against the islands.

Despite a strong desire to locate the three-drum cache, common sense dictated shelter, and I looked for a long-deserted Hudson Bay Company hut on Perry Island some twelve miles short of the cache. We found the hut hidden around the bend of an island fjord and anchored the boat off its horseshoe beach.

For twenty-four hours the storm bottled us up on the island. There was rain and sleet as usual but inside the old wooden shack we were okay with sleeping bags on the floor and buckets under the leaky parts of the roof. Our sodden boat suits did not dry out, but at least we did. I trudged across mossy rock to the south of the island, disturbing on my way a snowy owl with a lemming in its beak, two ptarmigan and a gyr falcon. Ollie, I thought to myself, would have been ecstatic.

Quite suddenly I happened on an Eskimo village of six one-room shacks. Seal pelts, bear skins and moose antlers littered the shingle. Broken sledges and rotten fishnets lay about, but not a soul answered my calls. I fixed up the radio but Ginnie did not answer. A friendly operator from Gladman Point DEW site some two hundred miles to the northeast, and our next port of call, did pick up my call and wished us good luck.

On August 10 the storm showed no signs of letting up, and my patience ran out. We dodged between islands to keep away from their exposed shores. Sometimes we hitched up the out-boards and waded the boat over rockbeds. At noon we came to the island of our cache, but mud banks extending from it meant leaving the boat two hundred yards away and trudging through shallows with the jerry cans. Since the mud was soft and deep our boots sunk in and were often held tight with suction, especially on our way back with full cans. Two weary hours later we were ready but found that the boat, heavy with fuel, was now stuck in the mud.

As though from heaven, an Eskimo in oilskins chugged up in a long, low river boat. He spoke no English but pointed toward Perry Island. Perhaps he came from the huts I had seen but he and the other inmates were all out on a summer fishing trip. We fixed a line to his stern, and after many jerks with the two of us heaving knee-high in mud, we eventually unstuck the whaler. Twice more we became jammed on unseen shallows but each time our Eskimo guardian angel helped us away.

Clear now of the mud channel, we again came to a maze of isles, rock isles and shoals. The sea had calmed down and for ten hours we headed east, sometimes out of sight of land except for ever more isolated islands to the east and south. Since the compass was useless and the sun made no appearance, I kept my nose glued to the chart.

At dusk the wind again raced down from the north, and we plunged off creaming breakers. Twice the whole heavy boat was flung into the night as great black walls of water struck us broadside.

'We'd better not do that last bit again,' Charlie yelled into my ear. 'Remember, we're not allowed to fly. This is a surface voyage.' I saw his teeth grinning in the dark, then grabbed at the handrail as another unseen surge sent us keeling madly to the starboard.

Not long before midnight, in the middle of a timeless, bucking nightmare, a thin moon scudded clear of the racing cloudbank, not for long but long enough for us to spot an indent in the silhouette of the cliffs ahead. Since our current progress was clearly suicidal, I shoved my beard against Charlie's dripping hood and said, 'We'll go in here till dawn – but watch out for rocks.'

The indent proved to be a well-sheltered inlet. Charlie steered us in without a bump, and I sloshed up the beach with the painter. We put up our tent, peeled off the boat suits and lit a wood fire. Charlie located some whisky. I'd always thought it disgusting stuff, but when you're very cold it has, no question, distinct advantages. Three hours later the bottle was all but finished.

Streaks of livid orange announced the break of a new day and the cold shapes of rock and seashore imposed on our salt-stung eyes. I made a waking-up noise and Charlie groaned. By dint of much shouting at the sky and running on the spot I persuaded myself that I was not only alive but could just about face the awful moment of climbing back into the clammy confines of my boat suit. The fact that sand from the beach clung to its inside did not help especially in the neighbourhood of my crotch ... the insides of my thighs were red-raw from the long days of salty chafing.

*

The next fourteen hours we weaved our weary way through innumerable gravel islands and along a bewildering slalom course with north as its basic ingredient. The distant dome of Gladman Point under a low black sky was a wonderful sight, but despite a yearning for warmth and sleep, this was no place to stop – the bay provided little shelter given a storm. The station boss gave us fuel and hot black coffee.

Gjoa Haven, the Eskimo settlement which marked for me the halfway point of our journey, was only seventy miles to the east. For five days, we were told, fishing parties of Gjoa Haven Eskimos had been stranded by the bad weather at various points between Gladman Point and Gjoa Haven. We could stay until the storms subsided if we liked, the DEW boss told me. It would be safer ... the Eskimos knew best. If they did not think it safe to travel we would do well to follow their example. I thought back to the Yukon Indians and decided to press on. It was not a question of deriding the local people's judgement but purely a matter of time-and-distance mathematics. The local fishermen could afford to sit tight and wait for safe conditions. If we did so, we would undoubtedly fail.

By evening we reached Gjoa Haven and, almost drunk with weariness, secured the whaler between two Eskimo boats. The narrow bay was where Nansen's *Gjoa* had spent a winter during her three-year epic voyage through the passage, the first in history.

In Gjoa Haven we were warned that sea ice almost certainly blocked the Humboldt Channel and the Wellington Strait to the north. Better to head up to call in at the last settlement before Resolute Bay, a hamlet at the head of Spence Bay Fjord. After Spence Bay we must take guides and be ready to turn back should ice block the northerly passage ...

For once we set out in good weather and no mist, following the coastline of King William Island until, at Matheson Point, I took a bearing off the sun and headed across Rae Strait. For a short while in mid-crossing there was no land anywhere, then inverted mirages of the coast danced over the horizon and we made good time to the great rock-girt inlet of Spence Bay, arriving late on August 13 at the isolated Eskimo hamlet named after the bay.

Our morale was high. From now on we would be travelling north once more. True, time was running short and soon we would meet ice, but we were already further by far than could have been managed in a year of even average ice conditions.

We moved into a 'guest cabin' for one night and plonked our kit in the living room. Once we had moved into our rooms I took my spare set of maps out of Charlie's boat bag and settled back to read through the notebook that he used as a diary.

Charlie and I both tended to read anything we came across, but an old saying goes that eavesdroppers never hear good of themselves. The same might be said of those who, on expeditions, read other people's diaries. Since, as the official book writer of the expedition, I believed that, as after our polar training, I would be reading the contents of all the expedition diaries, I felt no qualms about reading Charlie's. When he came back I tackled him at once. I was upset and angry at his entries and told him so. Why, I asked him, had he said I was lost off such and such a place? Because, he replied, I had said so myself. Yes, but surely he realised I only meant in terms of our exact position vis-à-vis two river mouths, not as regards our overall position?

But, said Charlie, he had not written that I was lost overall. No, but only he and I knew what had actually happened, and if he were to die no one would believe my interpretation of his diary. Didn't he realise that a diary can become accepted as 'historical evidence'? As far as I could see his own notes were misleading . . . Not at all, said Charlie, that was how he saw things, and anyway his diary was not for general consumption. Was I trying to censor him? Stop him writing a diary at all?

No, of course not, I bit back, but couldn't he understand my feelings? I had thought how very well we were getting along together and now realised that I was under permanent review. Like having a KGB agent in the back of the car taking critical and, in my view, inaccurate notes of my every action and word and then attributing supposed motives to them. Would he like it if I did the same?

He shrugged. Go ahead, he said. He wouldn't mind at all. I was too damn sensitive to criticism.

I left things at that. Maybe he was right.

But at heart I felt strongly about the matter, and my relationship with Charlie was never quite so free and easy again after Spence Bay. Openly all was fine and friendly when we were together and alone. But the presence of a third party tended to bring out in him a prickliness toward me which he made no attempt to disguise. Which in turn encouraged me to keep quiet whenever possible unless we were alone, in which case he relaxed and normal conversation was again possible. And since the vast majority of the time we were isolated from third parties and worked exceptionally well as a two-man team, there should have been no basis for worry.

So why did I worry? I think mainly because of a long-held belief that it is not just the facts of the matter that form the lasting records of an event but the participants' written testimony. I also believe that diaries, traditionally held to be incontrovertible evidence and accurate statements of events, are often rather subjective, even prejudiced tomes of inaccuracy. Often the writer will pen his accounts of events by way of letting off steam at the end of a day of frustration. Understandable enough, but he may well be in a fairly volatile state, interpreting the words and actions of his companions, as well as himself, from a distorted viewpoint.

In any event, whatever latent antagonism or rivalry there might have been between Charlie and me was certainly not apparent when we were on the move. Perhaps because our energies were fully taken up with coping with mere progress from A to B. It was only when we emerged from the lonely wastes to some warm, relaxing outpost that symptoms of unrest arose.

Two other boats left Spence Bay ahead of us. We followed in convoy. They too were eighteen feet long and outboard-powered. Included in their crew were the Spence Bay mountie and a local Eskimo hunter with an unrivalled knowledge of the region.

An hour or two north of Spence Bay the other boats turned aside and beached. We hovered off shore. What was wrong? 'There's a storm coming,' the mountie shouted, 'a bad one. Our friends will go no further and advise you to stop here or head back to Spence Bay.'

The sky was clear and there was no more than a light breeze from the west. I told the mountie we had better press on and would camp if the storm materialised. He shrugged and waved as we pulled away.

Three hours later the wind had indeed risen. Storm clouds poured across the sky, and on the western horizon a rugged run of ice edged the blackness of the sea.

'Sheep,' I shouted to Charlie, pointing at a small cream-coloured animal moving along the beach. As we approached, it turned into a polar bear patrolling its patch of the coastline . . .

For a hundred miles we moved north through increasing signs of ice, thick banks of fog and winds of up to sixty knots. Since the coast we followed was unindented and the waves smashed its shore with mounting fury, there was nowhere we could stop.

The next fuel cache was a low sandspit somewhere in Pasley Bay. With luck we would find shelter from the storm within the bay and camp until the winds abated.

After six hours of drenching in ice-cold water our eyes were inflamed and our fingers ached with the cold. The moment we reached the mouth of the bay, conditions altered. For the worse.

The whole of Pasley Bay writhed with the power of the storm. Serried lines of wind-lashed breakers smashed into every shore. There was no shelter. We could not go on, we could not turn back. To turn broadside onto the rushing walls of water, even briefly, would be to invite immediate swamping. I squinted at the chart and noticed a stream that looped its way into the bay dead opposite to the mouth. If we could just cross the two-mile reach from mouth to stream we might find shelter.

Off Perry Island we had experienced bigger waves but none so powerful, so steep or so close together. The bows plunged off one six-foot wall vertically down its front and into, not over, the next. The boat's floor was quickly awash with cans and kit floating about our feet. The wave tops completely covered the prow and smashed down into the cockpit. Most of the time visibility was nil – as soon as we opened our eyes a new deluge cascaded over our heads. The water, rushing down the insides of our suits, was far colder than it had been further south.

Never did two miles seem longer. But finally a brief gap in the pounding beach surf revealed the river's mouth. We nosed upriver, delighted at the wonderful calm and the depth. We had feared shallows. A mile or so upstream on a lee shore we moored the whaler to a piece of driftwood and struggled to erect the sodden tent. The wind whipped out the tent pegs, so using our remaining full cans as weights, we half-fixed up the tent, brewed coffee, ate chocolate and slept as soon as our slimy suits were off.

Next day there was no wind and the bay was smooth as a millpond. Hard to imagine how so pretty a cove could boil in fury as it had only six short hours before.

Our fuel drums were cached on a nearby spit where the Polar Continental Shelf Project's Twin Otter had left them the previous month.

We continued north. For an hour we enjoyed a weak wan sun, then fog closed dense and yellow all about the boat and we nosed between chunks of ice and the coastline for a while before deciding to pause until we could see something. Camping on a tiny shingle bar we watched a herd of beluga or white whales pass dolphin-like through nearby shallows ... flashes of white and black as they rubbed old skin off their stomachs along the gravel. Belugas are not hunted commercially, but the Eskimos catch them in nets and eat the fat, the meat, even the skin, which they say tastes like the white of an egg. Herds of beluga have been seen in Arctic rivers many miles from the ocean, which makes sense since their worst enemies are sharks and polar bears.

When the fog dispersed we kept going along a craggy coast with well-defined mountains and bays that made navigation a delight. We passed by the maw of Bellot Strait, which in years when Peel Sound is blocked is the only way through the passage. We ourselves, I realised, might yet have to turn back and pass through the hazardous channel. There was just no telling how much further north the ice would allow us.

From time to time lonely bergs, grounded until the recent storm, sailed by us without posing a threat until, at the end of the day, we reached the great cliffs of Limestone Island, spattered with the droppings of a million seabirds, at the northwest tip of Somerset Island.

Ahead lay Barrow Strait and, on its far side, Resolute Bay, the only settlement on Cornwallis Island. The crossing was forty miles wide, and pack ice stretched across our front from horizon to horizon. There was also little fuel left, and our last cache before Resolute Bay was another twelve miles around the island's north coast.

So we edged on beneath the cliffs. Carefully, because the sea was full of chunks of half-drowned ice, from marble to man-size. We progressed down an ever-narrowing corridor between the cliffs and the pack. A strong breeze blew from the north, which worried me because the pack could shift south with the wind and close in behind us.

Soon we were nudging along channels in the pack with ever-decreasing sea room. With ten miles to go to the cache I decided to turn back until the north wind stopped blowing. We might well reach our cache, but the chart showed no place near it that was likely to afford protection from invading ice.

Back the way we had come by some twenty miles there was a deep inlet, Aston Bay, which looked as though it would provide cover unless a west wind blew for long enough to pour the pack back down Peel Sound and trap us in the bay.

Charlie did not look happy at the idea of turning back, but I had long ago learned that you can't keep all the people happy all the time. I was content to take risks if I had to, but was damned if I would when any alternative course remained open. Not presuming a comparison, but I recalled how my mother always told me my father respected his boss, General Montgomery, for his never moving forward, if he could help it, until the cards were stacked where possible in his favour. Neither nature nor Rommel would be likely to hand out second chances. I sort of took that as my text, and in a situation like this I usually avoided asking for the opinion of others. Why? Charlie probably nailed my reasoning process correctly . . . He once said: 'I think Ran finds it very difficult to talk of the logistic side for the simple reason that I will see something and say, "Well, how about doing it such and such a way?" That might mess him up from his own thinking as to how he wants to do it. Obviously there is more than one way of playing any ball game, so if he airs his views to me I will come back and say, "Well, why don't you do this or that?" Then he's got another something churning around in his head, so he'd rather not listen. So he keeps it all to himself and I think it eats him away slightly.' Could be . . .

The fjord down which we did retreat was almost ice-free and several miles deep. We eased over a shallow sandbar to the terminal bay in a wide gravel valley. Shale slopes overlooked us and water from the summer melt tinkled its way down to the fjord via several outwash gullies.

Using the tent and an oar for antennae masts I contacted Ginnie. The bay at Resolute was full of ice, she said, and added that a Japanese with a boat equipped with sail and outboard had been waiting there for two summers to cross Barrow Strait. This was his third year, she pointed out, so I shouldn't be impatient. That kept me quiet for a few hours, but when we were still in the little bay three days later, I began to champ at the bit.

Each day more ice floes appeared along our protective sandbar. Some smaller ones sneaked over it at high tide and crunched against the side of the whaler, though they were as yet too small to do much harm. As yet. It would be foolish to be caught in the bay like a rat in a trap with floes pressed up solidly against our sandbar exit.

On the morning of the third day a skein of new ice sheened the water all about the whaler, a sinister reminder of perilous winter. In eleven days or so the remaining open sea would begin to freeze. True, in a week or so Giles and Gerry were to arrive at Resolute with the Twin Otter and help guide us through any pack ice in our way, but a week was too long to wait. By a lucky stroke, an old friend of ours from the Arctic training days happened to come to Resolute for a month's pilot work. Dick de Blicquy, most famous of Canada's still-working Arctic bush pilots, met up with Ginnie, learned of our predicament and agreed to guide us across the strait as soon as the weather looked right.

On the fourth morning of our stay in the fjord the wind dropped, the mist lifted and we sneaked over the ice-choked sandbar, sped around Somerset Island to our cache at Cape Anne and entered the pack three miles north of the coastline.

For four hours we responded to radio instructions from Dick de Blicquy who circled above Ginnie and Simon in the PCSP Twin Otter. Sometimes it was necessary to push floes apart with oars and our feet; sometimes a route that looked good from above proved a cul-de-sac from our point of view in the boat. But in the end we reached the mouth of Resolute Bay, two hours before fogbanks poured over the cliffs of Cornwallis Island and blanketed the pack ice.

Tugaluk was as big as Bothy now and only happy when destroying some useful item like a mukluk or a set of vital maps.

'I thought you were going to get rid of her,' I meanly reminded Ginnie.

'I am. Don't flap. We'll be around for at least another week and there are plenty of folk here who would love to own such a beautiful dog.'

I let that one lie ... Within a few hours of our arrival a wind change brought pack ice back into the harbour, nearly crushing the whaler. This prevented our departure for four critical days of mist and sleet. During this stay I received a message from our chairman in London suggesting that my route should be north of Resolute via the Wellington Channel. At the channel's north end there is a narrow neck of low land west of the Douro Range that blocks any sea route through to Norwegian Bay. To avoid known hazards of going east around Devon Island and from there north up either side of Ellesmere Island, our chairman was suggesting that we abandon the whaler at the northern reach of Wellington Channel, camp there until the sea froze, then carry on by Skidoo. In a message four days later he said: 'As we have mentioned previously, more haste, less speed. It would be sensible to use the sea ice as far as possible by Skidoo to Tanquary Fjord and then on land to Alert.'

As a cautionary move in case the chairman's suggested course became necessary I asked Ginnie to check out our light inflatable boats with skids, which would be portable across the narrow isthmus west of the Douro Range and struck me as a better bet than Skidoos for the conditions of ice *and* water which characterise early winter.

Ginnie exchanged messages with Ant Preston in London, who advised us that Dr Hattersley-Smith, the polar-regions expert, had again stressed to our chairman: 'I must say that I have always been very sceptical about the feasibility of this journey in one season and told Ranulph so three years ago.'

I walked over to the Resolute meteorological research station and asked a technician if we could get through the strait east of Bathurst Island. No, he said. It was jammed solid with ice and likely to stay that way. How about out into Lancaster Sound and up the east coast of Ellesmere Island? Again, no. Likely to be ice- *and* storm-bound. How about a giant detour around Devon Island and through Hell Gate to Norwegian Bay? Possible, but inadvisable, owing to the hazardous sea conditions off Devon Island's east coast. All in all he had discounted all options beyond spending the winter in Resolute.

But that was the one thing I could not take – doing nothing – so I plumped for the easiest-looking option, a race around Devon Island for six hundred miles as soon as the ice allowed our whaler out of the harbour. Ginnie was unable to contact our chairman but got a message through to Colonel Andrew Croft, whose Arctic experience was considerable. He replied with approval for my plan.

I realise it might seem strange that I should check such moves with the committee back in London. Surely the man on the ground knows best? Often true, but I had never been in the Northwest Passage, nor had Charlie. So it seemed not unwise to sound out the options of people with experience. Having received such options, I still felt the final choice should rest with me.

Maybe this was wrong.

Charlie's view was: 'Ran runs the show. He's the leader in the field but you've got to remember he has a committee back in England. They run the expedition. This does cause problems, as you can imagine. In the sense that if Ran wants to do something, he does it, and the board of directors, the committee, they try and change it . . . He now feels the strain. I can see it. Because he has to be diplomatic. He can't say, "Well, I'm going to do this or that without telling the committee."'

And yet at the same time Simon wrote: 'Ran seems to be the only cheerful one of our team at the moment . . . Charlie is sharing my room. He seems to be sparring with Ran in a funny way – overtly brash and friendly but needles underneath.'

As the race against time intensified, all became a bit tense. With nine hundred miles to cover in six days, if we were to reach Tanquary Fjord by the end of the month, there was no more time for delays. Early on August 25 the ice moved out of the harbour and hung around a couple of miles off the coast. Before a south wind stirred to bring the pack back in again we went in silence down to the harbour in our boat suits and set off to the east.

(An American geologist, the founder of the Arctic Institute of North America, watched us leave. He would write to Andrew Croft: 'When we were in Resolute the Fiennes group came through. They moved off in a snowstorm when the harbour ice had cleared sufficiently – but I tell you none of us would have changed places with them, sitting high without benefit even of windscreen.')

All that day the mist remained alongside or near to the gaunt cliffline that we followed east. At the sheer cliffs of the Hotham Escarpment we left Cornwallis Island and crossed the stormy seas of Wellington Channel.

Relieved to make land now and the shelter of the cliffs of Devon Island, we steered into an inlet called Erebus Bay ... *Erebus* and *Terror* were the two sturdy ships of Sir John Franklin, the sixty-year-old leader of an 1845 expedition to locate the Northwest Passage. One hundred and twenty-nine men had set out. Some had wintered in this same bleak spot. A few days before the expedition began Franklin's wife, spotting him dozing off in a chair, tucked him up with a flag she was sewing for the expedition. He awoke startled and cried out, 'Union Jacks are for corpses.' In this case he was right. Both ships and all the men disappeared, and despite forty separate search expeditions, many of them great feats of endurance, over the next ten years no survivors were found. The disjointed discoveries of the searchers put together some idea of the drawn-out suffering of Franklin's men, but they also produced new mysteries. Did Franklin's senior officer, Crozier, die with the rest or did he, because of his unique personal knowledge of the Eskimo tongue and methods of survival, live on with an Eskimo family? Why were two of the skeletons, found in an abandoned ship's boat, missing their skulls, and why did each hold a rifle that had fired a single shot? Did Eskimo hands pull down the survivors' cairns and destroy their records? Did they murder the stragglers? Both ships were immensely strong. One of them, *Terror,* had once spent three months stuck on a floating iceberg but survived and returned to England. Six years after the ships left for the Arctic, there was an official sighting by the master and crew of the English brig *Renovation.* They reported seeing two three-masted ships, black in colour, marooned high on a passing iceberg off the northern coast of Canada. Did some of the survivors resort to cannibalism? Dr John Rae, one of the searchers, recorded: 'From the mutilated state of many of the bodies and the contents of the kettles it is evident that our wretched countrymen were driven to the last desperate alternative as a means of sustaining life.'

The terrible fate of Franklin and his men was very much on my mind as we anchored on the eastern side of Beechy Island and waded ashore where an old ship's bowsprit protruded from the gravel beach. On benchland some way above the high tide mark were the crumbled foundations of a small shack, and the shattered remains of wooden barrels and rusty iron hoops. Beyond the bowsprit were gravestones. Some of Franklin's men had died here, of scurvy perhaps, but the majority had continued on to die further south.

Charlie cut his name into a slab of slate and left it on the beach, and for an hour we sat together and stared at our desolate surroundings . . .

Then we pushed on for the one hundred and sixty miles to Croker Bay. En route we crossed the mouths of many bays, and looking north saw the crown of the high ice field that lay over the eastern half of Devon Island and sent its tentacles down the coastal valleys to emerge into the sea fjords as icebergs. As evening closed in we moved in the cold dark shoulder of huge cliffs through an ink-black sea. There were seals and whales and many birds and, increasingly, icebergs of great height and length.

At Croker Bay, as night fell on us from the ice-laden cliffs above, a storm rushed north over Lancaster Sound and caught us ten miles short of shelter. The propellers struck unseen ice with heart-stopping thuds. To be immobilised between the jostling icebergs would not be healthy.

'Monster to port,' Charlie shouted in my ear. I stared into the gloom where he pointed and saw the foaming silhouette of a giant wave strike a nearby chunk of ice. A wall of spray rose above us.

The world kicked and danced in unseen turmoil, and I strained my eyes at the rock heights to spot the indent of Dundas Harbour, once the site of a Hudson Bay Company store but now abandoned to the elements. I found the entry, but icebergs crashed together in the high swell across the bay mouth and only with a goodly slice of luck did we thread our way safely through to the haven of shallows to the wonderful sight of three little shacks by a low bar of shingle.

One shack was almost rainproof. I fitted up my antenna on the roof and Charlie soon had a log fire spitting under our stewpot. For an hour we sat by candlelight, our suits strung up to dry, and chatted about army days long ago in Arabia.

East of Dundas Harbour the inland glacial mass poured icebergs down vertiginous valleys which split the mountains. The sea was awash with ice, bergs that had clashed in the stormbound fjords; a million water-coloured chunks floated off the coastline like lethal frog spawn. Waves broke against the seaborne giants all about us. Spray shrieked by in horizontal sheets. The storm that day raged along the southern coast of Devon Island, and from Resolute Ginnie reported drifting snow and overlying ice.

With but four days to the end of August I decided not to wait for improvement. An hour after setting out we rounded the gaunt rocks of Cape Warrender, where waves smashed the shore in a thundering welter of surf. A course running parallel to the cliffs and four hundred yards out seemed least dangerous. Several times the boat shuddered as unseen ice hit the hull or propellers. Then a shearpin went. Charlie closed down the now useless port outboard and we limped on at half power, gradually drifting nearer to the cliffs.

For four miles we found nowhere to land but knew we must change shearpins and quickly. At any moment the other propeller might strike ice, at which time we would quickly be the fibreglass version of matchwood.

Suddenly a tiny defile with a shingle beach appeared between cliff walls. On our way in we passed several hundred beluga whales, nosed between madly jostling ice blocks and grounded bergs to fight through to the little beach.

And then Charlie grabbed my shoulder and pointed dead ahead. One of the grounded bergs on the beach, at the very point selected for our landing, turned out to be an adult polar bear. Perhaps the bear knew the beluga, its natural prey, were accustomed to basking in the shallows off the beach. In any case, to disturb a polar bear is generally a poor idea. We, however, had no alternative. According to my chart unbroken cliffs stretched twenty miles to the east.

Charlie nosed the boat in as far as he dared, and I went overboard. One of my suit leggings, having developed a tear, filled up with water to the thigh. Holding the bow painter, I trod the slippery rocks while Charlie unsheathed his rifle.

The bear, unfamiliar with shiny white eighteen-foot-long whalers, withdrew slowly and disappeared among boulders which ringed the beach.

For thirty minutes I struggled to hold the boat as steady as possible while Charlie worked with freezing hands to replace the shearpin and both propellers ... we discovered they were hopelessly battered and one had a blade missing.

I also kept a wary eye out for the bear. As we left the beach it passed us, swimming with only nose and eyes above the water. Startled, it dived. For a moment its great white behind rose skywards, then nothing.

The waves beyond the immediate lee of the cliffs were as big as any I had ever seen. For a hundred and twenty miles we were to buck and roll between heaving icebergs, mesmerised by the size and power of the waves. Bergs bigger than bungalows rolled about like beach balls in the sixty-knot gale, and many a time I held my breath as we squeezed between highly mobile ice monsters. Freezing sleet, fog and gale force winds forced us to spend a night at Cape Sherard, but on August 27 at midday we left the coast of Devon Island and crossed Jones Sound to Ellesmere Island.

At Craig Harbour, under dizzy cliffs, we paused to relax beside a king berg complete with blue arched caverns. Then on and on until, feeling much like soggy bacon rind, we reached the deep and shadowed reaches of Grise Fjord, the only Eskimo settlement on Ellesmere . . .

Back in Resolute Bay, Ginnie knew the dangers of Devon Island's east coast. For twenty-eight hours she had waited for my call, 'her face getting more introverted, frowning and bitter all day as she heard nothing,' according to Simon's comment.

I fixed an antenna up by two Eskimo houses, threading my way through wooden stretch frames of drying harp-seal pelts. Ginnie's voice was faraway and faint, but I heard the happiness in it as she acknowledged our position.

The last three days of August passed by in a blur of black cliff, freezing spray and, above all, increasing ice. In thick mist the oil-black cliffs of Cape Storm, Bear Head and Walrus Cape slid by disembodied from the sea. At the mouth of Hell Gate, escape route from Jones Sound, and beneath a cliff called Cape Turnback, I decided the conditions looked evil and the currents treacherous. We turned west and passed Devil Island, north into Cardigan Strait.

Again, hours of anxiety in wind-writhed waves, but once through the strait our long detour was over. In Norwegian Bay we were once more on our original axis north from Resolute Bay. The gamble had paid off, and there were still forty-eight hours in which to cover the final four hundred miles.

That evening the surface of the sea began to freeze for the first time, congealing silently and fast. We had to speed on. A twenty-mile bay bites into Ellesmere Island to the south of Great Bear Cape, and there we again hit pack ice. Again and again we nosed up channels and leads. To no avail – the pack became more solid to seaward and impenetrable within the bay. There was nothing for it but to retreat, and again new ice covered the open sea in oily sheets.

We beached in an unnamed bay and talked little to each other that evening. I radioed Ginnie, and she reported a sixty-mile belt of pack ice in Norwegian Bay that stretched west to Axel Heiberg Island. Our Twin Otter had still not arrived and so could not help us through the ice barrier. But an hour later Ginnie came back with great news. Russ Bomberry, one of the finest bush pilots in the Arctic and a chief of the Mohawk Indians, was in Resolute Bay with his Twin Otter. He had agreed to give us two hours 'ice flight' the next day.

The mist stayed away. The temperature dropped. I slept little that night. Only three hundred and twenty miles to Tanquary Fjord, but we could be one short day too late if this last ice belt delayed us long enough to snare us in the new ice of the coming winter.

At dawn we were up, teeth a-chatter, and loaded the whaler in readiness. At midday Russ Bomberry circled overhead, and we left for the ice belt. The new ice was already thicker and filled every open lead in the pack. The young frazil ice and ice rind burgeoned like active yeast. In places the whaler could no longer plane through it but meshed with it like a bug in a spider's web.

In the middle of the bay a light wind arose and opened channels in the ice rind. This helped. Russ ranged in wide circles northeast over the Bjorn Peninsula and northwest toward the snowy peaks of Axel Heiberg Island.

While he was gone we nosed about in the centre of the pack, and I wondered if Russ did not return or if a fog closed in how long it would take us to extricate ourselves from so complex and ever-changing a labyrinth as we were in.

Once back, Russ wasted no time. To get us north to Great Bear Cape he led us west, east and even south a good deal of the time. From the air our course must have looked rather like a dish of spaghetti, but three hours later Russ dipped his wings and left us. We were clear of the close pack. The rest we could handle.

A mile or two out of the pack, the steering linkage broke down. Charlie glared at it, smoked two cigarettes in contemplation of its mechanics, then fixed it in an unorthodox but neatly effective fashion ... During the next two days we slept five hours as we moved north through narrowing channels. A hundred miles up the winding canyons of Eureka Sound to Eureka itself was an isolated camp set up by the Canadian government as a weather station. A strong wind kept the new ice at bay in the fjords during the night of August 30, and next day we began the last run north up Greely Fjord for a hundred and fifty miles to Tanquary Fjord itself, a cul-de-sac deep in glacier-cut mountains.

Tiers of snowcapped peaks now shaped the horizons as we snaked ever deeper into a twilight world of loneliness and silence. Wolves stared from shadowed lava benches, but nothing moved except ourselves to sunder in our wash the mirror images of the darkened valley walls.

Twelve minutes before midnight we came to the end of the fjord. The sea journey was over. Within a week the sounds behind us would be frozen.

Chapter Twelve

We are the pilgrims, master:
We shall go always a little further:
It may be that beyond that last blue mountain
Barr'd with snow,
Across that angry or that glimmering sea . . .

SAS REGIMENTAL MEMORIAL TO THE DEAD

Five great ice caps surround the head of Tanquary Fjord, but it is possible to reach Alert, a hundred and fifty miles to the north-east, by a chain of stream valleys. On our arrival at Tanquary these valleys were snow-free but the streams themselves had frozen.

There was a temptation to set out at once before the temperatures began to plummet, but this could not be because the gravel strip and three little huts at Tanquary camp were to form one of the two bases for the Twin Otter during our coming attempt to cross the Arctic Ocean. It had been Ginnie's idea to use Tanquary as an additional base to Alert. The mists in April and May were so bad at Alert, she said, that we would save weeks by having Tanquary, beyond the reach of sea mists, stocked up as a second Twin Otter base.

Giles and Gerry were due at Tanquary in a week's time with the first of the base equipment from Resolute. This would need careful sorting and repacking, since some was to stay at Tanquary and some would go on to Alert. I had to do this before we could leave. And another reason argued for delay: Charlie and I were body-weak from more than a month of inaction in a cramped boat, in no condition for a long journey on foot.

Ginnie and Bothy had flown into Tanquary the previous day by Twin Otter from Resolute. Simon and Tugaluk stayed behind to run things for the aircrew.

There can be few places in the world at once as remote and idyllic as Tanquary camp. Ginnie and I walked along the frozen course of the creek that tumbles from Bedrock Glacier. Bothy chased Arctic hares. Yapping with joy he ignored Ginnie's orders to return and scampered away over moss-clad benchland unaware of his danger . . . Two wolves, white like Bothy, and probably attracted by his barking, loped down the hillside toward him. Ginnie fired her pistol in the air. The wolves ignored her, closed the gap to Bothy. Ginnie screamed. So did I. Bothy took no notice but lost the hare-trail and turned back. The wolves stopped, gazed at us and then moved away toward the camp.

That night three adult wolves with three cubs came down to the huts. Watching them through a window, the little wolves looked cuddly but we resisted the temptation to go outside and see if they liked to be stroked.

(Arctic wolves are slightly smaller than their southerly neighbours, the timber wolves. They often prowl alone, but when hunting caribou, their main source of food, they operate in packs. Survival of their pups depends on the food supply that varies season by season. Not long ago all wolves were shot on sight in the Canadian Arctic; now only the Eskimos can kill them and sell their pelts.)

*

On September 6 Giles and Gerry arrived from Resolute with a full load of cargo, then immediately flew back for another load, the weather holding fine.

Finally, on September 11, leaving Ginnie to look after the base, we set out on foot with eighty pounds of gear apiece. Because the Viking Ice Cap blocked our way northeast to Lake Hazen, we trudged southeast along the valley of the Macdonald River – in reality a piddling little stream that meandered along gravel beds and was frozen over anyway. Charlie carried a .357 magnum rifle instead of his pistol.

The first day's going was easy, with a light breeze and clear sky. Mountains rose on both sides, but the valley was wide and grazed by Arctic hares. To us they were just white rabbits, pretty and comical. Some would carry on feeding until we were a mere ten yards away, then off they went on their rear legs, holding their front paws daintily like old ladies poised with teacups. Musk oxen in groups of twos and threes munched at the sere sphagnum, cow-sized shaggy bundles with stubby legs and runtlike horns. The skyline glaciers and the wide rock valley formed a primeval backdrop to the Arctic oxen. As we approached they pawed the mossy ground, heads lowered in defiance. (The explorers of eighty years ago shot many of them, took the soft wool beneath their long brown hair – this *qiviut* was valuable to the Eskimo, and the meat was vital to the existence of any man so far north.)

We put nearly two miles behind us each hour for four hours. Where the melt water from the Bedrock Glacier entered the Macdonald Valley we stopped beside a frozen pool. Our tent was light and small, easy to set up. Charlie smashed the ice with his knife and collected water in his mug. The sole of one heel was blistered, but he showed no concern.

Next day the valley narrowed down. Now the sunlight was shut away by canyon walls. We turned northwest up a side valley that climbed for six miles to an unnamed glacier that tumbled down from the Viking Ice Cap in an ice fall that landed in our valley and turned it into a cul-de-sac.

Summer floods had burrowed a tunnel underneath this barrier. Arriving at the resulting culvert, I found there was plenty of room to pass through it if well bent over, but the ceiling looked insecure. I paused to wait for Charlie ... Eventually I heard him shout my name with note of urgency, but I could not see him for the ice chunks and boulders all around. I shrugged off my rucksack and scrambled back down the valley, then realised I'd left my pistol behind and there might well have been a bear. Grabbing a rock, I plunged on around a corner.

There was Charlie, hunched over a rock in the middle of the frozen stream. No bear but plenty of blood. His head was leaking from below his hairline and one eye was full of blood. He had slipped on ice and come down with his head hard against a sharp-edged rock. He looked white. I quickly took out the tiny first-aid pack from his rucksack, plastered a gauze pad over the cut and had him shove his head low until the dizziness went. The plaster seeped blood for a day or two, but the wound, fortunately, stayed healthy.

Charlie had received a nasty jolt and now moved a bit slower. I took the tent from his pack in exchange for my sleeping bag. After eight hours we had covered eleven miles, but a mist came down and snow settled on my tracks. I could not see Charlie behind so I stopped and put the tent up. He arrived after forty minutes – blisters on both his soles had broken and several had formed on his toes. He also ached all over.

As for me, there was a big bump on my right calf above the boot rim, squelchy to the touch but painless. My underclothes were wet with sweat. Both our boots and socks and trouser legs were soaking from breaking through the ice crust time and time again into the stream below.

But it was easy going, and the weather was still only just below freezing. We were in good time. Charlie, a rugged individualist, did not need my walking just ahead or behind him to encourage him. So long as he could see which way I had gone he preferred to be left alone, to go at his own pace. My own preference was also to carry on at my own best pace, not to dawdle. Charlie knew this and he never complained. Two different people and attitudes, but we managed to accommodate each other.

Subsequently our film crew could not understand why we did not walk together like normal folk, why I didn't hold back with Charlie like a good leader would. Should? Later, Charlie would be asked about this . . . Did he hate walking? 'Yeah, I don't like it but I wouldn't say I hate *every* step of the journey. I mean the first step was okay and the last step was absolutely beautiful. The rest of it was hell. I knew it was going to be hard keeping up with Ran. He has always punished himself in the walking field. There was a race in Wales we all used to train for and he was always up front. He's always pushing himself. He *can't* do it the easy way. I don't know what drives him but he always pushes himself. I'm not that way inclined. I'm a slow plodder. I *will* do the trip but in my own time. Ran must do it in the fastest possible time. It was a mental thing. I knew I was going to do it in *my* time and I had to realise that if I tried to keep up with Ran I wasn't going to make it. Whereas Ran can kill himself each day, I can't. I have got to space myself out.' Did that bother Ran? 'The speed difference would bother him for the simple reason that he would have to wait for me. He travels for two hours, then he stops. I might be half an hour behind him, in which case he has got to wait for me and therefore he is going to get cold. That would worry him and hurt him.'

The third morning dawned grey and dismal. Ice crystals lined the tent for the first time, but we were a mere thousand feet up into the mountains. Snow covered the valley floor. Charlie's left eye was closed, and the skin around it was puffed up in yellow swellings. His back and knee and blisters all hurt, and the blisters looked very nasty. The whole of his right heel was raw and weeping. He no longer wanted his rifle. 'How about the bears?' I asked him. 'If a polar bear attacks me,' he replied, 'it'll put me out of my misery.'

The first ten minutes of the day's walk must have been purgatory for Charlie, but he kept at it and we covered fourteen miles in ten hours. I missed one Y-junction of valleys in the mist but picked up the second without trouble and forked further north up the Very River bed. Gravel benches fashioned by the retreat of long-ago glaciers gave us shelter from a bitter wind, and Charlie managed to cook a delicious rehydrated stew.

The Very River moved down its own floodplain, a chain of pools or lakes leading to its mouth at Lake Hazen. But a mixture of fine sand, ice and snow covered the lakes and the lonely moraines all about them. A strong wind came down from the ice caps to our north and whipped up the dust of the sand bowl. With strange light shifting wan and sombre through the storm and our boots sinking deep in the grey-white dust, we might have been on the moon. Minus 7 degrees Centigrade.

Gradually the valley opened out until the lake itself was visible stretching west and north to the horizon. Forty miles long and up to six miles wide, the lake was bounded to the south by rolling tundra spattered with streams and pools, and to the north by the towering ramparts of the central ice cap.

I chose to follow the lake's northern flank because halfway along was a single deserted hut by the lakeside put there by scientists twenty years earlier. A fairly flat gravel bench beside it was said to be suitable for a Twin Otter, and I felt we ought soon to change from rucksacks to pulk sledges, from walking boots to mukluks and skis. Two weeks earlier we might have completed the journey on old crusted snow and bare tundra, but new snow now lay thick in windscoops, indicating the conditions likely at two thousand feet to which, after the lake, we would have to climb in order to swap watersheds. At the northeast end of the United States Range we would find river valleys leading down to the Arctic Ocean. Until then the frozen waterways all led to the eastern channel between Ellesmere Island and Greenland.

On reaching Lake Hazen, already frozen over at its southwestern end, I headed north, aiming for the glistening blue wall of the Henrietta Glacier ... frozen reeds and bloody remains of Arctic hares, the zing and twang of ice strain underfoot ...

By the outwash from the Turnstone River I set up our tent a few yards from the side of the lake, open at this point. All night a sound similar to Rice Krispies reacting to milk lulled our intermittent sleep ... new ice forming in the shallow along the beachside and rafting slab upon slab.

By now Charlie's left eye was closed and swollen over. Both his knees were watery and his feet were balloonlike. He was understandably worried that they might not fit back into his boots the next day. The mornings, then, were especially painful for Charlie. Putting his raw heels and bloody toes into frost-hardened boots made him grit his teeth together.

Late on September 15 I reached the old hut below Omingmak Mountain. A family of nine musk oxen galloped snorting off the hillside. Two hours later Charlie arrived looking half-dead. It was obvious that his feet were getting worse, so we changed the bandages and he took penicillin in an attempt to fight infection in the blisters.

Next day Giles came into the little strip beside the hut, bringing our pulk sledges, skis and snowshoes. He also took Charlie's rifle and gave him a pistol. I made weak contact with Ginnie, who warned me communications were fading fast. She had spent two days alone at Tanquary earlier in the week, and although she found the white wolves most attractive to look at, was not altogether happy with the way they stood up at her hut windows during the night and looked in at her, nor with their loud and discordant howling that made sleep difficult. They themselves seemed to sleep little, since by day five of them followed her about the camp and ignored her pistol shots. She took to using my FN rifle instead, but firing that frightened her more than it did the wolves. Part of the problem seemed to be the two dogs ... the wolves had obviously decided Tugaluk and Bothy would provide good eating and hung about the camp waiting their chance ... Ginnie now faded out and I was unable to raise her or anyone else again for the next two days despite alterations of frequency and antenna. The polar sun was soon to disappear for the winter, and communications are often poor at this time of year.

There were yellow-paged books in the hut which Charlie read, his poor feet propped up on a bench. Giles had taken one look at his knees and feet and suggested we wait at least a week before going on.

After two days there was little sign of improvement. I loaded the two pulks with care. With enough food for ten days the loads came to one hundred and ten pounds apiece, an easy load. Taking a pulk with cross-country skis I climbed the foothills of McGill Mountain, itself a mere molehill beneath the looming ice caps. The skis were awkward, so I changed to basket-type snowshoes, which made uphill work much easier.

The air was cold and clear. To the east lay mile upon mile of rock and ice beyond the lake, the weird tundra polygons of Black River Vale and, fifty miles away, the frozen cliffs of Robeson Channel. The sad remains of Fort Conger, itself but fifty miles south of Alert, still stood beside Robeson Channel, mute testimony to two brave

Arctic pioneers – the great American Admiral Peary, who tried five times to reach the Pole and had seven gangrenous toes cut off at Conger in 1904; and twenty years later Lieutenant Greely who experienced the hardships of an Arctic winter along the same coastline ... He and his men suffered intense cold and bitter frost, slow starvation, insanity and death. To these unpleasantnesses historians have added the probability of cannibalism because the rescue party found corpses with large chunks of flesh missing. Only seven out of Greely's twenty-five men survived to be rescued by the relief ship, and one of these, who had lost his hands and feet through gangrene, soon died.

(Despite the inhospitable terrain and climate, humans have survived on eastern Ellesmere Island on and off for centuries. Now no one lives there, but seven thousand years ago Vikings are believed to have settled in the area. The Thule Eskimos from Alaska are believed to have migrated east and colonised parts of Ellesmere Island prior to further expansion to Greenland. They were a tough crowd from necessity. In 1950 a band of three hundred still lived by hunting in the region of Thule. Their customs included throwing weak husky puppies to the pack as food and hanging dogs once they reached eight years old. Aged or infirm members of the tribe were simply left outside to die. Food was too valuable to waste on nonproductive members of the society. In the 1950s Denmark put a stop to traditional ways of life, and drink and venereal diseases were introduced for the first time along with refrigerators, Skidoos and outboard motors.)

From Tanquary Fjord to Lake Hazen we had passed no single man-made object, no paths, no refuse, nothing, and I reflected that it was comforting to have been somewhere where humans have left no lasting mark whatsoever on their environment. I began to shiver, the sun having passed behind the outline of a glacier ...

Back at the hut, Charlie showed me his feet. The swellings had subsided and the blistered areas looked clean. It would be an untold number of days until new skin replaced the raw places, yet further movement would probably reopen the sores. Every day now the temperature dropped and the dark hours grew longer. I had to make an unpleasant decision.

'If you feel okay tomorrow, we should set out early.'

Charlie made no comment.

Wearing snowshoes, there was less pressure against Charlie's sore feet. The weight we dragged now was on sledges behind us, not on our backs, which also helped him. At first he went well and we made good time.

But the cliffs beyond the Abbe River came down to the lake leaving no narrow shingle strip to follow. I detoured up a ravine in a thick mist. The pulks were now hard to pull because the slopes were steep and icy. Under the balls of our feet and attached to our snowshoes were metal claws, which helped. For several miles we pushed through dense fog along cliff ridges, down snowfields and rock gullies. Twice I tried to swing back to the lakeside, and twice I was again forced uphill where there was no beach.

By late afternoon the hills fell back from the lake, leaving flat going beside it. The temperature dropped four degrees and our beards were now frosted. Once I waited forty minutes after only an hour's travel. Seething inwardly, I pummelled my hands and feet. What the hell was holding up Charlie? When he arrived I asked him. 'The pulk keeps overturning on boulders.' 'Maybe you've stacked it wrong.' 'It makes no difference.'

Angrily I unloaded his pulk, repacked it and lashed the kit down tightly. Maybe it would make no difference, but anything was worth trying ... All the time, of course, I realised that the fault was entirely mine. Charlie was suffering considerable pain in moving at all. I should be moving at *his* pace, then I wouldn't have to freeze my noodles off waiting. There was no good answer to this. Once or twice I did try setting off slowly but I just couldn't keep it up.

That night the temperature dropped to minus 18 degrees Centigrade and the lake froze over. We began to travel over its surface. This was excellent for Charlie's feet and knees, and we made good time. Of course if you trod in the wrong place where the ice was weak, it broke, and often it buckled and protested noisily.

At noon on September 21 we left the lake behind and entered a wide, featureless valley. Musk oxen, startled by our sudden appearance through the thick yellow murk, thundered off, their wide hooves sinking into drifts, their loose fur coats swinging kiltlike.

I took the line of least resistance and proceeded to count my paces. Without lake or closed valleys or river line for boundaries it would be easy to get lost, and so I also began to use the compass with care. After all, the North Magnetic Pole was now a long way to our south. The needle was sluggish but seemed to settle with some consistency. I took a magnetic bearing of 130 degrees and tried to ignore the temptation of easier routes which veered off their course. The three-mile-long Turnabout Lake was snow-covered and invisible. Not surprisingly we crossed it without knowing it. Afterward there were no recognisable features, just a confusing land of mist and snow and hillside ...

We finished the lake water in our water bottles during the morning and grew thirsty. Once we stopped, we became quickly cold. Now we were climbing all the time. Snow covered the tundra hummocks, and our snowshoes often sank deep, jamming in potholes. Ice hid all lakes and pools, covered the streams. In the freezing fog we progressed no more than one mile an hour, and our sweat froze when we stopped. I followed iced-up riverbeds which meandered in every direction. To keep to the bearing, I sometimes had to leave a stream and head over featureless tundra to seek out another valley. The musk oxen, shaggy monsters in the mist, snorted and stampeded. I ate handfuls of snow which did little to slake my growing thirst. Charlie kept close now, which was just as well, because sometimes there were streams where the glass-ice left no mark of our passing.

For hours we floundered up valleys of soft snow on our clumsy snowshoes, staggering through drifts, tumbling down snowbanks and hauling on all fours at our pulks up the near vertical banks of moraines. We listened in the gloom, and once, hearing the tinkle of water from an iced-over stream through the heavy silence, plunged our knives into the ice, hoping for water to slake our thirst. There was no water.

Toward evening we did find a slow trickle two feet below the iced surface and drank greedily and filled our bottles with the muddy liquid, keeping them inside our shirts so the water would not freeze.

Since the whiteout removed all shadow and perspective we blundered on at the whim of my compass needle . . . After twelve hours' travel, fat snowflakes began to fall softly through the mist. We set the tent up. It was a wet snow and our clothes were sodden. One of Charlie's little toes hurt him. 'Still,' he rationalised, 'it takes my mind off the usual aches and pains.'

I contacted Ginnie on my whip antenna. She had flown from Tanquary Fjord to our old huts at Alert. I was able to pass on our rough position but conditions were too bad for anything else.

The cooker would not start, no pressure at the pump. There was ice around the plunger leather so we covered it with margarine. Once the cooker came to life, life began again . . .

The mists retreated overnight, and soon after dawn I clambered up the nearest hill. Minor valleys ran off in all directions, separated by snow-covered mesas like my own vantage point. It would have been as illuminating to have climbed onto a hedge in the midst of a maze. My dead reckoning from the previous day's travel put us along the bed of the Turnabout River at the spot it turned west to the Turnabout Glacier. But since no glaciers or high ground were anywhere visible, I could well be way off. Presuming I was somehow correct, for want of proof to the contrary, I carried straight on up a subsidiary valley where the main riverbed next jinked sharp left. Charlie stayed close by. Ever since we swapped from tight leather walking boots to canvas mukluks his feet had improved; he was also pleased to get rid of his heavy rucksack.

In an hour the new valley began to descend sharply and then bear eastward. No good. Slipping on boulders, I turned about and retraced our trail to where the prints of musk oxen climbed a narrow defile up one side of the valley system. By hauling up our pulks six feet at a time we finally reached a ridge top. Luckily this ridge was attached like a rib to a main spine that led westward for a mile, cutting through the labyrinth of canyons to a high plateau of snowfields.

Once there we found a lake leading northeast, and to my astonishment this placed us on the map precisely where the dead reckoning had indicated.

The pulks partially broke through the ice crust of the lake and sludge clung to their hulls. Once in contact with the air this sludge froze solid. We now dragged jagged-bottomed sleds, which effectively doubled their weight. We chipped the tough ice clay away, and, after four murderous miles, they ran free once more ...

Five hours later I found another long valley climbing to the 1,500-feet contours. We edged up to it onto the topmost ice plateau, which rose slowly to the feet of the glaciers. Now the snow was soft and deep. Snowshoes sank in twelve inches, sometimes double that, before the surface was solidified to take our weight and the transferred drag of the sledge, which itself dragged low ...

Late that afternoon we reached the foot of the Boulder Hills at twenty-two hundred feet and camped beside a frozen gulley.

For three long days we plodded single file through the deep snowfields, with temperatures at minus 20 degrees. Because movement was continuous we wore only two layers of clothing, as for walking in the Welsh hills, and only felt cold when we stopped for more than two minutes to drink or eat snow. The stillness was immense. No musk oxen now. Nothing. And no one ...

On September 23 we camped at the foot of the great Eugenie Glacier, its well-formed snout armed with layers of glistening teeth, stalagmites from a previous summer's brief melt.

Mist rolled over the plateau from the east, but now the very rim of the Grant Ice Cap brushed our left flank and, spurred on by the increasing cold, we limped at last to the northern tip of the plateau. There were many steep snowbanks to climb up or slither down, and on one of these Charlie bruised his hip.

In a kind of awe now, we laboured beneath the towering ice-falls of Mount Wood. Here twin glaciers tumbled two thousand feet down to a lonely lake. Here everything had a contorted, temporary look. The gigantic blocks of ice were scarred and smudged with alluvial muck, and blackened walls of ice reared up like monster waves frozen in the act of crashing against some puny dam. In the wary hush of this place where no birds sang, it was as though some new and cataclysmic upheaval was ever imminent. Crane your neck up to ease the pain of the sledge harness and the sky-high icefalls appeared to teeter from their summits.

Thankful to leave, I sought a tiny stream outlet from the lake. Fingers of mist crept over the primordial environs, and we literally stumbled into a corridor, some ten yards wide, between two boulder outcrops. This narrow rock-girt passage immediately descended, in curves and steps, to the west-northwest. There could be no doubt we were in the upper canyon of the Grant River, a winding ravine that fell for thirty miles to the sea. Once in it there was no further need to navigate, there being no branch-off valleys.

The only place to camp was on the river ice. All game followed the river too, and myriad small hoofprints of fox, hare, lemming, caribou and wolf dented the snowdrifts all about. But the metal spikes of our snowshoes, long since blunted by rock and slate, no longer gripped the sheet ice, and every few minutes evil language echoed off the narrow canyon walls as one or the other slipped and crashed over onto the rocks. Often our snowshoes smashed through the ice and dropped two or three feet down to the stream bed. Still, thanks to the snowshoes, awkward though they were, there were no sprained ankles.

Our pulks also plunged through the ice; as they wet their hulls they clogged up, just as they had on the plateau lake. More scraping and cold fingers. The sledge harnesses broke from the violent stop-start effect of jamming against boulders, overturning and crashing into sharp rocks. Using parachute cord, we repaired the breaks and carried on . . .

The canyon kinked and snaked, was blocked with high black boulders and once even seemed to climb, which must have been an illusion. One night was spent in a bottleneck some twelve feet wide between high black walls. Our tent stood suspended on ice above a neat round pool. We swallowed our soybean stew and bet each other how far it was to the sea. Already there was far less snow, and in places we hauled the sledges over nothing but rock for hundreds of yards.

Despite the hills all around us there was good contact with Ginnie at Alert, and I fell asleep thinking blissfully of the warmth of the huts there . . .

On September 26, toward noon, the riverbed plunged thirty feet down a frozen waterfall. From the top of this cleft we looked out at the Arctic Ocean, where an inlet, Black Cliffs Bay, edged in to meet the mouth of our river valley. A jagged vista of contorted pack ice stretched away to the polar horizon.

Travelling along the edge of the frozen sea, we came by dusk to the four little huts that we knew so well, the most northern habitation on earth. Alert.

We had travelled around the polar axis of the world for 314 degrees of latitude in seven hundred and fifty days. Only 46 degrees to go, but looking north at the chaotic ice rubble, 30 feet high in places, there was no doubt in my mind that the hardest nut was yet to be cracked.

Twelve hundred miles to the far rim of the Arctic Ocean.

Chapter Thirteen

> As soon as preoccupation with security begins to dominate human life, the scope of human life itself tends to be diminished.
>
> GABRIEL MARCEL

Winter in the Arctic would for us last but half the span of our Antarctic winter. Now there were three of us – Ginnie, Charlie and me – instead of four, and two dogs, not one. The dogs were to live in a tiny shack on the slope between the huts, which was also to be our lavatory. There was straw on the floor and a bucket with a plastic seat we had sent out from England.

On reaching Alert the first thing I noticed was a large black dog. 'Where,' I asked Ginnie, 'is Tugaluk, the dog you said was half Bothy's size?' 'This is her,' she replied indicating the monstrous black affair which was at least three times as big as Bothy. 'Don't flap, she's probably fully grown, she's two months old now.'

Our first night in the huts was better than the night we flew into Alert back in 1976 in midwinter. This was autumn, a few hours of sunlight still graced each day, and the temperature hovered around minus 10 degrees Centigrade.

The 'Chosen Frozen' was what the Canadian soldiers and weathermen at Alert called themselves, proud to be the most northerly men on earth. The nearest manned base was Thule, four hundred miles to the south. There was no possibility of visitors by sea or land, nor, when the weather was bad, by air. The battered remains of a transport aircraft and the nine graves of its occupants rested close to our huts, mute testimony to the hazards of reaching Alert.

A message arrived from our chairman in London suggesting that we should continue to travel without delay out onto the sea ice in the hope of gaining valuable mileage toward the North Pole. Colonel Andrew Croft was not in favour of this, saying, 'The proposal is dangerous. Ran is already planning to set out three weeks earlier even than Admiral Peary in 1909 and one month earlier than in 1977 when one of his own colleagues had to be returned to base with frostbite.' The suggestion was not pursued.

Giles and Gerry completed our cargo flights from Resolute to Alert and Tanquary in the first week of October. Before Giles left I asked him to drop some fuel and rations a hundred miles west of our camp and along the coastline. We took off at the beginning of the daily quota of sunlight, by then only three hours, and flew west, Giles's one-thousandth flying hour for Transglobe. The coast was rough. The sea ice was broken and reared up in huge waves of rubble that smothered the shoreline. The mountains were steep-sided and mostly hidden by active glaciers. Deep fjords cut into them.

Giles inspected Cape Columbia, the dark promontory where I intended to turn north onto the sea ice when the time came. There was nowhere remotely suitable for a landing. Giles veered back east. The next feature, Cape Aldrich, was also out of the question, but four miles further south Giles circled over an unnamed glacier that flowed east from Mount Hornby. Close to its snout on the beach of Parr Bay we came in fast and low-landing on an uphill slope of hard ribbed snow. There were bumps but we hardly felt them – Giles was no ordinary pilot. Quickly we unloaded the rations, jerry cans and orange marker flags. When next we came here there would be no sunlight.

By October 6 Giles had finished his supply flights; he took off and circled once, diving low over the three of us waving from the cold foggy strip. It did not seem like a year since the day he had left us to winter in Borga.

Simon and Gerry also went back to England, but David Mason came to Alert for two days on a Hercules, unloaded over two hundred drums of fuel, four Skidoos we had last seen at Borga and a good deal more ex-Antarctic gear. The work involved in transporting it all to London from the far south, servicing and repairing it, then getting it up to Alert via Thule, Resolute or Montreal had taken David many long months and late nights. After leaving us, David flew back to Thule with a further load of stores destined for Ginnie's most remote radio base, Station Nord in East Greenland, a place she would fly to in the Twin Otter if and when we ever reached the North Pole . . .

I woke suddenly one night to hear Ginnie moaning from her stomach pains, which had become increasingly frequent. But something else had awakened me. As I watched the ceiling in the dark I noticed a horizontal gap along its edge, through which I saw moonlight and stars. The roof had parted company with the walls by a good four inches. At the same time the whole hut shook as a violent gust struck the camp. For two minutes the camp hummed with the rattle of antenna wires and the clash of metal on metal from the stores hut. Then, as suddenly, silence. Throughout the night successive windstorms slammed through the camp. In the morning our room was covered with a thick carpeting of snow. I spent the day lashing the wooden roof down with wires and ropes. Out to sea the moonlight revealed huge black rents in the pack ice.

I checked the thermometers in our beehive screen: minus 4 degrees Centigrade. Such warmth so late in the year was not good for us. We needed a cold hard winter to make the ice grow thick and solid, the better to resist the rupturing stresses of the winter storms.

In the last week of November, Alert meteorological station recorded minus 9 degrees Centigrade, the warmest temperature on record so late in the year by eight degrees. Continued bad news for us, though the dogs loved their mild starlit wanderings in a fruitless search for fox and hare. Bothy followed Tugaluk nose-to-tail wherever she led.

By mid-December, one of the coldest winters ever recorded in Britain with temperatures on the *south* coast of minus 28 degrees Fahrenheit, we were basking in Alert at a mere minus 26 degrees Centigrade. Throughout that winter the three of us lived in a pretty fair state of harmony – no arguments, even few awkward silences. Mostly we talked of the goings-on up at the main camp, news from England and especially from the Transglobe ship, then berthed in Southampton for a refit.

On one cool night in December we went up to the camp on two Skidoos to a party given by the men of the sergeants' mess. When Ginnie and I left it was midnight and a balmy minus 32 degrees Centigrade. Charlie said he'd return later. Next morning when I shouted outside his hut that breakfast was ready, there was no reply. I went in and found him in bed. He had skidded on an icy bend and ended up in the ditch. His back hurt him badly but at least he could move. A few hours motionless in the ditch and he would have quickly frozen unnoticed, since nobody used the road by night.

This was the fifth time he had come a spectacular cropper off his Skidoo. Twice in the Arctic, three times in Antarctica. But this might not be so funny, because in only seven weeks we both needed to be fit and ready to go. For days Charlie hobbled about painfully and slowly like an old man. I gave him Deep Heat embrocation, but it did him little good. His coccyx, he felt, was badly bruised.

In the evenings after supper we played cards or dominoes, but the kitchen hut was usually too cold to stay in for long. Sometimes Alert radio spewed forth taped versions of the world news from Ginnie's transistor: 'Snow storms over Europe. A lifeboat lost off Cornwall with all hands. Repression in Poland. Unemployment all over the place . . .' It made you think the Arctic wasn't such a bad place after all.

I spent long hours each day preparing every item for the coming journey, weighing, greasing, modifying, packing. I checked pistols and rifle after leaving them loaded outside for a couple of days. I mock-loaded the eight-foot six-inch steel sledges as well as the fibreglass manhaul pulks. I cut up and redesigned aluminium bridges with which to cross frozen sea-leads. My hand compass I checked for variation when used on the Skidoo and off it, with engine running and switched off, when held in my left hand wearing a quartz-powered watch and in the right hand above metal-spiked snowshoes. Charlie tried to rest his back when not working on the generators.

While we worked at our preparations, four other groups announced their intention to reach the North Pole in the spring. A French team intended to travel with Skidoos from eastern Greenland to the Pole and from there to Svalbard. A group of Spaniards aimed to sled from Svalbard to the Pole, and three Russians held a press conference in Montreal to announce a plan to cross from Siberia via the Pole to Canada. All these schemes were due to begin in nine weeks – March being considered the optimum start-date. And the year before, four Canadians set out from Cape Columbia, but six kilometres out from the coast gave up and were evacuated. Not until Christmas time did we learn of a three-man team, a Canadian Eskimo and two Norwegians, under the leadership of Ragnor Thorseth, Norway's best-known contemporary explorer.

The Christmas Canadian Hercules brought mail to Alert that included some news clippings about a month old sent by Ant Preston, including this from the *Svalbardposten* in late November:

> The Scott-Amundsen duel looks as if it is going to be repeated in the new year. It will of course be at the other end of the world, but be as before Norwegian and English expeditions in a race to a pole. As far as we know the English expedition is aiming to leave from the same place as Thorseth. The leader of the English is a lord who is very well-equipped. It is rumoured that on a recent North Pole attempt he took prostitutes with him so that the hardships would not be too severe. Scott had horses with him on his tragic South Pole expedition. The question now is whether prostitutes will bring better luck to the expedition team than horses.

And in mid-December the *News of the World* announced:

> ARCTIC TEAM BLASTS SEX SLUR
>
> Members of the Arctic expedition sponsored by Prince Charles are furious at allegations that they are taking good-time girls with them. The claims are made in a Norwegian paper under a banner headline, 'Lord to North Pole With Prostitutes.' The lord is Sir Ranulph Fiennes, who is leading the expedition. A Norwegian expedition with the same aims will depart at the same time and the allegations are part of a dirty tricks campaign to stir up hostility between the two teams.
>
> Robin Buzza, the British team's representative in Spitsbergen, said the allegations were 'a load of old codswallop'. After Buzza

complained the relevant editor printed an apology, saying he had been given wrong information. But he added, 'Competition does exist and the race is starting long before they hit the ice.'

'Good old Buzza,' I said.

'Who's Buzza?' Charlie asked.

'He's our representative on Spitsbergen.'

'How do you know?'

'It says so here,' I said, tapping the clipping.

'I know, but who appointed him as our representative?'

'Good question, but it doesn't matter, he's doing a job. Probably appointed himself.' Charlie became abruptly silent.

'I know what you're thinking, Charles,' I said. 'Get that wistful look off your face. We'll be taking quite enough baggage as it is, and anyway there are certain things that are impractical at minus forty degrees.'

Back in London our committee discovered the Norwegian endeavour long before we did and quickly told us to ignore 'competitive urges'.

We had somewhat more serious matters on our minds. While we continued to sweat out our apprehension about the fatally warm winter and had nightmares about thin ice ahead, in North America a record cold front killed fifty-eight people in a week, Chicago suffering an all-time record of minus 32 degrees Centigrade and Atlanta, a minus 21 degrees Centigrade, its lowest since 1899. I visited the little meterological station on the edge of the main camp, where the met-man was not enthusiastic about our chances. 'Warm weather means less ice thickness. Taking last week's measurements, we have thinner ice, even in the sheltered bay by your huts, than at any previous Christmas since 1978, which as you may remember resulted in open sea the following summer.' I winced inwardly and thanked him, not wanting to hear any further elaboration.

On Christmas Day we went up to the camp, where the commanding officer gave us a radio message he had received from Ottawa. It was from Bill Berry, the commanding officer at Alert when we last wintered there: 'I understand you have as neighbours a group of delightfully mad English persons hanging around the Polar Shelf camp waiting for a sunrise departure for the pole. Please tell them from me – I was convinced back in '77 that you folks were absolutely stark raving mad. Having watched your exploits since then I remain more than ever convinced ... but if anyone can complete the journey, you will. If I can help in any way, you need only pull my chain.'

As the old year faded I walked to the end of the isthmus over wet, ill-formed snow. Forty-mile-an-hour gusts blew from the south but the temperature held around minus 16 degrees Centigrade. I listened. From beyond the great angular shore chunks, sinister in the semidarkness of the moonlit noon, came a rushing sound, as of gravel pouring from a great height onto concrete. In a while my eyes grew more accustomed to the darkness, and I could make out wide rashes of black sea not far behind the coastal rubble. Then followed the sounds of a muted struggle, muffled thuds and the splintering crash of ruptured floes as wind countered tide. I thought of climbing over the immediate ice blocks to get a better look, but an old saying flashed through my mind: 'Sufficient unto the day is the evil thereof.'

In mid-January, three short weeks before we were to set out onto the sea's creeping crust, I again saw the met-man. And once again his news was bad. The bay ice was 87 cm thick, thinner than that of any previous January on record, the average being 105 cm.

It came – but awfully late ... the true coldness that crackles the nose and ears like burning parchment, congeals the blood in fingers and toes like rapid-setting glue and fixes the sea ice slowly but surely into a precarious platform to the Pole. Well, better late than never. The tent could now be erected on the bay ice, and I spent a night in it with Ginnie testing the naphtha heating for fumes, listening as the ice about us spat and cracked and boomed as the floes contracted. At the camp they recorded minus 51 degrees Centigrade with a ten-knot breeze. Safety lines were fixed between huts. In the kitchen we ate in duvets, boots and woolly caps, but our morale was now high ... the sea ice was surely growing out there, and it just might not be too late ...

Charlie's back had slowly mended, and we began to take daily exercise together. He ran through the details of Skidoo servicing and repairs with me and I took him up on the hillside with a theodolite to shoot some stars. Each evening I practised Morse with a key and a recorded tape prepared by Ginnie.

In London Prince Charles radioed through to Ginnie and mentioned he had heard rumours of a race with the Norwegians. 'No racing,' he told me. 'No, sir,' I replied, 'we will not race.'

But suddenly I remembered how he loved a race whether briefly during polo matches or out on hazardous four-man crosscountry steeplechases, and I knew he would not object to our indulging in a little healthy competition in a quiet sort of way. I decided that whatever the Russians, French and Spanish might do, we must not let the Norwegians complete the Arctic Ocean crossing before us even if they were to reach the Pole first. In a small way it would be nice to avenge Scott's much-heralded defeat at the hands of Amundsen three quarters of a century earlier.

The rest of January stayed cool for us. Although the larder was in the centre of the kitchen and well insulated, Ginnie had to use a hammer to batter frozen soup out of bowls stored there. Raw eggs emerged from their shells like golf balls, although they did not bounce quite as well due to their shape. To offset my mania for an open window at night Ginnie began to use a hot water bottle under her blanket. One night a fox outside our room barked us awake, and she found her bottle frozen solid by her feet.

We remembered our fear of the cold when we first came to Alert in 1977, how in our greenhorn state we touched metal without mitts on, a mistake not usually repeated, since up here uncovered flesh stuck fast to metal and, if torn away, left the skin behind, burning the hand just as though it had touched a flame. Much laughter over the memory of Ginnie visiting our lavatory shack and the plastic seat slipping off the rim of the metal bucket. She had received a long cold burn down the left cheek of her backside and rushed back to our hut to comfort the afflicted area in front of our iron stove. Sadly she had got too close for comfort and branded herself with an even worse hot burn on her other cheek.

The closer our departure date, the easier to laugh.

On January 29 I saw clearly for the first time the aurora borealis, not just an electric flicker on a summer night such as is common in the Scottish Highlands, but the full brilliant display of green-and-white curtains evolving from one marvellous pattern to another and fading away only after an hour of, for me, almost hypnotic fascination.

With no moon and an average temperature of minus 41 degrees Centigrade, a succession of crisp clear nights also provided some good navigation practice, my favourite target stars being Regulus, Arcturus and Vega, all too bright and easily located to be mistaken for other nearby bodies when pinpointed in my theodolite's narrow field of view.

It was five years earlier that I'd learned for the first time to shoot stars in the dark and the cold from this same patch of snow between the huts. It was a painful, painstaking, frustrating time, and I'd recorded some of it this way . . .

Though there was no moon the sky was alive with movement, scattered clouds moving fast over some parts while elsewhere an entire quarter of the sky remained for a while brilliant with stars – so clear and so numerous that individual constellations were less easy to identify than is normal further south. I flattened the snow by marching on the spot until a patch the size of a kitchen table was fairly solid. The tripod's telescopic legs dropped down as I loosened off their holding screws, the three pointed feet digging well into the snow ... Once the instrument, a T2 model, was centrally screwed to the tripod I began to level the vertical and horizontal bubbles to ensure the T2 was correctly set. Until the two bubbles were central, the instrument's readings would be useless. The bubbles in the alcohol moved in an unusually sluggish and insensitive fashion, moving to the left or right with slow lurches but refusing to settle centrally. The bubbles used to take me two or three minutes to level in Greenland. Now they took twenty-five minutes. I turned on the battery box to light up the graticules in the eyepieces. Nothing happened. The three new U2 batteries had gone dead. I unplugged the lighting system and set it aside. My flashlight would have to do instead. I looked up to find a suitable star to shoot, but my head would not move because the woollen balaclava had set rocklike. I felt a slab of ice a quarter of an inch thick from my bottom lip down to that part of my neck where the balaclava fitted into the wolf-skin parka. My nose and mouth dribbled constantly. The result was an immovable area of balaclava. By bending from the waist I faced upward, keeping my back to the wind. Usually quite quick at picking out stars, I was now confused by the multitude available. After several tries I traced Capella, certain of her identity because of the obtuse triangle of tiny stars beside her called the Twins ... Carefully noting her position relative to the dark silhouettes of the nearby huts, I set about spotting her through the main eyepiece of the T2. Since this was a telescope that picked out only a few stars at a time, it was not too easy to be sure which of the many pinpricks was actually Capella when no general picture of the sky could be seen as was the case with the naked eye. Fairly certain that the scope was finally trained on my chosen target, I quickly tried to light up the inner eyepiece markings by shining my light directly into a little hole on the side of the T2 while looking through the scope and twiddling the control knobs with my free hand ... It would take less than a minute for the moving star to cross the scope's view and disappear unless I could pan the T2, with the lit-up crosshairs directly on the star, at the same rate. My aim was to record on my Rolex watch the precise moment at which Capella moved across the horizontal line in the centre of the eyepiece. If my watch was accurate and I recorded the correct reading from the smaller eyepiece, which gave information as to the instrument's lay compared with the true horizon, then I would know the altitude of Capella at that time. My computation tables would later enable me to work out my own position on the surface of the earth along the backbearing from Capella. Computed backbearings from two other stars in different sectors of the sky should then provide my actual location ... The finely sprung control knob, which normally allowed me to adjust the scope horizontally to keep pace with a rising or falling star, was jammed. The only way I could move the scope now was to crudely push it up and down until the hairline and star coincided. Then, at that precise moment, to glance at my watch. An error of only four seconds would put my position wrong by a mile ... Further delays were caused by my eyelash sticking to the metal of the scope (despite the chamois leather covering over the eyepiece itself) and by my nose succumbing to the first symptoms of frostnip. To avoid this I pulled the inner silk balaclava over it. Unfortunately this directed some of my breath on to the eyepiece. It froze instantly, preventing any further use of the scope until I could extricate a gloved finger from the inner mitten and quickly rub the lens. Which started finger problems. I flung my arms about to restore the circulation. One hand brushed against the tripod leg and dislodged the set of the bubble. After fifteen minutes I managed to reset the instrument but then experienced an uncontrollable urge that had nothing to do with navigation. It would not be sensible to respond outside, especially with my present iced-up clothes and numb fingers, so I retreated to a hut where we kept polythene bags for this purpose. This was quite sanitary since the bags went rock-hard in double-quick time, our huts always being well below freezing at floor level. On returning to the T2 I discovered that Capella had vanished behind clouds. Fortunately Spica was visible, although too low in the sky for use. Her position points along a curving line to another bright star, Arcturus, and, on the same arc, to the curve of the Great Bear. Although the Great Bear was covered by cloud, the rudimentary knowledge that a V-shape across the night sky is formed by Arcturus, the Great Bear and Vega, the brightest of all the stars, enabled me to locate Vega's neighbour, the easily recognised Altair. This was in a clear patch, and I soon had the crosshairs in position ... Inside the hut my eyelashes had collected moisture, which soon turned to little balls of ice that slowly grew in size. They were now clogging my vision ... On that first night I shot one star after an hour and fifty minutes. By itself the star was virtually useless. The next night I obtained three stars in just over two hours but then there was only a ten-knot breeze. I thought how much simpler a sextant would be, but Wally Herbert, who was adept with both instruments, had counselled us strongly against the less accurate instrument.

One session with my theodolite in England would have taken me no more than twenty-five minutes. Sometimes I wondered about my ability to keep track of our position on the drifting floes of the Arctic Ocean.

By the last day of January I needed to make up my mind exactly when we would set out. To decide, I thought of those who had tried before us and of our own failure in 1977 when we tried to travel as far as the Pole, less than half the distance that faced us this time. We had failed convincingly. Then we had left in early March, but one of the team, Geoffrey, got frostbite in eight of his fingers. So as a group of three we'd set out again in mid-March, and after fifty unpleasant days we'd found ourselves a hundred and sixty miles short of the Pole and surrounded by a sea of moving slush ice, too thin to travel over.

This time we must get further sooner. To be precise, we must reach the Pole by mid-April at the latest. Once in its vicinity we would be out of the grip of the Beaufort Gyral current, which floats ice *backward* toward Alert, and into the pack ice of the Transpolar Drift current, which heads over the top of the world and down toward Greenland and Svalbard. Thereafter for some two thousand miles of floating travel we could expect to move wherever the by-then fractured pack might take us. One hoped the *Benji Bee* would try to penetrate the pack along its southern fringe and, if possible, remove us without herself getting crushed.

Could such a journey be made in one Arctic summer season? Impossible to predict, since it had never been done before. Wally Herbert, the only man ever to have crossed the Arctic Ocean, had taken *two* seasons ... 'I think,' he said, 'the big physical problem of crossing polar pack ice is that, at least initially, you travel in very cold weather and, in order to get to your destination before the ice breaks up, you have to put in a lot of travelling time which means being exposed to temperatures of minus 45 degrees, minus 50 degrees for up to fifteen hours a day. Now minus 45 degrees is not very cold by northern Canadian standards but if you are exposed to it for that length of time *and* you have to knock your way through pressure ridges and across open leads, then it is a big strain. At the times when you really need to push hard, it is going to be twilight, or even dark. It is going to be a lot colder and you will be moving a lot longer across moving ice which can swallow you up at any time or which physically needs a lot of effort to knock down. So you might be burning up to the region of 7,500 calories a day. That is pretty high going.' And Charles Kuralt, writing about the four-man Plaisted group, the only men to have reached the Pole without dog teams, said: 'There is only a short span of time, mid-March to mid-May, when man can safely walk on the Arctic ice. Earlier in the year darkness and severe cold can make travel hazardous. Later the rising sun turns the ocean snow cover to mush and high winds break the ice pack into thousands of individual floes.'

Back in 1977 our final start date was March 14. I decided to cut this by a month to February 14 and then subtract a further week for good measure and unforeseen troubles. What worried me most was the likelihood one or other of us might get frostbite in the dark. The only way of avoiding amputation of a frostbitten limb would be evacuation to an intensive care hospital with the right equipment. Until sun-up, in early March, this would be out of the question, since even an efficient ski-plane like our Twin Otter with a brilliant pilot such as Karl Zberg would not land on the Arctic pack ice before sun-up. With this hazard very much in mind I nonetheless had no option but to plump for a 'dark' start in the first week of February.

But first I had to be flown to Thule by the weekly Alert-to-Thule Hercules to have a broken tooth and other dental problems repaired.

While waiting for my return Hercules a United States Army colonel took me around the missile warning centre. 'All kinds of things here have been screwed up because of this warm weather,' he told me. 'Normally, we have a drivable ice road across the bay. It saves a long detour. But this year the ice is only three feet thick instead of the normal six or seven feet. So no road. Usually the whole bay is solid in October. This winter she only began to freeze in late November.' And when on February 10 the next weekly Hercules took me back to Alert via Eureka, as we roared low through the starry gloom to land at Alert the navigator pointed down at the sea just off the coastline. 'Those lakes of darker shading,' he shouted in my ear. 'Either open water or freshly formed ice.'

I digested this unhealthy news and grinned back in sickly fashion.

On departure day, February 13, my diary recorded: 'Poor Ginnie has a sharp and persistent headache which really stuns her. This is despite four Parahyphon pills in the last twenty-four hours. She's really down-and-out and tired tonight and looks miserable. I hate the thought of leaving her.'

The night before we left a radio message came from Wally Herbert in the form of a rhyme:

With my very best wishes for the final dawn,
I send tips to help win the fight:
Beware of the calm that follows the storm
And the floes that go bump in the night.

Never trust ice that appears to be dead,
And if you want peace of mind
Steer well clear of the bear up ahead
And cover that bear behind.

I left Ginnie a file of details on camp logistics to give Simon. Included was a note suggesting, should anything happen to Charlie and me, that he and David Mason carry on from where we left off. I silently recalled Ollie's diary-comment the night before we left Alert in 1977: 'We are all prepared now. This is the biggest and most dangerous thing I have ever done.' He spoke for us, once again.

The weather was clear as we left. The thermometer read minus 45 degrees Centigrade. For four hours shortly after midday there would be conditions of twilight, enough to steer by.

The camp commanding officer and six others came down to the camp to see us off, their flashlights darting about below the halos of freezing breath. They had been good to us. I said only a quick good-bye to Ginnie. We had spent the previous night in our hut closing our minds bit by bit to reality. Over the years we have found it better that way. The wrench of leaving her was perhaps worse than in Antarctica, for we both knew the latter would prove to have been a rose garden compared with the journey ahead.

As I jerked my sled away and headed out of the pool of light between the huts, I saw Ginnie crouched by the dogs and looking up at the passage of darkness by which we had left. I kept the memory in my head like a photograph, as a squirrel will keep a last nut for the winter ahead.

Using the brief hours of twilight and the memory of our previous journey along the same coastline five short years before, we made good speed and no mistakes. There was nothing clever about this; simple familiarity tends to make light of even the worst conditions whereas ignorance, as they say, can founder at the easiest fence.

The second morning, in Patterson Bay, we spotted the round pugmarks of a bear. They were known to range this coastline when there was open water about and so fishing access. We checked our individual weapons and kept them close to hand. The ice pressure against the shoreline was in places heavier and higher up the beaches than previously. In others it was clear going where before there had been walls of rubble.

Until Cape Delano I held to the route as planned, but bare patches of gravel west of Dana Bay, murder for our soft Tufnol sledge runners, forced us too far north over the mountain passes of Feilden Peninsula. As the twilight hours dwindled I found myself caught on a sheer-sided slope between Mary Peak and Mount Julia. Charlie tried to follow my tracks but that was often more difficult than taking a virgin route with more purchase for the Skidoo's slithering tracks. Twice Charlie's sledge overturned. Both times he managed to reright it by himself, but each time he was a touch lower down the snowfield on the side of the mountain just below which were the cliffs of a narrow ravine. With great caution we skirted this cliff and reached another steep slope down which we lowered the sledges bit by bit.

It was dark by the time we camped along the rim of James Ross Bay. There were no animals and no birds about. Spring, after all, was yet a long way off. On February 15 we sneaked through a defile between mountains on the Parry Peninsula and descended to Sail Harbour, which was surrounded by snowfields on every side. New snow lay soft and deep in this bay, and the going was slow. The hills fell away on either flank to reveal a view of frozen wonder – Clements Markham Inlet, a giant sea loch ten miles wide at its mouth and penetrating deep into the interior mountains. Although the sky was dark enough to see the major stars, the air was clear all the way to the looming bulk of Mount Foster, the western sentinel of this wild majestic fjord.

(Of the rare and time-scattered men to travel west along this coast some were never seen again. As late as 1936 Kruger, leader of the German Arctic Expedition, was lost along the coastline further west with two companions. No trace of them was ever found.)

We camped eighteen kilometres west of the fjord. It was truly cold. So easy to make a little mistake in the darkness, to allow the creeping nip to stay that little bit too long in a finger or a toe.

It is not necessary to be a weak-minded person, nor ill-equipped nor even inexperienced, to die quickly in the Arctic. The longer a man is out in the cold and eating dehydrated rations, the lower his strength. Resistance will slowly sink.

Late the next day, February 16, I spotted our food and fuel cache well south of our route over the Cape Aldrich ice shelf. We spent an hour there replenishing and repacking, then camped a short distance to the north – it was already dark and minus 46 degrees Centigrade.

Next day, February 17, we set out early. The coast steamed with the brown murk of frost-smoke, sure sign of open water in the vicinity. At a guess the coastal tide creek had opened up during the night. This was surely an ominous sign. In the depths of winter long before sunrise and at a point of maximum coastal pressure, the ice should not be open.

Skirting the steaming slits, I kept as near to land as possible until rubble fields forced me out onto the sea ice. Every few minutes I turned in the seat to check that Charlie didn't falter or fall out of sight for long.

Between the encroaching walls of pressure ice from the sea and the tumbling glaciers that descended from Mount Cooper Key there was a narrow corridor, in places merely ten yards wide, and into this we crawled, because there was no other way west. To our right frozen waves of snow lay shoulder-high, where five years before I had seen pellucid green blocks piled layer on layer to a height of twelve metres – testimony to the great driving and cutting power of the pack ice.

We had no trouble in the gloomy corridor, and emerged at the foot of a steep snow slope just short of Cape Columbia. This we ascended to its top, and I spent a while observing the immediate area since, any time now, I must find a route north onto the sea ice.

The black slab of Cape Columbia stood out to the south. A short distance west, the rolling white layers of the Ward Hunt Ice Shelf thrust north into the sea for a distance of over ten miles. The ice shelf was formed by thicknesses of sea ice forming off the coast and attaching themselves, in most places still afloat, to the original coastline. Each year the shelf grows upward because of seawater with low saline content freezing to its lower surface, and at the same time summer melt-water from inland refreezing to its upper surface. As with all Arctic ice, the ice shelf was subject to immense strains and could fracture with no warning. In 1961 massive calving from the Ward Hunt Ice Shelf reduced its area by some six hundred square kilometres. The resulting islands floated away east and west, and aerial study of their routes suggested that Cape Columbia lay at the spot where westerly and easterly currents separated – which would make it the best start-point for anyone wanting to travel north without being too powerfully influenced by the pull of either current.

At the base of our hill were large chunks of pressure ice piled in places to a height of forty feet. They formed a wall between snowfield and frozen ocean, but in places there were narrow gaps. We descended the hill, slithered down a ramp after some axe work to bridge a twenty-foot void and – we were at sea.

We had already covered a hundred miles or more on a somewhat devious route, and travelling many days earlier than any of our predecessors.

On February 17, two weeks before sun-up, we camped for the first time on sea ice ... and I remembered my thoughts following the bitter acceptance of defeat five years earlier. I had known I would come back. It was somehow wrong to be beaten. Peary, after one of his two-year polar attempts had failed, said: 'The lure of the North is a strange and powerful thing. More than once I have come back from the wild frozen spaces ... telling myself I have made my last journey thither ... It was never many months before the old restless feeling came over me and I began to long for the great white desolation.' Dr Frederick Cook, his arch-rival and co-claimant as first man to the North Pole, was equally emotional: 'A new and absorbing passion which ever since has dominated my life – the voice of the Arctic, the taste for the icy response of the polar sea. Something keeps calling, calling, until at last you can stand it no more and return, spell-drawn by the magic of the North.' The Danes have a word for this polar attraction – *polarhuller.*

As we erected our tent three hundred yards out from the coast on the edge of a seemingly limitless field of impenetrable rubble, and I pressed one mitt to the raw end of my nose, I felt not the remotest tinge of *polarhuller,* merely a ghastly realisation of what was to come and a host of crowding memories of what had passed the last time we tried to pit our puny wits against the Arctic Ocean.

Chapter Fourteen

> Even a man with perfect circulation and the best clothing combination designed by man, will suffer terribly under the worst Arctic conditions.
>
> WALLY HERBERT

As a result of our 1977 failure to reach the Pole I had planned a pessimistic schedule that allowed for initial progress of only half a mile per day.

During the first day's twilight labour we fell short of this scheduled distance, but only just, since we also cleared eight hundred yards of rubble. The passage we axed and shovelled was exactly the width of a Skidoo and zigzagged between ice walls and isolated boulders.

During the next six months there were many times when we felt truly at the end of our tether but not once did we consider giving up. The thought of facing the crew of the *Benji Bee* having failed was not something I could even contemplate. But would it have been more sensible, more responsible, to have given up? Who can say? As will be seen later, even our Arctic experts were to counsel evacuation, and with good cause. But in those first twilight days, we did not think of *anything* but the next few yards of slow and frozen toil.

According to Wally Herbert we would have to travel 825 miles in order to cover the 474-mile beeline distance to the pole. This took into account a 75 per cent detour percentage. Wally – and nobody knew better than he – said we were unlikely to succeed unless we reached the Pole before April 17. With this date in mind we could afford only minimal delays.

No man has ever crossed the Arctic Ocean without resupply by air. Wally's support came from Canadian air force C-130 aircraft. If our own lifeline, the Twin Otter, was 'off the road' for any reason at any time it could critically delay our progress. Ever since Giles and Gerry had so nearly been marooned in the midst of Antarctica by engine start problems there had been concern over the possibility that the aircraft suffered from some major but intermittent technical fault. Charlie and I had set out before the Twin Otter arrived at Alert, but its welfare was seldom far from our thoughts. We knew Gerry, the engineer, was ill; instead, Simon was to accompany Karl on the long flight from England, but he knew nothing about aircraft engines. Karl himself was luckily an experienced engineer as well as a pilot, but polar flight engineers work when their pilots are catching up on vital sleep. Karl's handwritten notes told of his mounting worries about the temperamental engine of the Twin Otter. Karl and Simon did reach Alert in the darkness of February 15, two days after our departure, but Karl's worries stayed with him. Any droplet of water, for example, in the fuel system could have stopped and would stop both engines in mid-flight without warning.

On February 19 we axed our way north in a fifteen-knot breeze and minus 42 degrees Centigrade. By the end of the twilight hours a further two hundred yards were hacked away, and I decided to bring the Skidoos up the one thousand prepared yards from our first coast-site camp.

Despite the work we had done, there was pushing and pulling, bouncing and sweating. The sweat turned to ice particles inside our underwear as soon as the work stopped, even briefly. I broke off half a fingernail but felt no pain; the finger was too cold.

Like myself, Charlie weighed 185 pounds, so between us we could, by using our weight jointly, shift the 800-pound-laden Skidoos and 600-pound-laden sleds bit by bit over each new blockage. But progress was hardly the word for it. More like a couple of geriatric snails on a Sunday outing. Luckily the visibility remained passable during the hours of twilight so we did not lose track of our hardwrought 'motorway'.

But much damage was done to the Skidoos, since there was no way of negotiating the more or less cleared route other than at full speed rebounding off walls and iron-hard ice rocks. Not surprisingly, just short of the roadhead my drive axle snapped. That did it. I decided to switch to manpower and abandon the Skidoos.

The previous winter, in preparing for just such a switch, I'd tested out two eight-foot-long fibreglass manhaul sledges and lightweight survival gear to go with them. That night I asked Ginnie to get the Twin Otter to us the next day. We would try to find a flat place where Karl could drop the kit without smashing it.

In the morning Charlie worked to change the sheared shaft – at prevailing temperatures, not at all an easy job. I ferried the sledges slowly back to the coastline and was able to find a 400-yard strip of flat ice without a bump.

I axed down to forty centimetres and struck no water. After twelve hours the weather cleared to coincide with the time of twilight. There was no wind; blowing ice crystals but no mist. Minus 37 degrees Centigrade. Relatively good conditions, but nonetheless there was probably a mere handful of pilots in the world who could have and would have landed in those conditions. Karl did. We shook hands with him and his duvet-covered passenger Simon. The pulks and ancillary gear were taken off and our steel sledges loaded together with boxes and fuel.

'Leave the Skidoos and the big tent here,' Karl said, 'and I'll come back when it's light to collect them.'

I asked Simon to prepare the two light Skidoos, only 250-cc and easily manhandled by one person. When the rubble zone ended, or at least cleared up a bit, I hoped to try them out to see if, as I had been told, they were indeed better than our heavy 640-cc models.

Karl described the scene this way: 'I left some kit and food for the team. The temperature was minus 43 degrees Centigrade, and the ice crew's faces were all frosted up. I was glad to climb back into my plane and turn back for a warm base camp.'

So on February 22, in semi-darkness, we began the long haul. I thought of Wally Herbert's words: 'There can be few forms of polar misery more physically exhausting than hacking a route through pressure ice when it is cold and there is scarcely enough twilight to see the joke.' ... After eight hours our underwear, socks, facemasks and jackets were soaking wet or frozen depending on which part of the body they covered and on whether we were hauling or resting at the time. Each load weighed a hundred and ninety pounds. The new tent was only nine pounds compared with our hundred-pound Antarctic tent and was difficult to keep 'warm.' Small and igloo-shaped, there was little room for drying clothes other than on a suspended net from which the drips fell onto us, our bags and our evening stew. It was never possible to dry clothes out, but with some effort they could be improved from wet to damp.

Our eyes stung when the cooker was burning but never as badly as during 1977 – now we burned naphtha, never petrol. There was the occasional fire alarm resulting from refilling the cooker tank inside the tent. Some fuel invariably spilled and ignited, and a quick dousing of the tent-floor area with a sleeping bag was the best response. I was forever putting sticky tape over holes burned in my bag, and our beards were usually dusted with feathers.

For four long days of twilight gloom we hauled, sweated and froze over the endless rubble.

I suffered from the problem that one gets in warmer climes from sitting on hot radiators or wet grass, which made the constant hard tugging at my harness an altogether unpleasant experience. Charlie's legs and back were also displeased with life. But by the end of the four days we had completed eleven long miles. I realise that doesn't sound very impressive, unless you have seen pressure rubble for yourself and travelled through it in the dark and in the minus fifties. (The previous year a team of four sturdy Canadians set out for the Pole from the same spot as ourselves, and with the benefit of sunlight. After five miles they were evacuated, one with bad frostbite. They were well trained and knowledgeable, but their luck was out.)

As on Ellesmere Island and even back in the Welsh mountains four years earlier, Charlie plodded on at his own slow but solid pace. Unable to go any slower than my 'natural' pace, I ended up every hour stomping around in circles, banging my hands together, kicking my mukluks hard against the nearest ice block and singing loudly. At such times my thoughts often wandered to the local fauna. But on the move it was stupid to keep glancing over one's shoulder to check on polar bears . . . this would only invite painful trip-ups. In any case, plain exhaustion soon overcame any fear of bears, but I often thought about the best action to take if attacked, remembering the words of a friendly Greenlander in Thule: 'The old bears, going blind, die slowly of starvation as they roam the pack ice, less and less able to find a meal. But they retain their scent for hot-blooded animals and a human will suffice if they happen to smell one.' And so remembering, I kept my pistol available on the pulk at all times. On February 27 we came onto a wide pan of smooth ice thick enough to be a multiyear floe, ice three or more years old. We struggled to part ourselves from the mountains but they seemed to move with us. The day when we could no longer see them would mean much to us both. We longed for some visible sign of progress.

I tried to avoid stopping in rubble fields. How stupid to be caught napping by a sudden storm, yet it was often tempting to camp wearily on a small slab of a field of rubble liable to instant crackup and massive fracturing. Often, exhausted and sore, I gave in to my weakness and camped in just such fragile places in full knowledge of the danger of it. But the best sleeping places were chunks of consolidated pack ice, where many floes were frozen together. They were never completely flat but, if made up of older multiyear floes which had somehow survived disintegration for several summers, proliferated with well-rounded hummocks polished by years of wind and sun. You could cut away chunks from the yellow-white hummocks on these old floes and find, on melting them, that the water was salt-free, or nearly so.

On March 2 we woke up as usual with steaming breath and feeling cramped. Outside the tent the temperature held at minus 44 degrees Centigrade. Inside our body heat improved matters to minus 38 degrees Centigrade, but to be honest I noticed little or no difference. We did not start the cooker in the mornings but quickly drank down a mug of coffee brewed the previous night and kept in a padded flask. This was breakfast and gave us the courage to unzip our bags and climb into frosted clothes and boots.

At this time we were dragging behind us, man for man, as

much as Scott and his team. Amundsen, of course, used dogs and so did not normally experience long periods of manhauling. The difference between our clothing and Scott's was minimal except for our footwear, which was superior as long as the boots were carefully dried out when camping. I wore a pair of cotton socks under woollen stockings, a cotton T-shirt under a zip-up, windproof jacket and a pair of army windproof trousers over a pair of cotton longjohns. Charlie wore much the same, and we both wore facemasks. Our cooking habits were also much the same as Scott's except that we ate only in the evenings and – a vital difference – our dehydrated rations were supplemented by vitamin pills.

For us the weather conditions for three weeks were far more severe in that we travelled in lower temperatures and in semi-darkness. Like Scott we were spurred on, to be honest, by the knowledge that a team of Norwegians shared the same goal, though details of their progress to our flank were not known to us. The terrain that we struggled over was, of course, ribbed with high walls of ice which Scott did not face in Antarctica. This horrific region stretched one hundred miles ahead of us before, supposedly, it would improve and we would, hopefully, be able to have our Skidoos brought in by Karl.

Our main peril lay in thin ice and the crushing motion of the floes; Scott's in the hidden crevasses which we had ourselves so disliked in Antarctica. He would fear unseasonable blizzards; we were worried about abnormally warm and loose pack conditions. He could suffer by not locating his prelaid depots; we by a single electronic failure of our pocket beacon, which sent a pulse some forty miles into the sky. If the beacon failed due to the cold or a malfunction, or if my navigation erred by over forty miles – not too difficult on drifting pack ice after many days in thick mist with no landmarks – then we could be lost forever in five million square miles of ever-shifting rubble. In such circumstances no amount of searching aircraft would necessarily locate us. Scott moved over land-girt ice and his route was predictable. Ours had to move for six long months very largely at the whim of the ice floes on whose skin we hitched a lift.

I mention these comparisons because it is assumed that travellers of the 1980s move in a cocoon of protective comforts compared with their predecessors of fifty years ago. Most of any physical feats of today is automatically set against the activities of our forebears in the days of no radios, no aircraft and no maps. Actually, in much of Antarctica and throughout our Arctic Ocean journey we too had no maps, only empty white charts. Our means of navigation, like Scott's, were a compass and the sun, its position and its altitude. As for radios, they seldom helped us travel from A to B, although their fragility and weight were not something our predecessors had to cope with. As many a modern polar traveller has discovered, radios break down easily in cold temperatures. Actually two North Pole expeditions had to be withdrawn *because* their radios ceased to work – the Simpson and the Hempleman-Adams expeditions. Injury in a crevasse or serious frostbite required evacuation to avoid death; during much of our Antarctic crossing sastrugi would have prevented Giles's landing near us had we required evacuation, and in the Arctic darkness, mist, rubble or slush would likewise more often than not have prevented Karl from reaching us. The epic travels of Amundsen, Mawson, Peary, Scott and Shackleton deserve always to stand out in the annals of polar travel, but the notion held by some that polar journeys postdating the invention of the radio should be relegated to relative picnics does not exactly stand up to close scrutiny.

Not being masochists, we were not, in fact, trying to suffer for the sake of it, but when things were truly bad day after day, night after night, week after week, we found ourselves mere humans with scant comfort from radios that brought no warmth and very often no reply on account of ionospheric conditions, nor from a distant aircraft that in average Arctic winter conditions could not locate us visually, let alone land by us.

On March 3, despite a slight lowering in the temperature, our world took on a new rosy glow, as the blood-red ball of the sun slid briefly along the rim of the frozen sea.

The sun was, of course, our true number one enemy. Its ultraviolet rays would soon begin their work on the ocean's skin, eating at the sea ice until, in a few weeks' time, travel would no longer be possible by any means and we would need to float at the whim of whatever floe we might choose as host body. Nonetheless, after a four-month absence the sun was, for a while at least, like a welcome friend.

Whether the coming of the sun made me unusually optimistic or whether the surface did that day begin to improve for the first time I cannot say, but I did feel there was a chance we could now progress using light Skidoos. Our normal 640-cc machines were still where we had abandoned them. When Karl had last flown over them he reported: 'I will not be able to land for at least ten days. The ice looks like a shattered window with the Skidoos sitting in the middle of it. I hope that the movement stops, or we could lose them.'

However, there were two small, almost toylike machines called Elans at Alert, and Ginnie radioed they would be brought to us the next day, weather and ice conditions permitting . . .

At Alert Simon went out to the stores garage to prepare the Elans and decided to leave them inside for the night. Easier to start in the morning.

At 3:00 A.M. Ginnie's alarm went off and as usual she climbed off her bunk to listen for the ice group. By then a field telephone had been rigged between her room and the Canadian camp two miles to the south. Just before 4:00 A.M. its bell jangled. It was the duty watchman. 'I think there's a fire somewhere by your huts,' he said. 'I can see flames down at your place.' Ginnie looked out her own frosted window and saw an orange glow from the garage. The dogs sensed something amiss, the big black Tugaluk cowering under Ginnie's table, little Bothy putting up a strident yapping.

Ginnie, forgetting the temperature, which was minus 40 degrees Centigrade, rushed across to the garage and tried to pull back the main sliding door. 'It was just a fireball inside,' she said later, 'with smoke coming from all the seams in the walls, and flames filling the windows. I shouted "Fire" but nobody heard me. I moved around to the rear end of the hut where there were eight forty-five-gallon drums of gasoline stacked beside the wall. We had once tried to remove them but they had been there many years and were frozen deep into the ice.'

She hoped, of course, to rescue the precious Elans, but found she was too late. The garage was a mass of flames from end to end. The scientific gear, including a valuable seismometer, was already destroyed, as were machines, spare parts, rations and all the items I had modified during the winter, including ladders to see us over so-called porridge-ice and open canals nearer to the pole. Ginnie tried using fire extinguishers but she might as well have spat into hell.

Rushing down to the other huts, she woke up Simon, Karl and Beverly Johnson, one of the film crew. None of their efforts were of any use. As they watched, the eight drums of gasoline exploded and soon fusillades of rocket flares and 7.62 FN bullets enlivened the scene.

We will probably never know the cause of the fire, though Simon

Charlie about to erect our home for the first ever crossing of Antarctica by a single team (Hillary & Fuchs used two teams from both sides of the continent)

Our open boat is frozen in at Tanquary Fjord

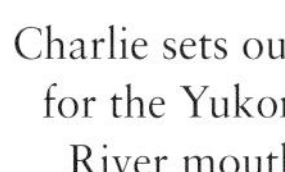

Charlie sets out for the Yukon River mouth

Look closely and you can see our boat dodging ice floes in the North West Passage

Charlie after his accident in the ice tunnel

At Alert I favour the 'new' material Gore-Tex. Charlie prefers his old wolfskin

The Alert base camp on fire

After our base camp is burnt down

Trouble with my skidoo on a patch of thin ice

Oliver watches and waits for a freeze-up

Wind-cut ice shapes

A young pressure ridge beginning to form

A moving lead between two converging floes

The first two humans ever to reach both Poles by surface travel. From L to R Charlie and Ran

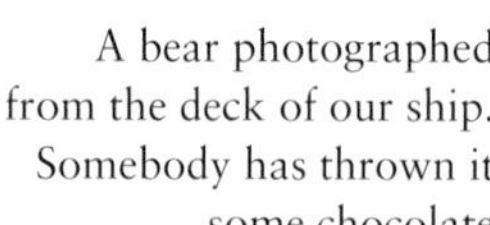

A bear photographed from the deck of our ship. Somebody has thrown it some chocolate

Jimmy Young from New Zealand keeps watch from the main mast to try to spot the sledge group north of Greenland

Charlie with ice prod on a home-made ice raft

The Ship's crew at last reunited with the Ice Group after the latter's long and hazardous float across the North Pole from Canada

Ginny and Ran in the Arctic

believed it probably had something to do with the electrical wiring. There was also an ironic side effect of the fire. Our expedition had managed to cross Antarctica in sixty-six days and navigate the entire Northwest Passage in four weeks without causing much of any interest in the world. Suddenly newspapers and televisions all over the world were giving forth with 'Conflagration at Polar Base' and 'Polar Expedition in Flames'. We seem to relish bad news, so long, of course, as it doesn't affect us personally. In any case, after the night of the fire nearly every action that we took, and one or two that we didn't, became news from London to Sydney, from Cape Town to Vancouver . . .

But out on the ice we had other things to think about when Ginnie told us everything, the result of seven years of painstaking sponsor-getting and equipment-testing, was burned.

Within an hour of assessing the damage Ginnie managed to get a message to David Mason in London. He was due to fly out to Alert that week to be ready as our first reserve and to man our alternative airstrip at Tanquary Fjord. Now he agreed to delay his coming for as long as it took to obtain the more vital replacements for our fire losses. And Prince Charles sent us a message of sympathy, as did the crew of the *Benji Bee*.

Out on the sea ice we had food for eight days, so we tried to close our minds to the disaster at Alert and concentrate on the job of immediate concern, that of covering the next few miles or, to be precise, the next few painful yards.

As our resistance imperceptibly lowered day by day, the effects of the unremitting cold began to tell and our pace to slow. I found the worst of it was the trail-breaking, the sinking of each snowshoe at every step into the deep soft snow on the floes and the deeper traps of hidden holes between ice blocks. My legs ached, and the pain from the piles did not let up. Our shoulders were raw from the day-long tug of the sledge traces. My nose, red raw at the nostrils for two weeks now, had become frostnipped on its bridge. This too now lacked skin and bled as the rough and frozen material of my facemask rubbed across it. As in 1977 we failed to solve the face-mask problem. Heavy breathing and the continuous involuntary dribble from nose and mouth resulted in a plaster cast of ice around the neck, to which my beard froze solid. I could not wipe my nose to stop this happening since, being raw, it preferred not to be wiped. By night we thawed out the armour-plated facemasks above the cooker, where they soaked up the smell of our rehydrating meal, so every day we slogged along breathing in the aroma of yesterday's supper. We ate nothing at all by day, being unable to force food through the little mouth hole in our masks and unwilling to open up the masks once they were frozen into position for the day. Attempts at reaffixing a frozen but disturbed facemask usually failed to prevent frostnip to nose, forehead or cheeks. So daytime snacks were out.

The worst troubles at night were also with the face. Generally speaking, polar travel would be quite pleasant if one didn't have to breathe. If you tried to snuggle down inside your sleeping bag, tying up the drawstrings above your head, your breath formed a thick rime of frost all around your head, particles of which fell down your neck or settled on your face and in your ears. If, on the other hand, you left a hole at the top of the bag just big enough to frame your nose and mouth *and* you managed to keep them in that position through the sleeping hours, then your nose grew most painful as soon as the temperature descended to around minus 40 degrees Centigrade, which it did once the cooker's heat faded away . . .

By March 7, my thirty-eighth birthday, we had lived and hauled for three weeks at temperatures much colder than a deep freeze with winds usually above fifteen knots. Both of us now well knew why people did not venture about on sea ice in these latitudes before the coming of March. It had taken a lot out of us; perhaps too much. Charlie was to say of these days:

> Instead of drinking something like six pints a day, which we needed, we were only getting about two pints so we suffered from dehydration. As you get dehydrated you get weaker. If you are out for a long period of time and don't stop to recuperate you get weaker and weaker until you simply can't even pick up an axe. You start hammering away, and after about five minutes you collapse and gag and don't know what to do with yourself. You start to suck ice and snow. I can remember times when Ran and I couldn't pick the axe up. We both had to go back absolutely exhausted to the tent because we could not pick an axe up any more. We were absolutely shattered. So, so tired. We dragged our way back, hardly raising our feet off the snow and crawled into the tent and went to sleep like dead mutton. But there is always the light at the end of a tunnel, and this is what you've got to think about the whole time you're killing yourself.

On March 8 Ginnie advised us that the French had arrived in Greenland to start their Arctic crossing attempt. The Norwegians had set out on Skidoos three days earlier, four men including an Eskimo, from Resolute Bay. Their resupply flights were to be provided partly by chartered Twin Otter and partly by the Royal Norwegian Air Force with C-130 aircraft. She thought they would set out from the coast at more or less the same spot as ourselves.

Late the same day, in a brief gap between snowstorms, Karl found us in a flat but narrow alleyway and managed to land and off-load two Skidoos – not the Elans we wanted, which had burned up – but a slightly heavier model called a Citation.

Manhauling we had averaged six to seven miles per day and covered over a hundred miles of the worst sort of pressure ridging. Now, with the Citation Skidoos we reverted to one mile on the ninth and two on the tenth. Admittedly there was nonstop whiteout and high winds, but these were not unusual. The problem was the old one: Skidoos, unlike dogs and manhauled sledges, simply would not negotiate small heaps of rubble, let alone walls of ice blocks.

So the days passed in endless hauling and pushing, bogging down and overturning with inevitable breakdown delays. And all to little avail in terms of progress. Plus Charlie's back hurt from the strain of dragging the 400-pound machines up rubble walls . . .

Just south of a twenty-foot-high wall, the top of which was lost in mist, my Skidoo's drive system showed signs of malfunction. A reconnaissance on foot, with both of us heading separate ways along the west-east barrier, proved fruitless, neither of us able to spot a possible route in the thick fog. So we camped and waited and all the while floated slowly back toward the coastline from which we wanted so much to distance ourselves.

When Karl brought us the Citations he also removed the manhaul sledges, so we could progress only by these ineffective machines or, if Karl could ever retrieve them from the ice, by waiting until he brought us our original old Alpine models. It was a four-day wait because the whiteout stayed clamped down around the pack and the winds increased. During that time we managed to reach a slightly bigger floe with a possible airstrip down its middle, but in doing so the drive shaft of my vehicle sheared.

I made use of the enforced delay to take a look at our overall chances. It seemed that time was ripe to encourage our London end to put plans into action that might cope with our failure to meet the tight schedule. If we should succeed, there was no problem, but if not, I didn't want sudden panic at home among the sponsors, especially the owners of the Twin Otter and the *Benji Bee*. Best to make them well aware of troubles *before* they occurred.

An alternative would be an optimistic assessment of our chances, but I remembered and went by the advice of the Roman sage, Publius Syrius: 'Never promise more than you can perform.' Or perhaps even as much.

I sent Ginnie a message intended to worry the committee and Ant Preston into immediate action. They must make ready enough fuel and food for an extra year back at Alert in case we failed to reach the Pole by the breakup likely to occur in mid-May. Then again, in case we reached the Pole not before the end of April, they must prepare extra food and fuel for the remote Greenland base of Cape Nord. I ended the message: 'I fully appreciate that a delay in our schedule will mean a difficult decision for sponsors, committee members and members of the expedition team, whether ship, aircrew or Londoners. It will mean extra requests for financial aid and materials, mainly food and fuel. I feel we cannot too quickly put the likely eventualities to all concerned. This way, if key sponsors do drop out there will be time to replace them.'

This note, despite being sent off so early in the day, did not, unfortunately, have the required effect. Everything had gone too well in Antarctica and the Northwest Passage, and a dangerous attitude prevailed at home that was soon to cause critical troubles . . .

All about our floe, as the wind steadied around forty knots from the west, a sound of roaring water came to us through the fog and the blown snow. The pack was on the move. There was no knowing in which direction.

It was easy to worry yourself sick inside the tiny tent. At times the wind tore away the windward side of the fly sheet. I shovelled a wall of snow around us and double-pegged the guy ropes, but each new crack and boom from outside made my ears prick up and the skin crawl down my back.

As we waited out storms in the Arctic I thought of a comment Prince Charles made in a radio broadcast after our Antarctic crossing: 'I think a great lesson to be learned is that the power of nature is still immense and that it should remind us of our frailty as human beings, that we aren't as great as we think we are, that out there still is something so much more powerful than we are, even with our sophisticated technology and our ability to communicate to people so rapidly and create vast and deadlier weapons, that nature is even more deadly in many ways than we are, and we should respect that and recognise our place within the natural environment, because if we lose that I think we should lose touch with everything.'

I found it very easy to agree with this when sitting in a tent among the crashing floes, with seventeen thousand fathoms of cold sea just beneath my sleeping bag.

The four days of wind acting on sea ice far less compacted than after an average winter caused widespread fracturing over thousands of square miles and vast regions of open water where for at least another two months the ice should have remained solid. Fortunately we were not able to see a satellite photograph of our overall predicament.

(Also, although we could not know it, the Norwegians arriving at Yelverton Bay, not far west of Cape Columbia, had found to their surprise nothing but seawater where solid fields of rubble should have pressed up against the Yelverton Peninsula. The Eskimo and one of the Norwegians decided to give up. The Eskimo was brave as a tiger when it came to facing polar bears or extreme low temperatures, but he had relatives or friends who had died out on the sea ice and he could sense more clearly than most that things were far from normal this year in the Arctic Ocean.)

On March 14 Karl and Simon managed to rescue the two stranded Skidoos at some considerable risk and flew north to our battered floe. Within minutes of their leaving us, a fogbank closed over the floe and the wind rose, moaning over the shattered pack. Still, we were keen to press on now that our old Skidoos were back. Heavy and battered they might be, but we at least knew their every idiosyncracy; we had, after all, crossed the Southern Continent with them.

So we set off into a curtain of snow blown from the northwest that settled over the many slits and trenches freshly opened up by the wind. We could see very little to the front . . . flying ice particles stung our eyes. Twice I lurched down into camouflaged patches of sticky nilas and held my breath as the Skidoo tracks slithered and clawed for purchase. Both these places were invisible due to a dusting of blown snow. I should have been warned, but it was so good to be moving again that I carried on into the gathering gloom of dusk. Each time a new split caught me unaware I signalled wildly to Charlie, who shoved a hand up to acknowledge the warning and took care to avoid my route.

The canals began to proliferate and widen. Soon there was a spider's web of open canals cunningly concealed by the poor light and the newly fallen snow.

From time to time I turned to check the whereabouts of Charlie in the twilight murk. This I did once too often and narrowly missed a wide canal zigzagging across my front. No sooner did I come clear of this cutting than a divergent channel with four-foot-high banks barred my new course. Again I swerved. This time too late. Skidoo and sledge skidded into the trough, flinging me toward the far bank. My legs broke through to the knees, but my chest was against the further wall and I managed to scramble out.

But the Skidoo was beyond reach and already settling fast, like a cow caught in a quagmire. Within minutes it was gone, its 900-pound laden weight pointing down at the black ocean floor far below. The steel sledge tilted slowly despite the air trapped between items inside the sledge boxes. The front of the sledge was just within reach and I grabbed at a lashing strap. With a twist around my leather mitt, the strap could not slip ...

I shouted for Charlie. He was twenty yards away, unaware of my problem and unable to hear me above the noise of his Skidoo. I could not stand up to attract his attention but did so lying down with my free hand. Charlie saw it and came up. 'She's going down,' I shouted somewhat unnecessarily. 'Try to save the tent.'

The tent was in a rear-mounted box. Each box had a separate lashing strap, and since the sledge had already been briefly immersed in salt water ditches that day, the straps were covered with a sheen of hard ice. Charlie found he could only just reach the rear of the sledge and with his thick mitts couldn't unlash the straps that held the tent box to the sinking sledge. He took his mitts off, a thing we *very* rarely did outside our tent, and began to work at the frozen strap.

As he did, the sledge settled slowly but surely, and my arm began to feel stretched to its limit. I couldn't hold on much longer. My body, laid out on the ice bank, was slowly pulled over the edge ... With my free hand I opened the second box and pulled free the radio and search beacon. Charlie couldn't get at the tent, but he loosened the lashing of another box and retrieved my theodolite. He also removed a bundle of tent rods tied separately to the sledge. But by then one of his hands had lost all feeling, and my own arm could take it no more ... 'I'm letting go,' I warned him, and did.

Within a minute the sledge had silently disappeared. The tent went with it.

Long ago we had learned that warmth had to be very quickly applied to frozen limbs. But warmth meant a tent. I connected the long aluminium tent poles and pushed their ends into the snow to form the skeleton of a small igloo. Over this I flung the light tarpaulin with which Charlie normally covered our Skidoos at camps. With Charlie's shovel I covered the tarpaulin's edge with snow to keep it taut over the skeleton.

All the cooking equipment and half the rations were on my sledge somewhere below us, but Charlie carried a spoon, mug, a spare tin pot and a spare petrol cooker. Also a spare set of navigation almanacs. While I fixed up the shelter Charlie worked hard to keep his worse hand alive, flinging it from side to side, trying to force some blood down his arm and into his white, unfeeling fingers. And once the spare cooker was lit we bundled what gear we had into the shelter and Charlie began the wonderful but painful process of regaining his fingers.

The temperature fell back to minus 40 degrees Centigrade during the night. Two of us could in no way fit into Charlie's down sleeping bag, but it came with an outer waterproof cover and an inner cloth liner, both of which Charlie gave me.

There was much chattering of teeth that night, and halfway through it I made us a cup of coffee. Charlie's face staring at me in the dim light from a candle balanced between us looked skull-like.

'You look half-dead,' I told him.

'Thanks. You don't look too healthy yourself.'

I had made a stupid mistake and we both knew it. In my eagerness to press north whatever the conditions, I had lost precious equipment and, very nearly, some of Charlie's fingers.

Each day since we had left the coast I had recorded details of the ice conditions, incidence of open water, dimensions of major pressure walls and apparent age of floe systems. All my records had sunk along with my personal gear, spare clothing, photo of Ginnie. Gone, too, was my oilskin container with the only two items to have travelled every foot of the way with me, Gnome Buzzard and Eddie Pike's mouse.

Still, we were both alive and at least no further from our goal. I thought of Peary's companion, Marvin, who, returning toward Ellesmere Island, had disappeared beneath the ice. And the Thule Eskimo hunter, Mitsok, who fell through sea ice close to his sledge. Searchers found the place later the same night through the howling of Mitsok's dogs. The moon lit up an expanse of ice fragments made during his last struggles. His body was retrieved with hooks and his torn nails showed how, clutching at the ice, he had struggled to climb out.

At midnight, with my small radio none the worse for its brief immersion, I called Ginnie on our emergency night schedule. As usual she was listening and picked up my faint call sign through the permanent crackle, static and plethora of Morse signals. She sounded calm but concerned when I told her about our situation. Since all our replacement gear was destroyed in the fire I worried about a bad delay, but Ginnie said the sledge Ollie had always used, with its standard load, had been in the snow clearing outside the garage. She promised to get it and the camp runabout Skidoo as soon as possible. If I sank that, she said, there would be *nothing* else; even the skis were burned.

As soon as the weather cleared Karl set out and found a clearing half a mile from the site of my accident, where he landed . . . just. I couldn't imagine many other pilots even considering such a site. On his way back to Ellesmere Island Karl warned us that the ice was now horribly broken. 'Whole areas of open sea,' he reported . . .

The wind soon dropped to eighteen knots, and a new fogbank swirled about us, messing up my navigation and slowing our progress to a blind limp. I counted seven wide leads of grey jellied ice that flexed beneath our Skidoos and broke under the heavier sledge runners. In such places we crossed at different points and at maximum speed, 'swimming' the sledges across on long towropes with less danger to Skidoo and rider.

Pressure ridges averaged twelve feet high, sometimes reaching twenty-five feet, with two or three to a mile. Between them lay rubble fields through which a crisscross of alleyways snaked, at least allowing us to progress without the nonstop preparatory axe work of the more southerly pack.

On March 16 we woke up to find a forty-knot wind battering the tent and showering the layer of frost that skimmed the inside of our flysheet onto our faces and into our bag openings, where it promptly melted.

In semi-whiteout we nosed north. There was no sign of the sun, so I applied an error of some 92 degrees to my compass bearing and hoped for the best.

The temperature had shot up to minus 6 degrees Centigrade, a sinister sign and unprecedented so early in the year. By evening conditions resembled a lily pond, with ourselves hopping from one floating leaf to another. The powerful west wind fortunately ensured that most ice chunks touched each other at some point. If they did not, we retraced our route and tried a new one. There was, of course, a good deal of west-east travel involved with trying to head north, and much axing of ice blocks to make bridges.

Not long before dusk our best bridging efforts failed to span a twelve-foot-wide lead and, when we tried to get off the floe the way we'd arrived, we found our tracks led into a new canal that opened further even as we watched. So we camped in the centre of our floating islet. I climbed a thirty-foot-high hummock and looked around. Leads meandered all about us. The wind rose to fifty-five knots as we set up the tent, and all about us the sound of shattering ice competed with the roar of the elements.

We both knew that small isolated floes were highly susceptible to crackup not only when larger neighbours weighing millions of tons began to nip them but simply because of lateral wave action bending and straining the natural flaws in the ice. Such knowledge helped sleep evade me for much of that noisy night.

In the morning I made contact with Ginnie, but only briefly because the frequencies were shooting up and down like yo-yos. The aircraft, she said, had been damaged in the storm. Gerry and David and a radio operator named Laurence Howell, who had come to man the Tanquary Fjord with David, had arrived the previous day.

When news of our recurring problems reached London the press began to sound off with some notes. 'Today,' said one paper, 'two and a half years and 300,000 kilometres after the expedition's start, things are going disastrously.' I suppose this was a reasonable assessment . . . One John Akass of the *Daily Express* went further: 'If Fiennes's critics have their way, there may now be questions asked as to his sponsors' choice of leader.'

When Ginnie warned me how things were going back in Britain I decided to change my approach to the crossing attempt. I would forget the various other teams racing us across the Pole, even the Norwegians. I would no longer press on as far and as fast as we could stand the pace. From now on I would try to conserve our strength day by day and concentrate on the long-term aim – to reach the ship before winter brought a new freeze-up, probably in October. That way I might avoid any more dangerous foul-ups like the ones that had set the wasps buzzing back in London.

All day on March 17 we remained cut off, and a new crack opened up some twenty yards from the tent. Although this happened soundlessly we both felt the sudden temperature change as warmer air came from the unzipped sea beside our tent. The temperature lowered a touch to minus 26 degrees Centigrade and the wind held at fifty-two knots. The main lead to the north was now a wind-whipped river some forty feet across.

In such conditions a sleeping pill was the only way to catch up on much needed rest ... the noise and the vibrations were truly spectacular once the ice got on the move. The fracture and pressure sounds were varied, but the most awe-inspiring were the booming and crunching type. Like the pipes and drums of an approaching enemy horde the distant rumble and crunch of invading ice floes that grew louder and closer hour by hour were impossible to ignore, or become adjusted to.

The minor noises, too, had a chilling effect on a tent-bound listener. After hours of silence a sudden sharp trill or zing immediately below your ear as you lay on a thin mat on the ice could bring you instantly alert and ready to run – if it weren't for the clumsy constriction of your zipped-up, laced-up sleeping bag. The ice beside your ear acted like a huge acoustics chamber.

Next morning the wind dropped, as did the temperature to minus 36 degrees Centigrade. At 7:00 A.M. I scouted around our floe and found a narrow junction point at its southern extremity. There was a good deal of grinding and whining at this point and much flaking off of ice from our side of the touchpoint.

An hour later we were packed and with a little axe work managed to manoeuvre the sledges across the moving junction of the floes. Only a few miles to the north we entered a miasma of brown gloom, a certain sign of open water, and soon afterward stopped before a sea of dirty sludge that moved across our front. In the mist we could see no limit to this marsh.

Back at the base, after thirty hours of work in bitter cold and using an old fibreglass kit, Karl and Gerry managed to repair the damaged wingtip, then flew high over our own area at about 85 degrees north and 70 degrees west. Karl described our situation in a way we couldn't comprehend at the time ... 'The ice is very rotten and much in motion. I'm sure that the ice group are stuck for a week or more until the ice can settle and refreeze. They are in a trap. To their east, north and west there are high ridges and open water all around. I can see only one way out. They must retrace their tracks for half a mile and then go west for one and a half miles where I can see some ice bridges. Then they can try to go north. If they miss any part of my prescribed track there is no way out ...'

Ginnie made contact with a pilot operating out of Cape Nord in northeast Greenland, the area we would have to float past sometime during the next six months. At this time of the year it would have been mostly solid pack ice, but he reported: 'No ice older than second-year floes and all the younger ice appears thin, weak and broken up. Even three hundred miles north of here the sea is like a watery mosaic.'

That night Ginnie said, 'When I look to the north of the camp here I should see an expanse of unbroken ice. All I see is open water to the horizon.' And back in London Ant Preston wrote, 'At this stage it is fair to say that there is no one immediately involved in the expedition who would give much for its chances of reaching the Pole this year.'

From our camp by the sludge marsh we went out on long journeys on foot, taking with us weapons and axes. The first two trips led us through much impressive scenery and evidence of wide upheaval. I thanked God we had not been camped anywhere in this region during the recent high winds. It was as though the floes had been shaken through a great sieve and dropped back into the sea like croutons into chilled consommé. A most unpleasant region to travel through, even on foot.

We retreated to the tent, and I took down some advice from Karl after his recent overflight. His route obliged us to fill in two twenty-foot-deep ditches, which took us four hours, and after fourteen hours' travel we managed to progress six miles to the north before a new lead stopped us.

(Karl later wrote: 'I was very, very curious if they could make my route and I must say in that respect Ran is an excellent navigator because next morning Ginnie told me they had made it out of the ice jungle and were some miles north of it.')

The next ten days passed in a haze. Brief excerpts from my diary are as revealing of my comprehension of the conditions as anything, even though they are but a clutch of fleeting glances:

> We have come nine miles today to 84°42′. Only 318 miles to the Pole. Another thousand or so on the other side but that is not even worth contemplating yet. It was at this point that the Simpson expedition gave up and turned back. Plaisted's first attempt with Skidoos petered out 66 miles to the south and Peary's first two attempts – Eskimos, dogs and all – got to 84°17′ and 83°38′ respectively. For a while this evening we bridged our way over a multi-year floe with great splits in it just narrow enough to fill in with shovel work. Looking down you can see twelve feet and more to the level of the sea. We are stopped here by a two-mile field of green, ridging blocks. Spent an hour axing a path before coming back and erecting the tent. Quite a few rips in the flysheet now ... My chin was numb when I came in and lit the cooker. Must have pulled my frozen facemask off too hard. When thawing it out and picking the ice bits from around the mouthpiece I found a one-inch-diameter tuft of my beard complete with skin and implanted in the ice. It took a while to remove this from the wool. Where the skin has come away there is now an open patch of raw flesh the size of a large coin. In a while my chin warmed up and began to bleed. Now it is just weeping liquid matter ...

A big switchback wall held us up this morning. After a rough time we got over. I saw Charlie's track looked wrong. One track adjuster bolt had sheared and I left him to fix it. For an hour I scouted and chopped and then went back. Charles was cursing away, unable to fix the new bolt in place without damaging its thread. Together we heaved at the track until at last the bolt screwed home. Charlie's fingers took a while to revive before we could continue. Mechanical work at minus 44 degrees Centigrade with a twenty-knot breeze is no fun ...

Both sledges were dunked today and now all our lashings are frozen stiff. You need to crack the ice off with the back of an axe to get at the buckles. If we used ropes it would be hell to undo knots, even with needle-nose pliers ... Tonight we've had a fire. Charlie restarted the cooker but a leak around the pump caused flames all over the safety blanket and on the tent floor. We chucked the flaming cooker out of the tent in case the tank decided to explode, then beat out the flames. Now we are using the spare cooker and patching up the holes in our bags with black cloth cut from a marker flag ... One of Charlie's towropes frayed through today but we had a spare. Two hours of axing and shovelling were necessary in a rubble field just north of here before camping. So our clothes are very damp and steaming above the cooker. My chin aches nonstop now but it is all right by day when it is normally numb ...

Charlie's leg went through today as we tried to pull out a sledge jammed in a moving trench. Dead on minus 40 degrees Centigrade all day and wind steady from the northwest bang into our eyes. All the world is misty. We've been out here well over a month and I can't wear goggles on the move, they mist up and navigation becomes impossible. I just can't spot that vital line of least resistance through the murk that is the key to success or failure. At midday clouds of black steam rose up right across the northern horizon. There is no noise, just the steam. Impressive and a touch uncanny. The equinoctial tides may well be shifting the sea and so fracturing the ice ... Have just finished trying to patch up my chin. The raw place is now down to the bone. I can see it in the mirror of my compass. I look a disgusting sight. Charlie confirmed this ...

Ginnie's signal was weak again on March 21, almost unreadable. She said the Norwegian team needed fuel and had called in a chartered Twin Otter fitted with tundra tyres. Thinking the surface to be fairly solid snow, they landed the plane but could not take off again. After a two-day delay another Twin Otter carrying spare skis arrived and eventually rescued the first one. Karl had been called in to help when the rescue plane was unable to locate the Norwegians' camp; he spotted them and guided the other Twin Otter down. When they later ran out of naphtha Karl dropped them some of ours.

The French team, Ginnie said, had bickered among themselves while preparing to set out from their base in East Greenland and had flown back to France. It struck me that perhaps the French leader had selected his team from experts ... a doctor, a mechanic, a navigator, a radio operator, a scientist or two ... in short, a nest of prima donnas, likely ingredients for internecine strife. Our expedition had from time to time certainly suffered from its *lack* of experts, but that to my mind was the lesser evil.

On March 22, fearing our days of drifting had taken us too far east into the looser conditions above the outflow channel west of Greenland, I steered us to 15 degrees to the west of due north. It was unusually cold. My duvet jacket's zip gave up the ghost. I used some string as a belt, but my heat loss all day was considerable and did me no good.

That night my chin throbbed like a tomtom. Not having any more antibiotic cream I applied the cream I used for hemorrhoids. Charlie found this pretty amusing ... 'He's got piles on his chin,' was how he put it. It was lucky that we shared a weird sense of humour ...

More of my diary:

> A hairy time today with some dicey crossings. One was via a little pin of an island in a twenty-metre lead. Charlie almost slid into the sea as it tipped sideways. Several of the crossing points were in motion with heavy blocks bobbing up like corks one moment and dropping out of sight the next. Once you mount these places you must keep going to the other side at all costs. Stop halfway over and you risk being churned up, crushed and dunked for good ... We had our first good day. Fifteen miles in eight hours, though not all of it to the north by any means. Then a great barrier of blocks stopped us. Averaging twenty-five feet high and over two hundred yards from side to side it stretched west and east beyond the limits of my vision. We clambered up the wall and agreed it would take a day at least to axe a route to the other side. Leaving the sledge we drove east through a maze of high sculptured blocks and after a mile came to a wonderful sight. Somehow an acre or two of four-foot-thick floe ice, in the grip of hidden forces, had been forced twenty or thirty feet upward without fragmenting and formed a ready causeway over the barrier wall. For two hours we chopped and hammered with our axes to make a ramp by which to descend the other side of the wall. My axe slipped and cut through one mukluk but I felt no pain and assumed my inner boot had protected my toes. Winding our way, soaked by exertion, back to the sledges we erected the tent on this paddock. It is not an old floe and the water is very salty. Charlie has looked at my foot. The axe blade

seems to have cut right through the nail of one toe and deep into the meat beneath. But there's not too much blood and Charlie has bound it up with gauze and plaster treated with cure-it-all pile cream . . .

Another good day and extremely cold. This morning my chin was swollen up like a golf ball so Charlie gave me broad-spectrum antibiotic pills. After covering the raw chin with pile cream and gauze plus a tissue I place a stocking bandage over my head from chin to the back of my skull, then on go the two facemasks . . . Within twenty minutes of leaving the tent the facemasks have begun to freeze into position, and a matting of ice from nostrils to chin accumulates. The discomfort of the long hours' travel into the wind, which averages eighteen knots, at minus 40 degrees Centigrade is well worth it. We need the cold to repair the ice and stave off further breakup . . . At midday we stopped at a fifteen-foot-high barrier and trudged toward it with axes and a shovel. Charlie grabbed my arm. 'Listen,' he said. A grinding, squeaking moan as though from a concrete mixer issued from the wall of ice, and despite the intense glare of the sun we watched fascinated as blue-bellied blocks the size of small houses spewed up from the wall's centre and fell down its leading edge. At the same time splits appeared in the floe itself and green water surged up and along the foot of the moving wall . . . At the time there was little or no local wind but great shearing powers were at work to cut and shift those heavy blocks. The theory that pressure ridging results from the squeezing of newly frozen leads and not from the interaction between the grinding edges of two senior floes did not tally with the impressive activity of that particular ridge . . . Since there was no way around and no point in waiting indefinitely for the movement to cease, we gingerly worked at the blocks as they slithered and fell, taking great care to avoid being crushed. A few minutes before we were ready to attempt a crossing, all movement ceased and there was absolute silence ... The wind rose again during the afternoon, and Charlie was frostnipped along the bridge of his nose; myself on one eyelid. Navigation was becoming almost instinctive with or without the sun. Perhaps unknowingly I was responding to the lie of the ridges or the wind or even the direction of the light source that I couldn't consciously determine ...

March 27: Minus 41 degrees Centigrade with twenty-three knots from the northwest. Every hour we have to stop and restore the blood to our hands and feet. Fingers get numb with the axe work. My neck glands are now puffed up and swollen like my chin, so I keep taking the antibiotic pills. I notice in my compass mirror that the whites of my eyes are all red. I still can't wear my goggles, but much of today there was a sort of ice rain, the little freezing nuclei particles in the air that hit the retina as tiny spicules and sting ... We camped here at 5:00 P.M. on a solid enough floe, though a small one. There seemed to be no movement about. Yet at 6:00 P.M., just as Charlie had boiled the ice water and made coffee, a violent shudder passed through the floe like an earth tremor, and within the second a shock wave of air, similar to a distant bomb blast, grabbed at the tent and caught at our breath. Coffee spilling all over the floor, we clutched for the tent-door zipper, fearing that a giant floe had hit ours and was about to raft over us. Outside there was no wind, no movement and no sign of anything untoward. Warily we rezipped the entrance flap and mopped up the coffee puddles ... 'Odd,' I said ... 'Strange,' said Charlie ... We feel uneasy on this floe ...

During the night of March 28 we awoke sweating inside our damp bags. The atmosphere was oppressive and there was dead silence. I thought of a line from Wally's doggerel: 'Beware of the calm that follows the storm ...'

Outside, our rubble-strewn paddock was surrounded by mottled marshes of steaming sludge. The light of the sun, a sick yellow, appeared to flutter and fade from minute to minute. Neither of us spoke as we raised camp and tightened the lashings of our sledges.

To the northeast a brown-skinned lake disappeared into the gloom. Elsewhere the marsh was broken by floes not unlike lumps of molten cheese on the surface of onion soup. I heaved a lump of ice onto this marsh ice. It settled slowly into the jellied crust, then in a leisurely manner disappeared. I looked at Charlie. His eyebrows lifted and he shook his head slowly.

We walked to the eastern side of our island and slung a chunk out into the brownish skin of the lake. There was a rippling motion away from the point of impact, but no breakthrough. Again I looked at Charlie. He remained expressionless. I shrugged and we made for the Skidoos.

There followed five hours of hell. By rights we should not have tried to travel. Our route was about as straight as a pig's tail and went where the perils of the moment dictated. Much of the time to stop would mean to sink. For a thousand yards we moved over this first lake, which was in reality more like a wide river. I intended to get off it quickly, but high banks of ice boulders prevented that.

After ten minutes we saw that the surface was undulating ahead of us, a sort of forward wash spreading out in front of our slow advance. And the brown skin actually ended in open water a short distance to our left flank ... open water that hissed with vapour that curled and billowed.

A solitary floe chunk with one low edge gave us brief respite, and from it we listened for signs of what lay ahead in the yellow murk ... A soft squeaking and grinding came from nowhere in particular. A sort of private Satan's cauldron, if I may be permitted some dramatic indulgence. Maybe Marlowe did some Arctic travel before he wrote in *Doctor Faustus:* 'Ugly Hell gape not! Come not Lucifer.'

Often that morning we lost sight of each other in the fog. Sometimes we moved on foot, Charlie waiting on some bump suspended in the marsh halfway from the Skidoos and shouting to guide me back. We were afraid that a new fracturing would cut us off from the sledges. If that happened we couldn't, we knew, expect to live for long. By noon we were worn out with apprehension, since for all we knew the marsh stretched on for many miles.

But then the mist grew less dense and in a while it cleared away altogether and fourteen miles of *solid* ice rewarded our morning's efforts. I felt wonderfully good and forgot about my chin and nose and toes and all the vast distance ahead. Nothing, we felt, could ever be so bad again. If we could travel over *that* we could cross anything. Such a sense of elation and conceit didn't last long, but was great while it did . . .

We stopped at 87° 02′ within nine miles of our furthest north in 1977 and forty days earlier in the season. If our aim had been solely to reach the Pole, we could perhaps have felt confident.

That night in a new fogbank I took a little while to work out in which direction Ginnie was in order to lay out the radio antenna on the correct plane, then did hear her Strength 2, but fading in and out like the noise of the seashore . . . The Spanish team, she said, had set out for the Pole from West Svalbard. After three miles from their camp beside Longyearbyen Airport their sledges gave trouble so they abandoned them and went back to Madrid. The Norwegians on the other hand had covered an astounding 120 kilometres in a couple of days and were now only 176 miles to our south waiting resupply by the Norwegian air force. How they had stormed through the worst possible pressure zone which had taken us weeks I only learned some days later. The breakup that had held them up at Yelverton Bay froze solid during the ensuing cold front and presented a virgin highway to the north. Taking their chances they had carried on without sleeping until they came to older ice and ridging and fractures. But 176 miles is a long, long way on the Arctic Ocean so I decided to take note of Prince Charles's winter advice and put aside any thoughts of racing. 'The Norwegians may catch us before we reach Spitsbergen but not before the Pole,' I told Ginnie. 'Be careful,' she replied, 'remember the Convergence.'

This was not a feature I was likely to forget, since it was stage one on the way to Nirvana as far as our crossing attempt was concerned. Once past the Convergence we would be out of the Beaufort Gyral, the current that flows in a giant clockwise circle between the Pole and the top of Canada. For a while we would be in a sort of no-man's-land where floes might or might not find themselves spat back into the Gyral. But within a few miles of the Geographical Pole we would enter the Transpolar Drift proper, which heads over the Pole from the USSR and down toward Greenland. Where these two currents met and diverged there was, of course, corresponding surface disturbance that in places tore floes apart, in others jumbled them together. We believed this highly mobile belt to be at around 88 degrees, 120 miles short of the Pole . . .

As we crept north in early April the general movement and noise of the floes increased. It seemed as though we were rushing pell-mell in an unseen tide race to an invisible sink-hole – the maw of the world.

Wanting to keep tabs on our position and warned by Karl of the unpredictable behaviour of the Twin Otter's navigation system, I checked out my theodolite on April 2 shortly before Karl was due to drop us rations. Three sun's altitude shots gave me a position of 87°21′ north, 76° West. But when Karl came in, his Omega put us at 87°23′ north, 75° West, a difference of some five miles. The

Omega I decided was more likely to be accurate so I asked Karl to bring in my second theodolite once we reached the Pole. This had been kept in Ginnie's hut and so was not burned, although two others of different types had been destroyed.

Somehow Karl managed to land at our strip, although it was far from even. Simon, who was with him to collect bags of snow for a pollen check for the Polar Shelf Project, made these entries in his diary: 'At our furthest point today we were the most northerly men on earth with nothing below us but fractured ice and black open leads . . . When we got back to Alert, Karl said, "Well, we survived another landing." We'd had a short takeoff, barely flying, and the stall warning sounded off as Karl pulled up to clear a ridge.'

When Karl left I tried to make up time by setting out at midnight – a wearisome, bitter ten miles with much axing through rubble with no perspective to indicate possible routes. We camped amid a hopeless muddle of blocks.

The sting of the ice-rain, the glare of the whiteout and the fumes in the tent made my vision poor. I didn't think I had sun blindness, but however much I blinked I just saw an indistinct haze up ahead. I prayed hard in the tent for my sight to come back properly, and fortunately it did.

For three days we struggled on with some solid old floes, many breakdowns and two occasions when a sledge sank into a lead and its Skidoo was simultaneously jammed in the sludge. As long as both of us were close by when this happened we could usually tow the stricken units out frontward or backward. But there were too many near squeaks. Bad for the nerves . . .

At 87°48′ north we were stopped by the most massive wall I had seen in the Arctic, not in height but in sheer bulk – first a ten- or twelve-foot moat, fortunately frozen, then a sheer-sided twenty- to thirty-foot-high buttress a hundred yards in depth, then a jagged rubble belt ending in another rampart that almost twinned its parallel neighbour. There was no causeway over this barrier and no detour around it, so we fashioned a devious zigzag route over it and four hours later bounced down the far side to eighteen miles of better going and no leads of any consequence.

Throughout the day black shadows along the line of the horizon, similar to rainstorms seen on steppe-lands, helped me steer clear of open water. A helmsman in polar seas knows by 'ice blink' – a portion of brightness in an otherwise dark ocean sky – just where to his front he will find floes. Conversely, black smoke, known as steam fog or frost smoke, tells the ice-bound pilot where he may find an escape route from the pack. The steam comes from cold air striking warmer water ... the rapid and visible discharge of moisture and heat into the atmosphere.

Ginnie came through clearly on April 4. The Russian expedition, she said, had never set out because the Canadians refused it a landing permit. The Norwegians were doing well but no longer closing on us. Dundee University in Scotland had sent Ginnie a message describing a satellite picture of the sea ice ahead. For weeks they had told her nothing, owing to fog or clouds, but now a clear picture was available. At 88°31′ north and again at 89°20′ massive surface disintegration was under way, and both areas appeared to consist only of thin ice.

Given that the first such zone might be the Convergence belt, we tried to speed up our progress and next day managed twenty-one miles in spite of open canals, wide rubble fields and much axe work. We were operating well together, and the magic of knowing we were north of 88 degrees tended to work wonders.

My diary has it this way:

April 6. Bitter cold day and movement everywhere. Whole fields of thin new ice, but a weak wind seems to be holding it together.

Have stopped with black smoke rising right across the southern horizon. But ahead seems clear at present. Only sixty-five miles now . . .

April 7. A real fight today. To think we have believed for years that a flat and smooth 'highway' existed to the north of 88 degrees. Charlie said this morning that today's conditions were as bad as anything along the coast. He may well be right but at least there are a few good bits *between* the zones of chaos . . . Charlie nearly sank this morning. After two hours' hacking through an eighteen-foot-high wall we filled a sludge ditch with cutaway blocks. As he mounted them, they disappeared under water. He leapt off, and together we hauled until his rubber tracks were clear. How many more cat's lives? . . .

April 8. Crossed sixty-two sludge cracks today and two major ridge features. But the bit is between our teeth. Twenty-one miles done, and no more than thirty-one to the Pole . . .

April 9. Charlie's sledge swam for twenty yards today, but the breaking nilas never quite caught up with his Skidoo. This area is a dreadful mess. My neck swelling has gone and my chin is almost healed, so no more antibiotics . . .

Suddenly, some twenty miles short of the Pole, the ocean's surface improved and remained almost unbroken with hardly any obstacles in sight.

At midday on April 10 a theodolite sighting put us at 60 degrees west. Our local noon was at 1630 hours Greenwich Mean Time.

The last miles to the Pole were flat with but three narrow leads that caused no problems. I checked the miles away with care after the noon sunshot, not wanting to overshoot the top of the world.

We arrived there at 2330 hours GMT, and I contacted Ginnie at 0215 hours GMT on Easter Day, 1982.

I had to think for a while when laying out the antenna to point due south at her, since *every* direction was due south.

The temperature was minus 31 degrees Centigrade.

We were the first men in history to have travelled over the earth's surface to both poles, but the *Benji Bee* and the edge of the ice were still many hundreds of miles and many cold wet months beyond our immediate horizon.

Chapter Fifteen

The middle course is best.

CLEOBUS

Following our arrival at the Pole the London *Daily Mail* said: 'On the anniversary, almost to the day, of Robert Falcon Scott's tragic death in Antarctica in 1912, there is something very satisfying about Englishmen beating Norwegians at the other end of the globe. For it was Norway's Roald Amundsen who vanquished Captain Scott at the South Pole.'

I thought of the Vikings' famous saying, their equivalent of not counting chickens until they are hatched: 'Praise no day until evening, no wife until buried, no sword until tested, no maid till bedded, no ice until crossed.' We had not crossed our ice or even reached the halfway point.

Karl, ever the realistic Swiss, said: 'At least one part is over, but now the last leg must be done and this one will not be so easy at all because it is an unknown and treacherous task. On the way to Spitsbergen the sea currents are much stronger, the temperatures start to get warmer and with these conditions the ice is bound to break up. I've seen in previous years the ice in certain patches so badly broken up you figured you were looking at a river in spring breakup.'

The sea ice breakup, after which we would be unable to travel and must seek a solid floe on which to float, was unlikely to occur before mid-May. Which gave us four weeks in which to zigzag a thousand miles to the edge of the ice and the safety of the *Benji Bee*. At the Pole the weather for once was excellent, but we could not take advantage of it because, back in London, an arrangement had been made for the *Daily Mirror* to send two of their staff to the Pole by Twin Otter.

Wary of accusations that we had never reached the Pole, we welcomed this visit. Flying on a given bearing from the Ellesmere Island coast for the correct mileage after computing the wind speed, the pilot and crew would be able to ascertain that we were exactly and precisely at the top of the world. Also, with three spaced altitude shots of the sun my theodolite could provide proof of our position – but only Charlie and I would know this, and that would satisfy no potential critics, as Admiral Peary and Dr Cook would readily agree from their graves.

David, Simon and Bothy were to spend a while at the Pole with us if the weather held, but Ginnie and Laurence Howell were to remain at their respective radio watches at Alert and Tanquary Fjord as Karl's rear links.

Karl's landing was made on April 12 on what he called 'suspect' ice. He was proven right a few days later when another Twin Otter, chartered by a group of Japanese tourists determined to land at the Pole, came down safely enough but then sank through the ice and disappeared.

Prince Charles sent us a message, saying, 'What wonderful news ... you have achieved a remarkable feat and we are all praying for endless square miles of solid smooth ice between the North Pole and Spitsbergen.'

Bothy was unimpressed. He trotted about on the floe and peed close to but not on the Union Jack and the other flags which we had planted there.

Karl took a walk over the airstrip and checked the holes that Charlie had drilled for ice depth. He was not happy. Taking me to one side before he left, he advised me to head down the Greenwich Meridian for at least a hundred miles from the Pole and then aim off to the east to counteract the prevailing westerly currents.

Once the Twin Otter and our friends had gone away, we packed up and set out in the evening; I had decided to travel by night and sleep by day . . . that way the sun would be behind us and throw the shadow of my body ahead of the Skidoo, allowing me to use it as a sundial and so dispense with a compass for much of the time. Also, there would be less glare and more perspective.

In the absence of any firm policy, speed might have seemed the safest way to proceed, just as it had in Antarctica and the Northwest Passage. Yet a single error in judgement or an over-hasty move might easily upset everything. The chairman and one or two others counseled an attempt to reach the coast of northeast Greenland and then to sledge over the ice cap to some part of the coast that the *Benji Bee* might reach. But Andrew Croft, who had experience as extensive as anyone else, disagreed and suggested we keep to my original plan, which was to head east toward the northern coast of Spitsbergen.

Although I trusted Andrew Croft I also feared the current signs of an unusually early breakup. At Cape Nord an American meteorologist had said the pack ice was more loose and broken north of Fram Strait than at any time in the last thirty-seven years. This being so, I was equally shy of heading too far west or too far east. It seemed better to stay halfway between the two islands, almost on the Greenwich Meridian, where the southerly current was thought to be strongest. So I made up my mind to follow local evidence rather than outside opinions.

I had my hopes pinned on the *Benji Bee,* but I knew she could not hope to penetrate pack ice in the way an icebreaker could. The only way she might reach us was through the skill and spirit of skipper and crew acting in unison with Karl as their eyes in daylight and summer ice conditions. Such conditions existed only for five or six weeks in an average year, from late July until late September, and we had to reach at least 81 degrees of latitude and preferably well east of the Greenwich Meridian by that period, otherwise even the best efforts of the *Benji Bee* would be to no purpose. For the ship to linger after the end of the short Arctic summer would be to invite disaster on herself.

Our Skidoos could not cope with mush ice and open water because, unlike dogs, they were not amphibious. The *Benji Bee* could not penetrate pack ice as well as the far larger H.M.S. *Endurance* of Wally Herbert's 1968 team, nor did she possess any helicopters. So it would be foolish for me to attempt to follow Herbert's route, even assuming the 1982 breakup was to be in late May, as it was in 1969.

I decided to steer a middle course: to head south under our own steam and at a speed comparable to Herbert's while the temperatures remained reasonably low and the pack relatively stable. But once local conditions deteriorated to the point where I considered a breakup imminent, I would search for a floe to float south on toward the best pickup point, somewhere close to the Zero Meridian, not too far west or east of it. That way we might reach the *Benji Bee*'s limit-of-penetration point before winter darkness and new ice forced her out of the Arctic. No man had crossed the Arctic Ocean in one summer season before, but given a few more weeks of solid ice and skilful handling of the old *Benji Bee,* conceivably we just might make it. I reckoned we had between ten and fourteen days before the April sun, beating on the ice twenty-four hours a day, would start to crack it up. From then on, more or less open water leads would bar our progress. We would zigzag to try to find crossing places where floes touch. If storms came our way over the next few days the ice would break up sooner, but with luck we would use the latter half of April to leave the Pole about three hundred miles behind. If so, the month of May would find us at 85 degrees north, which would leave us another three hundred miles to float south. We hoped to drift at three miles per day, which would take us to the edge of northwest Spitsbergen by mid-August. Although the pack ice would extend well south, our ship would attempt to penetrate the pack and retrieve us before our chosen floe got crushed or disintegrated.

This projection was not to prove too accurate. The distances were, of course, straight lines, and we were never able to travel or float in straight lines . . .

For four nights of travel from the Pole the weather was never below minus 28 degrees and despite signs of recent upheavals there was no open water to be seen. We averaged twenty-two miles of southerly sea travel.

During the night of April 22 I noticed the prints of an Arctic fox at 88 degrees north, many hundreds of miles from the nearest land. Although there were no bearprints in evidence, it was safe to assume that the fox could only have survived so far from the source of any of its natural prey, such as hares, by shadowing a bear and feeding off its leftovers.

As we moved away from the Pole our distance from Alert was at the very limit of Karl's operating distance, so Ginnie decided to start closing down first Tanquary Fjord and then Alert in readiness to move to her next base, Cape Nord in East Greenland.

On the night of April 18, over a hundred miles from the Pole, we crossed a narrow lead between two pools of green water. Then confronting us was a belt of grey sludge that bubbled cauldronlike and moved as we watched to the southwest, transporting a load of broken floe bits trapped in its nilas. The noise of a giant heartbeat emanated from this canal and we listened fascinated at its edge. Two skins of nilas rafted one over the other with rhythmic jerks, and this we decided was the source of the cardiac beats.

Long ago we had learned that a single skin of nilas was likely to collapse beneath a Skidoo, but two, buckle and bend as they might, usually held our weight. So we headed out and across the canal. That day we made thirty-one miles in fourteen hours; probably our best night's travel . . .

Over the next three nights of twenty-four, twenty and twenty miles respectively, our relatively easy-going conditions slowly deteriorated. There were many regions of ridges and rubble as bad as any to be found off the Ellesmere coast . . . 'Makes you laugh,' said Charlie as we axed our way through a twenty-five-foot-high blockage. 'Both sides of the Pole between eighty-eight and eighty-nine degrees have great heaps of this muck just where we've always expected good going.'

He was right. Peary and Cook and Plaisted and Herbert all experienced a marked improvement to the north of 88 degrees. Maybe we just happened to hit unusual conditions . . .

From 88 down to 86 degrees was a continued decline. Rubble fields grew more frequent, with many more open water leads. Potential airstrip floes were correspondingly more rare. I'd become accustomed to keeping an eye open for airstrip potential. In the Arctic no one could tell when a flat floe of at least twenty-four-inch thickness might not become a life-saving necessity. For forty miles through the night of April 20 and 21 there was no potential strip of any sort. The pack ice was far too broken and, for huge areas, too thin. Nothing I saw in all that time could have served us for a floating platform to head south on.

The temperature was by now in the minus 20s and rising. No

longer was it necessary to wear a facemask. By rights I could count on four more weeks until breakup, given normal conditions. But this was no normal year, and I daily became more wary as the weather grew more balmy.

On the early morning of the 21st many open leads blocked our route and required careful bridging to negotiate. At one such obstacle we lopped off enough fragments to make a temporary pontoon and I crossed at full speed. Charlie, watching the pontoon disappear under my sledge runners and black water surge over the slipway, prudently said he would find some other crossing point.

'I'll wait here,' I shouted. 'If you find nowhere else within fifteen minutes we can build this place up again.' I took a mitt off and shoved my five spread fingers into the air three times, then tapped my watch. Charlie nodded, then disappeared.

Twenty minutes later he had not returned and I began to axe away at the bank of the canal to rebuild the slipway, my only way of getting back to follow Charlie's tracks ... After forty minutes he was still gone and my mind was filled with visions of telling Charlie's wife and parents how it had happened and why we had separated. I imagined him trying to claw himself out of some morass of moving nilas. Sweating profusely I was about to take a header at the clumsy slipway blocks when I saw Charlie emerge further down and on my side of the canal.

My relief was laced with some annoyance and I may have been a little brusque. Why hadn't he come back within fifteen minutes? Simple: he'd misunderstood my hand signals, which weren't, after all, written in some universal code ...

Open water, pools and leads began to occur many times a mile with no signs of new ice forming over them. Often I walked ahead with an axe to find a way through webs of canals. Charlie would station himself halfway between the sledges and me and within sight of both. If and when he saw some canal become active he would shout and signal and I would run back to him as fast as possible so we were not cut off. There was, of course, no one to keep close watch on the channels between Charlie and the sledges, but that was a risk we could hardly avoid ... There were many acrobatics and near misses those last days, many wet sledges and legs and, on two occasions, Skidoos caught wallowing in mobile ridge joints with only a minute or two for Charlie and me to haul them out before they sank ...

On the night of the 21st a whiteout closed over us as we camped in a tiny paddock we had reached by way of a tortuous route through sludge fields and 'lily pond' conditions. The wind rose to twenty-five knots and blown snow brought visibility to nil. In such broken ice it would be silly, I decided, to travel, so we stayed there for forty-eight hours ... Two nights later the wind rose to thirty knots from the south, and the whiteout lifted enough for a wan yellow light source from the northwest to provide a means of navigation. The temperature had risen to minus 14 degrees Centigrade.

Two hours of axing through low walls of green rafted blocks gave us access to a weird region of winding couloirs of new-looking ice. All around were black pools of wind-ruffled water. In fact, the whole area looked ready to go ... several times, approaching grey sludge, I sank into water-logged ice that had seemed firm.

Along the side of one narrow canal I tripped and fell headlong. The hand holding my axe shot out to ward off a heavy fall. It disappeared through the surface as did my arm up to the elbow and somehow one leg up to the knee. I was partially soaked but, fortunately, the snow-covered sludge held my overall weight.

Seven miles later seawater cut us off in all directions, so we camped. The wind still blew at thirty knots with the temperature steady at minus 13 degrees Centigrade. Chunks of ice floating across pools and along canals all seemed to be heading east. In the tent I told Charlie I would start searching for a floe suitable for a float south. For three days no sun shot had been possible, but a rough estimate put us at 86°10′ north. Charlie was not happy. He felt we should not attempt a float-out until we had travelled to at least 83 degrees – another 190 miles. Any less, he felt, and we might not make it in time. I could see his point of view. After so many weeks out on the ice the one thing we both wanted was to get the hell off it as soon as possible. Indeed, the risk of stopping so early and so far north must have seemed something like wilful masochism.

But for many hours over the past three days I'd been turning over and over in my mind the pros and cons of my alternative course. To my mind *everything* came second to whichever course of action promised the greatest chance of eventual, not short-term, success. I tried to make Charlie see things my way but he just could not. He must be mentally exhausted, I thought, not to be able even to consider any course which did not promise speedy removal from our current environment. And he in turn felt that I must be mentally exhausted from the stresses of day-to-day travel and simply wanted to stop regardless of our chances of escape from the Arctic Ocean.

In spite of our contrary views we didn't argue, a credit to Charlie's strength of character. He must have badly wanted to dissuade me from my course. He simply made his position very clear. If I decided we would at once begin our search for a suitable floe, so be it; but I should remember in the days ahead that it was my decision, not his.

Fair enough. But what, I asked him, would he do if the decision were his?

'I'd continue until mid-May,' he said, 'providing the temperature stays at minus twelve degrees or below. But I would keep a sharp watch and should a sudden rise in temperature and wind conditions become severe and indicate a breakup I would at once adopt the float mode.'

'But, Charlie,' I argued, 'adopting a float mode is not something you can do at once. There are, as we've seen for the last fifty miles, very few suitable floes to float on. I'd also like to carry on further before floating, but the choice is either stopping *after* the breakup signs have become apparent, as you suggest, in which case it's likely no suitable floe will be attainable and I'll be like the proverbial foolish virgin – wise but too late in the day – or I can risk being accused of overcaution and try to find a reasonably safe floe while it's still possible to get to one.' Charlie may have agreed that these were the only two alternatives, but he still did not go along with my decision to follow the latter. The next day I wrote out a radio message for the committee in London making clear my intention to seek a suitable floe. A few days later when they met to discuss my message Colonel Andrew Croft suggested it had been 'written by an exhausted man', that I should have travelled along 30 degrees east of the Greenwich Meridian and that it was my 'failure to follow this course that had resulted in the present predicament'. The official reply, however, assured 'fullest support and agreement with your decisions'. So I was free to stop when I felt it best; after thirty-eight years of behaving like a bull in a china shop and deriding the canny and the cautious, I'd decided to join their ranks just when it was the least popular thing to do. Clearly the popular course all round would be to bash on. But between us Ginnie and I had put twenty years of our lives into this expedition and we were at last on the home stretch. The current was now with us. My natural instinct to hurry on conflicted with an intuition at this point to be careful.

Of course the outcome of starting to float too soon from too far north might prove to be that we ended up well short of the ice edge and out of reach of the *Benji Bee* when the new winter ice formed in September or October. If so, the fingers would point squarely, and fairly, at me.

(In a later comment Charlie showed that he understood my

dilemma and the irony of it ... 'I was the one who wanted to get moving, to get it over with as soon as possible. And I know that Ran is like that too. Yet this time he was the one who decided to float. It must have been a hard decision for him to take. He alone decided it – everyone else wanted to keep moving.')

Of course, it was one thing to decide to float and quite another to locate a suitable floe. For a week I had simply been heading between 15 and 30 degrees to the east of due south whenever the terrain allowed.

By the evening of April 24 the wind had softened to ten knots. There was light snow. The temperature hovered at minus 15 degrees. That night, bathed in a pale pink light, we stumbled over an obstacle course of streambeds that bounced, sludge mires, cracked canals, the banks of which moved laterally in opposite directions, and wide plains of thin new ice ready to fragment at the least pressure from wind or current. A precarious place to travel over and one where at any time we were liable to enter a cul-de-sac from which our exit might crack away as fast as a portcullis can descend.

Many times that day, on reaching open water, we split up to check both ways for a crossing point. Meeting again in the middle we would report our findings and decide on a solution. If no natural bridge was available either way we would follow the obstacle for two or three miles until some narrow place gave us some chance to build a bridge. More often than not these narrow places moved apart as we worked and the chunks we flung in simply submerged and floated away.

I noticed pools, protected from the wind, where the water lay quite still, yet no new frazil ice platelets formed on their surface. The winter healing process appeared to have stopped.

Around midnight, crossing a deep ditch in which we had made

a clumsy ramp, Charlie touched his engine 'kill' button by mistake and came to a halt at the critical moment he needed momentum. His sledge quickly began to sink. I slung him a medium-size towrope, something both of us carried close at hand at all times, and in moments he clipped it onto his towbar. Then he pulled his starter rope, and with both our Skidoos straining and slithering, the sinking sledge came clear, water surging off its flanks . . .

That night, despite long hours of travel, we managed a mere five miles. We did get through to a medium-sized floe of first-year ice, the first viable airstrip I'd seen in some sixty miles, but it wasn't old enough ice for a floating home . . . At that camp Charlie woke up to feel the floe shuddering under the impact of an unseen collision.

The next night a wide lead delayed us for some hours at the far side of this floe, but we crossed it on sludge and, to my delight, landed on a good-sized second- or third-year floe dotted with well-rounded hummocks which, apart from two easy fracture lines, allowed us easy progress for four miles to the south. An odd-looking lead of two colours, grey and brown, put a stop to our advance. We patrolled far to the west and east but found no improvement. In fact the river of sludge seemed narrower where we first ran into it, at which point it was a hundred yards across.

Charlie described our attempt to cross the lead this way: 'It wasn't completely open. There was ice on it, bad ice, rather like sponge rubber. We tried to cross it. I gave Ran a bit of a start, then followed. But I saw him stop, swing around and turn back toward me and at the same time I felt a motion beneath me rather like being on a roller coaster. I looked back. The ice was actually breaking into waves, and I realised the same thing must be happening to Ran. He was trying to get off. When these two waves meet, mine and Ran's, I thought, I don't want to be on this lead. So I turned in a big sweep and managed to run up onto some firm ice, and Ran went past me and got back to the floe where we'd left it. We chatted about this.

We'd been on this sort of ice before but had *never* encountered such big liquid waves before . . .'

There being no way around or over the lead, we camped on the floe and for the next four days periodically walked out to check it with an axe. Once I reached some two-thirds of the way across before the surface was obviously too rotten to take my weight. However, I knew a Skidoo could cross where I could not, so I told Charlie all was well and we packed up. Back down on the lead the temperature was minus 24 degrees Centigrade, and I felt sure the nilas, though still of an odd tinge – part grey, part brown – would by now hold our weight.

Charlie watched carefully as I ran over the grey stuff and headed obliquely toward the weaker brown band in the centre. To my surprise my sledge cracked straight through the grey sludge where I had only an hour beforehand been happily walking. I swerved immediately back toward Charlie and the bank. We put up the tent again some ten yards from its last position. That night I reread the notes and records of Papanin's drift and noted in my diary: 'If we float from here at Papanin's rate, we will get to 80° North 8° West by August 15.'

I walked to the edge of the floe at the narrows and climbed up a twenty-foot-high ice boulder. A clear view to the south.

The ice looked as mouldy and riven with pools, canals and mush zones as the sixty miles to the north of the floe. Dark patches on the underneath of clouds showed where open lakes were reflected in the sky.

It was apparent even then that the overall conditions were those of an early breakup in spite of the continuing low temperatures – which could only have been due to the abnormally warm winter of 1981.

Five days after our arrival and first crossing attempt I managed to walk right across to the far side of the lead, but it still felt tacky;

the same sticky texture which, during colder weather, would firm up within twelve hours.

A day after my walk-over new patches of grey and pools of open water again cut up the lead. We might well have crossed that lead and perhaps several more like it but whether we would have ended up on a reasonably solid floe that would carry us as far south as we needed to go was quite another matter. Still, as the days passed, I began to accept that Providence had brought us a reasonable piece of real estate and that we must just make the best of it.

On April 30 Ginnie closed her base at Alert, said a sad farewell to the Canadians up at the camp who had been such kind friends for so long and joined Simon and the air crew for the flight over the Robeson Channel and the Greenland Ice Cap to Cape Nord.

While Ginnie began to set up her radio gear, Karl flew north over our beacon and gave us a position of 85°58′. After three weeks of poor visibility and strong northern winds we had floated some forty-four miles further south than could be expected under normal conditions. Such helpful winds never occurred again.

Ginnie's first call from Nord confirmed that the *Benji Bee* had set sail from Southampton for the North Sea. Also that the Norwegian ice team, having finally reached the North Pole, had decided to give up their attempt to cross the Arctic Ocean. A Twin Otter managed to evacuate them to Cape Nord – a military radio base manned by five Danes that served as the northern depot for the Syrius dog teams that patrolled the northeast coast of Greenland every summer – where Ginnie had a long talk with their leader Ragnor Thorseth, a strong individualist but a likeable man.

Karl told me we were lucky, since apart from a single floe four miles to our north, the last fifty miles were either new ice or fragmented floes. To our south, he said, the pack was already in a very bad state. Whether our own floe would safely weather the journey south he was not prepared to predict.

During the first week of May I sent a message to London via Ginnie saying that 'we must just rely on floating until the ship can get to us or as close as possible to us so we can close the gap, probably in July or August.'

My original plan to travel over mush ice, where Skidoos would be as useless as walking or boating, had been to use water shoes and tow light handsledges. But the 'shoes' we ended up with did not fill me with much confidence. Even crossing the Thames on a choppy day had proved awkward. So now that the prospect of travel on mush was only two or three months away I asked Ginnie to procure a couple of light canoes. She radioed this to Tony Preston and warned him that they must somehow reach Spitsbergen within three weeks, otherwise the surface of our floe would be too slushy for Karl to land on and one could not, certainly, drop canoes by parachute.

Ginnie was feeling lonely without Bothy and Tugaluk, both of whom had been flown out of Alert to spend six months' quarantine in England. Ginnie had grown isolated from Simon and the aircrew in Alert, largely due to her job, which kept her alone for long hours . . . 'Back at Alert,' Karl had written, 'we got ready to move the base camp to Cape Nord but I had quite a quarrel with Ginnie because I wanted to do it my way. After I calmed down, Ginnie and I had a talk together and I think we both hoped to do our best, but it never was the same again as before. I know she is very tired. Often she was on the radio watch for twenty-four hours a day, had lots of pressure from the office in London and the operation up north. I maybe could have spoken a little more frequently with her but, well, I am sometimes also very stubborn.'

On May 9 the *Benji Bee* arrived off Longyearbyen in Spitsbergen, the most important of a group of islands called Svalbard.

Norway has the sovereignty over these islands although there are two thousand resident Soviet citizens along with twelve thousand Norwegians. Both groups are concerned almost exclusively with coal mining, often from cliff faces a hundred feet or more above ground level. The islands were first discovered by the Dutch in 1596 and used for centuries as a base for summer whaling settlements. The Russians arrived in the early 1700s to collect the pelts of reindeer, Arctic fox and polar bear.

For three days the *Benji Bee* failed to penetrate the long fjord up which Longyearbyen is situated, but on May 12 she finally butted her way to the main quayside through fairly thick pack. Anton, remembering the Antarctic days, wrote: 'As always, everyone gathers on the bridge and, at each swipe at the ice, turns to their neighbour and quietly suggests how *they* would have done it.'

'We have been twelve days in this tent,' my diary recorded. 'Today I cricked my back and can now move only with difficulty. It's noisy around the floe ... Despite the continued whiteout the surface of the floe is becoming slushy. Signs of last year's melt pools, shiny green patches, are daily more in evidence as the actual snow-cover decreases. Radiation from solar rays is gnawing at our precarious floating platform and eating it from under us ...'

Wally Herbert wrote that 'There is no surface more unstable nor any desert more mistily lit than the Arctic ice pack in the month of May.'... On the night of May 11 and without a sound, our floe unzipped five hundred yards to the east of our tent, not, as far as I could determine, along the seam of an old ridge or any other fault-line. Our territory was suddenly a third smaller than it had been the previous day. Bending over the new canal I saw that the floe was some five or six feet deep.

Early in the morning, after three months without seeing a bird or an animal, a single faint cheep awoke me. Peeping out of the tent flap, once my eyes were accustomed to the glare, I spotted a snow bunting, the size of a robin redbreast, perched on a ration box. Somehow I felt full of hope and certainty. The bunting soon departed into the damp mist, God knew to where. It ignored the bit of army biscuit I threw out onto the snow ...

Hope was conditioned by back pains, which stayed with me for ten days, and I began to go for a daily walk to exercise ... who knew how long we would stay on the floe?

When Karl finally landed on the floe he brought us two eight-by-five-foot tents. In the centre of our floe an old weathered ridge provided a narrow mound four or five feet above the general level of the snow surface that I levelled out with an axe, and on it we tried to erect the tents end-to-end so we could sleep in one half and eat in the other. This didn't work because one part of the mound was lower than the other, so we left a small gap between them and agreed we would each live in one. I would keep the radio gear in mine and Charlie the cooking kit.

Quite apart from being together more or less nonstop for over six years, we had lived cheek by jowl in the same small tent in somewhat trying physical conditions during the previous ninety camps. Tempers could be expected to be frayed. We had one long discussion during which Charlie accused me of having a 'negative disposition'. I stoutly denied this. Then he said I was 'highly devious'. This I found more difficult to parry, since I knew he had heard both my mother and Ginnie accuse me of the same trait. I counterattacked that he was naturally argumentative, following a disagreement about the direction of northwest compared to the position of our tent door. That, I think, was the most risky conversation we held, and within minutes we were busily discussing the merits of putting snow around our tent skirting.

During the entire time of our Arctic Ocean journey we had no flareups, no bad atmospheres. Back in 1977 things had not been so trouble-free, and I am unsure why this was. Perhaps we had just gotten older and wiser. Perhaps we recognised each other's stress points so well that we knew almost subconsciously when to steer clear of a delicate topic.

(Charlie said about himself: 'People either like me or dislike me. I have a manner which can be abrupt and I am basically a shy person – although nobody believes that. I myself either like or dislike people, which is a terrible thing. I have tried to get myself over it. I don't like people who try to push themselves or push me too far. There are limits to what I can take but if someone is a pain I will listen quietly, I am good at listening.') Since the tents were cramped we could not stand up. The floors of axed ice were uneven and daily became more sodden with melt water – which made sitting impractical, so we lay in our sleeping bags to keep out the damp and cold. I raised mine above the melt water on ration boxes and a wooden board to help my wonky back.

Most days we were enveloped in sea fog, so there was no chance of Karl landing on the floe even though the surface in mid-May was still firm enough. One day the sun shone from a perfectly clear sky and we actually sunbathed beside our tents, but the weather soon changed.

On May 17 Ginnie reported that the *Benji Bee* was stuck firmly inside Longyearbyen Fjord because of a wind change. For a week of gloomy whiteout a south wind roared over the floes and pushed us back north toward the Pole. By the end of the month we were well behind my schedule. The wind also caused new fractures and a second major split right through the floe to our west that joined up with the eastern canal and effectively halved our original 'safe' area.

Each day I walked around the floe's perimeter. There were no signs of bears so I took only a pistol. Although I lost sight of the tents after a few yards there was no chance of getting lost because I could always retrace my own footprints, and anyway, there was now open water all around our floe, in places up to forty yards wide and edged with huge upright slabs.

I wrote in my diary: 'June 1. Tonight Charlie plucked three grey hairs out of my mop. "Poor old man," he said, "getting past it." I reminded him that he was a year older than me and that his bald patch had doubled in size since we left Greenwich ... He checked his diary and discovered this was the one-thousandth day of the expedition ... It seems as though we have been here for eons but strangely we aren't bored. A conversation about even the simplest matter seems to take forever. This evening there was a fifteen-minute discussion about faggots in Hyde Park and why a chunk of wood should become a generic term for gay gentlemen.'

Charlie's face and hands were by now black with carbon deposits from the cooker fumes. Our beards were wild and tangly and our clothes ragged, though the sores of our earlier travels were mostly healed up. Day by day my tent sank lower and became wetter and Charlie's grew more and more precarious as our mound melted slowly. The ice under the edges of his tent began to disperse, and items including his bed slipped downward and outward into the open ...

Late in May two members of the committee flew to Longyearbyen from Copenhagen and then, with Karl, flew out over the sea ice between Svalbard and our own area. Returning to London they warned the rest of the committee on June 2 that the chances of success this summer were remote.

As a result of the advice from his committee, our chairman said he was not prepared to take the risk of allowing us to continue floating and that he felt sufficiently strong about the matter to resign over it.

Ant Preston, David Mason and Paul Clark attended the meeting and all spoke strongly against evacuation of the ice team. George

Greenfield and Colonel Tommy Macpherson did not agree with evacuation and asked that their names be absent from any evacuation directive sent to the ice group.

The outcome of all this was the drafting of a message to me that set out the options considered and stated that the committee 'unanimously concluded and in complete agreement decided that the only prudent course is to use the expedition aircraft while still available to recover you and your equipment within the next fifteen days. The committee does not believe that such action would invalidate in these circumstances the aim of the expedition as opposed to later air/sea rescue by non-expedition means.'

What precipitated this decision, apart from the report from Spitsbergen, was that Ant Preston pointed out to the committee that in about two weeks' time the surface of our floe would be so sodden that neither the Twin Otter nor any other aircraft would be able to land. Nor would any helicopter have the range to reach us. Therefore, if there were any evacuation it would have to be within a fortnight. When Ginnie received the committee's radio message she immediately contacted Portishead Radio Station who in turn fixed up a phone patch with the committee. It became clear that the original message was intended to convey the point that the final responsibility was mine.

Only then did Ginnie contact me, and I sent a reply back assuring the committee of our determination to carry on with the original plan and agreeing to take sole responsibility for the consequences.

All members of the ship's crew and air crew were vociferous in supporting a continued float attempt . . . This was of course easier for them than for the committee who could not be guided by their emotions but had to make the life or death decisions, when necessary, on the facts available. This was not always easy since up-to-date information was often not available to them. 'It was inevitable,' Anton Bowring said, 'that members of the team in the field and their London advisers should, at that stage, have different views. In the field it was possible to study conditions at first hand. In London our advisers could only read reports of ice movements, temperature, wind speed and direction. Two wholly different sets of reactions developed. In the field there was optimism while in London there was growing concern. As it was, we knew, with time and perseverance, we had a good chance of taking the ship close to the ice team. We knew they must eventually leave the floe but only if we could give them a distance of less than twenty miles of alternating floe and open water to cross in what had always been recognised as the final and most dangerous stage of the whole journey . . .'

During the first week of June the surface of the strip became too sodden for Karl to land, but the canoes arrived in Longyearbyen and as Karl flew to collect them, Charlie looked about our floe for an alternative strip and found one starting twenty yards to the west of our camp and running for three hundred yards toward the open water along our floe-rim. Karl landed there on June 3, and we unloaded the two light aluminium canoes with paddles and wooden ski adaptations for manhauling over floes.

By mid-June this second strip was also water-logged and we were cut off. As far as evacuation by any means was concerned we were on our own . . . My diary:

> Strong westerlies on June 6 and average temperatures of minus 3 degrees Centigrade. Nonstop fog. Last night our floe was blown against its easterly neighbuor. Where they met, a fifteen-foot-high wall of fragments has reared up. It is thirty metres long, noisy and spews up new blocks as you watch. I am bailing out the water from my tent floor every other day now. Communications are awkward to Ginnie. She has a blackout to

England and to the ship, and the Danes can't raise anyone. I get through to Ginnie only with Morse and then only on 9002 megahertz on the brief upsurges of that frequency ... We have been on the floe fifty days and nights and not a bear. Excellent! On my evening walks it is too wet now to use snowshoes so I wear waders and take ski sticks for balance ... June 15. We are spending twenty-one hours a day in bed. After my walk I found my pulse rate was 125. Getting old. And we're going scatty too. Every time a passing seagull shrieks in the mist outside we both shout back, 'Hello, Herbert.' All types of gulls are Herbert to us, as we're not much good at identification without Ollie. I *think* our most common visitors are jaegers, kittiwakes and ivory gulls. No more snow buntings ...

One thing was certain – sooner or later we would run into polar bears. What did we know of them? Little more than was printed in our Canadian and Norwegian booklets:

The polar bear, near man's habitats, is not normally dangerous. It is inquisitive and often approaches man. It attacks when very hungry or when feeling threatened. At close quarters the bear may suddenly feel threatened. Therefore do not allow it to get close. The bear's behaviour will tell you whether it is being curious or aggressive. When attacking, the bear often gives a signal like an angry bull and gnashes its teeth. But an attack can take place without warning and will often come in great supple leaps. Aim at the chest or shoulders ... Large males weigh half a ton and measure eight feet long. Erect they tower to twelve feet tall. Yet for all their size they glide over the ice with a fluid grace. A grown male can easily snatch up a 200-pound ringed seal or kill a 500-pound bearded seal with a single blow of his 50-pound paw. A young bear has been clocked galloping along a road at 35 m.p.h. Bears can swim at 6 m.p.h. and travel nonstop for a hundred miles and more. Their sense of smell is legendary. Eskimos say they can smell a seal from 20 miles away. They hunt basking seals by creeping over the floes from hummock to hummock and even, the Eskimos say, push lumps of snow ahead of them to hide the giveaway blackness of their eyes and nose. Approaching via a lead, they can ease themselves into the water with scarcely a ripple and swim underwater or with just their noses and eyes on the surface.

I had seen bears at the London Zoo, and viewed from behind bars they had seemed cuddly, lovable animals. I had also heard unlovable stories. In 1977 a group of Austrians with children camped at Magdalene Fjord in Svalbard. A polar bear wandered into the camp and snuffled at a tent. The man inside unzipped the door flap and the bear seized him by the shoulder, dragged him down to the sea and onto an ice floe, where it slowly ate him in front of the other Austrians, who had no firearms.

I was in my sleeping bag one evening when I heard snuffling sounds beside my head, which was up against the single canvas skin of the tent. The noise went away in a moment or two but shortly afterward, close to the gap between our tents, a ration box began to make scraping noises. 'Ran?' Charlie called.

His voice came from inside his tent. He had not, after all, been snuffling around my tent nor scratching at ration boxes. My hackles rose at the implication. A third party! 'I think we have a visitor,' I called back.

Donning waders and jacket over my longjohns and vest I grabbed my camera and revolver and peeked with great care out of the door flap. All I could see was Charlie doing likewise. We emerged very slowly. Charlie was dressed precisely as I was and held his rifle at the ready. I thought of the *Goon Show.* I looked around his tent. 'Nothing there,' I said. He peered around mine. 'Nothing by yours either.' We relaxed. Then I saw Charlie stiffen. His eyeballs seemed to grow larger. 'Correction,' he said, 'we *do* have a visitor.' A large polar bear stepped out from behind my tent. Its front legs were across the guy ropes some three yards in front of us. It licked its lips and impressed me with the length of its long black tongue.

The official warning notes came back to me – 'Do not allow polar bears to get close.' There was not much we could do now about that. Without remembering to focus or adjust the shutter speed I took a couple of photographs, hoping not to irritate the great beast with the clicks.

The bear eyed us up and down for a while, then slowly walked away. Like a poodle that barks ferociously once a bulldog has left its immediate vicinity, I began to shout 'Shove off' at our visitor, when it was well clear of the camp.

Next time we were not so lucky. Again, the bear moved about by the tents for a while, with each of us thinking its movements were the other man working outside. When we twigged and emerged armed, the bear was close by Charlie's tent. We shouted at it and I fired my revolver over its head. All this was studiously ignored.

Charlie's .357 rifle was bolt-action and at the time he had only two bullets. I had plenty of ammunition, but my .44 Ruger magnum revolver had been ridiculed by some Canadians as inadequate for effectively stopping an aggressive bear. This had affected my confidence in it.

For ten minutes the bear padded about us in a half-circle between our ration boxes while we shouted abuse in three languages, clashed our pots together and sent revolver bullets past its ears.

If its motives were curiosity it should have been put off. After fifteen minutes Charlie lay down on a sledge and took careful aim. I stood behind and to one side and fired off a parachute illuminating flare. The rocket blasted by Charlie's head and struck the snow in front of the bear, fizzing brilliantly. This was also ignored, and the bear crouched down in the snow, facing us and waggling its rear end slightly in the manner of a cat stalking a mouse. It began to approach us.

'If it comes within thirty yards . . . over that snow dip . . . I'll fire one shot at it,' I whispered to Charlie.

The bear, a beautiful-looking creature, continued to advance and I aimed the pistol at one of its front legs. The shot went low, through the foreleg and probably close to the paw.

The bear stopped abruptly, as though stung by a bee, hesitated for a moment, then moved off sideways and away.

There was no sign of a limp but splashes of blood marked its spoor. We followed it to the end of the airstrip, where it jumped into the sea and swam across to another floe. There seemed little point in trying to kill it since it could only have a flesh wound and the salt water would probably prevent infection.

Nonetheless, I felt guilty. Would it have been better to have killed the bear? Perhaps I should not have shot it in the first place. A dead bear lying beside our camp or even floating in a nearby lead might attract other visitors.

How close should one allow a bear to get before shooting it? To my mind, no closer than you feel is the distance where, if it does charge, you can shoot it dead with your available firepower before it can reach you even though it may be half-dead when it does. A single raking scratch from the paw of a dying bear was, it seemed to me, to be avoided by individuals who couldn't be evacuated by any means and whose first-aid know-how would have been sneered at by the Battersea Girl Guides.

During the weeks that followed, a goodly number of bears wandered across our floe, and eighteen made it up close to our camp.

Each one seemed to react differently to our scare tactics. Their visits surely kept us from being bored. (So, too, did the shrinking nature of our floe.) Any noise outside the tents had us listening intently. There were many false alarms. One night I awoke in a gale. Among the wind noises I heard a rhythmic scuffling that I was certain must be a bear. It turned out to be the sound of my heartbeat against the canvas earflaps of my nightcap!

Whether or not the presence of nonexpedition members, the five friendly Danes, affected relations within our little base group at Cape Nord is difficult to say. Perhaps it was the strain about the uncertainty of our progress. Whatever the cause, morale was not high . . . 'Everyone at base is jumpy as it looks like we're not going to make it,' Simon wrote in his diary.

On June 22 Anton Bowring flew across with Karl from Longyearbyen to Nord and stayed there for a few days. 'Poor Ginnie,' Anton wrote, 'has all the worry and aggro from the committee and their decision. Apart from their recent advice to withdraw Ran, we now hear that they wish to have Ant Preston resign. Oh well, our patron Prince Charles had a seven-pound son last night, so there's some good news about. Ginnie and I chatted for a long while about the various problems and I am convinced she is a very honourable person who is struggling against her sensitivity and the inevitable flak that has been flying.'

Ginnie's sense of isolation from the others, making her feel they were hostile, sapped at her will. But perhaps above all it was the nonstop noise that unsettled her. Once in Antarctica I spent an hour on listening watch waiting for a call from another winter base. All I heard was a low whine, a fuzz of crackle and a high-pitched whistling that quickly deafened and irritated me. I turned the volume down, but this made it impossible to pick up the low dah-dit-dah of the Morse signals I was waiting for. Either you put up with the cacophony or, as likely as not, you missed the message when it came. For me an hour was more than enough.

After Antarctica Ollie had said: 'I don't think Ginnie enjoys it but she does it. Why? Perhaps, purely because of Ran's involvement. But then, as she's often said, she treats all three of us very much on an equal basis. Whether it is something I want – a mechanical thing, or Charlie for the field radios, or Ran for the general running of the expedition, she treats us all very much the same. But she has got an extremely difficult job.'

The underlying threat that weighed on all minds, whether on the floe, at Nord, at Spitsbergen, or back in London, was the Marginal Ice Zone. What would it do to our own floe? Where and when would we be drawn into its vortex? Could the *Benji Bee* somehow get through the heavy pack to reach us before we entered its danger zone? The only answer was wait and see. But nobody likes to sit and do nothing when they feel they should be up and active. This was especially true of the skipper and crew of the ship.

What we knew of the Marginal Ice Zone (MIZ) in Fram Strait was impressive and did not bode well for the continued existence of our floe after entering it. The MIZ is known to glaciologists as an ice pulverisation zone. It is perhaps useful to describe the natural forces involved, the most striking of which is the East Greenland current. This body of water sucks a tongue of heavy polar ice out of the Arctic Ocean through the gap between Greenland and Svalbard. Bearing in mind that over two million square miles of the Arctic Ocean are covered by pack ice and that one third of this load is disgorged every year through Fram Strait, it can be seen that the strait acts as a giant drainage plughole.

Five quite separate types of ice come together prior to entering the strait: paleocrystic ice, which is heavily deformed and originates from the zone just north of the coasts of Greenland and the Canadian Archipelago; old floes from the Eurasian side of the

Arctic basin; Siberian ice from the area north of the Soviet Arctic islands; Spitsbergen ice, which has drifted around the Spitsbergen coast from south to north; and locally formed thin ice. These different masses flow together with a great deal of turbulence and churning into the narrows of Fram Strait, where they're broken up and mixed irretrievably together through the massive forces extended individually on each fragment. By the time the East Greenland current reaches 78 degrees north within the strait it is rushing its chaotic burden of ice south at an incredible thirty kilometres per day. The speed of the surface current increases by as much as 100 per cent as it passes through the narrows of the strait.

Anton Bowring and skipper Les Davis were both keenly aware of our approaching danger and decided to try their luck without delay. On June 28 the *Benji Bee* reached the outer rim of the pack ice. Karl tried to help, but thick fog hid the ship and ice much of the time. Les did not set much store by the accuracy of the position-fixing instruments in the Twin Otter, but he had, of course, his own navigation aids and continued to push north.

Les had to keep in mind that damage to the ship within the pack could be fatal. Far more so here in the Arctic Ocean than down in those Antarctic waters, where he had successfully negotiated the pack of the Ross Sea. Antarctic pack is usually far younger and lighter.

There is little information available to skippers of merchant vessels such as the *Benji Bee* wishing to penetrate the pack ice of the Greenland Sea. Normally only icebreakers have business in the area, and they have no need to heed the warnings of the *Arctic Pilot*, which are:

> The Greenland sea pack ice is in general unnavigable. In the northern part the pack may be up to 6½ feet thick. As a result of pressure due to wind or current the pack ice may be hummocked to a height of 25 to 30 feet. Typical forms of damage to vessels

> by the ice are the breaking of propeller blades, rudders and steering gear, damage to stern and plating causing leaks in the forepart of the vessel and the crushing of the hull. Also due to ice pressure the buckling of plating and the tearing out of rivets causing seams to open and leak ... When the air temperature is below the freezing point of seawater, water from heavy seas will freeze to the superstructure. This frozen matter will rapidly increase with falling air and sea temperatures. This, in extreme cases, had led to capsize; most recently in 1955.

For two days we lost contact with the ship, but on July 2 we heard she had been forced back. After this failure Anton thought it best to stay close to the edge of the pack and so moor at the tiny coastal settlement of Ny Alesund rather than return to Longyearbyen. Les came around to agreeing with this, which left our various expedition components scattered about the Greenland Sea. Since I could not reliably communicate with Ny Alesund or Longyearbyen, Ginnie stayed with the five Danes at Nord while Simon and the aircrew lived in the little Portakabin at Longyearbyen Airport.

At her most northerly point the ship was a hundred and fifty miles away from our floe. During their brief essay our floe had hovered about, almost static, due to strong south winds.

Although I liked to think we would continue to head more or less due south at a uniform rate, there was good reason to fear, especially in July and August, that we might enter an anticyclonic area of lighter and more variable winds. Sea ice moves three ways. Each floe rotates when it can, each local wind and current has its own specific effect, and the whole ice pack is subject to gravitational movements and the earth's axis effect to which all oceans respond. But the main cause of the drift in the Arctic Ocean is the direct driving force of the wind.

Between 80 and 81 degrees north and east of the Greenwich Meridian in summer there is a dead spot where ice floes can go round and round much as though they were in a river eddy. It was this that I feared as much as, too far *west* of the Greenwich Meridian, being sucked by the local currents toward the east coast of Greenland itself.

By July 3 80 per cent of our floes were covered in slush from eighteen inches to seven feet deep in the bigger lakes. Our camp was surrounded by one such lake on three sides.

The floe was often jostled by surrounding bodies of ice. Sometimes we came off best. At others, new fractures opened up from the rim of our floe and ran inward. Some of these narrowed and disappeared as they neared the heart of it, others petered out in a few yards. After windy periods you could visit recently released touchpoints and watch fragments of ice as large as double-decker buses moving slowly over on their sides.

On July 10 I managed to shoot the sun at midday. We had been on the floe seventy days and were still north of 82 degrees. Preparing the theodolite for the noonday shot took me fifty minutes wading about slush pools. Since the tripod legs kept settling slowly it was necessary to readjust the theodolite's leveling bubbles after nearly every shot, and each readjustment took five or six minutes before the bubbles were reasonably level.

The sun was a faint white circle, too indistinct to be visible through a dark or even a blue prism, so I had to use the telescope with no protection against retina burns. From the noon latitude shot I also obtained my longitude because Time equals Longitude. On this occasion we were at 01°88′ East.

Although still some sixty miles to the north of the latitude to which a phenomenon called 'Whalers' Bay' can in freak summers extend open water, our floe was showing signs of disintegration. A complete chunk of some two acres had broken away from our southeast corner. Our northern neighbour had overridden one sector of the floe over a forty-yard front and rafted up to squash our ice into the sea. New ridgewalls rose up daily with a good deal of noise where we struck against our neighbours. Off our seaside edges, the wind whipped up wavelets on the great expanses of black water where regattas of broken fragments sailed by before the wind. All around us the ice was bare of snow-cover, so that weak seams now showed up clearly like varicose veins.

Day after day there was no sign of the sun, and the low-hung sky reflected the dark blotches of great expanses of open water to the south and north of our floating ice raft.

When in mid-July the Dundee University satellite managed a reasonable picture of our area and was shown to our committee there appeared to be a major loosening of the pack between our floe and the Greenland Sea. Captain Tom Woodfield, whose previous experience skippering British Antarctica Survey vessels included interpretation of satellite pictures of sea-ice conditions, looked at the Dundee picture and saw no reason why the ship couldn't get through that loose stuff! He offered to fly out to Longyearbyen and personally take the ship north into the pack.

However, satellite picture or no, by July 20 things were a touch unsettling on the floe. Hardly a day passed without a bear, sometimes two. We stood beside the tents waiting with guns, hoping that each new visitor was not a hungry one. For a while they came at us only from our remaining 'dry' side, but as this narrowed down they took to swimming across the melt-water lake that hemmed us in. They could swim almost silently despite their bulk.

The noise of the wind and the surf-sound of the sea were now joined by a gurgle of drainage, the melt pools having eaten away a network of sluices from pool to pool and finally off the floe into the sea. In the water all about us huge floating chunks jostled, and humpback whales, surfacing with much resonant splashing, swam back and forth, like dolphins except for their Moby Dick tails. Often they would snort like horses, and by night their unearthly music floated clear over the misty ice field: sometimes like the howl of werewolves; at others a soulful dirge.

We were now separated by some distance from other solid bodies of ice except when a strong wind blew us briefly against another, causing much peripheral damage. At times I would wake up suddenly and listen intently. Was it a bear close by or a new upheaval around the floe? For an answer more often than not came the plunging roar of many tons of ice breaking off our floe-rim, followed by echoes as miniature tidal waves broke against obstacles in the leads.

As we headed south into the maelstrom of Fram Strait, the floe began to gyrate like scum descending toward a plughole.

The sun hovered imperceptibly lower each day, and by nights now the surface of the melt pools began to freeze.

Captain Tom Woodfield arrived in Longyearbyen to initial hostility. The skipper and crew had tried to reach us and failed but they saw no reason why some ice maestro should be brought in from outside even if he was a member of our committee and one of the board who had three years previously selected most of the crew. But Tom Woodfield was no fool. He brought a peace offering of whisky, accepted the flak that came his way and openly discussed the situation.

'Les and Tom had a real ding-dong battle,' Anton Bowring reported, 'and both threatened to leave. But they resolved things and now have a working relationship although there is an uncomfortable atmosphere that everyone feels.' Later after they had set sail for the north: '0730, we are shuddering violently. Tom at the controls and hurling the ship at six- to seven-foot-thick floes, which are breaking without too much difficulty. But the ice is more solid and further to the south than on our last attempt. Evening: We are stuck solid at 82°07′ North 01.20° East, eighty-two miles south of Ran. One or two people went overboard by rope ladder and Jimmy Young spotted a cracked weld in the stern. Ken and Howard have gone over with welding kit to fix it.' . . .

The crew had set out with much excitement. It seemed as though, with Tom's success at crashing through medium pack, nothing would stop the *Benji Bee*. Bryn Campbell had arrived from London and Mike Hoover, the leader of our film crew, had flown out from the U.S. to be in at the kill. But the sea temperature dropped 5 degrees in twenty-four hours and the wind moved around to the south. The pack began to tighten up dangerously, and after four days battling the floes, the ship reluctantly turned away, having by some ten miles not even reached the most northerly point of her earlier attempt. Morale was very low. A major letdown.

Back in Spitsbergen Mike Hoover returned to the U.S. and Tom Woodfield went back to London, where he told the committee: 'There's nothing to be done but wait for the ice to ease off.'

During the last week of July there were seven bears in our camp in five days. We could not hear them approach because of a strong south wind that prevailed and the roar of the surf that drowned out all sound but the crash of segments breaking from our floe-rim. All through the night of July 28 I lay awake listening to the rumbling explosions from the sea, as though elephants were bellyflopping off skyscrapers. In reality, it was the depletion of great chunks from the western side of our floe. We were daily decreasing in size.

On the 29th Charlie warned me that the bare seams in the floe between our lavatory shelter and the tents were widening, as were those between his tent and the nearest part of the melt lake. Any thoughts we might have nursed of getting off the floe were dampened by Karl. On July 30 he flew over Fram Strait in patchy weather and caught but brief glimpses of the surface. He did not like what he saw … 'Ran and I agreed that he should not leave the floe unless the ship was within twenty miles because I could see from the air that the going will be tough and hazardous. It would have been sad and chilling to have an accident so close to our victory like it turns out with some climbing expeditions. They have the victory so close to their hands, then they make a mistake because they can't wait to grab it and without thinking make a mistake and pay with their lives …'

At noon that day I caught brief glimpses of the sun, sufficient to plot our position as 80°56.2′ north, 01°39′ west. Ginnie relayed this to Les Davis and Anton. The wind about the ship began to veer to the north after days of southerlies.

All on board the *Benji Bee* knew the state of our floe and realised that our entry into the MIZ was imminent. Les decided to sail at once to the edge of the pack, and at the first sign of its loosening up to fight north toward us. So on the first day of August, our seventh month on the sea ice, the *Benji Bee* slipped into the low mist.

Shortly before, Ginnie, certain at last that she could communicate with our floe from the ship or Longyearbyen, had left Cape Nord and the Danes. Now she too was on board and only Simon manned the little Portakabin. 'It is wild and wet and windy. I have lashed the hut down with wires against the violent gales,' he wrote in his diary.

Late in the evening of August 1, I heard Anton speaking intermittently to Simon. The ship was forty-nine miles from our last reported position and moving slowly through medium pack and thick fog.

Progress between the larger floes was hampered by wedges of ice small enough to be pushed under the bows but too tough to break. They had to be nudged aside by the bows and swept past by the draw of water from the propeller, a frustrating business that took considerable skill from the bridge.

In fits and starts, with many detours, the *Benji Bee* moved through an ever-changing and ill-lit icescape, occasionally startling seals and bears and Menke whales and gradually gnawing away at the edges of the floes that barred her progress.

'The shuddering and grinding of the hull,' wrote Anton, 'is a constant accompaniment. The lurch as we strike each new floe often throws us off our feet.'

Many of the crew spent long hours on deck in foul-weather gear peering into the gloom and clinging to the railings. A cautious and expectant mood of optimism slowly surfaced. 'All around us,' wrote Anton, 'we see leads between the floes filled with soft porridge which could neither be walked on nor paddled through. I am convinced that the decision to float was the right one. To have moved off the floe prematurely would have been extremely rash.'

Late on the afternoon of August 2 the fog rolled away from the *Benji Bee* and Karl took off from Longyearbyen at once. After circling for a while he began to talk Les Davis through the labyrinth of broken floes and, with great skill, guided the ship to a jagged twelve-mile lead heading northwest toward our floe.

At that time the crew noticed the ominous signs of a wind change, and within the hour a southerly breeze picked up. Any stronger and the pack would begin to close about the ship, now deep inside the MIZ, too deep to escape if the floes concentrated.

Throughout the long night the whole crew willed the ship north, yard by yard, and despite much battering and many a retreat, the *Benji Bee* squeezed through.

At 9:00 A.M. on the third I made contact with Ginnie. She sounded tired but excited.

'We're seventeen miles north of your last reported position and jammed solid.'

I shouted the news to Charlie. We must be ready to leave as soon as possible. Both of us hoped that somehow the *Benji Bee* would smash a way through right up to us. Even half a mile of travel from our floe might prove disastrous. Everything was in motion about us, great floating blocks colliding in the channels and suspended nets of porridge-ice marauding the open sea lane.

At noon I shot the sun and sent our position to Anton: 80°43.8′ north, 01°00′ west. The ship was to our southeast. To reach it we had to move over the sodden surface of the racing pack for some twelve nautical miles and cross the Greenwich Meridian en route.

At 2:00 P.M. on our ninety-ninth day adrift we stowed three hundred pounds of gear, rations and our glaciological records into the aluminium canoes and trudged away from the two bedraggled tents.

I had a compass bearing to the ship at the time we set out – the longer we took to reach her the more this would alter. The wind was a stiff twelve knots as we paddled across the first choppy land.

The wooden ski attachments for hauling the heavily laden canoes over floes broke off within the first hour. After that we simply dragged the naked hulls over the rough ice and prayed they would not wear through.

Arriving at each successive pool, river and lake we lowered the canoes off the crumbling ice banks with care.

The strain of the haul was considerable. Charlie was nearly sick with the effort. We'd lain for so long in our bags, twenty-one hours out of twenty-four, with little or no exercise.

Every so often I filled my water bottle from a melt pool and we both drank deeply.

At one stage a swamp of porridge and floating fragments barred our way. Then once into it we were committed. That hour we progressed only four hundred yards. But normally, spotting such marsh zones well ahead by clambering up the high ridges, I took long circuitous detours to avoid their hazards.

We simply waded through melt pools several feet deep, hauling on our two ropes . . . Trying to negotiate a spinning mass of ice islands in a wide lake, I looked back to check that Charlie was following, just in time to see two high blocks crunch together. The impact sent a surge of water after my canoe. It was only luck that Charlie had not yet entered the moving corridor and so avoided a certain flattening.

Our hands and feet were wet and numb, but at 7:00 P.M., climbing a low ridge to scout ahead, I saw two matchsticks on the broken horizon along the line of my bearing. I blinked and they were gone. Then I saw them again – the distant masts of the *Benji Bee*.

I cannot describe the joy of that second. I found tears smarting at my eyes and I yelled to Charlie. He was out of earshot, but I waved like a madman and he must have known. I think that was the single most wonderful and satisfying moment of my life. Until then I could never bring myself to accept that success was within our reach. But now I knew, and I literally felt the strength of ten men in my veins. I knelt down on that little ridge and thanked God.

For three hours we heaved and tugged, paddled and sweated. Sometimes we lost sight of her briefly but always, when again we saw her, she was a little bit bigger.

Shortly before midnight on August 3, Jimmy Young, up in the crow's nest with binoculars, shouted down to the bridge, '*I see them . . . I see them.*'

On the bridge, gazing into the low wan sun, one by one the crew identified among the heaving mass of whiteness the two dark figures that they had dropped off so long ago at the mouth of the Yukon River on the far side of the Arctic Ocean.

Down below decks a tired Kiwi, John Parsloe, was just turning in to his bunk when Terry, the bosun, rushed down the gangway shouting, 'Up, up! The boys are home.'

At 0014 hours on August 4 at 80°31′ north, 00°59′ west, we climbed on board. The circle was complete.

Each one of us retained the image of that moment on our ship among the floes. We would never forget. At that moment we shared something no one could take from us, a warm sense of comradeship among us all, Swiss and American, Indian and South African, British, Irish and New Zealander.

Ginnie was standing by a cargo hatch. Between us we had spent twenty years of our lives to reach this point. I watched her small, tired face begin to relax. She smiled and I knew what she was thinking.

Our impossible dream had come true.

Afterword

Once on board the ship I radioed Longyearbyen and spoke to our base there. Karl wrote: 'They are arrived! In my joy I could have made a somersault. Right away I woke up Simon and Gerry and with no hesitation went to my bag for my bottle of champagne that I carried over the whole North Pole route for this special occasion. I couldn't sleep anymore and I paced the hut up and down and it felt so good because of the released pressures I had carried with me for the last seven months.'

For twelve days the *Benji Bee* strained to escape the pack ice. But she was jammed solid. By good fortune the angles of the two floes that enclosed her accepted the transverse pressure and protected her from the enormous internal forces of the pack.

Karl tried to help when visibility allowed, but there was nothing he could do . . . 'It looked to me like some washing in a washing machine. You never had the same conditions for more than half an hour,' he said.

On August 15 the wind finally changed and the *Benji Bee* was little by little released from the pack.

We called at Longyearbyen Fjord to collect the base cargo and say good-bye to the aircrew, who would now begin their flight back to Britain.

Karl wrote: 'As the ship arrived, Ran gave me a good handshake and Ginnie gave me a big hug and then I knew I did something right and I could almost cry. She is a great hardworking girl. So many times over the months I thought she would break down in tears but she never showed any signs of it. It sure has been an experience in a lifetime. I have met a lot of great people and I won't forget them. All the hardship is now over for us all.'

The so-called real world impinged upon ours with local drama. First, two drunken Norwegian fishermen came aboard and broke into the cabin of the Buzzards, who had no clothes on since they were asleep. Annie screamed and Ginnie saw them off with her most killing expression. But they were soon back and this time were surrounded by Les Davis from Carlisle, Cyrus from Bombay and the Kiwi, Jimmy Young, who, under provocation, threw them down the stairway and were about to become more violent when I arrived and tried to cool things down, bearing in mind that there were but twenty Transglobers and over fifty Norwegian fishermen moored alongside.

That afternoon two Polish scientists with a portable radio escaped from the inland base where they were working with the Russians and sent a message to the Norwegians. The Russians monitored the signal. Norwegian and Russian helicopters rushed to the escapers' location. The Norwegians arrived first, and the Poles were given asylum. Three years away from it all was definitely coming to an end. Next day, the cargo lashed in the hold, we moved away from the wooden jetty ... our last leavetaking after three years of departures from remote harbours and ports. One of those who saw us off was Robin Buzza, the local expatriate who had stoutly defended us against the allegations of taking prostitutes to the Pole. He later wrote to me: 'I felt sad on the day your band of global adventurers left Longyearbyen for the last time. Transglobe has sustained me for many months and I was only too glad to have been of assistance to a really great expedition. When the *Benjamin*

Bowring sailed out of the fjord last week, a part of me went with her.'

From the lonely islands of Svalbard we sailed south through the Greenland Sea and finally the North Sea until the beacons of fire from the oilfields and the orange night sky of Aberdeen passed us by.

Cyrus noted with pride that the *Benji Bee* averaged 10¼ knots on the journey home, well above her normal best. 'She always does that,' he said, 'puts on a bit of speed when she's coming into port for a rest. All ships have special characters you can't explain, and the older they are, the more they show it. The *Benji Bee* is very special.'

Cyrus, perhaps more than most, was going to feel the wrench when he had to leave the ship. He would not get his job back with the P&O Line and would not be the only one to join the ranks of the unemployed, which since we first left Britain had increased to over three million.

On August 29 His Royal Highness Prince Charles joined us on the River Thames and brought the ship back to our start-point, Greenwich, almost three years to the day since we had set out. The Thames sparkled with a stiff breeze and the warmth of a lovely summer's day. Colourful bunting and ten thousand cheering people lined the banks.

The journey was over.

Was the expedition worthwhile? Was it worth so much effort, so much risk and the peripheral involvement of so many people? I've no single answer to this, though I've tried to suggest a few positive ones. And of course some humans will always respond to the old call of 'Because it's there,' whether *it* happens to be Mount Everest, the moon or the polar axis of the world.

Whether or not Transglobe was any sort of inspiration to people whose lives are necessarily full of the prosaics of making a living is hard to say. But the retired and the young by the thousands have taken the trouble to write to us from all over the world. The Transglobe Club attracted members from eleven different countries, the oldest member being ninety-eight years old and the youngest eight. We have books of watercolours from children showing the way they imagined our experiences. Many raised money for us without being asked.

Our team has melted away, of course. Charlie is at work attempting to raise sponsorship for a boat to enter for the 1985 Round the World Yacht Race. Gerry has signed on as an administrator with the British Antarctic Survey. Giles is back with Britannia Airways, and Karl with Bradley Air Services in the Arctic. The Buzzards now live and work at Mount Maunganui in New Zealand, Eddie Pike and Les Davis are back in the Merchant Navy, and Simon is married and settled in Australia. Terry Kenchington works in his hometown of Bath. Anton Bowring will be organising the occasional reunion, so perhaps we will all meet again one day . . . to remember how it was.

A few months after our return, Ken Cameron purchased the *Benji Bee* from the Bowring Steamship Company. On a cold day in January 1983, he held a renaming ceremony at a deserted quay in the London docks. The ship looked ghostlike. Ken only employed Cyrus and Dave Hicks; no one lived on board. They had reluctantly repainted the ship. No longer did the words 'BENJAMIN BOWRING' and 'TRANSGLOBE' stand out proudly from her familiar hull. Ginnie, with help from Dave Hicks, Ollie and Charlie, smashed a champagne bottle against the bow and renamed her *Arctic Gael*. The *Benji Bee,* remaining link of our memories, was no more.

As for myself, I'm not certain of the future, but I will try to keep fit, for one day Ginnie may come up with another idea.

Appendix A

Involvement

This book focuses more on the 'land travelers' and of necessity omits some of the experiences of other members of the team. In 1984 a book by Antony Bowring will be published telling the full story of the voyage of the M.V. *Benjamin Bowring*.

It is of interest that, during the course of the expedition:

H.R.H. The Prince of Wales, our patron, married Lady Diana Spencer and Prince William was born.

Antony Bowring married our ship's cook Jill MacNicol, and Virginia (Mini Ginnie) was born.

Charlie Burton married Twink Petts in Sydney. They had met in England before we left.

Ken Cameron married Janet Cox of our London office. Simon Grimes married Shane Tarlington who organized our trade show in Sydney, where they now live. Mick Hart married Rose Mabey. Sir Edmund Irving, our chairman, married Elsa. Terry Kenchington married Pam.

Elizabeth Martin of our London office, married to Peter Martin of our aircraft committee, had a daughter, Anna. David Mason married Monique and Natalie, Ginnie's goddaughter, was born.

Geoffrey Newman married Mary Gibbs. Gerry Nicholson married Katharine.

David Peck married Stella whom he met in Vancouver where they now live.

Anthony Preston, married to Mandy, had two sons, Alexander and Sam.
Martin Weymouth married Annie Stanley whom he met in New Zealand. Annie then joined the ship's crew as assistant cook.

In all there were sixteen members of the expedition who were married, thirteen marriages, and six babies were born.

The Patron of the Expedition
His Royal Highness The Prince of Wales K.G., K.T., P.C., G.C.B.

The Executive Committee/Board of Directors

CHAIRMAN:
*Rear Admiral Sir Edmund Irving K.B.E.,C.B. (1978–1983)
*Mr Peter Bowring (1983–)

MEMBERS:
*Sir Campbell Adamson, Abbey National Building Society
Mr George Capon, Touche Ross & Co.
*Colonel N.A.C. Croft D.S.O., O.B.E., Arctic Adviser
*Sir Alexander Durie C.B.E., Financial Adviser
*Sir Ranulph Fiennes Bt, Expedition Leader
*Sir Vivian Fuchs F.R.S., Scientific/Antarctic Adviser
*Mr Simon Gault LLB., Marine Lawyer
*Mr George Greenfield, John Farquharson Ltd
Mr Tim Halford, Occidental International Oil Inc.
Mr Anthony Macaulay, Herbert Smith & Co.
*Colonel R.T.S. Macpherson C.B.E., M.C., T.D., Mallinson Denny Ltd
*Mr Peter Martin, Aviation Lawyer
Mr Jim Peevey, Mobil Oil Company Ltd
Captain C.T. Pitt O.B.E., C.T. Bowring & Co. Ltd
Mr Alan Tritton (Honorary Treasurer), Barclays Bank Ltd
Mr Peter Windeler, The Chubb Group of Companies
Captain T.E. Woodfield O.B.E., Corporation of Trinity House
*Brigadier W.M. Wingate-Gray O.B.E., M.C., Expedition Commander

HONORARY AUDITORS:
Touche Ross & Co. (Formerly Mann Judd Ltd)

HONORARY SOLICITORS:
Herbert Smith & Co.

*denotes director of Transglobe Expedition Ltd

Export Promotion Advisory Committee

CHAIRMAN:
The Rt. Hon The Lord Hayter K.C.V.O., C.B.E. (1978–1981)
Mr Jim Peevey (1981–1983)

MEMBERS:
Sir Campbell Adamson, Abbey National Building Society
Mr John Barker, British Linen Bank
Mr Eddie Carey, Racal Group Services
Colonel S.W. Chant-Semphill O.B.E., M.C., C.T. Bowring & Co.
Mr John Cornwell, The Observer
Mrs Carol Dear, C.T. Bowring & Co.
Mr Colin Eales, Transglobe P.R.O.
Mr P. Evans British, Overseas Trade Board
Sir Campbell Fraser, Dunlop Ltd
Mr George Greenfield, John Farquharson Ltd
Mr Eddie Hawkins, Marlow Ropes Ltd
Rear Admiral Sir Edmund Irving, Executive Committee Chairman
Mr D. James, Central Office of Information
Commander Mike Lethbridge, Tri-Wall Containers Ltd
Colonel R.T.S. Macpherson, Mallinson-Denny Ltd
Mr S.J.D. Nowson, London Chamber of Commerce & Industry
Mr Reg Pilgrim, The Chubb Group of Companies
Mr Derek Price, John West Foods Ltd
Mr P. Probert, British Overseas Trade Board
Miss Pru Raper, Dunlop Press Office
Mr Robin Sandberg, Thornton Sandberg, Brockbank Ltd
Mr G.M. Ward, James Neill Holdings Ltd
Mr Peter Windeler, The Chubb Group of Companies

The Aircraft Committee

CHAIRMAN:
Mr Peter Windeler (1978–1981), The Chubb Group of Companies
Mr Peter Martin (1981–1983), Transglobe Aviation Lawyer

MEMBERS:
Mr Bill Bryce, Brymon Airways
Mr Jack Clifton, Civil Aviation Authority
Sqn Ldr Bert Conchie Royal Air Force
Mr Peter Cook, Royal Aircraft Establishment
Mr C. Cresswell, Civil Aviation Authority
Mr Trevor Davies, Royal Aircraft Establishment
Mr Richard Griffiths, Air Associates Ltd
Mr Bill Hibbert, Royal Aircraft Establishment
Captain Giles Kershaw, T.G.E. Antarctic Pilot
Mr Tony Medniuk, C.T. Bowring & Co. Ltd
Mr Jim Peevey, Mobil Oil Company Ltd
Mr Reg Pilgrim, The Chubb Group of Companies
Mr Gordon Swain, The Chubb Group of Companies

The Ship Committee

CHAIRMAN:
Captain T.E. Woodfield O.B.E. (1978–1982)
Captain C.T. Pitt O.B.E. (1982–1983)

MEMBERS:
Mr Peter Bowring, C.T. Bowring & Co.
Mr Simon Gault LLB., Marine Lawyer
Rear Admiral Sir Edmund Irving, Executive Committee Chairman
Mr Jim Peevey, Mobil Oil Company Ltd
Mr Jack Smith, Westralian Farmers Ltd
Mr Chris Mercer, Westralian Farmers Ltd

Public Relations Committee

CHAIRMAN:
Colonel S.W. Chant-Semphill O.B.E., M.C.

MEMBERS:
Mr Eddie Carey, Racal Group Services
Mrs Carol Dear, C.T. Bowring & Co. Ltd
Mr Colin Eales, Transglobe P.R.O.
Mr George Greenfield, John Farquharson Ltd
Mr Tim Halford, Occidental International Oil Inc.
Mr Jim Peevey, Mobil Oil Company Inc.
Miss Pru Raper, Dunlop Press Office
Mr Peter Windeler, The Chubb Group of Companies

Appeals/Merchandising Committee

CHAIRMAN:
Rear Admiral Sir Edmund Irving K.B.E., C.B.

MEMBERS:
Sir Campbell Adamson, Abbey National Building Society
Mr John Barker, British Linen Bank
Mr Peter Bowring, C.T. Bowring & Co. Ltd
Mr George Capon, Touche Ross & Co.
Sir Alexander Durie C.B.E., Financial Adviser
Mr George Greenfield, John Farquharson Ltd
Mr Anthony Macauley, Herbert Smith & Co.
Colonel R.T.S. Macpherson C.B.E., M.C., T.D., Mallinson Denny Ltd
Mr Allan Tritton (Honorary Treasurer), Barclays Bank Ltd
Dr Paul Clark, Transglobe Merchandise Organiser

All committee members donated considerable time and advice to Transglobe.

I would like to express my sincere gratitude to all members of the committees and where relevant to their employees, who spent considerable time and gave invaluable advice to the Transglobe Expedition.

. Expedition Team

Ice Group

Ranulph Fiennes, Expedition leader/ Navigator/Photographer

Charles R. Burton, Cook/Mechanic/Radio operator

Oliver W.N. Shepard (until 1981), Mechanic/Medic/Meteorologist/ Radio operator

Geoffrey Newman (until 1979), Radio operator/Meteorologist

Reserves

David Mason

Anthony Birbeck (who also spent one year in Antarctica base)

Base Camp

Virginia Fiennes, Communications/Base commander

Simon Grimes, Mechanic/Cook

Laurence Howell, Radio operator at Tanquary Fjord

Mary Gibbs (until 1979), Cook/Medic/Mechanic

U.K. Radio Base

Jack Willies, R.A.E. Cove Radio Station

Graham Standing, R.A.E. Cove Radio Station

Crew Of The Twin Otter Aircraft

Captain Giles Kershaw, Pilot for Antarctic and Northwest Passage

Karl Zberg from Switzerland, Pilot for Arctic Ocean

Sergeant Gerrard Nicholson REME, Aircraft engineer full-time

Full-Time Crew Of M.V. Benjamin Bowring

Antony Bowring, Marine coordinator, 33 years old. Joined Merchant Navy in 1969 but left to become mate on a number of small vessels which took him to many countries from Bangladesh to Greenland. From Suffolk.

Cyrus Balaporia, Chief officer, 33 years old. Joined British India Steam Navigation Company in 1970 (later P&O Line). He qualified as master in 1976. From Bombay, India.

Kenneth Cameron, Chief engineer, 30 years old. After three years at an engineering college he joined Denholm Ship Management in 1975. From Fort William, Scotland.

Howard Willson, Third engineer, 30 years old. After school was in Royal Navy working with submarines. In 1976 joined Shaw Saville. From Isle of Grain, London.

Terry Kenchington, Bosun, 33 years old. Joined Merchant Navy in 1966 initially on R.M.S. *Queen Elizabeth*. From Wiltshire.

Edward Pike, Carpenter, 44 years old. Joined Merchant Navy in 1956 and worked many years with Bowring Steamship Company. From Essex.

David Hicks, Steward, 40 years old. Many jobs but essentially a professional photographer. From Kent.

Martin Weymouth, A.B., 26 years old. Joined Merchant Navy in 1973 and experienced one previous journey to Antarctic waters. From Leighton Buzzard.

Also serving with the ship in various capacities, and some for more than two years, were:

Poul Andersson, Denmark
Jill Bowring, Sussex
Paul Clark, U.S.A.
Nigel Cox, Eire
Les Davis, Cumbria
Mick Hart, Suffolk
Geoffrey Lee, New Zealand
Edwyn Martin, Somerset
Dr Christopher McQuaid, Northern Ireland
John Parsloe, New Zealand
David Peck, Suffolk
Peter Polley, Canada
Commander David Ramsay, Buckinghamshire
Leslie Rickett, South Africa
Annie Stanley, New Zealand
Admiral Otto Steiner, Isle of Wight
Nicholas Wade, Surrey
Stuart Weldon, London

Mark Williams, New Zealand
James Young, New Zealand

There were a few other individuals for short periods when the ship was on charter.

London H.Q. Staff

Mr Anthony Preston, Expedition secretary/Administration
Miss Janet Cox, Personal assistant to Anthony Preston
Mrs Joan Cox, Transglobe Club secretary and General assistant
Mr Colin Eales, Public relations officer
Miss Susan Klugman, Secretary/Export promotion
Mrs Elizabeth Martin, Assistant secretary to Anthony Preston
Mr David Mason, Logistics coordinator in London and polar zones
Mr Roger Tench, Photographic library / General assistant
Mr Paul Clark, Merchandising Officer
Miss Margaret Davidson, General assistant
Mrs Muriel Dunton, General assistant
Mr George Doherty, Barclays Bank representative
Mr Norman Williams, Barclays Bank representative
Mr Roger Elliston, Touche Ross & Co. (for annual audit)
Mr Bob Hampton, Touche Ross & Co. (for annual audit)
Mr Arthur Hogan-Fleming, Touche Ross & Co. (for annual audit)

Considerable secretarial/administrative help prior to departure:

Miss Jan Fraser
Miss Jane Morgan
Miss Gay Preston
Mrs. Dorothy Royle
Miss Annie Seymour
Mrs Sally Travers-Healy

Outline Details of the M.V. *Benjamin Bowring*

Built by: Aalborg Vaerft A/S of Esbsjerg in 1952

Originally owned by: J. Lauritzen of Copenhagen

Engined by: A/S Burmeister and Wain. Six cylinders. Bore 350 mm. Stroke 620 mm.

Reg. output 1560 IPH. Contract output 1200 LPH

Dimensions: Length, 212 feet. Breadth, 36 feet. Mean fully laden draft 19 feet 8 inches.

Height of masts: 77 feet

Gross tonnage: 1244 tons

Speed: 11 knots (average 9 knots)

Appendix B

I would like to thank the following companies and individuals in the United States for their support and advice which made the expedition possible. I sincerely apologise to any whose names have been inadvertently omitted.

Arbor House Publishing, New York.
Armand Hammer Productions Inc., Los Angeles, Ca.
Bird Electronics Corp., Ohio
The Coleman Co. Inc., Wichita, Kansas
Disneyland, Los Angeles, Ca.
The Explorers Club of New York
Hendersons & Co., South Wilmington, Ca.
International Longshoreman's and Warehousemen's Union, Local 13, Wilmington, Ca.
Jaeger International Shop, Beverly Hills, Ca.
Los Angeles City Council, Los Angeles, Ca.
Port of Los Angeles, Los Angeles, Ca.
The Mara Corporation, Long Beach, Ca.
Marsh and McLennan Companies, New York
Marsh and McLennan Inc., Los Angeles, Ca.
William Mercer Inc., Santa Ana, Ca.
Mikuni American Corporation, North Ridge, Ca.
Mobil Oil Inc., New York
M. Morgan Stanley & Co. Inc., New York
The National Science Foundation, Washington, D.C.
The Navidyne Corporation, Newport News, Virginia
Occidental International Corporation, Washington, D.C.

Occidental Petroleum Corporation, Los Angeles, Ca.
Outboard Marine Corporation, Waukegan, Illinois
Pacific Telephone, Pasadena, Ca.
Poppy Food Company, Los Angeles, Ca.
Rolls Royce of Beverly Hills, Ca.
Rotunda Inc., Los Angeles, Ca.
San Pedro Scout Troop 210, San Pedro, Ca.
Security Pacific National Bank, Los Angeles, Ca.
Star Kist Foods Inc., Van Nuys, Ca.
Systron Donner Inc., Concorde, Ca.
Tecumseh Products Co., Tecumseh, Michigan
Toshiba Corporation, Ca.
United States Department of Commerce, National Oceanographic and Atmospheric Administration, Rockville, Md.
Unitor Ship's Service Inc., Long Beach, Ca.
VDO Argo Instruments, Winchester, Virginia
Wisdom Imports Inc., Irvine, Ca.
Wrather Hotels (Queen Mary) Long Beach, Ca.

I would also like to express our sincere gratitude to Marsh and McLennan Group of Companies who owned the ship M.V. *Benjamin Bowring* and Mobil Oil Inc. who provided all the fuels for the ship, aircraft, etc. My special thanks to everyone in these two companies, in New York and all over the world, who did so much for the expedition.

Reg Abbis
Eric Anderson
W.J. AuCoin
Major Joe AuCoin
Gerry Austin
Bebe Axelrod
Joe Baird
Steve Barnard
John Bianchi
Kay and Roger Bierly
'Jumper' Bitters
John Bocstoce
Richard Bona
Greg La Brache
Sandra Bradley
Commander John Brandon
Art Brown
Bob & Celia Brown & Family
David Budge
Don Burgess
George Castle
Ernie Chase
Eric Chiang
Col. Church-Watkins

Nick Clapp
Norm Corlew
Pat Cornelius
Otto Dedrick
Col. J.H.V. Dicks
Caroline Ferriday
Don Fine
Gordon Finlayson
Al Fowler
Kennedy Galpin
Gary Gillenwater
Bob Greenham
Peter Haggland
Armand Hammer
Betsy Hammett
Bill Harper
Andy Heiberg
Tom Hill
Mike Hoover
Chuck Huss
Greg Jensen
Beverly Johnson
Jim Joiner
Mary Jones
Mike Kilborn
Bob Kleist
Admiral Knapp
William Kronick (Uncle Bill)
Tim Leistico
Ken Locker
Taylor Maiser
Admiral Manning
Fred Manse
William McCann
Sgt McClamrock
McMurdo Base Commander and all at McMurdo Base between January–March 1981
Ken Mendes
Ken Moulton
Gary Moskowitz
'Murph' Murphy
Steven Oates
Willie Odinzoff
Bill Overbay
Alvin Owletuk
William Penton
Richard Perryman
Pete Peteroff
Tom Plyler
Jack Reagan
Gordon Reece
Paul Richards
D.J. Riggs
Col. Saravo
Keith Savoy
Bruce Schnitzer
Walter Schob
Walt Seelig
Philip Smith
Ray Smythe
SOUTH POLE – All at Scott-Amundsen Base between December 1980–February 1981
John Stagnato
Sully Sullivan
Dick Taylor U.S.C.G.
Matt Valley
William Tavoulereas
Anthony Thompson
Dr Edward Todd
Archie Thurmond
Jules Uberuaga
Thomas Vojtek

Jack Wadsworth	Noah White
R.F. Wallace	Vince Zimmerer

I would like to express my sincere gratitude to Dr Armand Hammer for making the documentary film *To the Ends of the Earth* and all his support throughout the expedition.

I would also like to give special thanks to Jack Reagan, William Tavoulereas, Tom Hill, Bruce Schnitzer, Mr R. F. Wallace, Jack Wadsworth and Bob Greenham for their continued support and encouragement throughout the expedition.

Lastly I would like to thank Bill Kronick, Mike Hoover, Beverly Johnson and Gary Moskowitz for their help and friendship.

Appendix C

List of Selected Antarctic Expeditions
by P.M. Booth, Transglobe Research Assistant

650 A.D.	According to legend, Ui-te-Rangoria, a Polynesian chief, sailed to the frozen sea in the south.
1520	Ferdinand Magellan circumnavigated the world, confirming that it was round.
1570	Ortelius published a map called *Theatrum Orbis Terrarum* which showed an Antarctic continent: 'Terra australis non dum cognita.'
1578	Sir Francis Drake passed through the Magellan Straits. For two centuries it was thought that Terra del Fuego was part of a huge polar landmass.
1642	Abel Tasman discovered Tasmania.
1675	A British expedition under Antonio de la Roche may have discovered South Georgia.
1738–39	Captain Jean-Francois-Charles Bouvet de Lozier sailed in the *Aigle* and *Marie* to annex Terra Australis (the South Land) for France. He discovered Bouvet Island (54°S in the South Atlantic) on January 1, 1739.
1762	The ship *Aurora* reported discovering the Aurora Islands (53°S 48°W) now known as Shag Rocks.
1768–71	Lieutenant James Cook R.N. in the *Endeavour* circumnavigated the world. One of his tasks was to find Terra Australis before the French. He did not do so, but he did

establish that the land if it existed at all must be south of the latitude 40°S.

1771–72 Yves Joseph de Kerguelen-Tremarec in the *Fortune* discovered Kerguelen Island (49°S 70°E) on February 12, 1772, but thought it was part of the polar landmass.

1771–72 Marion-Dufresne in the *Mascarin* discovered the Prince Edward Islands (January 13, 1772) and the Crozet Islands January 23, 1772).

1772–75 Commander James Cook in the *Resolution* and Captain Tobias Furneaux in the *Adventure* attempted to find Bouvet 'Land' but failed to do so because its position had been incorrectly reported. Cook then sailed south and became the first European to cross the Antarctic Circle. In 1774 he achieved a latitude of 71°10'S before being stopped by pack ice. By 1775 he had circumnavigated the polar continent in high southern latitude and crossed the Antarctic Circle four times. On occasions he was within a day's sail of land, but never saw it. He took possession of South Georgia for King George III (January 17, 1775) and discovered the South Sandwich Islands (January 30, 1775). He ended his southern travels uncertain as to the existence of a southern continent.

1776–80 James Cook in the *Resolution* and Charles Clerke in the *Discovery* visited and named Prince Edward Islands, and visited Kerguelen Island.

1778 British sealers started to use South Georgia as a base for their operations, followed by the Americans three years later. From this time sealers and whalers worked in the Southern Ocean regularly, visiting Kerguelen Island, Crozet Island and rediscovering Bouvet Island in 1808. This activity increased and in 1820 over 35 sealing and whaling expeditions took place, mainly British and American found. Stocks of fur seals were soon exhausted.

1810 An Australian sealing expedition in the *Perseverance* discovered Macquarie Island, on July 11.

1819–20 William Smith, an Englishman, was blown off course in the *Williams* and discovered the South Shetland Islands on

February 18. Returning later in the year he landed and took possession of the islands on October 16. The *Williams* returned once more to investigate the discovery with Edward Bransfield as master under the instructions of Captain Shireff RN, Senior British Naval Officer, West Coast of South America. On January 30, 1820, Bransfield landed on the northwestern coast of Graham Land; he was probably the first man to land on the Antarctic Continent.

1819–21 Czar Alexander I sent Captain Thaddeus Bellinghausen and Captain M.P. Lazarev in the *Vostok* and *Mirnyy* to find the Continent. Bellinghausen circumnavigated the world to the south of latitude 60°S, and six times crossed the Antarctic Circle. He probably sighted land twice, but did not realise it; the first occasion was on January 28, 1820 (two days before Bransfield landed on Graham Land) when he probably saw Kron-prinsesse Märtha Kyst. Thus it is likely that Bellinghausen is the discoverer of the Antarctic Continent. He also discovered Peter I Island and Alexander I Island in January 1821.

1820 The American sealer Nathaniel B. Palmer in the *Hero* saw the peaks of Graham Land at Palmer's Coast on November 16, 1820.

1821–22 The British sealer George Powell in the *Dove* and Nathaniel B. Palmer in the *James Monroe* discovered and charted South Orkney Islands on December 6, 1821.

1822–23 Benjamin Morrell, an American sealer in the *Wasp*, probably reached 70°14'S in the Weddell Sea. He also made the first recorded landing on Bouvet Island.

1822–24 James Weddell, British, achieved 74°15'S 34°16'W (in the Weddell Sea) in the *Jane*.

1828–31 Henry Foster in H.M.S. *Chanticleer* charted Deception Island and made pendulum and magnetic observations. He also charted part of the Palmer Coast.

1829–31 The first American government-sponsored exploring expedition led by Benjamin Pendleton in the *Seraph* visited South Shetland Islands in 1830. The *Seraph* reached 101°W south of 60°S.

1830–32 John Biscoe, British, in the *Tula* and Avery in the *Lively* circumnavigated the Continent; reached 69°S 10°43'E; discovered Enderby Land on February 28, 1831, Adelaide Island on February 15, 1832 and the northern Biscoe Islands. On February 21, 1832 he discovered land (an extension of Bransfield's and Palmer's discoveries) which he called Graham Land.

1833–34 A British expedition under Captain Peter Kemp in the *Magnet* discovered Heard Island on November 27, 1833 and Kemp Land on December 26 of the same year.

1837–40 The Frenchmen J.S.C. Dumont d'Urville and C.H. Jacquinot in the *Astrolabe* and *Zelee* discovered Adelie Land on January 22, 1840, claiming it for France. They then discovered Clarie Coast (now Wilkes Coast) a few hours after Charles Wilkes on January 31, 1831.

1838–39 John Balleny, British, in the *Eliza Scott* and H. Freeman in the *Sabrina* discovered Balleny Islands on February 9, 1839 and saw land east of the Sabrina Coast.

1838–42 Lieutenant Charles Wilkes led the United States Exploring Expedition of five unsuitable and badly equipped ships. The coast of Wilkes Land was charted, although some of Wilkes's work was later found to be erroneous. Nevertheless his contribution was considerable, and he was the first to recognise the land as a continent. William Walker in the 96-ton *Flying Fish* sailed to 70°S 105°W before being stopped by ice; Cadwalader Ringgold in the *Porpoise* achieved 68°S 95°44'W.

1839–43 James C. Ross in H.M.S. *Erebus* and Francis R.M. Crozier in H.M.S. *Terror* circumnavigated the continent and entered the Ross Sea. After discovering and charting the coast of Victoria Land and landing at Franklin and Possession Islands, they discovered Ross Island and the Ross Ice Barrier. Mount Erebus, an active volcano, was named by the expedition. They had achieved a furthest south of 78°10'S 161°27'W.

1844–45 T.E.L. Moore in the *Pagoda* reached 67°50'S 39°41'E while carrying out an important magnetic survey.

1872–76	George S. Nares took a steamship, H.M.S. *Challenger,* to 66°40′S 78°22′E. He carried out important oceanographical researches and scientific observations at various southern islands.
1874	American, British and German expeditions observed the Transit of Venus in December 1874 on Kerguelen Islands.
1892–93	Members of a British whaling reconnaissance expedition carried out scientific work in the Joinville Islands and Trinity Peninsula.
1892–93	A French expedition under Commandant Lieutard in the *Eure* reasserted sovereignty of Kerguelen Island and carried out hydrographic surveys.
1892–93	The Norwegian whaler Carl Anton Larsen in the *Jason* discovered Foyne Coast and reached 64°40′S 56°30′W in the Weddell Sea. He also collected fossils on Seymour Island.
1893–94	C.A. Larsen discovered King Oscar II Land and Robertson Island. He reached 68°10′S in the Weddell Sea.
1894–95	Norwegians Henrik J. Bull and Leonard Kristensen in the *Antarctic* reached Coulan Island (74°S). Lichens were discovered by Carsten Borchgrevink (a school master who had shipped as an AB) on Possession Island and Cape Adare. The latter was the first landing on Victoria Land (January 24, 1895).
1897–99	Adrien de Gerlache, a Belgian, accompanied by Amundsen and others, found the Gerlache Strait between Graham Land and the Palmer Archipelago (which he named). The *Belgica* was beset and drifted with the ice for twelve months, the first exploring vessel to winter in the Antarctic.
1898–99	Carl Chun and Captain Krech in the *Valdivia* accurately located Bouvet Island and carried out deep-sea surveys.
1898–1900	The Norwegian Borchgrevink led a British expedition which explored the coast of Victoria Land. Borchgrevink and ten men wintered at Cape Adare, the first men to do so intentionally in the Antarctic. The *Southern Cross* reached 78°21′S where it was stopped by the Ross Barrier (which had retreated south over the years). Borchgrevink and Colbeck

travelled over the ice to 78°50'S. Zoological, geological, meteorological and magnetic work was carried out.

1901–03 Professor Erich von Drygalski led a German expedition in the *Gauss* which discovered Kaiser Wilhelm II Land, exploring it by sledge.

1901–04 The British National Antarctic Expedition, led by Commander Robert Falcon Scott R.N., sailed to McMurdo Sound in the *Discovery.* Members of the expedition included Ernest Shackleton, Albert Armitage and Dr Edward Wilson. After wintering at the Sound, they discovered King Edward VII Land. Scott, Shackleton and Wilson attempted to reach the South Pole but were forced to turn back having achieved 82°17'S on December 30, 1902. They suffered from hunger, scurvy and exhaustion, reaching safety only with difficulty. W. Colbeck in the relief ship *Morning* discovered Scott Island.

1901–04 Otto Nordenskjöld and C.A. Larsen wintered on Snow Hill Island (east of Graham Land) with the Swedish South Polar Expedition. The first major sledge journey in Antarctica was made along the Larsen Ice Shelf to 66°S. The *Antarctic* was crushed and sunk by pack ice while trying to relieve them. All members were safely rescued by the Argentine vessel *Uruguay.*

1902–04 Dr W.S. Bruce led a Scottish National Expedition in the *Scotia,* discovering the Caird Coast and carrying out the first oceanographic survey of the Weddell Sea.

1903–05 Dr Jean Charcot wintered at Booth Island (off west Graham Land) in the *Francais.* He discovered and charted Loubet Coast, and mapped parts of the Palmer Archipelago.

1907–09 Ernest Shackleton led the British Antarctic Expedition which wintered at Cape Royds, Ross Island. Shackleton, Armitage, Dr Eric Marshall and Frank Wild travelled south over the Ross Ice Shelf, before crossing the Trans-Antarctic mountains (where they lost all their ponies). Hampered by very low temperatures (minus 70°F) and storms, they reached 88°23'S 163°E, that is, 97 miles short of the South Pole. Professor David reached the South Magnetic Pole and took possession of Victoria Land on January 16, 1909. Shackleton claimed the South Polar Plateau for King Edward VII on January 9, 1909.

1908–10 Jean Charcot wintered at Petermann Island (Biscoe Islands) in the *Pourquoi Pas,* mapping new regions of the Graham Land coast and carrying out scientific work.

1910–12 A German expedition under Wilhelm Filchner in the *Deutschland* discovered Luitpold Coast and the Filchner Ice Shelf, and was beset in pack ice for nine months.

1910–12 Captain R.F. Scott R.N. in the *Terra Nova* wintered at McMurdo Sound. After depots had been laid, Scott and eleven men climbed the Beardmore Glacier. There, 300 miles short of the Pole, four men of the support party were sent back. About two weeks later the three remaining men of the support party turned back, leaving Scott, Captain L.E.G. Oates, Dr Edward Wilson, P.O. Edgar Evans and Lieutenant Henry Bowers to continue manhauling their sledges south. They reached the Pole on January 17, 1912, just over a month after Amundsen. Bitterly disappointed, Scott and his men marched back, gradually weakening from starvation and scurvy. P.O. Evans died first from exhaustion, then Oates walked out of the tent, never to be seen again. Scott, Wilson and Bowers were trapped in their tent by a blizzard eleven miles from the next depot, where they died of hunger, cold and exhaustion. Their bodies and diaries were found by a search party in October on the Ross Ice Shelf.

1910–12 After establishing a base at the Bay of Whales, Roald Amundsen and five men reached the South Pole on December 14, 1911, using dogs and sledges. They spent three days in the area before returning safely.

1911–12 Lieutenant Choku Shirase, Japanese, landed at the Bay of Whales and sledged to 80°05′S 156°27′W in King Edward VII Land.

1911–14 Douglas Mawson led the Australasian Antarctic Expedition which discovered King George V Land, Queen Mary Land and the Shackleton Ice Shelf. Adelie Land was explored, as was the area of the South Magnetic Pole.

1914–16 The *Endurance* became beset in the Weddell Sea while carrying the British Imperial Trans-Antarctic Expedition led by Sir Ernest Shackleton. The ship sank after a 700-mile drift. With strenuous efforts, Shackleton took his party to Elephant Island in the ship's boats. Leaving twenty-two of his men there, Shackleton and five men sailed in the 22-foot, 6-inch boat *James Caird* to seek help. Through Shackleton's leadership and F.A. Worsley's brilliant navigation they safely reached the west coast of South Georgia. Shackleton, Worsley and T. Crean walked across the island to the whaling station at Grytviken. The main party was finally rescued by the Chilean vessel *Yelcho*.

1914–17 Captain A.E. Macintosh took the *Aurora* into the Ross Sea with the intention of linking up with Shackleton in the *Endurance*. A storm tore the *Aurora* from her moorings, stranding ten men on the ice. The ship was beset for nine months; during the drift Oates Land was discovered. Of the ten men stranded on Ross Island, only seven were still alive when rescued by Captain John Davis in the *Aurora* in January 1917.

1921–22 While en route for the Enderby Land area in the *Quest*, Shackleton died on January 5, 1922 at South Georgia. The expedition continued under Frank Wild, but failed to find any new land.

1928–29 Sir Hubert Wilkins was the first man to introduce the airplane and aerial photography to the Antarctic. He twice attempted to fly across the Continent from the Weddell Sea to the Ross Sea, but failed. From aerial photographs he came to the erroneous conclusion that Graham Land was an archipelago.

1928–30 Rear Admiral Richard E. Byrd, U.S.N., made the first flight over the South Pole from his base in Little America I on the Ross Ice Shelf on November 29, 1929. He also explored by air King Edward VII Land and Byrd Land.

1929–30 Sir Hubert Wilkins continued his aerial reconnaissance of Graham Land, unfortunately confirming the earlier erroneous discoveries.

1929–31 A joint British, Australian and New Zealand expedition under the command of Sir Douglas Mawson explored the area between Enderby Land and Wilhelm II Land, adding Princess Elizabeth and MacRobertson Lands to the map.

1928–37 The five Norwegian (Christensen) Antarctic expeditions explored various areas, notably Enderby Land and Dronning Maud Land.

1933–34 Lincoln Ellsworth, an American, attempted to fly across the Continent. His plane was wrecked on sea ice in the Bay of Whales.

1933–35 Byrd returned to the Ross Ice Shelf and established the largest base in the Antarctic up to that time. He carried out extensive aerial exploration and successfully used tracked vehicles on the ice. From his aerial photographs it was shown that Graham Land is a peninsula.

1934–35 Lincoln Ellsworth was prevented by bad weather from flying from Graham Land to the Ross Sea.

1934–37 John Rymill and the British Graham Land Expedition wintered in the *Penola* in successive years at the Argentine Islands and Debenham Islands. They sledged to 72°S in King George VI Sound proving the channels reported by Wilkins in 1928–29 to be nonexistent.

1935–39 Lincoln Ellsworth, piloted by H. Hollick-Kenyon, successfully flew across the Continent from Dundee Island to the Bay of Whales in November 1935. He named Ellsworth Land and landed four times during the crossing. He continued aerial exploration in 1938–39.

1938–39 Alfred Ritscher led a German expedition which photographed some 350,000 square kilometres of Dronning Maud Land, and claimed part of it for Germany.

1939–41 The United States established two bases under the command of Byrd at Stonington Island and Little America II on the Ross Ice Shelf. Much useful exploration and scientific work was carried out. The expected permanent occupation was not effected because Congress did not provide funds in 1941.

1945 The Falkland Islands Dependencies Survey (forerunner of the British Antarctic Survey) was established to carry out scientific work in that part of Antarctica claimed by the British. Work has been continuous at many different bases until the present day.

1946–47 Admiral Byrd led a vast American expedition involving some 4,800 men to Byrd Land. The aim of Operation Highjump was to test equipment in polar conditions: icebreakers, helicopters, aircraft, radar and tracked vehicles (Weazels) were all taken and used. Although the expedition was short in duration many aerial photographs were taken but there was little ground control.

1947–48 The United States sent two icebreakers with helicopters (U.S.S. *Burton Island* and U.S.S. *Port of Beaumont)* to establish ground control points so that photographs taken during Operation Highjump could be used for mapping.

1947–48 Commander Finn Ronne, U.S.N., led a privately financed expedition. He based himself and his party of 21 men and 2 women (one of whom was his wife) at Stonington Island off the west coast of Graham Land. Ronne explored large areas of the Continent by air, photographing some 450,000 square miles for the first time (but with little or no ground control). His party was assisted by and assisted a British exploratory party also wintering at Stonington Island.

1947–83 After World War II various nations, including Argentina, Chile, United Kingdom, France, Australia, USA, USSR, South Africa, New Zealand, Japan, Belgium and Norway set up permanent bases in Antarctica. All claimant nations agreed to free access during the International Geophysical Year 1957–58. With the signing of the Antarctic Treaty in 1961 all territorial claims were placed in abeyance. Under the Treaty only work of a scientific nature can be carried out and all military activity is restricted to support for the scientists.

1949–52 A Norwegian-British-Swedish expedition led by the Norwegian Captain John Giaever carried out scientific work in Queen Maud Land, making the first seismic traverse on the inland ice-sheet.

1955–58 The Soviet Comprehensive Antarctic Expedition established bases on the Knox Coast (Mirnyy), at the Magnetic Pole (Vostok) and at the Pole of Inaccessibility (Sovetskaya) (82°06′S 54°58′E) as part of the International Geophysical Year (IGY) effort. The two inland bases were established by using motorised sledges.

1956–57 During Operation Deep Freeze I, the Americans established bases on Ross Island (McMurdo Station) and at Kainan Bay. An airstrip was built on the Ross Ice Shelf. On October 31, 1956 Admiral George Dufek (Operation Deep Freeze II commander) landed at the South Pole. By February 1957 the Scott-Amundsen Base had been established by air. Other coastal stations were placed, and Byrd Station was established using tractors from Little America.

1957–58 International Geophysical Year. Twelve nations established 55 stations on the Antarctic Continent and its surrounding islands. Scientific work of many kinds was carried out, work which is still being continued today. The year was remarkable for the spirit of international cooperation which it engendered among those taking part.

1955–58 The British Commonwealth Trans-Antarctic Expedition completed the first land traverse of the Antarctic. Sir Edmund Hillary led a New Zealand team which laid supply depots from Scott Base on the Ross Ice Shelf and reached the South Pole on January 3, 1958. Meanwhile Dr Vivian Fuchs led a party from Shackleton Base on the Weddell Sea via South Ice Base to the South Pole, which he reached on January 20, 1958. Two days later Fuchs left for Scott Base which he reached on March 2, 1958, having completed a journey of 2,180 miles in 99 days. Seismic ice-depth soundings and gravity measurements were made throughout the journey. Much geological and glaciological work was accomplished.

1959 The Antarctic Treaty was initialled by twelve nations.

1961 The Antarctic Treaty was signed. It is due for review in 1991.

1979–81 Transglobe Expedition's Antarctic crossing.

Appendix D

Arctic Exploration

by P.M. Booth, Transglobe Research Assistant

320 B.C. Pytheas, a Greek colonist from Massilia (Marseilles) is reported to have circumnavigated the British Isles and may have crossed the Arctic Circle.

c. 500 A.D. According to legend, St Brendan sailed to North America from Ireland.

870 Rabna Floki, a Viking from Norway, sailed west to Iceland.

875 Ottar, another Viking, sailed to the Kola Peninsula and reached the White Sea. King Alfred the Great had Ottar's story translated into Anglo-Saxon.

982 Erik the Red (Eirik Thorvaldsson) discovered Greenland where he spent three years. He returned to Iceland and brought colonists back to Greenland in 986.

c. 1000 The Icelandic Sagas relate six tales of voyages to Vinland and Markland, which are probably the Newfoundland and Labrador areas of mainland America. One saga indicated that Bjarni Herjulfsson discovered America, another that Leif Eriksson did.

1025 Gudleif Gudlaugsson is believed by some scholars to have landed on the coast of America after being blown off course.

1059 Jon, a missionary, may have sailed to Vinland where he was murdered.

1121	Bishop Erik Gnupsson left Greenland to search for Vinland. According to legend he spent a long time there before returning.
1347	A ship from Greenland is known to have been on a routine voyage to Markland, probably to collect timber.
c. 1480–95	Bristol merchants are believed to have sent a number of ships to search for the 'Island of Brasil'. Some of the ships may have reached Canada.
1497	John Cabot discovered the cod fishing grounds off Labrador and Newfoundland while searching for the Northwest Passage. European fishing fleets soon regularly fished the area.
1498	John Cabot set off again to discover the Northwest Passage to Japan. He may have died in the attempt.
1500	Gaspar Corte-Real, a Portuguese, sighted Greenland or Newfoundland.
1501	Gaspar Corte-Real was lost after last being seen just north of Newfoundland while searching for the Northwest Passage. Miguel, his brother, suffered the same fate a year later.
1504–06	French and Portuguese fishing fleets began fishing off Newfoundland.
1508–09	Sebastian Cabot may have discovered Hudson Strait and Hudson Bay while searching for the Northwest Passage.
1513	Vasco Nuñez de Balboa discovered the Pacific Ocean and claimed its seaboard from North to South Pole for Spain.
1524–25	French and Spanish Northwest Passage expeditions reached Newfoundland.
1527	Henry VIII sponsored two ships at the instigation of Robert Thorne for the first known attempt at the North Pole. The expedition failed.
1527–28	John Rut may have reached 64°N before exploring the Labrador coast.
1534–36	Two French expeditions explored the Gulf of St Lawrence and the St Lawrence River.
c.1543	Jean Alfonse, a Frenchman, probably entered the Davis Strait.
1553	Sir Hugh Willoughby and Richard Chancellor sailed in three

ships to find the Northeast Passage. Willoughby and his crew died in the attempt, but he may have reached Novaya Zemlya. Chancellor eventually travelled overland from the White Sea to Moscow.

1556 Steven Burrough reached the mouth of the Pechora River.

1558 The Zeno Map was published.

1569 Mercator published his map which possibly shows Ungava Bay.

1576–78 Martin Frobisher sailed on three consecutive years to Baffin Island, mainly in search of gold. His ships brought back 1,200 tons of 'ore' but it proved to be worthless. He had sailed some way into Hudson Strait which he called Mistakyn Strait.

1580 Charles Jackman and Arthur Pet in the *George* and *William* were the first West Europeans to navigate in the Kara Sea.

1584 A Dutchman, Oliver Burnel, tried to penetrate the Kara Sea but failed.

1585–87 John Davis three times attempted to find a Northwest Passage to Cathay. He achieved a farthest north in Davis Strait of 72°12'N in the *Ellen,* a ship of less than 50 tons.

1594–97 The Dutchman William Barents explored Spitsbergen and Novaya Zemlya. His surveying achievements were considerable. After wintering at Ice Haven, Novaya Zemlya in 1596–7, he and his crew successfully completed a remarkable voyage in small boats to Lapland some 1,600 miles away. Barents himself died near North Cape on June 20, 1597.

1602 Captain George Weymouth sailed with letters for the empress of Cathay in the *Discovery* and *God speed.* Unfortunately his crew mutinied in Davis Strait and he was forced to return. He claimed to have reached 69°N.

1606 Captain John Knight sailed in the *Hopewell* to find the Northwest Passage. His ship was damaged off the coast of Labrador. Knight went ashore and was never seen again. He was probably killed by Eskimos.

1607–08 Henry Hudson attempted to sail across the Arctic Ocean and achieved 80°23'N near Spitsbergen. He also landed on Novaya Zemlya.

1610–11 Henry Hudson took the *Discovery* with a crew of twenty men and two boys in an attempt to find the Northwest Passage. After wintering in Hudson Bay, some of the crew mutinied and cast him adrift in an open boat to die. With him were his seven-year-old son and seven men. The ship was brought back to England by Robert Bylot.

1610–11 Jonas Poole sailed to Spitsbergen with the intention of sailing across the Arctic Ocean. His attempt degenerated into a fishing venture.

1612–13 Captain Thomas Button took the *Discovery* and *Resolution* to Hudson Bay to find the Northwest Passage. After losing five men in a fight with Eskimos and more through hardship and cold during the winter at Fort Nelson, he returned in 1613. He decided the passage existed (if at all) through Roe's Welcome Sound, which he entered to 65°N.

1612 Captain James Hall was killed by Eskimos in Greenland. His death ended an expedition of which William Baffin was the pilot.

1614 William Baffin visited Spitsbergen and may have seen Franz Joseph Land.

1614 William Gibbon in the *Discovery* was prevented from entering Hudson Strait by heavy ice.

1615 The *Discovery* set off for the fourth time to find the Northwest Passage, commanded by Captain Robert Bylot (who had sailed with Hudson and Button), and with William Baffin as pilot. They reached Nottingham Island at the west end of Hudson Strait before returning.

1616 Baffin and Bylot once more sailed in the *Discovery* with the aim of travelling up Davis Strait to 80°N, and then heading southwest until they reached Japan. They achieved 78°N and named Smith Sound, Jones Sound and Lancaster Sound, but did not enter the last two. Baffin's discoveries in Baffin Bay were later disbelieved and ignored for some 200 years.

1619–20 Jens Munk with two ships entered Hudson Bay and wintered near Churchill. Only Munk and two of the 65 men with him survived the winter and the voyage home.

1620–35 Dutch fishing and whaling fleets occupied Spitsbergen and

Jan Mayen Island in the Greenland Sea during the summer months. The fleets numbered about 300 ships manned by some 15,000 men.

1625 William Hawkeridge in the *Lion's Whelp* spent some time in the north part of Hudson Bay, but accomplished nothing.

1631 Luke Foxe in the 70-ton *Charles* sailed with a crew of 22 to Hudson Bay, meeting the *Henrietta Maria* by chance near James Bay. He later crossed the Arctic Circle in Foxe Basin before returning safely without loss.

1631–32 Captain Thomas James in the *Henrietta Maria* spent the winter in James Bay, saving his ship by the drastic measure of deliberately sinking her in shallow water. Several men died from accident or scurvy before the remainder returned safely.

1636–39 Elisha Busa explored the area of the Lena Delta (130°E) by land.

1640 Postnik discovered the Indigirka River (150°E).

1644 A Russian trading post was established in the valley of the Kolyma River (160°E).

1646 Isai Ignatiev sailed east of the Kolyma River to trade in walrus ivory.

1648 Deshnev, Alexiev and Ankudinov sailed from Kolyma in seven ships and entered the Bering Straits from the north-west. Only Deshnev and his crew survived after being shipwrecked on the coast of Kamchatka.

1651–52 Jacques Buteux twice tried to reach Hudson Bay overland from the south to claim it for France. He was killed by Indians.

1666 Wood and Flaws were shipwrecked on the coast of Novaya Zemlya.

1670 The Hudson Bay Company was formed. Thereafter temporary and later permanent trading posts were established at various places in the bay. Regular supply voyages from England took place. The area was the scene of constant and deadly conflict between the French and the English for many years, with some posts being captured and recaptured many times.

1715–16 William Stewart of the Hudson Bay Company walked inland from York Factory to an area between the Great Slave Lake and Lake Athabasca.

1719–21 James Knight and 27 men in two ships attempted to sail to the Coppermine River through the Northwest Passage. They were never seen again. Forty years later two sunken ships and the remains of a house were found at Marble Island, 300 miles north of Churchill in Hudson Bay. Eskimos said that they had all died of hunger and disease.

1721 In the 14th century communications with the two large settlements in southwest Greenland lapsed. The Norsemen died out suffering from malnutrition and rickets, some probably being killed by the Eskimos. Eventually the region was recolonized by the Norwegian missionary, Hans Egede.

1725–28 Vitus Bering, a Dane engaged by Czar Peter the Great, named St. Lawrence Island in Bering Strait, but turned back at 67°18′N 170°W without sighting the American mainland.

1728 Paars attempted and failed to cross Greenland's inland ice cap.

1729 Henry Atkins of Boston sailed to Davis Strait while whaling.

1733–42 The Great Northern Expedition of 570 men under Vitus Bering left St Petersburg and travelled overland for 3,000 miles eastwards. In 1740 Bering and Chirikov sailed from Petropavlovsk on the Kamchatka Peninsula. The former landed on Alaska between Capes St Elias and St Hermogenes. Later his ship was wrecked on Bering Island, where Bering died of exhaustion and despair. Chirikov reached Cross Bay in Alaska, where he landed some men. They were never seen again.

1741 Captain Christopher Middleton attempted to find the Northwest Passage in the northwest of Hudson Bay. He discovered Wager Inlet or Bay.

1746 William Moor explored Wager Bay in the belief that it might be the Northwest Passage.

1749 William Coats explored the east coast of Hudson Bay.

1751 Dalager attempted and failed to cross Greenland's inland ice-cap.

1751 Captain MacCallum of the Greenland fishery reached 83½°N.

1755 An Act of Parliament offered £5,000 reward to the first ship to sail within 1 degree of the North Pole.

1761 William Christopher in the *Churchill* sailed 90 miles up the Chesterfield Inlet. The following year he returned and confirmed that the inlet did not contain the Northwest Passage.

1767 Synd landed at Cape Prince of Wales, Alaska, while searching for the Northwest Passage.

1770–72 Samuel Hearne and an Indian guide walked from Churchill to the mouth of the Coppermine River, a round trip of about 1,300 miles. He was probably the first white man to stand on the northern shore of Canada.

1773 Captain C. J. Phipps M.P. sailed in the *Racehorse* and *Carcass* with the intention of reaching the North Pole but not going past it. He was stopped by ice at 80°48′N near Spitsbergen.

1777 Walter Young in H.M.S. *Lyon* achieved 72°42′N in Baffin Bay.

1778 Captain James Cook in the *Resolution* attempted the passage from the Pacific but was stopped by ice at Icy Cape, 70°41′N.

1788 Joseph Billings, an Englishman, who had served under Cook, worked for Catherine the Great of Russia to map the North Cape. He failed to complete his work.

1789 Alexander Mackenzie with a dozen Indians and half-breeds canoed down the Mackenzie River from the Great Slave Lake to its mouth in the Beaufort Sea.

1791–95 George Vancouver in the *Discovery* and William Broughton in the *Chatham* explored the coast of Alaska. There was much Spanish activity in this area at this time.

1806 William Scoresby, a British whaling captain, achieved 81°30′N 19°E north of Spitsbergen.

1809 Hedenstrom, Sannikov and Koshevin explored the New Siberian Islands which had been discovered by hunters in the previous few years. It was confirmed that the soil of Lyakov Island consisted of mammoth bone.

1809 John Clarke may have reached the mouth of the Mackenzie River.

1816 Otto von Kotzebue reached Cape Krusenstern (67°N) in Alaska.

1817 Two British whalers under Captain Muirhead crossed the north end of Baffin Bay at an alleged latitude of 77°N.

1817 William Scoresby Jr surveyed Jan Mayen Island.

1818 Commander David Buchan and Lieutenant John Franklin in the *Dorothea* and *Trent* attempted to sail to the North Pole past Spitsbergen, but were forced to give up when storms and ice damaged the ships. They achieved 80°37′N.

1818 An Act of Parliament was passed offering rewards of £20,000 for the discovery of the Northwest Passage.

1818 Commander John Ross and Lieutenant William Edward Parry in the *Isabella* and *Alexander* attempted to discover the Northwest Passage. After finding Smith Sound blocked with ice and passing by Jones Sound, Ross entered Lancaster Sound. He believed this sound to be blocked off by mountains and so returned. He was later criticised for this decision.

1819–20 Parry, in the *Hecla* and *Griper,* penetrated Lancaster Sound, passed Cornwallis Island and achieved 110°W on September 6 in Viscount Melville Sound, thus winning a bounty of £5,000 offered by Order in Council. They spent the winter on Melville Island and crossed it on foot, using pikes and blankets as tents. The expedition was remarkable for its high morale, excellent health and good discipline. It achieved a furthest west of 113°48′W.

1819 Franklin canoed and walked 5,550 miles with, among others, Hood, Back and Dr Richardson, and several Canadian *voyageurs.* His route was Hudson Bay–Lake Winnipeg–Pine Island Land–Lake Athabasca–Great Slave Lake–mouth of Coppermine River–Kent Peninsula—Bathhurst Inlet–Coppermine River–Great Slave Lake. They suffered terrible hardships and several men died. At the end they were reduced to eating lichen, deerskins and any bones they could find.

1820–23 Lieutenant Ferdinand von Wrangel, a Russian, surveyed the Siberian coast. During his travels he completed one epic 1,530-mile journey with his dog teams in 78 days. He was subsequently governor of Russian America, now Alaska.

1821–23 In yet another attempt to find the Northwest Passage through Hudson Strait, Commander Parry in the *Hecla* and *Fury* determined that Repulse Bay was landlocked and explored the Melville Peninsula. He named Fury and Hecla Strait and spent a second winter at Igloolik. Ice prevented him from passing through the strait so he returned in October 1823.

1822 The William Scoresbys (father and son) discovered Scoresby Sound and charted part of the east coast of Greenland; in the following year they published a highly informative book.

1823 Captains Clavering and Sabine in the *Griper* explored and surveyed the northeast coast of Greenland.

1824 Parry in the *Hecla* and *Fury* attempted to find the passage through Prince Regent Inlet. After wintering on the Brodeur Peninsula, both ships were damaged by storm and ice. *Fury* was abandoned and the *Hecla* returned.

1824 Commander Lyon failed to reach Repulse Bay after the *Griper* was nearly sunk by storms in Bay of God's Mercy and Roe's Welcome Sound.

1825–27 Franklin, Richardson, Back, Dease and others travelled down the Mackenzie River to its mouth in small especially built boats. In spite of ice in the Beaufort Sea, Franklin and Back sailed west for 374 miles to 148°52′W before returning. He discovered Herschel Island, Camden Bay and Prudhoe Bay. Meanwhile Richardson and Kendall travelled east for 900 miles to the mouth of the Coppermine River, and then walked to the Great Slave Lake, where both parties joined up again at Fort Franklin. More than 1,000 miles of the north Canadian shoreline had been surveyed.

1825–28 Captain F. W. Beechey in H.M.S. *Blossom* sailed through the Bering Straits to Icy Cape. He sent his mate Elson to Barrow Point in the hope of meeting Franklin who was expected from the east; no sign was seen. They were one year and 156 miles apart.

1827 Parry in the *Hecla* reached Treurenberg Bay, Spitsbergen. From there, dragging sledge boats, he set out for the North Pole. Although they travelled over 900 miles over the ice, drifts and currents caused them only to reach a point 172 miles north of the ship, at 82°45′N.

1829–33 Captain John Ross, largely financed by a gin distiller named Felix Booth, took a 150-ton paddle-steamer (the *Victory)* to Prince Regent Inlet, where he removed the engine which had proved unreliable. Over the next two years he explored the Boothia Peninsula on foot, raised the Union Flag at the Magnetic North Pole, and his nephew James C. Ross discovered King William Island. He was eventually forced to abandon the *Victory* and after much hardship was rescued in Lancaster Sound by his old ship the *Isabella*.

1833 Commander George Back explored and mapped the Great Fish River (now called the Back River). His map of the river remained in use until 1948.

1836–37 While commanding the *Terror,* Back entered the Foxe Channel but was beset with ice.

1837–39 Thomas Simpson and Peter Dease of the Hudson Bay Company travelled down the Mackenzie River to the Beaufort Sea where they turned west and reached Barrow Point. Moving east they travelled over Rae Strait without realising it (the strait was iced over), and mapped the south coasts of Victoria Island and King William Island.

1839 John Bell of the Hudson Bay Company explored the Peel and Rat Rivers.

1840 John Bell established Fort McPherson (as it was later known) on the Peel River.

1845–48 Sir John Franklin and Captain Francis Crozier sailed in the *Terror* and *Erebus* to find the Northwest Passage. After wintering at Beechey Island, both ships were beset with ice off King William Island and finally abandoned in Victoria Sound. Although they had provisions for three years, all 139 men perished in the ships or during the march south to the area of the mouth of the Back River. Some forty expeditions were sent to find them over the next ten years.

1847–48 Sir John Richardson, John Rae and John Bell searched between the Mackenzie River and Coppermine River for Franklin without success. John Rae had previously carried out surveys in the area of the Rae Isthmus.

1848 Thomas Lee, in the whaler *Prince of Wales,* sailed 150 miles into Jones Sound.

1848–49 Sir James Ross and Edward Joseph Bird in the *Investigator* and *Enterprise* sailed to Lancaster Sound in search of Franklin. They were beset by ice in Barrow Strait but made four sledge journeys in that area and along the shores of Somerset Island, and were on one journey nearer to solving the Franklin mystery than any search party until 1857.

1848–52 Captain T.E.L. Moore in H.M.S. *Plover* searched for Franklin from the west, reaching Barrow Point in boats.

1849 John Gravill in a British whaler entered Jones Sound. He carried out the first reported landing on the south of Ellesmere Island.

1849 Henry Kellett in H.M.S. *Herald* discovered Herald Island near Wrangel Island in the East Siberian Sea.

1849 The Royal Thames Yacht Club schooner *Nancy Dawson* commanded by Robert Sheddon assisted H.M.S. *Plover* in the search for Franklin from Alaska.

1849–50 James Saunders in H.M.S. *North Star* eventually reached Prince Regent Inlet while attempting to resupply Sir James Clark Ross's search party and look for Franklin in Smith and Jones Sound.

1850 Charles Forsyth and William Snow in the *Prince Albert* were sponsored by Lady Franklin to look for her husband. They were prevented by ice from going beyond Fury Beach, but then entered Wellington Channel where they found news of Franklin's winter quarters at Beechey Island.

1850–55 This was the period notable for a large number of relief expeditions.

1850–55 Captain Richard Collinson and Captain Robert McClure in the *Enterprise* and *Investigator* were ordered to conduct a search from the Pacific and Bering Strait. Collinson's voyage was the more remarkable since he sailed eastwards through the Northwest Passage and nearly reached King William Island. After four winters in the Arctic, he arrived home in 1855. Meanwhile McClure had to abandon his ship in 1853 on the north coast of Banks Island.

Captain Horatio Austin, who had previously been with Parry, spent two winters in the area of Barrow Strait, where he met Captain William Penny, the well-known whaling skipper. Austin's search parties sledged nearly 7,000 miles before returning home in 1852.

1852–55 Four ships were sent back to the Arctic the same summer under Sir Edward Belcher, a man with no Arctic experience. Captain Henry Kellett (H.M.S. *Resolute)* and Captain Leopold McClintock (H.M.S. *Intrepid)* wintered at Melville Island and found a report about the position of McClure's ship (H.M.S. *Investigator)* 160 miles away. Next year McClintock, who had previously wintered with James Ross and also with Austin, was in the field for 105 days discovering Prince Patrick Island and travelling 1,408 miles, the greatest distance covered by men hauling their own sledges. Lieutenant Frederick Meecham did a journey of 1,336 miles in only 70 days.

Leaving the *North Star* at Beechey Island as a base, Belcher wintered in Northumberland Sound in the *Assistance* and *Pioneer.* After a further winter in Wellington Channel, Belcher found that he was unable to reach Lancaster Sound. He abandoned his two ships and made his way to the *North Star.* There he joined up with the crews of the *Intrepid*, *Resolute* and *Investigator* which had all been abandoned. When the supply ships *Phoenix* and *Talbot* arrived, these two ships and the *North Star* carried all the crews back to England, where Belcher was court-martialled and only narrowly acquitted. (H.M.S. *Resolute* was later found drifting undamaged in the Davis Strait by an American whaling captain Buddington in the *George Herz* in September 1855. The U.S. government bought her, re-equipped her and gave the ship as a gift to the admiralty.)

1852 In another expedition sponsored by Lady Franklin, Edward

Inglefield achieved a farthest north of 78°28'N in Smith Sound. The *Isabel* later entered Jones Sound before sailing to Beechey Island through Lancaster Sound and then searching the east coast of Baffin Island.

1853–55 Elisha Kane, an American, sailed in the *Advance* through Baffin Bay and became iced in at Rensselaer Island on the west coast of Greenland. He achieved 80°35'N with sledge and boat parties and explored the Kane Basin before abandoning his ship and escaping by boat and foot to Godhavn.

1853 Seeman carried out hydrographical work in the Bering Strait.

1854 Dr John Rae of the Hudson Bay Company reported that, during a survey journey to the west coast of Boothia Peninsula from the Coppermine River, he had been told by Eskimos that they had seen about thirty white men dragging a boat southwards over the ice and that several bodies had later been found nearby.

When the Crimean War broke out, the Government declined to make any further search.

1855 James Anderson and James Stewart of the Hudson Bay Company approached Montreal Island from the mainland by way of Back River and found relics of Franklin's expedition.

1855 Lieutenant John Rodgers reached 72°05'N 174°37'W.

1857–59 Lady Franklin now engaged McClintock to command the *Fox,* a steam yacht of 177 tons. During his second winter, McClintock discovered a record left in 1848 on King William Island by Captain Francis Crozier who, after Franklin's death, had abandoned the two ships (*Terror* and *Erebus*) and was leading southwards 105 survivors. Relics of all sorts were later found, as well as two skeletons in a 28-foot boat; this boat was estimated to weigh 700–800 pounds and the sledge 650 pounds. Now, thirteen years after Franklin had left England, McClintock and other experienced Arctic travellers had lightened and considerably improved travel equipment. Such progress was, regrettably, soon forgotten.

1860–61 Isaac Hayes led an American expedition in the *United States* with the intention of sailing to the North Pole via Smith

Sound (many people still believing that the Arctic Ocean was free of ice). When his ship became iced in at Foulke Fjord in northwest Greenland, he sledged across to Ellesmere Island and claimed a farthest north of 81°35'N, but this was later disputed. He probably achieved 80°14'N at Cape Joseph Goode.

1861 Torrell and A.E. Nordenskiöld explored Hinlopen Strait by boat, reaching a farthest north of 80°42'N at Phipps Island and discovering Prince Oscar Land and the two islands Charles XII and Drabanten off Spitsbergen.

1863 Captain Elling Carlsen followed Barent's route round Novaya Zemlya's northern point and found his hut of 300 years before, undisturbed. He circumnavigated Spitsbergen for the first time.

1867 Whymper attempted but failed to cross the Greenland ice cap.

1868 Captain Von Otter commanded the *Sofia* with A.E. Nordenskiöld as scientific adviser and achieved a farthest north of 81°42'N 17°30'E.

1868 Koldeway led the first German North Polar in the *Germania* which was prevented from reaching East Greenland. A latitude of 81°05'N was reached.

1869–70 The *Germania* and *Hansa* under the command of Koldeway once more tried to reach the North Pole. The *Germania* only completed some local but useful discoveries on East Greenland. The *Hansa* was crushed by ice and her crew escaped after a 201-day and 600-mile drift on an ice floe.

1871 Lieutenant Carl Weyprecht in the Isbjorn attempted the Northeast Passage.

1871–73 Charles Hall led a United States polar expedition in the *Polaris*. After passing through Smith Sound, *Polaris* was stopped by ice at 82°11'N. While wintering at Thank God Harbour in Polaris Bay, Hall died in mysterious and suspicious circumstances, possibly from arsenic poisoning. On the return journey a party became separated from the ship on an ice floe. These men were finally rescued off the coast of Labrador after drifting for 1,300 miles on the pack ice over five months. The *Polaris* was abandoned in Foulke Fjord and the remaining crew were picked up by a whaler from their boats.

1873 D.L. Braine and Commander James Greer searched Smith Sound for Hall and the *Polaris*.

1872–74 Lieutenant Carl Weyprecht and Lieutenant Julius Payer were beset by ice in the *Tegetthof* within sight of Novaya Zemlya. After a year's drift, they discovered and explored the Franz Joseph Archipelago. Payer reached Cape Fligely (81°51′N) by sledge, the most northerly land in the Old World.

1872 A.E. Nordenskiöld reached Phipps Island (Spitsbergen) by sledge from Mussel Bay where the *Polhem* had established winter quarters.

1875 Allen Young in the *Pandora* attempted the Northwest Passage. After sailing down Peel Channel, he was forced to abandon the attempt by heavy ice in Franklin Strait.

1875–76 George Nares and Henry Stephenson in H.M.S. *Alert* and H.M.S. *Discovery* tried to reach the North Pole by way of Smith Sound. The latter ship wintered on the north side of Lady Franklin Bay on Ellesmere Island. The *Alert* continued through Robeson Channel to winter quarters at Floeberg Beach (82°28′N). From there Albert Markham and Alfred Parr sledged to 83°20′N. Meanwhile Pelham Aldrich travelled west along the north coast of Ellesmere Island reaching Yelverton Bay. He established Capes Aldrich and Columbia as the northernmost points of Ellesmere Island at a latitude of 83°06′N. The expedition suffered greatly from scurvy. One man from the *Alert,* and two from *Discovery,* died.

1875 Nordenskiöld in the *Proven* commanded by Kjellman reached the mouth of the Yenisei River in the Kara Sea (80°E). He repeated the voyage in the following year.

1878–80 Frederick Schwatka led an American expedition to search for relics of Franklin's expedition in King William Island.

1878–79 Nordenskiöld navigated the Northeast Passage from west to east in the *Vega* in an expedition largely sponsored by the Swedish government. As always, he carried out extensive scientific work.

1879–80 John Spicer in the American whaler *Era* discovered the Spicer Islands in Foxe Basin. His discovery was not confirmed until 1946.

1879–82 Commander de Long (U.S.N.) and G. W. Melville went through the Bering Strait hoping to winter on Wrangel Island which he believed to be continental. The *Jeanette* was beset by pack ice and drifted for two years in the Siberian Ocean before being crushed and sunk at 77°36′N 155°E near Herald Island. Henrietta and Jeanette Islands were discovered by them. After many hardships Melville and nine men reached safety in the mouth of the Lena. Two of de Long's party survived, de Long and eleven others dying at Bulun, where Melville found their bodies in 1882.

1880 Leigh Smith in the English yacht *Eira* explored the westerly part of Franz Joseph Land, discovering many islands. He made valuable marine and botanical collections.

1881–82 Leigh Smith once more explored Franz Joseph Land. When the *Eira* sank, he was forced to spend a winter there before escaping to Novaya Zemlya.

1881–84 Captain Richard Pike commanded the *Proteus* which took an American expedition under Adolphus Greely to Lady Franklin Bay, Ellesmere Island. The *Proteus* returned, leaving Greely and 24 men, who built Fort Conger at Discovery Harbour. They stayed there for two years, exploring Ellesmere Island by sledge. When relief expeditions failed to reach them, they sailed by boat south to Cape Sabine where they wintered. By the time Schley's relief expedition rescued them, many men had died of starvation and scurvy, one had killed himself, and one had been executed for persistently stealing food.

1882–83 First International Circumpolar Year. Twelve stations were established by various nations to carry out scientific studies in the Arctic.

1882–83 Leonard Stejneger, an American, explored the area of Commander Island in the Bering Strait.

1883–86 Lieutenants Garde and Holm of the Royal Danish Navy surveyed the coast of southeast Greenland to continue the work of Lieutenant Graah of 1829. From this time, the Danes sent many expeditions to Greenland.

1888 Fridtjof Nansen completed the pioneer crossing of Greenland's ice cap, from Umivik Bay to Godthaab.

1888 Joe Tuckfield, an American whaling captain, confirmed that there were many whales in the area of Herschel Island. From that time whalers sailed east of Point Barrow and used Herschel Island as a winter base.

1888–89 Lord Lonsdale became the first recorded tourist on Banks Island when he made a six-day excursion from the Mackenzie Delta to Cape Kellett while on a private expedition.

1890 Warburton Pike accompanied by James Mackinlay of the Hudson Bay Company explored the Back River area, the former for sporting reasons. They were the third group of Europeans ever to do so, the first and second being Back (1833–35) and Anderson and Stewart (1855).

1891–92 Robert E. Peary sledged from Inglefield Gulf on the west of Greenland to Navy Cliff in the north.

1893–95 Peary crossed the Greenland ice cap again from Whale Sound to Independence Fjord.

1893–96 Nansen and Sverdrup intended to use pack-ice drift to reach the North Pole in the specially constructed *Fram*. After becoming beset northwest of the New Siberian Islands, they drifted for 35 months, achieving a highest north of 85°57′N 60°E. Sverdrup eventually extracted the *Fram* from the ice west of Spitsbergen. Meanwhile Nansen and Lieutenant Johansen attempted to reach the Pole over the ice. They turned south 228 miles from their objective at 86°12′N 100°E. After many hardships and dangers they were rescued by chance in the Franz Joseph Archipelago.

1894–97 Frederick Jackson, an English sportsman, charted much of Franz Joseph Land. It was he who came across Nansen and Johansen and rescued them.

1897 Salomon Andrée, a Swede, tried to balloon to the North Pole from Danes Island, Spitsbergen. Although it was known that he reached 82°N 25′E, he disappeared. In 1930 the bodies of

Andrée and his companions were found on White Island, where they had walked after abandoning the balloon on the ice. Photographs found with the bodies were successfully developed.

1898–1902 Peary made his first serious attempt at the North Pole through Smith Sound in the *Windward*. Leaving the ship at Cape D'Urville he sledged to Fort Conger, proved that Bache 'Island' was in fact a peninsula, and returned to the *Windward* after suffering many hardships. He lost eight toes through frostbite. In later years he determined Greenland's northernmost point which he called Cape Morris K. Jessup (83°39′N). In 1902 he set off northwards from Cape Hecla and reached a farthest north of 84°17′N.

1898–1902 Otto Sverdrup in the *Fram* explored the area of Hayes Fjord (meeting Peary) and then Jones Sound. Sledging parties discovered Axel Heiberg Island and Amund Ringnes Island in the Sverdrup Islands group. They also reached Beechy Island in the southwest corner of Devon Island.

1900–01 Prince Luigi Amadeo, Duke of Abruzzi, led a North Pole expedition which sailed to Franz Joseph Land in the *Stella Polare*. Captain Umberto Cagni started with sledges from Teplitz Bay and achieved 86°34′N 65°20′E, which was 22 miles further north than Nansen had managed. Hampered by the ice drift, the party only just reached Harley Island and safety. Three men were lost during the expedition.

1901 Zeigler reached a record (for a ship at that time) 82°04′N in the *America*.

1903–06 Roald Amundsen in the *Gja* became the first man to navigate the Northwest Passage. His route was Lancaster Sound–Barrow Strait–Peel Sound–Rae Strait–Queen Maud Gulf–Coronation Gulf–Amundsen Gulf.

1903 The Canadian NWMP established a post at Herschel Island to control the behaviour of the American whalers there. It remained until 1964.

1905–06 The persistent Peary took the *Roosevelt* to Grant Land (Ellesmere Island). From there he set out for the North Pole with a large force of Eskimos and dogs. Bad weather and ice conditions prevented him from succeeding, but he achieved a record 87°06'N 70°W.

1905–07 Alfred Harrison led a private British expedition which surveyed Herschel Island and visited Banks Island. He met Stefansson.

1906–08 Ludwig Mylius-Erichsen led a Danish expedition to north-east Greenland which carried out the first survey of this unknown area. He, Lieutenant Hagen and Jorgen Bronlund died of starvation largely due to inaccuracies in Peary's 1894 map. A second survey party of Lieutenant J.P. Koch, Aage Bertelsen and Tobias Gabrielsen survived and during the following spring, discovered Bronlund's body, his diary, and a bottle containing Hagen's vital sketch-charts.

1906–07 Vilhjalmur Stefansson (who had Icelandic origins) took part in an expedition organised by Ernest de Koven Leffingwell. He studied the Eskimos in the Mackenzie Delta and Jones Islands.

1906–07 Joseph-Elzear Bernier patrolled the islands in the District of Franklin in the C.G.S. *Arctic*. His aim was to take possession of all the islands for Canada.

1907–09 Dr Frederick A. Cook claimed to have reached the North Pole on April 21, 1908, having set out from Axel Heiberg Island. This was disbelieved by many at the time, and is still in dispute. Whatever the truth is, Cook spent 14 months away from civilisation in the Arctic regions which was a considerable achievement of endurance.

1908–09 Bernier continued his task of establishing sovereignty over the islands. He also found and recovered many relics of Parry's and Kellett's expeditions.

1908–09 Peary claimed to have reached the North Pole on April 6, 1909, having set out from the *Roosevelt* which was in winter quarters at Cape Sheridan, Ellesmere Island. Ross Marvin drowned in a lead while returning with a support party. Peary's claim has been doubted by some because of the speed of his return. He travelled 485 miles as the crow flies in 16 days, an average of 30.3 miles a day at the very least.

1908–12 Stefansson in a joint expedition with Rudolph Anderson studied Eskimos along the north coast of Canada and found the 'Blond Eskimos' of Victoria Island.

1909–12 Ejnar Mikkelsen and Iver Iversen explored the northeast coast of Greenland and found messages from Mylius-Ericksen as well as two food depots, but failed to find his diaries. They learnt too that Peary's 'Peary Channel' to the west coast did not exist; this led to a terrible journey back to base, where the two exhausted men arrived after the ship had departed. They existed there for a year before being rescued.

1912 Three expeditions prospected Baffin Island for gold, but like Martin Frobisher 350 years earlier, did not have any success.

1912 Knud Rasmussen crossed Greenland from Inglefield Gulf to Denmark Fjord, having set out from Thule. The information he gathered confirmed that Peary's outline of northeast Greenland was wrong.

1912–14 Two Russian expeditions under Sedov and Broussilov ended in disaster while attempting to reach the North Pole. Sedov died in Franz Joseph Land and the expedition returned. Broussilov's *St Anna* drifted north in the pack ice of the Kara Sea to 82°55′N (a drift of 1,540 miles in 18 months). Only two members of the crew survived.

1913 J.P. Koch made the longest traverse of the Greenland ice with ponies travelling from east to west from Denmark Harbour to Upernivik.

1913–17 Donald MacMillan, an American, set out to find 'Crocker Land' which Peary claimed to have sighted north of Axel Heiberg Island. After reaching 82°30′N 108°22′W, he realised the land did not exist and returned.

1913–18 The Canadian Arctic Expedition under Stefansson was split into a southern party which was to carry out scientific work in Coronation Gulf, and a northern party which was to explore in the *Karluk*. In the event the *Karluk* became icebound in the Beaufort Sea where she drifted for 3½ months before sinking. Two months later the crew reached Wrangel Island after the loss of eight men in the moving pack ice. Twelve survivors were eventually saved as a result of a heroic

600-mile journey to the Bering Strait in 37 days by the ship's mate Captain Robert Bartlett and one Eskimo. Meanwhile Stefansson, who had left the ship in order to hunt for game, carried out independent sledge journeys exploring the eastern seaboard of the Beaufort Sea, crossing Banks Island and visiting the Sverdrup and Parry Islands. The southern party successfully carried out its work.

1915 W.E. Ekblaw discovered Tanquary Fjord in Ellesmere Island. It was next visited in 1961 by Geoffrey Hattersley-Smith of the Canadian Defence Research Board.

1915 The Russian Admiral Vilkitski navigated the Northeast Passage east to west and carried out much hydrographical work in the Siberian Sea.

1917 Knud Rasmussen, Thorild Wulff and Lauge Koch (a nephew of J.P. Koch) formed the Second Thule Expedition which explored the northwest of Greenland from North Star Bay. Wulff and an Eskimo died from hunger and exhaustion.

1920–23 Dr Lauge Koch led the Danish Bicentenary Jubilee Expedition to northwest Greenland to continue mapping the coastline.

1921–24 Rasmussen, on his famous Fifth Thule Expedition, spent 3½ years with a number of Greenland Eskimos and Danish scientists studying the Eskimos of Arctic Canada.

1921–24 George Binney was responsible for organising the first of three Oxford Expeditions, which carried out successfully considerable work in the Arctic between the two World Wars. After a botanical and biological programme in 1921 in Spitsbergen, he led expeditions to North East Land in 1923 and 1924, using wireless for the first time and latterly a seaplane, the *Athene*.

1923 Lt Mittelholzer, a Swiss pilot, made several short flights in the area of Spitsbergen.

1925 Amundsen and Lincoln Ellsworth tried to fly to the North Pole from Spitsbergen in two Dornier flying boats. Six men flew in all. They reached 87°43′N, where they were forced to land through engine trouble, and one flying boat was abandoned. They spent 25 days making a runway on the ice for the other flying boat, which then successfully took off, and all returned safely.

1926 Commander R.E. Byrd and Floyd Bennett flew from Spitsbergen, supposedly to the North Pole and back, in 15 hours on May 9.

1926 Sixteen persons (including Amundsen, Ellsworth, Malmgren and the pilot Umberto Nobile) flew in an Italian dirigible over the North Pole where they dropped American, Italian and Norwegian flags. They departed from Spitsbergen in the *Norge* on May 11 and landed at Teller, Alaska on May 14 after a flight of 3,300 miles.

1926 Hubert Wilkins and Carl B. Eielson explored considerable areas of the Beaufort Sea by single-engined airplane from Point Barrow.

1926 James Wordie, tutor of St John's College, Cambridge, who had previously been chief scientist on Shackleton's 1914–17 *Endurance* expedition to Antarctica, was on his fifth Arctic expedition mapping the area around Clavering Island in East Greenland. In 1929 the nearby Peterman Peak, the highest mountain then known within the Arctic Circle, was climbed. A cruise to Baffin Bay in 1934 was handicapped by difficult ice conditions but in 1937 he successfully carried out his cosmic-ray investigations, the excavation of Eskimo house sites and the survey of coastlines in northeast Baffin Island. One of Wordie's great achievements was to train men such as Sir Vivian Fuchs to carry on the work in polar regions which he had inspired.

1927 Twenty-year-old H.G. (Gino) Watkins led an expedition to Edge Island, Spitsbergen.

1927 Wilkins and Eielsen again flew from Point Barrow but were forced down by engine trouble many miles to the northwest of the point. After drifting on ice and walking, they safely made land.

1928 General Umberto Nobile, Dr Finn Malgrem and 16 other men flew over the North Pole in the airship *Italia,* which unfortunately crashed on the return journey to Spitsbergen. Half the party had died or were missing and presumed dead when the survivors were finally rescued. A further tragedy was the loss of Amundsen in a rescue airplane.

1930 Dr H.K.E. Krüger led the German Arctic Expedition from north Greenland across Ellesmere Island to Lands Lokk after which they were never seen again.

1930–31 Gino Watkins led the British Arctic Air Route Expedition which had the aim of mapping and surveying southern Greenland and studying the meteorology there, with an eye to an eventual air route between England and Canada. A meteorological station was established on the ice cap which Augustine-Courtauld manned by himself from December 3, 1930 to May 5, 1931. He was rescued by Gino Watkins minutes after the fuel for his Primus stove ran out.

1930–31 The German Greenland Expedition under Professor Alfred Wegener had one party working in West Greenland, one in the east at Scoresby Sound and a station on the ice cap. Wegener died returning from the ice-cap station.

1930–32 Ushakov, a Russian, mapped the islands of the unexplored Northern Land northeast of Cape Chelyuskin.

1931 Hubert Wilkins attempted to cross the Arctic Ocean in an American submarine, the *Nautilus*.

1932–33 The Second International Circumpolar Year manned 45 permanent research stations in the Arctic, Antarctica and to a lesser extent in the temperate and tropical zones. Thirty-four nations participated.

1932–33 Unable to raise sufficient funds to cross the Antarctic Continent, Gino Watkins returned to East Greenland with Riley, Rymill and Chapman. On August 20 Watkins went out hunting in his kayak and was never seen again.

1933 Alexander Glen led an 18-man summer expedition from Oxford to Spitsbergen to carry out a scientific programme.

1933–38 Tom Manning has spent much of his life surveying and doing research in the Canadian Arctic. After two years in the district around Hudson Bay, he returned to England to organise an expedition to Southampton Island. Rowley, Baird and Bray accompanied him there, but returned in 1937, leaving him alone. They returned in 1938, when Bray was drowned.

Manning, his wife Jackie, Rowley and Baird have had a great impact and influence on the opening up and development of Arctic Canada since the end of World War II.

1933–34 Lieutenant Martin Lindsay, who had been a member of Watkins's first expedition to East Greenland, Andrew Croft and Lt Daniel Godfrey R.E. successfully surveyed the then unknown mountains between Scoresby Sound and Mount Forel, including the highest peak within the Arctic Circle. They approached the area from the west coast of Greenland and carried out the longest self-supporting dog-sledge journey ever achieved, of 1,080 miles.

1934–35 An Oxford expedition, organised by Edward Shackleton and under the leadership of Dr Noel Humphreys, was based at Etah in northwest Greenland. The six members became too dependent upon Eskimos, who were short of dog food, and the exploration of Ellesmere Island had to be curtailed.

1935–36 A ten-man scientific expedition from Oxford, led by Glen with Andrew Croft as his second-in-command, carried out a comprehensive programme in North East Land. Two ice-cap stations were created and manned, and a very detailed survey made of the whole island, about the size of Wales. An intensive ten-month study of the ionosphere proved to be of considerable value in the development of radar. Croft and Whatman crossed Spitsbergen to Klaas Billen Bay.

1937–38 A survey of the east coast of Ellesmere Island, to the south of Bache Peninsula, was undertaken by John Wright and Richard Hamilton both of whom had previously been with Glen. Meanwhile the leader, David Haig-Thomas, sledged to Amund Ringnes Island.

1937–38 Ivan Papanin and other scientists landed at the North Pole by ski-plane in May 1937. There they began a well-organised drift on a large ice floe down to the east coast of Greenland, and were finally evacuated by icebreaker in February 1938 near latitude 70°N.

1937 Chkalov and Gromov, Russian pilots, flew over the North Pole nonstop from Moscow to North America.

1940–44 Sub-inspector Henry Larsen of the RCMP, commanding the

80-ton schooner *St Roch*, navigated through the Northwest Passage in 1940–42, following Amundsen's route but in a reverse direction, from west to east. In 1944 he sailed through Lancaster and Melville Sounds, thence southwards through Prince of Wales Strait to Vancouver, completing a classic voyage in 86 days.

1946 The end of World War II sparked off tremendous enthusiasm and initiative in opening up the Arctic regions. The Canadian army and air force set the pace by carrying out a highly successful 3,000-mile journey by snowmobile, called Exercise Musk-Ox, from Hudson Bay to Victoria Island and thence southward via Coppermine, Great Bear Lake and through the sub-Arctic to Grande Prairie, Alberta. The exercise was commanded by Baird, who had previously been in the Arctic with Manning, and Croft was the British representative. Many expeditions of all nationalities have worked and explored the Arctic regions. Most British ones have tended to be small, scientific specialised expeditions, often supported to some degree by the Royal Geographical Society and the Scott Polar Research Institute.

1948–57 A series of scientific expeditions were led by Paul Emile Victor on the Greenland ice cap.

1952–54 Commander John Simpson R.N. with Hamilton as chief scientist led a Joint Services Expedition to Queen Louise Land, Greenland. Twenty-one scientists and servicemen carried out geological, glaciological and geomorphological work and established a weather station. At one stage Sunderland flying-boats of the RAF were used to establish a temporary base on an ice-free lake 200 miles inland.

1953–72 Dr Geoffrey Hattersley-Smith and a team of 8–20 men carried out geological and other scientific research at Tanquary Fjord, Ellesmere Island, every summer throughout this period.

1954 Scandinavian Airline Systems started regular commercial flights over the Arctic Ocean.

1958 The nuclear-powered submarine U.S.S. *Nautilus* crossed from the Pacific to the Atlantic Ocean without surfacing, passing over the North Pole on August 3 and crossing the Arctic Ocean in 96 hours.

1959 The U.S.S. *Skate,* another nuclear-powered submarine, surfaced at the North Pole on March 17 by breaking through the ice.

1960 The nuclear-powered submarine U.S.S. *Seadragon* sailed the Northwest Passage from east to west.

1959–61 Victor led further French expeditions to Greenland.

1963 Bjorn Staib, a Scandinavian, reached 86°N and escaped by 'boarding' an American floating ice-station. Several such stations had been established.

1965 A Scottish expedition consisting of Dr Hugh and Myrtle Simpson, Roger Tufft and Bill Wallace crossed the Greenland ice-cap ski-hauling sledges.

1967 Ralph Plaisted, an American, attempted to reach the North Pole by Skidoo from North Ellesmere Island. He was evacuated at 83°36′N.

1968 Ralph Plaisted successfully reached the North Pole on April 19, having left from Ward Hunt Island with a team of 12 men on Skidoos.

1968 Dr Hugh and Myrtle Simpson manhauled their sledge to 84°42′N on March 26, north of Ward Hunt Island.

1968–69 Wally Herbert, Major Ken Hedges R.A.M.C., Allan Gill and Dr Roy (Fritz) Koerner of the British Trans-Arctic Expedition crossed the polar ice-cap using dogs, the first to do so. They left Point Barrow, Alaska, on February 21, 1968, reached the North Pole on April 5, 1969 and landed on one of the Seven Islands, just to the north of North East Land, on May 29, 1969. They had covered 3,720 miles in 476 days.

1970 Count Monzino, an Italian millionaire and sportsman, reached the North Pole on May 19, 1970. His five-man team was supported by 14 Eskimos and 300 huskies.

1971 The Anglo-Danish Trans-Greenland Expedition made the longest manhauling traverse over the ice cap under the leadership of D. Fordham and J. Andersen.

1974–76 Naomi Uemura, a Japanese, made a 7,450-mile solo journey with dogs from Greenland to Alaska.

1977	Wally Herbert and Allan Gill attempted to circumnavigate Greenland by dog sledge and open boat.
1977	The British North Pole Expedition (Sir Ranulph Fiennes, Bt, Charles Burton and Oliver Shepard) reached 87°11.5′N on Skidoos while training for the Transglobe Expedition.
1978	Naomi Uemura reached the North Pole alone from Cape Columbia, Canada, covering 450 miles in 57 days.
1978	A Japanese ten-man expedition led by Kaneshige Ikeda sledged to the North Pole.
1979	D. Shparo (Russian) led six skiers to the North Pole having departed from Henrietta Land.
1981–82	Transglobe Expedition.

Expedition Notes

Before John Parsloe left the ship to return to New Zealand he said to me: 'Our journey should provide good news, but I wonder if it will. People are so cynical these days about any achievement by other people. The fashionable reaction is to discredit and degrade those who achieve it.'

In a sense John was wrong. During the eight months since our return I have heard happy, proud reactions from acquaintances and strangers. I do not include the handful of professional critics who seem to earn their living through denigration. '*Real* exploration involves the pitting of Man against Nature without the assistance of technology,' they have said. At that point does exploration become *real*? Does the Shackleton era and all that precedes it qualify, or is Shackleton precluded because he took advantage of steam-powered vessels whereas *his* predecessors suffered only with sail? Perhaps the magic words radio and aircraft are the key. If so, the purist must accept that his *real* explorers never crossed the Arctic Ocean or Antarctica. He might then respond: 'Ah, but Shackleton would probably have crossed Antarctica had his ship not foundered on the way south.' This would, I feel, make a poor wager, bearing in mind that even using the short approach from McMurdo Sound Shackleton could not make the South Pole, never mind the far more problematic stretch on the other side.

The advent of the aircraft meant that man could continue to eat after he had consumed all that it was possible to carry with him from his base and his prelaid caches. As a result and for the first time in history, man was able to cross Antarctica and the Arctic Ocean.

Would critics encourage contemporary attempts at polar or desert journeys without radio or aircraft in circumstances where their absence would almost surely result in the death of those involved? Looked at from the other side of the coin, how much sympathy would the dead *real* explorers get, having tried and failed after ignoring the availability of radio and aircraft, which, of course, are themselves hardly immune to the elements.

The true main hazards in Antarctica are crevasses and the cold. Neither is lessened by one degree because you have a radio with you and an aircraft in some distant base. The same is true for the Arctic Ocean if you substitute freezing water and moving ice for crevasses.

For hundreds of long, cold miles we hauled our sleds or carried in rucksacks individual loads in excess of one hundred pounds. We navigated from A to B in the polar regions solely by the sun and pocket compass and my watch. For months we travelled at temperatures as cold or colder than those experienced by our predecessors of twenty years earlier. Minus 50 degrees bored through our damp wolfskin and duckdown in much the same way as it did through the finneskos and ventile of Scott's team. Aircraft could not help us over great tracts of our travels since they could not land in the darkness or in mist or on surfaces of sastrugi or rubble.

As for the benefits of dogs over skidoos. There is no clear answer. Each has its pros and cons. In Antarctica skidoos come out on top despite the outcry from the polar experts who, before we set out, castigated us for choosing them. In the Arctic Ocean dogs are clearly the winners because of the twin obstacles of pressure ridges and leads.

Scott, Shackleton, Peary and the other explorers of the early twentieth century used *their* most modern contrivances to cut down their privations. We did likewise. The size of our ice team was smaller, the length of our expedition far longer in time and distance. They suffered unpleasantness when they made errors or Nature caught them on the hop. So did we.

It might be instructive for critics to complete the Transglobe route to see for themselves how successfully they could cocoon themselves against danger and privation through the application of modern technology.

In April 1983, the London *Times* published an article that set out to make the point that 'Shackleton's Trans-Arctic Expedition was the last justifiable voyage of geographical exploration.' The writer, himself a polar traveler specialising in dog journeys in Greenland, hinted that the travel of Fuchs, Herbert and Transglobe could never achieve the scientific status of Scott and Shackleton. He hinted too that the motive of the three more recent expeditions were jingoistic, with science as a poor cousin, whereas the earlier endeavours stood up proudly as geographical feats. To see through the camouflage of time, it is helpful to get to the simple question: When is a scientific expedition not a scientific expedition but an adventurous, jingoistic journey with a secondary science-gathering motive tagged on for respectability?

The answer, I suggest, is one of categories. There are the static bases of the Antarctic governmental bodies such as the National Science Foundation and the British Antarctic Survey. These are purely scientific 'expeditions' as are the based expeditions of the Royal Geographical Society in such places as Sarawak and Northern Oman. The personnel involved in such activities can be physically feeble and still be useful members of the expedition. Next there is the expedition which has a genuine scientific goal in a specific area and when the team reaches that area it is truly involved in science. However, the journey *to* the area may be an awkward one and some adventurous experiences may be had by the team while en route. Sometimes scrutiny of the entry route will reveal that a far easier and safer way in could have been used but the scientists chose the difficult way for unashamedly adventurous reasons. The other type of expedition is either merely adventurous and involves no science, or it is semi-adventurous and semi-scientific. It is under this last heading that the vast majority of expeditions fit, including the journeys of Scott, Shackleton, Fuchs and Herbert. Scott and Shackleton were competitive, adventurous men, a fact which their journeys reflect. They also used the most modern travel aids available to them and as much sponsorship as they could get.

Consider the designation 'mega-expedition'. By announcing that a given endeavour has cost a great deal of money, the impression is given that the whole thing must have been fairly simple on the principle that cash smooths the way. Some eight months after our return to England, the London *Times* said it cost Transglobe '£5m. to reach the North Pole'. I worked out the actual expense of our crossing the whole of the Arctic Ocean, which was less than £15,000 – and that was largely due to the fire at Alert. The *Times* later printed a short apology and correction. In other papers and on television the expedition was at different times quoted as having cost 10, 20 and 50 million pounds. It depended on the whim of the reporter at the time.

If one was to tot up the cost of Scott's *three* support ships and work out the wages his men would have earned and the price of all the items he was given if he had had to buy them, the cost in terms of money values of his day would have been very considerable indeed. But what a totally pointless exercise. Without the men, ships and equipment Scott would not have completed what he did complete. If his aim had been small and easy, his needs would have been commensurate.

The cost of the first crossing of Antarctica by the teams under Sir Vivian Fuchs and Sir Edmund Hillary was largely because the expedition was supported by the British and New Zealand governments and so funds *were* available. Ships were chartered, participants were paid, equipment was purchased. On such a journey it is a necessary exercise to tot up the overall cost since the expedition has a budget to stick to.

Transglobe was only possible because we spent seven long years ensuring that the journey did *not* cost us anything. We had no budget. The equipment had to come from such as the advertising and the public relations budgets of hundreds of companies who would otherwise have spent the money on television time or in newspapers. They chose to spend it on providing us with their goods or services. So be it.

Working out our hypothetical 'costs' would reveal a truly major sponsor to have been the ship's crew itself. Their standard wages would have amounted to £460,000, but they took nothing. They were not independently wealthy, no more than we were.

We are proud that the journey was set up and completed on a budget of *nothing*, and it frankly incenses us to see enormous mythical figures pulled out of hats, journalistic, expert or whatever.

It is true that once we left Greenwich there was no one left in London to carry out our policy of 'everything for nothing', and costs then began to creep in. These totalled £106,000; our advance royalties from this book will come to a fraction of that figure. On our return to England, Ginnie and Anton spent seven months selling wall charts, T-shirts, pamphlets and leftover equipment until our debts were all paid off. £36,000 to the New Zealand government for upkeep costs to the *Benjamin Bowring* was the single largest bill.

There was also the charge: 'Of course, they had a ship and an aircraft and a team of twenty-three so they could not fail.' Which conjures up a picture of twenty-three persons crossing the ice caps with a ship and aircraft ever alongside. The truth, of course, is that we operated on a shoe-string. Hence, in Antarctica, the official criticism was that we would fail using only one Twin Otter because it was underpowered and if just one irreparable piece of damage or mechanical failure occurred the whole project would come to a grinding halt.

We crossed Antarctica with three men using open-to-the-elements Skidoos. We navigated the Northwest Passage with two men in a small open boat and the Arctic Ocean with two men using partly Skidoos, partly a long man-haul and partly a long float.

We penetrated the polar seas at four corners of the world and travelled through the roughest oceans in a thirty-year-old ship with a thirty-year-old engine, keeping her going through the ingenuity of our volunteer engineers and the industry of our volunteer crew. She was the smallest and cheapest vessel available that could have conceivably completed the voyage.

What about the old cry, 'Nothing new was achieved'? We travelled over more unexplored, unmapped terrain than Scott or Shackleton, Peary or Amundsen. And we brought back useable information from that terrain, over one thousand miles of it, between Borga and the Pole, ice-core samples and aneroid barometer heightings, the latter specifically for verification of satellite imagery mapping. Whether or not we would run into vast crevasse fields in that untravelled region before we went there was unknown.

Critics could point out that Wally Herbert, in crossing the Arctic Ocean, did nothing new because pioneers like Peary had reached the North Pole first and Papanin had already travelled south from the North Pole. Yet by tying up journeys to and from the Pole into a single crossing, Herbert was achieving a new geographical feat for and by mankind.

A parallel is the voyage of Sir Francis Chichester. Other lone sailors had at one time or another sailed over each of the various seas which made up his total circumnavigation, but no one had previously completed the whole.

Our own great circle of the globe did in fact include a route to the South Pole of over nine hundred miles of hitherto untravelled terrain, just as Herbert's route to the North Pole was a new one.

In the same way that Chichester, Peary, Herbert and most of the others' routes included numerous wriggles and detours off a geometrically straight line, so did ours. Our biggest detour was the Northwest Passage, an additional leg of one thousand miles and an experience I do not regret; it took us through the Canadian Archipelago and over the ice caps of Northern Ellesmere Island, regions remote and unspoiled. This may not always be so.

I have been asked if religion plays a part in expeditions such as ours. This is, of course, not something that can be answered across the board.

Often it seems only a terrifying experience will bring out a person's latent belief, not merely a visit to remote places and a sojourn close to the elements. Then, too, many lone ocean travellers have proudly announced their atheism or agnosticism.

Personally, I agree with Edwyn Martin, a Transglobe participant. On the way back from Spitsbergen he said, 'The important thing is an ability to draw on some kind of inner strength. When you are totally alone and in the dark and things are bad, religion can be an inspiration. Sometimes it helps you feel you can go through almost any nightmare.'

Some Random Thoughts

If two people agree all the time one of them is unnecessary. Too much agreement kills a chat. *Eldridge Cleaver*

A pessimist is a man who looks both ways when he's crossing a one-way street. *Laurence J. Peter*

To be a prophet, it's enough to be a pessimist. *Elsa Triolet*

You don't have to be intellectually bright to be a competent leader. *Sir Edmund Hillary*

Leadership does not depend on being right. *Ivan Illich*

The leader must know that he knows and must be able to make it abundantly clear to those around him that he knows. *Clarence B. Randall*

There is no formula for success. But there is a formula for failure and that is trying to please everybody.

Think sideways. *Edward de Bono*

The only way to get the best of an argument is to avoid it.

An ounce of emotion is equal to a ton of fact.

As you grow older you'll find the only things you regret are the things you didn't do.

To be alive at all involves some risk. *Harold MacMillan*

A test of what is real is that it is hard and rough. Joys are found in it, not pleasure. What is pleasant belongs to dreams. *Simone Weil*

Everyman, through fear, mugs his aspirations a dozen times a day.

We give people a box in the suburbs, it's called a house and every night they sit in it and stare at another box. In the morning they run off to another box called an office and at the weekends they get into another box, on wheels this time, and grope their way through endless traffic jams. *Caroline Kelly*

If the Creator had a purpose in equipping us with a neck, he surely meant us to stick it out. *Arthur Koestler*

If we live we live. If we suffer we suffer. If we are terrified we are terrified. There is no problem about it. *Alan Watts*

Scientific Appendices

Research A

OCEANOGRAPHIC RESEARCH based from M. V. *Benjamin Bowring*, Arctic and Antarctic; Atlantic and Pacific, December 1979–August 1982 by Dr. C. McQuaid and L. Ricketts, Cape Town University

Research carried out by the scientific officers of the *Benjamin Bowring* was designed as a series of interlinked projects covering a wide spectrum of the oceanic environment and arranged in four main topics:

1) Physical oceanography
2) Primary productivity studies
3) Zooplankton studies
4) Seabird and marine mammal distribution

1) *Physical Oceanography* (a) Expendable bathythermographs were used to derive temperature/depth profiles along a transect across the Agulhas Basin, the Africa/Antarctic basin and the Maud Rise between Cape Town and Fimbulisen in Antarctica. A second transect was carried out between Fimbulisen and Cape Town via Bouvet Island.

(b) The possibility of pH changes in the open sea was examined using a Schott-Gerate pH meter on 3m samples. Three aspects were examined: (i.) Diurnal / nocturnal alterations in pH as a consequence of changes in photosynthetic activity of phytoplankton. The ship's course allowed this to be extended by considering diurnal fluctuations under polar and temperate light regimes. Monitoring of pH at two-hour intervals over 24–90 hours was carried out in McMurdo Sound, Antarctica; off Sydney; off San Nicolas Island, California; and in Adventfjord, Svalbard. (ii.) Latitudinal changes in pH were examined by monitoring every four hours (except 4 A.M.) in conjunction with collection of meterological data and measurements of surface temperature. Transects were carried out from New Zealand to/from Antarctica; Sydney to Los Angeles; Yukon River mouth to Vancouver; Caribbean to England; England to/from Svalbard; Svalbard to/from the pack ice of the Arctic Sea. (iii.) As the working hypothesis was that photosynthesis can lead to measurable pH changes even in an open system such as the deep sea, depth-associated pH changes between the surface and 200m were measured at 50m intervals on a series of stations between New Zealand and Antarctica. A bathythermograph with gold plated slides was used to determine whether any pH changes were associated with the presence of a thermocline.

2) *Primary Productivity Studies* Phytoplankton productivity rates were measured using light/dark bottles with a modified Winkler technique incorporating a photometric and point detector. Samples were incubated for 24 hours *in situ* after bathythermograph and salinity measures had been taken. Subsamples were filtered with glass fibre filters for subsequent chlorophyll analysis. Productivity was measured in three high Arctic marine systems: the fjords of Svalbard; in the pack ice of the Arctic Sea; in the open sea both at high latitudes (Greenland and Norwegian Seas) and in the North Sea.

3) *Zooplankton Studies* (a) Zooplankton distribution was examined by using an N-100 Discovery pattern net for surface trawls in the Southern Ocean along four transects: Cape Town to/from Fimbulisen; New Zealand to/from McMurdo Sound. Salinity and temperature measures were taken and a continuous temperature recorder used to locate the Antarctic convergence. Samples were preserved in formalin and after sorting, counting and identification to species level, biomass values were obtained by drying to constant weight at 60 degrees Centigrade. Specimens of the euphausid *Euphausia superba* were sexed and aged for detailed information on populations of this important species.

(b) Selected subsamples were preserved in Analar grade formalin buffered with calcium carbonate. These specimens were handled only with plastic instruments and returned to Cape Town for heavy metal analysis by flame spectrophotometry following digestion by nitric and perchloric acids. Specimens of fifteen species in a series of samples were analyzed for nine metals in this manner.

(c) Temperature acclimation of two Arctic amphipods *(Gammarus setosa* and *Onisimus litoralis)* were investigated by acclimating individual animals at different temperatures in reagent bottles with ground glass stoppers and analyzing changes in oxygen tension over 24 hours using the Winkler method. Results were expressed in terms of O_2 consumption per gram dry weight.

4) *Seabird and Marine Mammal Distribution* Three hours of bird observations, during which all visible birds were counted and where possible identified, were carried out each day while at sea. The bird watches were each one hour long, at the same time each day, and divided into consecutive ten-minute periods. Watches were maintained over 360 degrees from the bridge deck (3.5m above sea level) using 8 × 60 binoculars. Records of the start/finished positions of each watch as well as visibility, ship's speed, etc. were maintained. Return voyages (e.g. Cape Town to/from Fimbulisen) were treated as single passages for the species lists and gave additional data on seasonal shifts in distribution. Species lists and distribution tables were drawn up for ten major sea passages: Cape Town to/from Fimbulisen; Christchurch to/from McMurdo Sound; Sydney to Los Angeles; Los Angeles to Vancouver; Vancouver to/from Yukon River mouth; Vancouver to Panama; Panama to Southampton; Southampton to Svalbard; Svalbard to/from pack ice of the Arctic Sea; Svalbard to Greenwich.

Marine mammal observations were made in conjunction with bird watches as well as on an incidental basis. Identifications were made where possible along with position and meteorological conditions and observations of behaviour, pod size and structure, etc. Regular sightings of polar beasts (*Ursus maritimus*) on the Arctic pack ice gave information on population density. A total of 37 species of Cetaceans, seals, etc. were at least tentatively identified.

Research B

CRUISE REPORT: ROSS SEA SURVEY 1981 *UN. Benjamin Bowring* by Dr F. J. Davey, Geophysics Division, DSIR, for New Zealand Antarctic Research Programme 1980–81: Event 9

PROPOSED PROGRAMME

The scientific programme proposed for the ship consisted of two parts. The main part involved primarily geophysical measurements in the Ross Sea during a McMurdo Sound to McMurdo Sound charter. The second part of the work was mainly oceanographic sampling of the water mass at a series of stations between New Zealand and McMurdo Sound during the ship's run down to Antarctica. During this latter work geophysical equipment was operated on a noninterference basis.

The main geophysical programme was designed to study three regions in the Ross Sea:

(a) Eastern Ross Sea basin and continental margin

Objectives:

(i.) To study the eastern basin in more detail, in particular to obtain the total sediment thickness in the basin, link the sedimentary reflectors, especially the deeper reflectors, to DSDP sites 270–272 and to the Eltanin 32 profile, on which basement reflectors were seen, along the ice shelf front.

(ii.) To study the continental margin of the eastern basin. Eltanin 52 data showed an apparent rift structure to the margin, basement being downfaulted by 2 km on the oceanward side, with a deep consolidated sediment layer outcropping on the continental slope. The conjugate margin for continental rifting is the southwest Campbell Plateau margin which shows no downfaulting. Gravity, magnetic, seismic reflection and refraction data along profiles from the ice shelf to about 73° along 170°W and 165°W were planned. A link to DSDP sites 270–272 would be made using existing Eltanin or Explora data.

(b) Western Ross Sea Graben

Objectives:

To study in more detail the sediment-filled graben trending north-south under Western Ross Sea. The Eltanin seismic measurements showed a large thickness of sediments underlying central Western Ross Sea; gravity data indicated a north-south trending graben coincident with this feature. More detailed information is required on the graben including better definition of its presumably faulted margin, especially in the west, its total depth and age of its formation.

An east-west profile from 180° to 165°E along latitude 75.5°S was planned. Gravity, magnetics, seismic reflection and refraction measurements were required. Seismic refraction measurements (sonobuoys) were important and needed to be well positioned.

(c) Transantarctic Mountains Front

Objectives:

(i.) To elucidate the nature of the boundary between the Transantarctic Mountains and the Western Ross Sea using, in particular, gravity data as a means to studying the deeper structure.

(ii.) To extend previous seismic work studying the extent and nature of the sedimentary basin lying along the eastern margin of the above boundary.

(iii.) To examine the relationship of the Franklin-Beaumont-Ross Islands volcanic centres to the regional tectonic pattern.

Six east-west profiles about 30 km apart, running westward from longitude 170°E to as near the Victoria Land coastline as ice conditions permit, were planned. Gravity, magnetic and seismic reflection and refraction data were required.

The oceanographic programme extended earlier work by D. Burns in the Western Ross Sea and had two objectives. The main objective (a) was to sample the water mass at depths down to 300 m to investigate the distribution of hard-shelled phytoplankton between New Zealand and the Ross Ice Shelf. The secondary objective (b) was to obtain seafloor sediment samples along the icefront in McMurdo Sound.

The main program (a) was planned to consist of water bottle stations at every degree of latitude from 46°S to the edge of the Ross Ice Shelf (about 78°18′S). The track would be from Lyttelton to 65°S 177°W and then due south down 177°W to 74°30′S, then to McMurdo Sound. The water bottle station required the ship to be stationary for about half an hour but underway marine gravity measurements were planned for between bottle stations. During the geophysics survey surface water samples were planned to be taken frequently while under way.

PERSONNEL

Dr F. J. Davey	Geophysics Division, DSIR	Cruise Leader, Principal Investigator – East and Central Ross Sea Geophysical Survey
Dr D. J. Bennett	Geophysics Division, DSIR	Joint Principal Investigator – McMurdo Sound and Coastal Victoria Land Survey
Prof. D. A. Christoffel	Victoria University, Wellington	Joint Principal Investigator – McMurdo Sound and Coastal Victoria Land Survey
Dr D. Burns	N.Z. Oceanographic Institute	Leader – Oceanographic Programme
Dr R. Grange	N.Z. Oceanographic Institute	Oceanographic Programme
T. Dean	Geophysics Division, DSIR	Senior Technician
K. Rose	Geophysics Division, DSIR	Technician

The assistance of Roger Clarke (OIC), Hugh Webb (DOIC) and staff at Scott Base was greatly appreciated; they made our preparatory work and problem solving at McMurdo much easier.

The master, Capt. L. Davis, and crew of M.V. *Benjamin Bowring* were very helpful during the survey and preparations for the survey. The Transglobe Expedition were concerned that the survey charter proceeded smoothly and responded quickly when the satellite navigator problem arose.

L. Diggle, D. Keen, L. Rickett, D. Clark and DARM Ramsey assisted with watchkeeping.

EQUIPMENT AND PREPARATION

The project involved equipping a ship for carrying out geophysical and oceanographic measurements. The ship had some basic equipment such as for navigation but lacked other essentials such as suitable electrical power supply, winches and depth sounder. This equipment had to be obtained and fitted and this aspect of cruise preparation took a large part of the time spent before the cruise. Supplementary funds were made available by Head Office, DSIR, for purchase of some of these extra items but others had to be borrowed or hired. Details of the main equipment follows:

a) *Electrical power*: The ship's electrical power supply was 220 V DC. Three-phase 240 V 50 Hz AC power was required for the compressor used with the seismic sound course, airgun, and similar single-phase power for other scientific equipment. A 60-kVA three-phase diesel generator was hired as main scientific power supply and a 12-kVA single-phase diesel generator, transferred to the division from INS, was taken along as back-up generator. These generators were installed in the number one tweendeck hold, fuel lines were run from the ship's engine room and appropriate exhausts systems were installed from the generators out onto the main deck.

b) *Compressors*: A Reavell 30-cu ft/min. high-pressure air compressor was purchased for the survey. It was driven by a three-phase AC motor to enable it to be used on most modern ships. Unfortunately the *Benjamin Bowring* is a DC ship; hence the diesel generators were required. A small (7-cu ft/min.) Ingersol Rand compressor was installed and fitted with a DC motor drive as a back-up unit for use with a small airgun in case of breakdown of the large compressor or diesel generator. Wiring and airhoses were installed between the generators, compressors, laboratory (see later) and the stern area.

c) *Winches*: There was a lack of suitable winches for handling 'over the side' equipment on the *Benjamin Bowring*. NZOI installed a small petrol-driven winch and davit amidships for the oceanographic programme. This encountered problems with flooding by seawater (see later). A small petrol-driven winch was installed on the boat deck for lifting the airgun. This proved only just powerful enough for the coring work also undertaken with it. For other towed geophysical gear the ship's warping capstan was used. It proved fairly satisfactory.

d) *Depth sounder*: Two 12-kHz echosounder transducers were already installed on the ship and the ship also had an echosounder system capable of recording depths to about 1200 m. After a lot of searching we managed to borrow an elderly 12-kHz Edo transceiver from the Royal New Zealand Navy which adequately matched in with the ship's transducers.

e) *Laboratory*: A laboratory space was essential for installation, operation and maintenance of electronics and recording equipment. The first plan for the use of a wood-lined container in the number two lower hold was curtailed by the eventual unavailability of a suitable container. Two options then arose: the use of a container fitted out for accommodation from the meteorological office or a caravan partially fitted out as a laboratory from PEL. The latter was selected and installed in the number two lower hold. Some minor modifications were needed to install our equipment. The space was a bit restricted so the echosounder transceiver and the gravimeter platform and sensor were installed in additional dust-free enclosures constructed in the same hold.

f) *Stern working space*: All towed gear was installed on the boat deck apart from the airgun firing board which was located in a sheltered position on the main deck aft of the accommodation.

Some equipment ordered from abroad was delayed in delivery, either not arriving in time for the survey, as with the magnetometer retermination kit, or involving large airfreight costs, as in the case of the Reavell compressor.

A reasonable amount of equipment was obtained on loan (Appendix I) and the use of it was greatly appreciated. A list of the main items of equipment installed on the ship is given in Appendix II.

Installation of the geophysical equipment started in early December, taking about a month to complete.

No significant amount of preparatory work at McMurdo was anticipated. However, faults developed in ship's equipment en route to or at McMurdo which required attention. Faults developed in the Weatherfax recorder (used for recording weather and ice distribution maps) and in the satellite navigator system. In attempting to resolve these problems we would like to acknowledge the assistance of personnel at McMurdo Station and Scott Base.

Transport to and from Scott Base from Christchurch was smooth; a total travel time of 28 hours between arrival at McMurdo Station from sea to arrival in Wellington was much appreciated.

SURVEY PROGRAMME

The tracks covered during the survey programme are shown in Figures 1 and 2.

A gravity base tie was made before the ship departed from Wellington for Lyttelton on January 5. At Lyttelton another gravity base tie was made, the ship loaded fuel and departed for the Ross Sea on January 6. On the voyage to McMurdo Sound the oceanographic programme and gravity measurements were carried out. The oceanographic programme consisted of carrying out water sampling to depths of 250 m at station intervals of 1 degree latitude. Rough sea conditions and violent ship motion curtailed the programme but seven stations were successfully occupied.

Gravity observations were made for most of the voyage but rough sea conditions shut down the meter for a couple of days and made data at other times marginal. Bathymetric data were recorded until depths of about 4000 m were reached, when signal strength was too small and no record obtained.

The ship arrived at McMurdo Station on January 20 and tied up at the ice wharf. The oceanographic party disembarked and three of the geophysics party joined ship. Technical assistance from McMurdo Station was used to try and fix the ship's Weatherfax recorder with no lasting success as the stylus belt and drive wheels were too worn, and no spares were carried by the ship. While working on this problem the satellite navigator developed a fault. No manual or spares were available but after working for two days a fault was isolated on the power supply board. No suitable spare ICs were available ashore. During this time spare module boards and manuals were flown down from the satellite navigator manufacturer's agents in Auckland. With the spare modules the initial fault was corrected but the main fault was traced back to the receiver module for which there was no spare or suitable test equipment (at Scott Base or McMurdo Station) to repair the module. The Transglobe Expedition, primary charterer of the ship, therefore decided to fly out a new satellite navigator from the U.S. This arrived in five days.

While awaiting the replacement satellite navigator the ship sailed to carry out some geophysical work in the McMurdo Sound region where navigation based on radar fixes was considered adequate. This short cruise acted as a 'shake down' cruise for geophysical equipment, especially the seismic reflection profiler. The sparker system was operated on a profile up the eastern side of McMurdo Sound to central Wohlschlag Bay. Seismic penetration of the system was limited because of the low power and level of 50 Hz background noise. A series of four coring stations for the Geology Department of Victoria University were occupied along a line from Wohlschlag Bay to Cape Bernacchi. Results were poor, the longest core being only about 50 mm long. The seismic reflection equipment was then deployed for a series of seismic profiles and gravity measurements across the sound up to Granite Harbor. This work was severely curtailed in extent by pack ice. Icing up of the air lines to the airgun were experienced at intervals of 6 to 12 hours which necessitated lifting the airgun to free them. The ice accumulated mainly in the firing board (valves and gauges) onboard and in the filter at the airgun. In the latter case the filter was eliminated and in the former case the firing board was insulated and a heater (light bulb) installed. An antifreeze drip feed system into the high-pressure airline helped to reduce the freezing problem. At the end of the seismic work a further two gravity core stations were occupied successfully obtaining cores up to 300 mm long.

On returning to McMurdo Station after the short survey the ship was held up by ice for several hours.

The ship stayed near McMurdo Station alongside the sea ice for one and a half days before the replacement satellite navigator arrived. The navigator was installed, tested and found to be operating correctly so the ship departed immediately on the main part of the Ross Sea survey. Gravity and bathymetric measurements were made from McMurdo Station to Cape Bird where the seismic reflection equipment was deployed. The seismic reflection equipment was in operation for the remainder of the cruise apart from two one-day periods when the airgun was brought onboard and the ship steamed at full speed to make up time to complete the survey programme.

The ship proceeded eastward parallel to the ice barrier to pass over Deep Sea Drill Project (DSDP), site 270, then headed to the ice barrier at longitude 170°W. The location of the edge of the ice barrier was noted as being about 20 km north of the 1962 location shown on most charts. A sonobuoy station was successfully occupied at longitude 176°E, at the south end of the Western Graben. A set of four sonobuoy measurements were made along the profile along longitude 170°W coincident with the axis of the eastern Ross Sea Basin. Pack ice caused this profile to be curtailed at 75°30'S and the ship traversed across to longitude 165°W and headed southward as far as the Bay of Whales. Three more sets of sonobuoy measurements were made along this profile. The next profile, northeast toward Marie Byrd Land, was curtailed by ice at 161°W. The ship then headed westward and the airgun lifted after crossing the 165°W profile for the first one-day high-speed run. At this time the echosounder record greatly deteriorated due to a worn-out stylus, so the bridge echosounder was subsequently used.

Starting at 75°30'S, 177°30'E a series of end-to-end sonobuoy measurements, nine in all, were made along an east-west profile across the western graben. Good data were obtained. The Victoria Land coastal survey then started with a profile in toward the Victoria Land coast just north of the Drygalski Ice Tongue. Pack ice at about 166°E stopped this profile short and the ship headed northeast to get around the ice. The ship then lost use of the main engine for six hours as one of the ship's generators broke down and the other had a jammed starter. The ship then worked into Terra Nova Bay before heading northward again. East-west profiles were then run into the coast on the northern side of Cape Washington, to within 30 km of the coast just north of Coulman Island, and to within 15 km of the coast at Mowbray Bay. The latter two profiles were limited in extent by pack ice which was just too thick to work in. The airgun was then lifted and the ship did its second high-speed run southward to Franklin Island. Profiles were then run in toward the coast, as close as possible in the ice conditions, at Tripp Bay, Granite Harbour and at Dunlop Island. The ship then headed south to the Dry Valley Drilling Project (DVDP), site 15, and a seismic profile was run from DVDP-15 to

MSSTS-1 site. The seismic gear was then recovered and gravity and bathymetry data obtained en route to McMurdo Station.

The ship was alongside the ice wharf at 1400 hours on February 12. The geophysical gear was then packed up in preparation for the voyage to New Zealand. A base reading was taken with the marine gravimeter. The geophysical party then left the ship for Scott Base. The party flew out from Williams Field at about 0630 February 13 arriving at Christchurch about 1500 the same day.

The ship returned to Lyttelton on February 27 and was ready for unloading on March 4. Original plans for unloading had to be changed due to industrial problems (rail ferry strike), so five people flew to Christchurch to unload the equipment and arrange for the transport back to Wellington by truck and rail wagon. Unloading took two and a half days. The gravimeter sensor was left onboard until Auckland as it needed special protective transport. The large generator was also left onboard as Auckland was its final destination.

Prior to the Ross Sea survey three members of the geophysical party were at Scott Base for a week awaiting the arrival of the ship. During this period additional geophysical measurements were made. An initial plan to extend the coverage of gravity measurements in the vicinity of the Dailey Islands was cancelled because of poor sea-ice conditions in the region. A revised program was set up. Dr Bennett joined R. Holdworth's party, Event K15, on the Erebus Ice Tongue for two days and carried out gravity measurements. Prof. Christoffel and Dr Davey carried out paleomagnetic sampling of basic igneous rocks at Castle Rock and Observation Hill, Ross Island, and of the lamprophyre dykes near Lake Vanda. This work supplemented work carried out earlier in the season by Prof. Christoffel as Event 13.

COMMUNICATIONS

Communications from the ship to Scott Base were always adequate. A daily sked on 5.4 mHz was always kept, usually at 1800, occasionally at 0835. The radios used onboard were Transglobe Expedition equipment. Communications with New Zealand, quite important at one stage, were good.

Information officer: No news service incoming to the ships as none was requested. It would be preferable if press relations about the survey work we were doing were released after we had done some work rather than before. A press release went out to say we had departed on a nineteen-day survey a few days before we in fact sailed and also before we had our extra charter time confirmed.

RESULTS

The results of the survey work undertaken as Event 9 can be summarised as follows:

a) Lyttelton to McMurdo Sound
3700 km gravity measurements
1000 km bathymetry measurements
8 stations oceanographic measurements

b) Ross Sea Survey
4200 km gravity measurements
3200 km seismic reflection profiling measurements
25 sonobuoy seismic refraction observations
6 shallow gravity core stations (5 successful)

c) Ross Island and Wright Valley
8 gravity observations on the Erebus Ice Tongue. Paleomagnetic samples taken at Castle Rock, Observation Hill and near Lake Vanda.

Overall, once the main Ross Sea survey started, the results were good and the survey can be considered successful. The main disappointment in the geophysics programme was the lack of magnetic data, especially in the Western Ross Sea area. Elsewhere magnetic measurements are considered to be of low priority as anomalies are few, and very large diurnal geomagnetic variations occur. For both the oceanographic and geophysical work the large amount of movement of the ship during the run down to Antarctica greatly limited the amount of data gathered. The gravimeter gyrotable reached its operational limits and a large amount of damage occurred to the oceanographic equipment on deploying and recovering it while the ship moved heavily.

Detailed analysis of the geophysical and oceanographic data will take several months to complete. Preliminary results of the geophysical, in particular seismic, data, however, are available and can be considered by regions.

a) *Eastern Ross Sea*: Two profiles were made along the north-south axis of the Eastern Ross Sea sedimentary basin. The seismic reflection data show sedimentary layers dipping steadily to the north, the dip increasing rapidly at the shelf edge. No basement reflectors were detected along the ice front as with Eltanin 32 data but the ice front had moved 15 to 20 km further north. The increase in sediment thickness northward is supported by the sonobuoy measurements which indicate over 4 km of section in the basin (Figure 3). The measurements in the eastern part of the basin show basement shoaling to the east with gently folded sediments along the eastern flank.
b) *Western Ross Sea*: A detailed set of sonobuoy measurements do not show the simple graben structure underlying Western Ross Sea inferred from early data. The new data shows a more basinal form with thick sediments occurring under central Western Ross Sea (Figure 4).
c) *Victoria Land Coast*: Reasonable seismic reflection data and eight good sets of sonobuoy measurements were obtained. Preliminary plane layered interpretations of these refraction lines are shown in Figure 5. Basement velocities (> 5 km/s) were only encountered on the eastern side of the region indicating perhaps that basement dips toward the coast. An intermediate velocity layer (4–5 km/s) occurs extensively west of the Coulman Island (CI) to Ross Island (RI) line. This may correspond to late Cenozoic basaltic flows but more likely would be associated with well indurated sediments typical of the Beacon Supergroup.
d) *McMurdo Sound*: The seismic data show sedimentary layers dipping and thickening eastward across the sound, as found on previously collected data in the region.

It is planned to publish the results of the work in various New Zealand scientific journals and at the SCAR symposium on Antarctic geosciences in Adelaide in 1982.

F. J. Davey

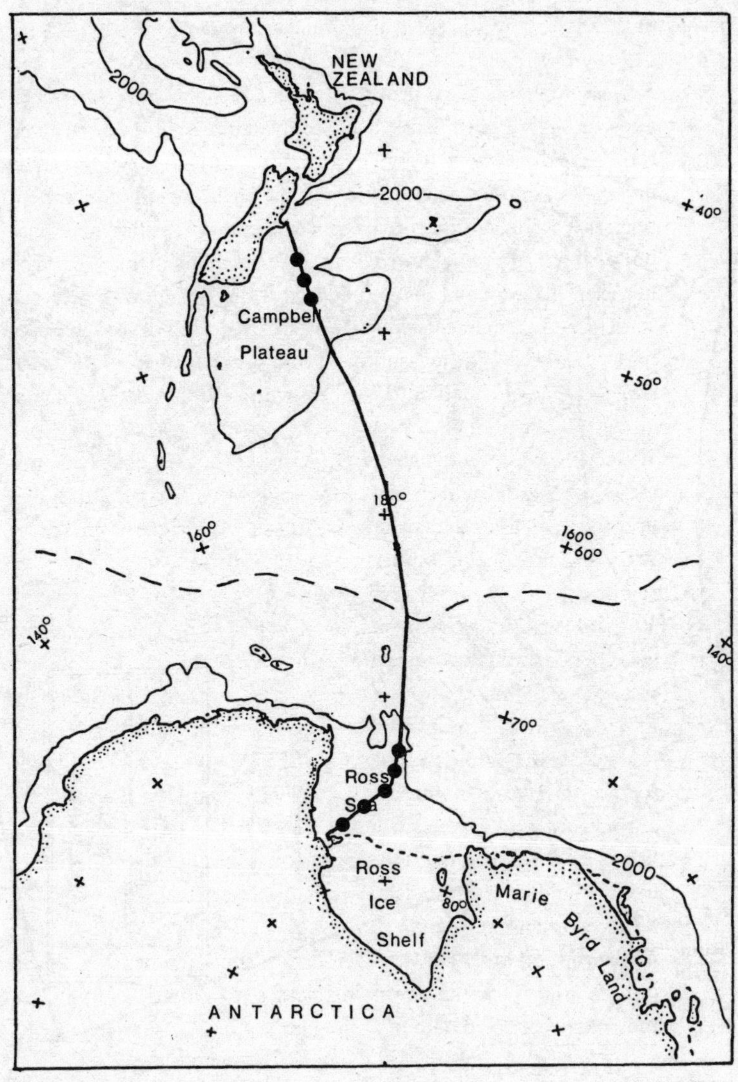

FIGURE 1
Oceanographic stations
Ship track

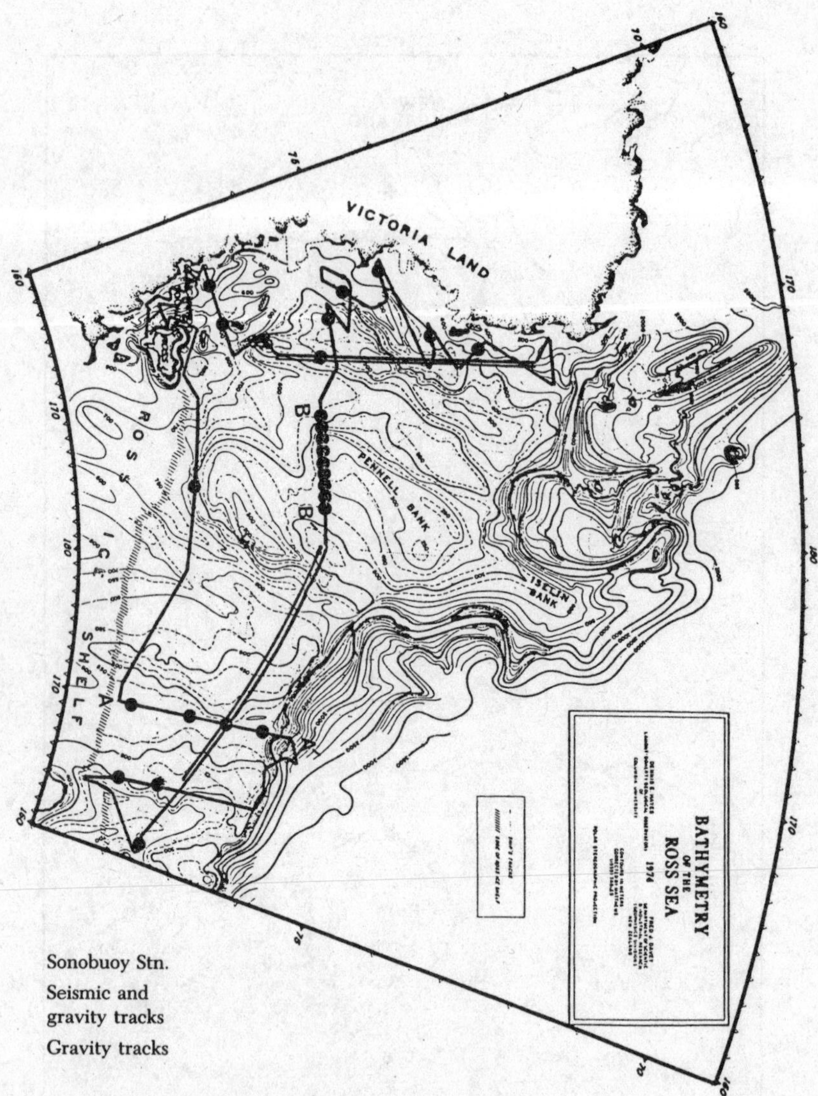

FIGURE 2
Bathymetry of the Ross Sea. Contours at 100-metre intervals, 500-metre contours shown by heavy lines, with 50-metre contours shown on the shelf area by a long dashed line.

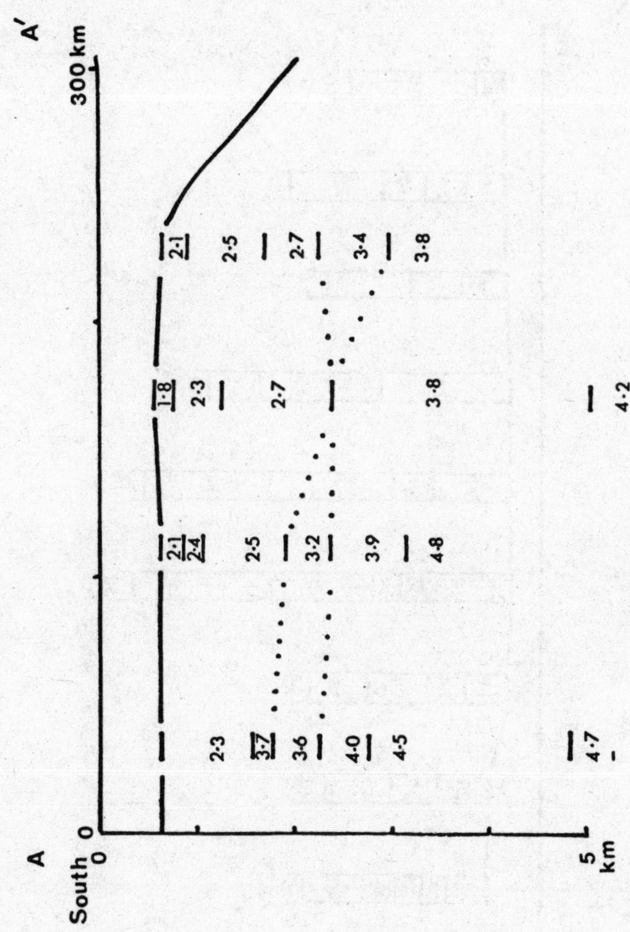

FIGURE 3
Sonobuoy seismic refraction results along profile AA′ located on Figure 2. Velocities in km/s.

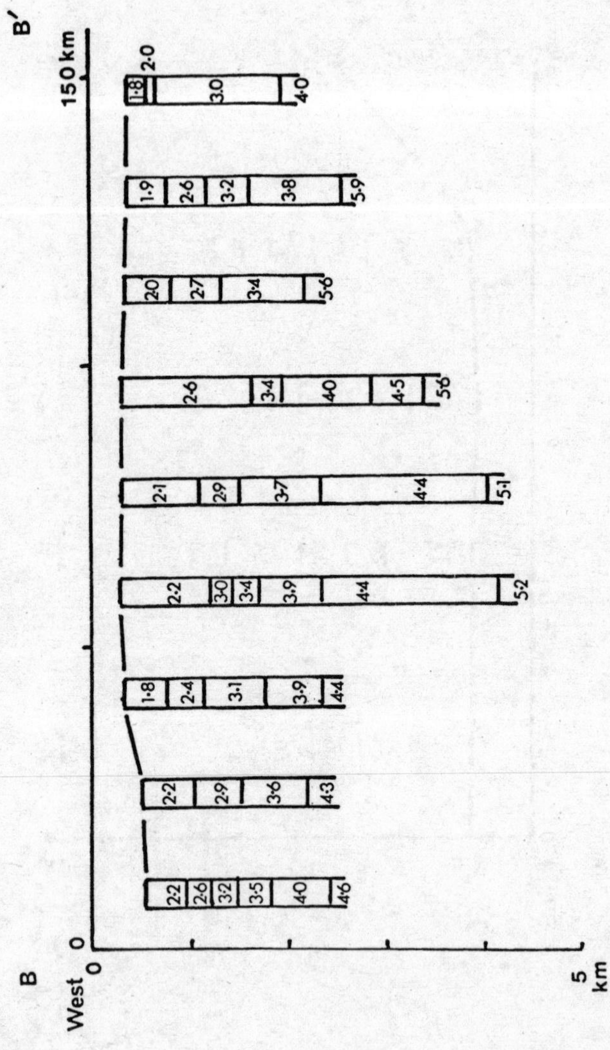

FIGURE 4
Sonobuoy seismic refraction results along profile BB′ located on Figure 2. Velocities in km/s.

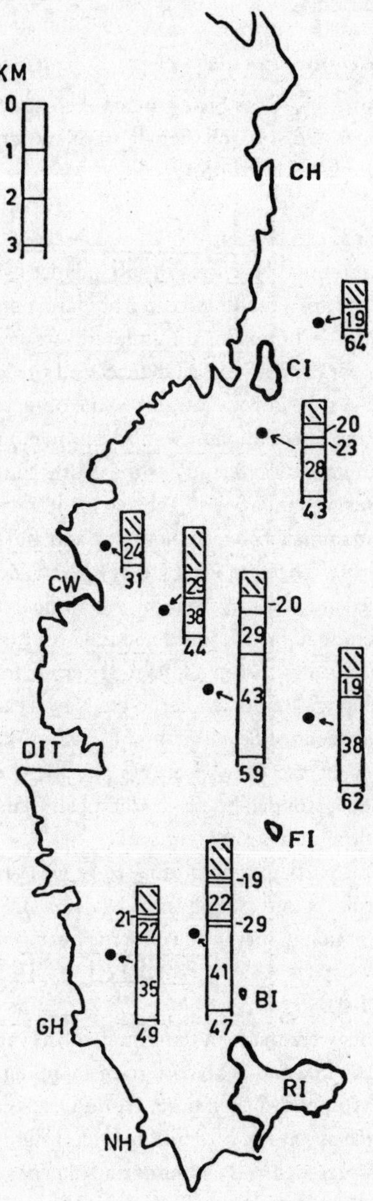

CH Cape Hallett
CI Coulman Island
CW Cape Washington
DIT Drygalski Ice Tongue
FI Franklin Island
BI Beaufort Island
GH Granite Harbour
NH New Harbour
RI Ross Island

FIGURE 5

Research C

BIRDS AND MAMMALS observed from M.V. *Benjamin Bowring* South Atlantic and Ross Sea. January–February 1981, by Jennifer Bassett and Graham Wilson (on behalf of New Zealand International Survey of Antarctic Seabirds (ISAS))

Seabirds can be relatively easily observed and, since their pelagic distribution presumably reflects the abundance of the marine organisms they prey on, they are a useful indicator of marine productivity over a wide area. The Scientific Committee on Antarctic Research (SCAR), when drawing up plans for the ten-year BIOMASS study, recommended that the first summer, 1980–81, be devoted largely to the observation and recording of the numbers and distribution of seabirds throughout the southern ocean. BIOMASS is an international study of the southern ocean ecosystem.

During January and February 1981 we made observations of seabirds and mammals between New Zealand and Antarctica from M.V. *Benjamin Bowring*. The ship left Lyttelton, New Zealand, on January 7, 1981 and arrived at McMurdo Station, Antarctica, on January 20. We made a three-day cruise in the McMurdo Sound area from January 25 to January 27. On January 29 we began a fifteen-day cruise in the Ross Sea, during which time the ship was under charter to the New Zealand Geophysical Division of the Department of Scientific and Industrial Research, to undertake a seismic survey of the Ross Sea. We left McMurdo on February 16 for New Zealand, stopped briefly at Campbell Island on February 23 and arrived in Lyttelton on February 27.

Our participation in this cruise was organised through the Transglobe Expedition and Geophysical Division, DSIR on behalf of New Zealand's International Survey of Antarctic Seabirds (ISAS) committee.

METHODS

Counts were made in ten-minute observation periods, and were recorded on Australasian Seabird Group mapping scheme cards. Up to six cards were completed each hour. During each count the numbers and activities of each species of bird and mammal sighted were recorded, as were date, time, presence and extent of pack ice or icebergs, weather and sea conditions. Our position and speed were recorded by satellite navigation system hourly; this was rounded down to the nearest degree latitude and longitude on the cards. New Zealand Standard Time (G.M.T. + 12 hours) was used throughout the voyage. Cruising speed was 9 to 11 knots, but was about 7 knots during most of the McMurdo Sound and the Ross Sea cruises.

Most observations were made from the bridge, 9 metres above sea level, giving a forward view of about 180°. Birds following the ship were noted at intervals, and in the subantarctic zone, where they were common, wake followers were noted during most ten-minute observation periods.

The sea was scanned by unaided vision and 10 × 35 or 7 × 35 binoculars were used to assist in bird identification or to count flocks. All birds and mammals seen within 400 m of the ship were recorded. With the exception of prions (genus *Pachyptila)* and shearwaters (genus *Puffinus),* only birds that were identified to species level are shown on these distribution maps. Prions and shearwaters often proved impossible for us to identify, but their numerical importance warranted their inclusion. Scientific names are given on the distribution maps.

Little allowance could be made for birds circling the ship or following behind, and some individuals were undoubtedly counted more than once.

In this report the data are presented as the number of sightings of each species in a twelve-hour period. The abundance of shearwaters, prions, penguins and other birds whose activities were not influenced by the ship's presence, was more accurately estimated than that of albatrosses, fulmarine petrels, black-bellied storm petrels, and white-chinned petrels, which were habitual ship followers. On the return voyage the data plotted on the albatross, mollymawk and giant petrel distribution maps is an aggregate of the highest number recorded on any one card during each clock hour of the twelve-hour period.

During the southward voyage, when only one observer (J.A.B.) was on board, continuous observations were impossible, but counts were spread out to cover as many of the daylight hours as possible. During the Ross Sea cruise and the voyage to New Zealand we alternated, and almost continual observations were made during daylight hours. Continual observations increase the likelihood of recording uncommon species, but, as birds accompanying the ship are counted several times, it does not give a good indication of bird abundance. Wake followers and birds accompanying the ship should not be recorded in a study of abundance.

More than 3,000 ten-minute observation cards were filled out and these will be incorporated into the BIOMASS study of the pelogic distribution of Antarctic birds.

Research D

PRIMARY PRODUCTIVITY research based from M.V. *Benjamin Bowring*, Svalbard region, May–July 1982, by J. Reynolds of Southampton University.

Primary production is of paramount importance in determining the distribution of carbon and oxygen in the sea and indirectly nearly all other biogeochemical processes. Since all other organisms are ultimately dependent on primary producers for food, the level of phytoplankton productivity establishes the basis from which energy flow through the ecosystem may be followed and provides an indication of the fishery potential of a given area. Although few data exist on productivity in Arctic waters, primarily on account of their inaccessibility and the inhospitable climate, it is generally considered to be unproductive. The Arctic is particularly interesting due to its light regime – in summer daylight is continuous, whereas in winter there are long periods with no light – and its complex zones of mixing that exist where waters derived from the Arctic Basin and from temperate regions meet.

Most of the information on Arctic productivity has been gathered from inshore and subarctic waters with a limited amount from drifting ice stations and from submarines operating in and under ice near the North Pole.

Sokolova and Solov'yeva (1971) making determinations off the Murmansk Coast found the highest values of primary productivity to be about 30 mgC M^{-3} day^{-1}. Measurements by English (1959) from Drift Station Alpha in the Arctic Basin also indicate low productivity. However, work by Digby (1953) at Scoresby Sound, East Greenland, suggests a level of phytoplankton pigment similar to that found in the English Channel, although no productivity measurements were made.

The Subarctic, by contrast, is a notably productive region as evidenced by the large crops of fish produced. The reasons for this high productivity are uncertain, but it is thought to result from a lifting of temperature inhibition by mixing of the Arctic water with warmer Boreal water, making possible the utilisation of nutrients in the Arctic water.

Productivity may be determined either by measuring carbon-14 fixation or by measuring oxygen evolution using either an oxygen electrode or Winkler titration.

Until recently, relatively low values of productivity could only be assessed on the basis of radio-labelled carbon assimilation (Steerman Nielsen, 1952). Difficulties in the interpretation of data suggest productivity values obtained in this manner may be unreliable.

The opportunity of joining the Transglobe Expedition vessel, M.V. *Benjamin Bowring,* in Spitsbergen and travelling with the ship into the Arctic pack ice enabled a study of primary production in these areas to be made using a recently developed oxygen technique of increased sensitivity attained through the use of a photometric end point detector (Bryan *et al,* 1976).

Although this technique is not as sensitive as the carbon-14 technique, there are many advantages to this method: the easy interpretation of data obtained, the elimination of the use of radioactive materials, the lack of sophisticated equipment and the simplicity and rapidity of the technique allowing immediate analysis of samples.

Productivity and ancillary measurements were made in three fjords in Spitsbergen in the open sea and in the pack ice. *In situ* incubations were carried out in the fjords, but the needs of the expedition necessitated on-deck incubations in the pack ice and open sea. Although *in situ* incubations were preferable, it was thought that on-deck incubations would give a relative indication of production levels and provide useful data on this process for Arctic waters.

The results showed low values of primary productivity throughout the area with the exception of a single station close to the seaface of a glacier in Kongsfjorden, Spitsbergen, where localised upwelling occurred.

J Reynolds

Research E

METEOROLOGICAL RECORDS by M.V. *Benjamin Bowring*, South Pacific, May–October 1980

To the Master: M.V. *Benjamin Bowring*

Dear Sir:

My thanks on behalf of the director general of the meteorological office for the latest meteorological logbook to be received from the *Benjamin Bowring* which covered the period May 2, 1980 to October 27, 1980. This is a first-class book; the observations contained therein are of a very high standard and reflect great credit both on the officers who made them and also on the radio officer who transmitted them to the appropriate shore radio stations. We were particularly glad to notice the use which the observers had made of the remarks column throughout the book, for recording shifts of wind, times and duration of precipitation, etc., as these considerably enhance the value of an observation when it is used for climatological purposes. The ocean current data recorded in this book are most welcome. As mentioned in our previous letter these are of great value to us in our work of updating admiralty pilots and compiling current charts. We look forward to further such data from your vessel whenever the opportunity occurs. Where applicable the interesting reports contained in the additional remarks pages have been forwarded to the appropriate experts and should we receive any comments concerning them we will be pleased to pass these on to you. Your reports of whales and dolphins observed between September 1979 and April 1980 were forwarded to the Dolphin Survey Project at Cambridge and they commented 'this is useful to have information from so far south. In almost all cases the animals are positively identified and therefore require no comment.' As usual, all these reports will be considered for publication in our journal.

It is obvious that you and your staff take the liveliest interest in our work of providing a meteorological service for shipping to which we are committed under the International Convention for the Safety of Life at Sea. Our sincere thanks to you and all concerned.

Yours faithfully,

Captain C. R. Downes
for Marine Superintendent
Meteorological Office

Note: Similar results were obtained by the M.V. *Benjamin Bowring* watch officers during the periods September 1970–April 1980 and November 1980–August 1982.

Research F

ZOOLOGICAL PROGRAMME, Algeria/Mali/Ivory Coast, September–November 1979 Completed by O.W.N. Shepard for British Museum, Natural History Department.

Following training at the National History Department of the British Museum, O. W. N. Shepard completed collections for the department as follows:

a) In the sand dunes 20 km north of El Golea in Algeria specimens of skink or sand lizard were trapped and preserved. These proved useful in establishing the location of subgenus of skink some 100 miles further south than previously thought to exist.
b) In the savannah region of Goundam in Mali specimens of fruit bat were trapped and preserved to complete gaps in the museum's collection.
c) In the rain forest zone of the Bandama Rouge river in the Ivory Coast, specimens of bilharzia-bearing water snails were collected and preserved for research under Dr C. A. Wright.

Note: Lists of bird sightings during the journey included 141 recognised species.

Research G

MAGNETOSPHERIC RESEARCH: ELF/VLF PROGRAMME, Completed at Ryvingen Camp, April–October 1980 by Virginia Fiennes for Sheffield University Space Physics Department.

The position at which the overwintering station was established (at an altitude of 1700 metres) had special advantages for the measurement of movements in the magnetosphere and changes in the precipitation of particles from it, as shown by ELF/VLF signals. This formed part of a major international exercise, of interest not only to U.K. scientists but also to South African, American, French and Argentinian organisations.

The programme had been formulated by Dr K. Bullough of Prof. Kaiser's Department of Space Physics, University of Sheffield, England. Suitable mobile equipment was designed and constructed at Sheffield. It consisted of twin-loop antennae, preamplifier and receiver, tape recorder, Venner oscillator, rechargeable battery power supplies, time code generator and goniometer.

This not only enabled ELF/VLF signals to be recorded, but provided a direction-finding capability showing where the signals come from. By operating simultaneously with other stations, it was possible to fix the point at which the signals penetrated the lower part of the ionosphere. The expedition's radio operator Virginia Fiennes was trained at Sheffield to use the equipment.

Any irregularities in the ionosphere diffuse rapidly along the tubes of force and thus generate radio guides linking one hemisphere with the other. Movements in the high atmosphere cause these tubes to move and thus it is possible to watch the circulation in the magnetosphere from the ground using naturally generated signals. The inner part of the magnetosphere co-rotates with the earth. The outer part forms a comet tail extending beyond the moon, which is approximately constant in form relative to the sun. The solar wind blows the outer part of this tail away from the sun, setting up a circulation with an inward flow near the centre of the tail. Changes in movement with time or position can cause acceleration of particles and thus precipitation of high-energy particles into the ionosphere which are then visible as aurora.

The most interesting and complex movements occur near the boundary between the co-rotating part of the magnetosphere, which has high-electron density, causing great delay of the signals, and the relatively rarified plasma of the tail. The mean position of this is strategically placed relative to Halley Bay (British Antarctic Survey), Siple (U.S. base), SANAE (S. African base) and the expedition's overwintering station, Ryvingen.

There is a major international effort to study such changes using an east-west chain along a constant magnetic latitude. It is very desirable that cross-bearings from widely separated stations should be supplemented by cross-bearings between a close triangle of stations. SANAE, Halley Bay and Ryvingen formed a useful triangle since Ryvingen is about 120 kms from SANAE and both are 600 kms from Halley Bay.

Observations made at the unmanned station at SEAL, 120 kms from Halley Bay during the relatively short periods in which this station was operating, have shown that interesting differences in behaviour can occur over a range of only 120 kms and that this separation is good for studying movements of ducts. A permanent station of the same type as the mobile station exists at Halley Bay and similar equipment of American design was recently installed at Siple and Palmer (U.S. bases) and SANAE. Thus observations made at Ryvingen can, in principle, be used in conjunction with SANAE as a short-base system, with Halley as a medium-base system using identical equipment at both ends, and with Palmer and Siple as a long-based system. This would complement the planned cooperation between Siple, Palmer, Halley Bay and SANAE. It is therefore to be expected that more than one of the national groups working in this field will be interested in using the data obtained at Ryvingen.

One of the major reasons for the international interest in the study of movements using ELF/VLF signals in the Weddell Sea sector of Antarctica is that conditions are exceptionally favourable for the generation and propagation of such signals. During winter between one and two orders of magnitude more signals are received than in the northern hemisphere during its local winter, and the great skewness of the invariant magnetic pole relative to the geographical pole in the south causes the circulation pattern to swing over an abnormally wide range of geographical latitude. Thus it is relatively easy to identify, and also to follow the movements of individual ducts for many hours, and also to obtain sufficient observations of each duct to minimise the random errors inherent in any radio direction-finding system.

In addition, the existence of much man-made radiation in these bands from the industrial zones of the eastern U.S. and Canada cause strong amplification of signals moving from north to south, thus enabling ducts to be followed over several thousands of kilometres, instead of a few hundred as is normal in the northern hemisphere.

REFERENCES:

Bullough, K. and Sagredo, J.L. 1973. VLF goniometer observations at Halley Bay Antarctica – 1. The equipment and measurements of signals bearing. *Planet. Space Sci.* 21, 899–912.

Sagredo J.L. and Bullouch, K. 1973. VLF goniometer observations at Halley Bay, Antarctica 11. Magnetic structure deduced from whistler observations. *Planet. Space Sci.* 21, 913–23.

Kaiser T.R., Orr, D. and Smith, AJ. 1977. VLF electromagnetic phenomena: whistlers and micropulsations. *Phil. Trans. R. Society* London B279, 226–38.

Research H

HIGH FREQUENCY PROGRAMME, Ryvingen Camp, April 1980-January 1981. Completed by Virginia Fiennes for Royal Aircraft Establishment, Farnborough.

Using equipment specially designed by R.A.E. Farnborough, transmissions were made through the expedition's radio equipment and recorded at Farnborough on an antenna specially erected for the purpose.

The results of these recordings will be analyzed and form part of a worldwide and long-lasting study of the reliability of high-frequency propagation.

The expedition's Ryvingen base provided a unique transmitting station for long-distance communication from the Antarctic, as few if any other Antarctic stations communicate directly to their home base over so long a distance on a regular basis.

Research I

GLACIOLOGICAL PROGRAMME, Antarctic Traverse, October 1980-January 1981. Completed by O.W.N. Shepard for Scott Polar Research Institute.

The programme included:

a) A traverse map with accurate positions of the observations completed and of the surface elevation. The latter is given in a separate chart as 'Altimetry'. The work was desirable for the verification of satellite imagery. During the next decade it is expected that the reconnaissance phase of airborne mapping of ice thickness and the accurate mapping of surface elevation by satellite altimetry should be completed. Our intention was that the surface positions of our observations be accurate to within one minute of latitude. Our heightings were measured as accurately as possible by means of a set of three calibrated aneroid barometers. The profile obtained, when analysis is completed, should provide finer detail of surface undulations than can be obtained by satellites at present.

b) At three predetermined sites, 10-metre ice core samples were retrieved and labelled as to source location and depth. A lightweight aluminium drill of Norwegian design was used comprising a one-metre drill barrel with one- and two-metre extension rods. All the 10-metre cores were sampled at a 5 cm frequency and returned to base camp where they were melted and bottled. These samples will in due course be analyzed for total B activity at the Labatoire de Glaciologie at Grenoble. The data should enable snow accumulation rates to be determined along the traverse route.

Mercury thalium thermometers were suspended in the drill holes overnight to help establish the mean annual temperature available at the relevant depths.

c) Oxygen isotopic determination work was carried out using the same drilling equipment. At or close to each degree of latitude crossed during the traverse, a two-metre was drilled. The purpose was to determine the variation of mean isotopic composition of the surface layers along the expedition's route.

A two-metre core penetrates several years of snow accumulation so its average isotopic composition was a close indication of the annual average.

Each core was melted slowly in a pressure cooker and three 25 ml subsamples of the total melt were collected in polythene vials. These samples were returned to Cambridge for analysis by Dr Dansgaard's team at the University of Copenhagen. Mercury thalium thermometers recorded temperatures at each two-metre site.

The results of the two-metre drilling programme have been incorporated in maps of isotopic ratios in Antarctica by Dr Gordon Robin of the Scott Polar Research Institute.

Research J

METEOROLOGICAL RECORDS, Ryvingen and Sanae bases, February 1980–January 1981. Completed by O.W.N. Shepard for W.M.O.

A fully equipped meteorological station was built at Ryvingen in January 1980, and for the nine-month wintering period synoptic reports were prepared every six hours and sent over the radio to Sanae which in turn passed them on to the U.K. Meteorological office at Bracknell. The meteorological phenomena observed were spectacular, with sun pillars, undersun, parhelion, antehelion, haloes and Aurora Australis all common occurrences.

The monthly temperature summary (in degrees Centigrade) at 1200 GMT was:

1980	Mean Ryvingen	Max. Ryvingen	Min. Ryvingen
February	-18.3	-12.5	-23.1
March	-24.2	-14.9	-30.6
April	-29.8	-17.6	-38.7
May	-31.8	-22.2	-44.5
June	-36.3	-21.6	-43.6
July	-34.6	-16.6	-45.5
August	-33.7	-22.1	-41.5
September	-33.7	-21.4	-40.7
October	-27.8	-15.9	-35.4

The daily recordings relayed to the W.M.O. included barometric pressure, ambient temperature, wind velocity direction and cloud formation.

An electrically operated anemometer and wind vane apparatus was installed at Ryvingen and used to record wind speed and direction on a 'nonstop graph'. SPRI studies of katabatic wind behaviour in winter are analyzing the graphs.

Antarctic Crossing Journey

ALTIMETRY FOR SATELLITE IMAGERY VERIFICATION Completed by O.W.N. Shepard for the Scott Polar Research Institute.

All heightings were measured as accurately as possible with a set of three calibrated aneroid barometers.

		ICE GROUP					RYVINGEN	
DATE	GMT	GRID REF	TEMP °C	BAROM 1	BAROM 2	BAROM 3	TEMP °C	BAROM
OCT 29	1800	73°36′ S 02°52′ W	−29.0	717.6			−24.0	781.1
OCT 31	0000	73°53′ S 02°48′ W	−44.1	686.2		685.8	−30.0	775.6
OCT 31	1200	74°32′ S 02°26′ W	−33.9	679.6		679.7	−22.0	771.0
NOV 1	1200	74°32′ S 02°26′ W	−34.5	670.8		670.6	−28.0	763.9
NOV 2	1800	75°12′ S 01°58′ W	−36.2	685.6		685.1	−21.0	773.7
NOV 3	1800	75°57′ S 01°21′ W	−35.1	691.2		690.7	−23.0	775.6
NOV 4	1800	76°45′ S 00°45′ W	−34.0	708.0	707.2	707.9	−22.0	781.5
NOV 5	1800	77°36′ S 00°30′ E	−34.6	720.8	719.2	720.7	−21.0	788.0
NOV 6	1200	77°36′ S 00°30′ E	−31.9	720.1	719.0	719.6	−21.0	786.0
NOV 7	1800	78°24′ S 00°28′ W	−27.3	722.9	722.3	722.8	−21.0	782.3

		ICE GROUP					RYVINGEN		
DATE	GMT	GRID REF	TEMP °C	BAROM 1	BAROM 2	BAROM 3	TEMP °C	BAROM	
NOV 8	1800	79°12′ S 00°40′ W	−27.7	730.7	730.0	730.7	−19.0	779.6	
NOV 10	1200	79°12′ S 00°40′ W	−30.7	735.0	734.1	734.6	−21.0	780.4*	
NOV 10	1800	79°12′ S 00°40′ W	−21.6	735.7	734.7	735.2	−21.0	779.6*	
NOV 11	1200	79°12′ S 00°40′ W	−30.3	734.5	733.7	734.8	−21.0	778.1	
NOV 11	1800	79°12′ S 00°40′ W	−29.7	733.8	733.2	733.6	−21.0	778.6	AT SAME SITE TILL NOV 25, 1980
NOV 26	1800	80°27′ S 00°45′ E	−21.5	742.6	741.4	742.1	−13.0	779.6	
NOV 27	1800	81°15′ S 01°12′ E	−20.0	744.7	743.4	744.1	−14.0	773.8	
NOV 28	1800	82°05′ S 01°20′ E	−16.7	747.0	746.1	746.8	−15.0	775.0	
NOV 29	1800	82°50′ S 01°20′ E	−23.0	728.1	727.5	728.0	−14.0	767.5	
NOV 30	1800	83°29′ S 01°30′ E	−22.9	721.4		721.1	−16.0	772.4	
DEC 1	1800	84°03′ S 01°30′ E	−23.5	715.5		715.3	−16.0	777.9	

*ESTIMATE

		ICE GROUP					RYVINGEN	
DATE	GMT	GRID REF	TEMP °C	BAROM 1	BAROM 2	BAROM 3	TEMP °C	BAROM
DEC 2	1800	84°26′ S 01°30′ E	−23.6	715.7		715.5	−16.0	782.2
DEC 3	1200	84°26′ S 01°30′ E	−10.6	717.0			−15.0	781.1
DEC 4	1800	84°32′ S 02°05′ E	−29.0	715.4		715.0	−15.0	781.0
DEC 5	1800	84°32′ S 02°05′ E	−21.4	714.4			−15.0	777.3
DEC 6	1800	84°32′ S 02°05′ E	−28.0	707.7			−15.0	773.9
DEC 7	1800	85°13′ S 02°05′ E	−26.0	698.7		698.9	−14.0	777.5
DEC 8		85°42′ S 02°05′ E					DETAILS	AVAILABLE
DEC 9	2200	86°12′ S 02°00′ E	−25.0	707.8		707.2	−21.0	784.3
DEC 10	1800	86°53′ S 01°30′ E	−23.9	711.7		711.2	−11	787.0
DEC 11	1800	87°22′ S 01°30′ E	−21.0	712.6		712.3	−11.0	785.8
DEC 12	1800	88°19′ S 01°32′ E	−25.3	704.5		704.1	−12.0	780.8
DEC 13	1800	88°59′ S 01°00′ E	−27.0	696.0		696.0	−14.0	776.6

		ICE GROUP					RYVINGEN		
DATE	GMT	GRID REF	TEMP °C	BAROM 1	BAROM 2	BAROM 3	TEMP °C	BAROM	
DEC 15	1200	90°00′ 00°00′	−22.0	686.2			−16.0	774.3	STAYED AT S. POLE TILL 22 DEC.
DEC 23	0600	89°35′ S 147°00′ W	−17.1	690.8	687.6	690.2			
DEC 24	0600	88°45′ S 147°00′ W	−21.5	679.6	676.8	679.4			
DEC 25	0600	87°49′ S 144°00′ W	−25.6	693.6	689.8	693.0			
DEC 26	0600	87°17′ S 146°00′ W	−14.3	725.8	722.8	725.8			
DEC 27	0600	86°58′ S 148°00′ W	−20.4	745.0	742.0	744.8			
DEC 28	0600	86°16′ S 151°00′ W	−11.3	839.9		839.7			
DEC 29		85°30′ S 151°50′ W							
DEC 30	0600	85°00′ S 152°00′ W	−0.9	936.8		936.4			
JAN 1 1981	0600	84°23′ S 160°10′ W	−3.9	973.6		973.4			
JAN 2	0600	83°43′ S 168°00′ W	−1.6	979.0		978.8			
JAN 3	0600	83°43′ S 168°00′ W	−0.9	978.5		978.3			

		ICE GROUP					RYVINGEN	
DATE	GMT	GRID REF	TEMP °C	BAROM 1	BAROM 2	BAROM 3	TEMP °C	BAROM
JAN 4	0600	83°43′ S 168°00′ W	−5.9	982.5				
JAN 5	0600	82°48′ S 175°30′ W	−4.5	982.6		981.9		
JAN 6	0600	81°34′ S 178°00′ E	−5.6	981.6		981.0		
JAN 7	0600	80°51′ S 175°20′ E	−5.1	986.6		986.2		
JAN 8	0000	80°51′ S 175°20′ E	0.0	990.9				
JAN 8	0600	80°51′ S 175°20′ E	−3.5	989.2				
JAN 9	1800	79°25′ S 170°40′ E	−4.4	986.1		985.8		
JAN 10	0000	78°03′ S 167°40′ E	−6.9	996.8		996.7		
JAN 11					ARRIVED	SCOTT BASE		

Research K

NONGLACIOLOGICAL PROGRAMME, Antarctica January 1980–January 1981. Completed by O.W.N. Shepard

a) *Urinalysis for British Antarctic Survey.* Throughout the crossing journey detailed records of the daily individual calorific intake together with details of individual urine content (taken from urine sampling sticks) were logged for a British Antarctic Survey study of the long-term effects of a high-caloric diet during a lengthy sledging journey.

b) *Cardiological study for Middlesex Hospital* During the wintering period and the crossing journey a study of stress on the heart was completed for the Middlesex Hospital through the use of miniaturised tape recorders. These were strapped to the waist of each individual with electrodes attached over heart and sternum. Heart rates and wave forms as an index of stress were recorded on tape over set 24-hour periods. The analysis is being carried out by Dr. Peter Taggart of the Middlesex Hospital Cardiological Department.

c) *Dental study for Royal Army Dental Corps* Throughout the period January 1980-January 1981 each individual's teeth were scraped for plaque smears and detailed questionnaires were completed regarding general dental state. These were returned for the records of the RADC.

Research L

ARCTIC OCEAN GLACIOLOGICAL PROGRAMME, Alert/North Pole/Svalbard, January–August 1982. Completed by Ranulph Fiennes for Scott Polar Research Institute and Polar Continental Shelf Project (Drs P. Wadhams and R. Koerner).

The Arctic Ocean work was curtailed owing to three unforeseen factors. The removal of O.W.N. Shepard after the Antarctic crossing, a polar base fire which destroyed all scientific equipment, including the SPRI seismometer and the sinking of a Skidoo and sledge load with two weeks' worth of snow accumulation and ice topographical records. Nonetheless three of the original six programmes were completed.

a) *Pollen sampling for Polar Continental Shelf Project* At six widely spaced sites surface samples were collected, bagged and labelled. They were subsequently taken from Alert to Toronto for analysis by Dr Koerner. These provided a pollen influx representative of the Ellesmere-Pole part of the High Arctic which were required to tie in with collections made simultaneously from ten ice caps in the High Arctic and from Northern Greenland and from Fram III (an ice floe some 2 degrees north of Spitsbergen). Analysis is taking place at the time of writing.

b) *Topographical log of Arctic Ocean traverse* Details of surface topography were carefully logged on a daily basis. Remarks concentrated on open water leads, extent and composition of ridges, percentage of rubble cover, details and direction of fracturing and extent and age of floes. Completed logs were sent to both SPRI and PCSP for their annual records of Arctic Ocean behavioural patterns.

c) *Snow accumulation and melt record* At each camp site from Cape Columbia/Pole/82°N, 01°30'E, snow depth average over a 20-square-metre patch was recorded in cm. During the period from June to August 1982, daily melt records were kept on a single ice floe between 86°N and 82°N. All records were sent to SPRI and PCSP for analysis.

Note: Throughout the journey Alert/North Pole/82°N, 01°30'E meteorological synops were sent daily to the W.M.O. via the expedition's forward base.

Glossary of Ice Terms

ablation	The process through which snow, ice or water disperses.
accumulation	The process through which snow, ice or water is added to a given surface.
bergy bit	A smallish piece of floating ice generally submerged or half-submerged.
brash ice	Floating ice in fragments of under two metres across.
calving	The breakaway action of ice chunks from seaborne ice bodies.
crevasse	Often hidden under snow bridges, crevasses are vertical splits in ice caps and glaciers.
first-year ice/floes	Ice which has grown, having formed on the sea surface, for up to 12 months and has reached a thickness between 30 cm. and 2 m.
floe	A piece of floating sea ice.
frazil ice	Fine ice plates suspended in seawater; a stage in the formation of young sea ice.
glacier	A mass of ice/snow moving under the influence of gravity.
grease ice	A later stage than frazil ice in the formation of new sea ice.
growler	An even smaller piece of floating ice than a bergy bit.
iceberg	Large pieces of ice in water which have usually broken off glaciers.
iceblink	A bright glare patch on the underside of a cloud

	which is the reflection of ice areas in the sea below the cloud.
ice cap	A dome-shaped mass of ice covering land and being less than 50,000 sq. kms. in size.
ice foot	A thin apron of ice attached to the coastline and not answering to tidal movement.
ice front	The cliff of ice that provides the seaward side of a land-based ice mass.
ice island	A tabular iceberg which floats within and from the Arctic Ocean. From 30 to 50 metres thick and from a few thousand square metres to 500 square kilometres in extent.
ice rind	A shiny skin of new ice formed from grease ice or by direct freezing.
ice rise	Usually dome-shaped and found on an ice shelf. Beneath it and not visible will be a rock feature which spawned it.
ice sheet	A mass of ice more than 50,000 square kms. in size resting on land or sea or both.
ice shelf	A floating ice sheet, some of which may be temporarily aground.
lead	A break in floating ice.
new ice	All types of newly formed sea ice including frazil, grease, nilas, shuga, ice rind and sludge.
nilas	Various thicknesses of new and growing sludge ice. Can be up to 10 cm. thick and is prone to rafting. Usually grey in colour.
nunatak	The top of a mountain or rock stack which protrudes through an ice sheet.
pack ice	Any floating ice which is not attached more or less permanently to land.
polynyas	Small patches of open water in an area of floating ice.
pressure ridge	A wall of floating ice fragments forced upward under pressure.
rafting	The activity of one layer of ice riding over another.
rime	A deposit of tiny grains of ice formed by the freezing of supercooled water droplets.

sastrugi	Abrupt wave-like ridges of hardened ice formed on a snow surface by wind. They usually run parallel to the direction of the prevailing wind.
shuga	An area of new, lumpy ice formed from sludge and grease ice.
snow bridge	The area of snow forming a roof to a crevasse. Caused by drifting snow, a snow bridge often hides the presence of a crevasse.
whiteout	The result of sunlight being diffused by reflection between an overcast sky and a snow surface. There is neither perspective nor shadow.

Index